The Complete Guide to NetWare® LAN Analysis

Third Edition

The first and second editions of this
book were published under the title
Novell's® Guide to NetWare® LAN Analysis.

Laura A. Chappell

Dan E. Hakes

San Francisco ■ Paris ■ Düsseldorf ■ Soest

Associate Publisher: Steve Sayre
Acquisitions Manager: Kristine Plachy
Developmental Editor: Guy Hart-Davis
Associate Developmental Editor: Neil Edde
Editor: Maureen Adams
Technical Editor: Roger Spicer
Book Design Director: Catalin Dulfu
Book Designer: Seventeenth Street Studios
Graphic Illustrator: Cuong Le
Desktop Publisher: Bill Gibson
Production Coordinator: Alexa Riggs
Indexer: Nancy Guenther
Cover Designer: Archer Design
Cover Photographer: Charles Krebs

This book is dedicated to Scott E. Spicer and Dan R. Hakes.

Acknowledgments

VERY SPECIAL THANKS to our business partner and technical editor, Roger Spicer, for his unrelenting technical reviews and advice on this project. Many thanks to our security guard, Drake Dougherty, for his persuasive way of getting us up out of our lab chairs every once in a while. . . and, of course, to Samuel Adams, patriot and Brewer. And, as always, nothing would get done without Jill Poulsen (Laura's lifeline to the "real world").

Our thanks to the vendors who were so supportive of our efforts and who provided us with their products, time, and expertise: John Corrigan (Madge Networks); Lance Sprung (Standard Microsystems Corporation); Eric Nohr (Eicon Technology); Kevin Rebman (Network Communications Corporation); and Quentin Liu, Mike Margozzi, Jon Rosdahl, and Bob Pratt (Novell, Inc.). Special thanks also go to Rosalie Kearsley of Novell Press for her continued support of our research and writing efforts.

Sincere thanks to our friends and family who put up with the late hours and evenings in the lab while this book was being developed and business was thriving.

Finally, we'd like to thank all the people who supported us as we ventured out on our own with our company, ImagiTech, Inc. (info@imagitech.com). We are experiencing a tremendously exciting third year in business—researching network performance and Internet/World Wide Web integration. We look forward to releasing many innovative products over the coming years.

Contents at a Glance

Table of Contents

Introduction

WORKING IN A LAN environment is fundamentally different from working in a stand-alone environment. Cabling becomes the bloodstream of the network, and communications protocols are used to transfer data and resource management information from one system to another. As NetWare LANs increase in popularity, so does the need for more detailed information regarding protocol performance, troubleshooting, testing, and optimization.

Over the past several years, we have studied, lectured, and written about Ethernet, Token Ring, and NetWare protocols. We received numerous requests for this third edition; specifically for information on NetWare Directory Services characterization and the latest on Service Advertising Protocol. This book addresses the most common questions posed by attendees of our full-day protocol analysis tutorials.

Who Should Read This Book?

This book is designed for all current and new NetWare users who are interested in learning the basic through advanced steps of protocol analysis in order to troubleshoot, test, and optimize their NetWare Ethernet and Token Ring LANs. Whether you have years of NetWare experience or are still mastering console utilities, this book will help you learn and troubleshoot the communications that occur "behind the scenes" in NetWare.

If you are a network administrator, this book will guide you through the techniques to fully document your network performance and identify growth trends, cabling, and server overload, as well as Ethernet, Token Ring, and NetWare errors.

If you are a network technician, this book will provide you with an insight into Ethernet and Token Ring frame structures and cabling systems. In the Ethernet sections, you will become familiar with frame errors that indicate an overloaded network segment, a cabling problem, a faulty LAN driver, and a faulty transceiver. In the Token Ring section, you will view the Token Ring management and data frames and learn to decipher the communications to locate a faulty lobe wire, MSAU port, or adapter. Finally, by examining the NetWare communications protocols, you will gain a thorough understanding of how the NetWare client/server communications system works, as well as how to optimize it.

For the instructor who presents technical lectures on the NetWare operating system and support, this book addresses many of the common questions asked in class. Used as supplemental instructional material, this book will provide insight into the Ethernet and Token Ring media access methods and NetWare communications for beginning through advanced students.

What You'll Learn

In this book you will learn the basics of Ethernet and Token Ring cabling, frame structures, and functionality. You will gain a thorough understanding of errors that occur on NetWare LANs and their effect on performance.

You will also learn about NetWare communications that provide services such as routing and server information, file and printer access, bindery access, connection-oriented and connectionless communications, large file transfer, diagnostics and configuration information, connection validation, serialization information, and network messaging.

This book also provides a comprehensive list of protocol analysis features and tools that are used to document network health and performance, test network cabling and server capabilities, optimize network performance, and troubleshoot Ethernet and Token Ring NetWare communications.

The Tools Presented in This Book

This book introduces you to two protocol analyzers: LANalyzer for Windows (Novell, Inc.) and NCC LANalyzer (Network Communications Corporation). Each analyzer offers a range of capabilities for examining networking protocols.

LANalyzer for Windows is an inexpensive MS Windows–based product that uses an intuitive graphical interface. Whenever a screen shot shows characteristics of this interface, you are looking at a demonstration of the LANalyzer for Windows, as in Figure I.1.

The NCC LANalyzer, on the other hand, uses the traditional NetWare C-Worthy interface and presents a text-based screen. Whenever a screen shot depicts a text-based screen, you are looking at the NCC LANalyzer product, as shown in Figure I.2. For more information on the LANalyzer for Windows, refer to Appendix C.

FIGURE I.1

LANalyzer for Windows uses the Windows graphical user interface.

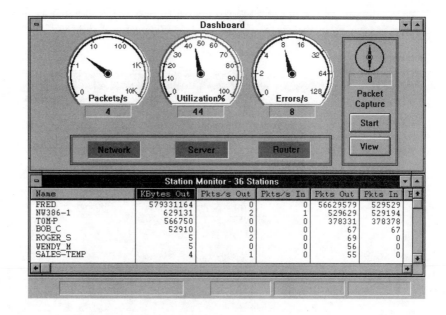

FIGURE I.2

NCC LANalyzer uses the traditional C-Worthy interface.

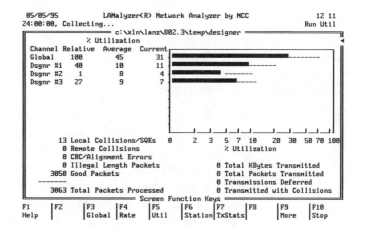

Novell's NetWare LANalyzer Agent is a distributed network analyzer. Net-Ware LANalyzer Agents allow you to analyze and capture traffic on network segments that are on the other side of a network bridge, router, or wide area link. The NetWare Management System provides a console that displays the data collected from various network segments, as shown in Figure I.3. The interface is based on LANalyzer for Windows.

FIGURE I.3

The NetWare Management System console interface is similar to LANalyzer for Windows.

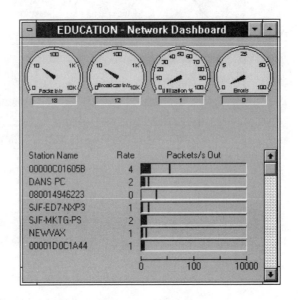

How This Book Is Organized

This book is divided into five parts, covering the Ethernet media access method; Token Ring media access method; NetWare protocols; performance benchmarking, testing, and optimization; and protocol analyzer features.

Part I, "Ethernet/802.3 LANs," details the Ethernet frame structures used in the NetWare environment, including Ethernet_802.3 (Ethernet "raw"), Ethernet_802.2, Ethernet_SNAP, and Ethernet_II. Part I also details cabling system configuration requirements and limitations, as well as cable testing. Finally, this part presents a complete listing of frame errors seen on NetWare LANs, along with their potential causes and possible solutions.

Part II, "Token Ring/802.5 LANs," details Token Ring network components, functional management stations and addresses, functional processes, and management frames. This section also compares performance of 4 Mb/s, 16 Mb/s, and Early Token Release, as well as examining frame structures, the

Source Routing/Spanning Tree Protocol, and Token Ring troubleshooting techniques.

Part III, "NetWare Protocols," examines the NetWare protocols, such as Routing Information Protocol (RIP), Service Advertising Protocol (SAP), Internetwork Packet Exchange (IPX), Sequenced Packet Exchange (SPX and SPX II), Large Internetwork Packet (LIP), NetWare Link Services Protocol (NLSP), NetWare Directory Services (NDS), and NetWare Core Protocol (NCP). Also included in Part III is an analysis of Watchdog and serialization protocols. Finally, the Diagnostic Responder Configuration Request and Response formats are defined and used for troubleshooting a NetWare LAN.

Part IV, "Performance Benchmarking, Testing, and Optimization," provides a thorough explanation of how to benchmark your network's performance, test network capabilities, and optimize your LAN. Also included in Part IV is a chapter detailing the communication that occurs during successful and unsuccessful attempts to attach to a server, log in, and create and delete files.

Part V, "Protocol Analyzers—Overview and Features," summarizes the many uses for protocol analysis tools by examining a variety of features that provide network short-term and long-term statistics gathering, station monitoring, setting of alarm thresholds and actions, packet filtering, packet capturing, transmission onto the network, and finally, protocol decoding. Throughout this part of the book, you are provided with examples of how to use features to troubleshoot and determine methods to enhance network performance.

Appendix A contains a glossary of terms used throughout the book. Appendix B lists books and articles used in researching this book; we recommend these resources for further study. Appendix C provides information about the LANalyzer for Windows product and Software Developer Kit. Appendix D details various Token Ring frame structures and lists Token Ring timers. Appendix E contains a hexadecimal-decimal-binary conversion chart. Appendix F provides details on the ImagiTech LAN analysis lab used to research Ethernet, Token Ring, and NetWare communications. This appendix also includes details on the products used in the lab.

Style Conventions Used in This Book

Throughout this book, many hexadecimal values are represented with a preceding "0x." Hardware and software addresses in the NetWare environment are shown in their hexadecimal format throughout this book, even if they do not contain the preceding "0x" indicator.

When new terms are introduced, they appear in *italics* and can be found in the Glossary (Appendix A). Material that needs to be typed appears in **boldface**.

With this book in hand, most NetWare communications and Ethernet and Token Ring performance issues can be easily solved. Using this book in conjunction with a protocol analyzer attached to your own network, you will be capable of tracking network trends, configurations, and performance characteristics. Upon completion of this book and the many analysis techniques presented here, you will have acquired a thorough understanding of the NetWare communication system on Ethernet and Token Ring LANs.

Ethernet/802.3 LANs

PART

Overview of Ethernet LANs

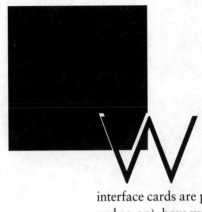

HEN INSTALLING A NetWare LAN, users must select a network access method that fits their specific needs. This network access method determines what type of network interface cards are placed in the workstations (Ethernet, Token Ring, ARCnet, and so on), how workstations access the cabling system, and how data is prepared and sent across the network.

The term "Ethernet" is used in this book to describe Ethernet II and 802.3 network specifications and functions, collectively.

The three common access methods seen on today's NetWare LANs are

- Carrier sense multiple access with collision detection (CSMA/CD)

- Token-passing ring

- Token-passing bus

Ethernet LANs use the CSMA/CD method, while Token Ring and ARCnet use token-passing ring and token-passing bus, respectively.

Currently, most NetWare LANs are Ethernet (CSMA/CD) systems; however, Token Ring networks have been steadily rising in popularity over the past several years. ARCnet LANs still hold third place in the "war" between the network access options.

These three access methods have unique ways of communicating over the network. On a CSMA/CD network, all workstations share a common cabling system, as shown in Figure 1.1. Because of this, they can (and sometimes do) send data at the same time on the cable, causing data signals to collide on the network. Each workstation must take certain steps to avoid sending at the same time as another workstation, and to retransmit if the last message was involved in a collision. These steps are defined by the Institute of Electrical and Electronic Engineers (IEEE). The IEEE 802.3 CSMA/CD specifications are covered in this chapter.

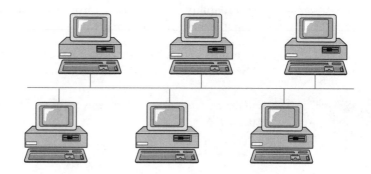

Token Ring and ARCnet LANs prevent workstations from transmitting at the same time by requiring each station to wait for a *token* that gives it permission to transmit data on the cabling system. Each workstation has an equal chance to transmit on the cabling system since the token rotates around the network from station to station, based on the station node address (ARCnet) or physical wiring (Token Ring). This type of access method is called *deterministic* since the token is passed in a well-defined process that guarantees access to the network.

This chapter explains how workstations use the CSMA/CD access method to send messages on the network. (Refer to Chapters 6 through 13 for information on the Token Ring/802.5 access method.)

Advantages and Disadvantages of Ethernet

THE PRIMARY ADVANTAGES of Ethernet include

Ease of installation: All workstations can be connected to a segment using a simple T-connector or transceiver. Ethernet LANs do not require a hub to connect systems.

Well-known technology: Businesses have been installing Ethernet networks for many years, and they are quite common.

Availability of inexpensive cards: The price of Ethernet cards has dropped significantly over the past two years.

Various wiring configurations: As shown in Chapter 3, Ethernet LANs can be configured using different cable types and cable layouts.

Chapter 3 discusses how hub systems and RJ45 (telephone-type) connectors can be used, if desired.

The main disadvantages of Ethernet include

- **Decreasing throughput on heavily loaded LANs:** On CSMA/CD LANs, as the load on the network increases, performance decreases. Although many feel CSMA/CD is Ethernet's greatest feature, others believe it is Ethernet's primary weakness, because a higher network load severely degrades performance.

- **Difficulty in troubleshooting:** Ethernet networks can be difficult to troubleshoot because of the common cabling system used for thinnet or thick Ethernet cable. If there is a break in the cable, the entire LAN segment is down. It can be very difficult to isolate a single node that is responsible for generating errors and causing problems on the network. The newer 10BaseT networks have solved some of these problems.

Before you begin working on an Ethernet LAN, it's important to understand how the access protocol, CSMA/CD, works. This helps you interpret the statistics, errors, and utilization information that are presented by an analyzer and throughout this book.

For details on the CSMA/CD protocol not included in this chapter, refer to the IEEE 802.3 specifications.

How CSMA/CD Works: Transmitting

BECAUSE CSMA/CD NETWORKS use a common cabling system, some rules must be set so that workstations avoid transmitting at the same time. However, if multiple stations transmit simultaneously, there must also be some way for them to find out whether their packet has been involved in a collision and when to retransmit. (The CSMA/CD protocol is similar to a party-line phone, a situation in which many people can share the line, talking at the same time. If everyone talks at once, you hear garbled chatter. If each person waits for a turn, however, you can understand each speaker, one at a time.)

Stations follow these five steps when transmitting on the CSMA/CD network:

1. Listen before transmitting.

2. Defer (wait) if the cable is busy.

3. Transmit and listen for collisions.

4. If a collision did occur, wait before retransmitting.

5. Retransmit or abort.

STEP 1: Listen before Transmitting

Stations continually monitor the cable segment for a *carrier on* signal, as shown in Figure 1.2. This signal on the cable is commonly recognized by a voltage indicating that the cable is in use. If a station does not notice "carrier on," it assumes the cable is free and begins transmission. (In terms of the party-line analogy mentioned earlier, this function is similar to listening on the phone line before speaking.) If the wire is busy (carrier on) when a station transmits, the station's packet will collide with the existing signal on the wire.

FIGURE 1.2

Stations monitor the cable for activity.

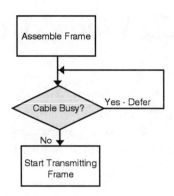

STEP 2: Defer (Wait) if the Cable Is Busy

In order to avoid collisions, stations must defer (wait) if they notice the cable is in use, as shown in Figure 1.3. A properly performing interface card will not intentionally transmit if it knows the cable is busy. (On a party line, if you hear someone talking, you wait until that person is finished before beginning to speak.) *Deferral time* is a set amount of time that a station must wait once the line becomes idle before attempting to retransmit.

FIGURE 1.3

Stations defer if the wire is busy.

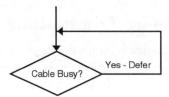

STEP 3: Transmit and Listen for Collisions

When the medium is clear (*carrier off*) for at least 9.6 microseconds, a station may transmit, as you can see in Figure 1.4. Frames are transmitted in both directions down the cabling system.

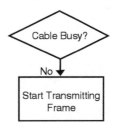

If another station on the segment has transmitted a packet at the same time, the packets collide on the wire, as shown in Figure 1.5. The packets involved in the collision are now only packet fragments on the cable. (If you began speaking at the same time as others on the party line, your conversations would collide, and the result would be a garbled message.) During transmission, therefore, the station listens for a collision on the segment. Collisions are recognized as a signal on the cable that is equal to or exceeds the signal produced by two or more transceivers simultaneously transmitting. *Transceivers* are electrical devices that physically transmit and receive data on the medium.

If a collision occurs but other stations haven't yet seen the collision signal, they may attempt to transmit. These stations would then be involved in yet another collision. To avoid this situation, stations involved in a collision ensure that all stations on the segment are aware that the cable is still busy by transmitting "jam," as illustrated in Figure 1.6. (*Jam* is specified as a minimum 32-bit transmission that cannot be equal to the CRC value of the prior transmission.) Stations involved in a collision increment their transmit attempt counter by 1.

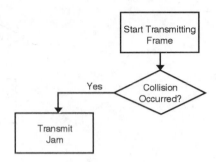

STEP 4: Wait before Transmitting

If stations retransmitted immediately after a collision, their second transmissions would also collide. It is necessary, therefore, to randomize the amount of time that stations must wait before attempting to retransmit.

To determine when they can retransmit, stations perform an algorithm, called the *backoff algorithm,* that provides several available times. When stations randomly select which time they will use, as shown in Figure 1.7, they reduce the chance of two or more stations retransmitting at the same time. (For example, on a party line, if two people begin talking at the same time, the messages are garbled. Both people will stop talking and then one will start up again while the other listens.)

STEP 5: Retransmit or Abort

If a station is on a busy segment, it may not be able to transmit without its packet colliding with another packet on the segment. A station may attempt to transmit up to 16 times before it must abort the attempt. NetWare 3.x and 4.x servers display the number of aborted server transmissions in the MONITOR utility under LAN Driver Statistics as "ExcessCollisionsCount," as shown in Figure 1.8. If the station retransmits and there is no indication that the packet was again involved in a collision, the transmission is considered successful. If a station is unsuccessful in 16 consecutive attempts, it will not transmit the packet. (On a party line, if you spoke when the line was not busy,

FIGURE 1.7

Stations use the backoff
algorithm to determine
when they can attempt
retransmission.

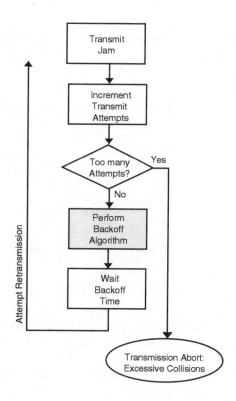

FIGURE 1.7

Stations use the backoff
algorithm to determine
when they can attempt
retransmission.

your voice would be heard clearly. If you attempted to get a message through
but couldn't because the line was constantly in use, you might give up.)

After each successful transmission, a station can ensure that its collision-
detection function is working correctly by performing a *Signal Quality Error*
(*SQE*) test. An SQE test is performed if the transceiver's SQE function is set
to "on."

*All repeaters must have SQE disabled; enabled repeaters think collisions are occurring and
"jam" the network.*

Understanding the way stations access the medium helps you determine whether the transmitting stations are accessing the medium efficiently
and whether they are following all the rules of CSMA/CD. The flowchart
shown in Figure 1.9 defines each of the steps a station must take in order

```
NetWare v3.11 (250 user) - 2/20/96          NetWare 386 Loadable Module

┌─────────────────────────────────────────────────────────────────┐
│                    Information For Server SALES1                  │
├─────────────────────────────────────────────────────────────────┤
│  File Server Up Time:     0 Days  9 Hours 47 Minutes  6 Seconds   │
│  Utilization:                  1 │ Packet Receive Buffers:   100  │
│  Original Cache Buffers:   3,643 │ Directory Cache Buffers:   50  │
│  Total Cache Buffers:      2,350 │ Service Processes:          2  │
│  Dirty Cache Buffers:          0 │ Connections In Use:         2  │
│  Current Disk Requests:        0 │ Open Files:                13  │
└─────────────────────────────────────────────────────────────────┘

        ┌────────────────────────────────────────────────────┐
        │      NE2000 [port=320 int=2 frame=ETHERNET_802.3]   │
      ┌─├────────────────────────────────────────────────────┤
      │ │ ▲  Hardware Receive Mismatch Count:             0   │
  ┌─┐ │ │                                                     │
  │NE20│ │    Custom Statistics:                              │
  │NE20│ │       CarrierSenseLostCount                     0  │
  └─┘ │ │       UnderrunErrorCount                        0  │
      │ │       ExcessCollisionsCount                     8  │
      │ │       TransmitTimeoutCount                      0  │
      └─├ ▼    TotalCollisionsCount                      197 │
        └────────────────────────────────────────────────────┘
```

to transmit on a CSMA/CD network. A station that does not follow these steps could cause the segment to become unusable.

In Chapter 3, you will use the NCC LANalyzer to identify stations violating the rules of CSMA/CD.

How CSMA/CD Works: Receiving

NOW THAT YOU have seen the process for transmitting on a segment, let's look at the receiving end. As discussed earlier in this chapter, when a station transmits a packet, it is sent throughout the attached segment. An active station on a segment must perform these four steps:

I. View incoming packets and check for fragments.

2. Check the destination address.

FIGURE 1.9

Transmission flowchart

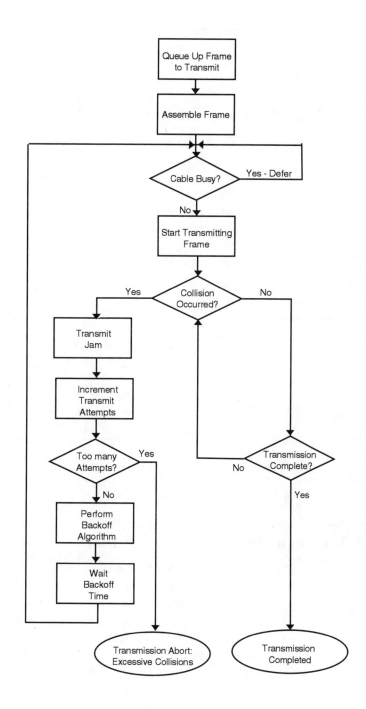

3. If destined for the local station, check the integrity of the packet.

4. Process the packet.

STEP 1: View Incoming Packets and Check for Fragments

On Ethernet LANs, all stations on the segment view each packet on the wire, regardless of whether the packet is addressed to that station. (This is similar to the party-line phone system; even though conversations are not intended for you, you can hear them.) As shown in Figure 1.10, the receiving station checks the packet to ensure that it is the appropriate length (minimum 64 bytes) and not a fragment caused by a collision.

FIGURE 1.10

When viewing packets, stations look for fragments.

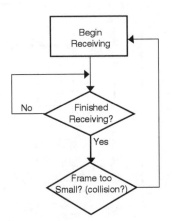

STEP 2: Check the Destination Address

After verifying that the packet is not a fragment, the receiving station checks the destination address of the packet to see whether it should be processed, as shown in Figure 1.11. If the packet is addressed to the local station, is a broadcast, or is to a recognized multicast address, the station checks the integrity of the packet. A *broadcast* is a transmission addressed to all devices on a network, such as a NetWare SAP broadcast. A *multicast* is a transmission addressed to a specific group of devices on a network, such as DEC routers.

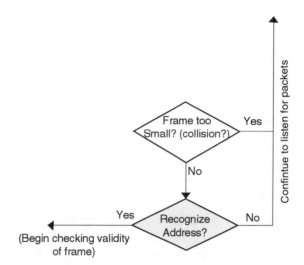

STEP 3: Check the Integrity of the Packet

At this point, a receiving station knows that the packet is not a fragment and
that it is addressed either to itself or to a recognized address. The station does
not know, however, whether the packet is properly formed. Receiving stations
can still read packets that have been corrupted on the cabling segment or were
not properly formed by the transmitting station. To avoid processing these
corrupt packets, the receiving station must check several of the packet's characteristics, as shown in Figure 1.12.

First, the receiving station must check the length of the packet. If a frame is
larger than 1,518 bytes, it is considered an oversized frame. Oversized frames
may be caused by a faulty LAN driver.

The receiving station must also determine whether one or more bits in the
packet have been "swapped" from a 1 to a 0 or vice versa (which also cor-
rupts the packet) while traveling on the cabling system. If the packet is not
oversized, the receiving station checks the packet to determine whether the
contents are the same upon receipt as they were at the time of transmission.
This is called a *Cyclical Redundancy Check (CRC)*. If the packet fails the CRC
check, the receiver then verifies the alignment of the frame.

FIGURE 1.12

Packets are checked for integrity.

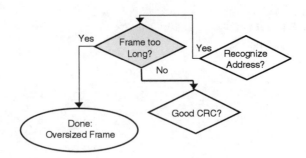

Misaligned packets do not end on an 8-bit boundary. All packets contain a set number of bytes (8 bits) and must end after a defined number of bytes. Packets that do not end on a byte boundary fail the alignment check. For example, a packet cannot be 72 bytes and 3 bits in length. It must be either 72 bytes or 73 bytes.

If the frame did not pass the CRC check but did end on an 8-bit boundary (proper alignment), it is considered a CRC error.

So far, the receiving station has checked the frame to see whether it is a fragment, whether it is too long, whether it contains a CRC error, and whether it is properly aligned. If the frame has successfully passed all these checkpoints, the station must now perform the final length check—to see whether the frame is too short. If the frame is less than 64 bytes but otherwise well formed, it is considered undersized. Undersized frames may be caused by a corrupt LAN driver.

All these checkpoints ensure that packets are valid in length and content before the receiving station processes them. If a frame fails to pass any of these checkpoints, it will not be passed to a higher layer protocol for processing by the receiving station.

The flowchart shown in Figure 1.13 defines the steps a station must take before processing a packet on a CSMA/CD network.

STEP 4: Process the Packet

If the packet has made it successfully through all the checkpoints, as shown in Figure 1.14, it is considered a valid, well-formed, legal-sized frame. If a station is still experiencing communication problems, you must look further into the

FIGURE 1.13

Receipt flowchart

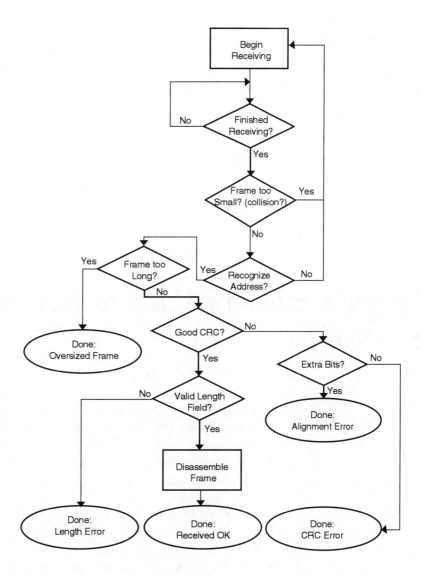

packet to find the problem. Perhaps the station is using the wrong frame type or has an error in the IPX/SPX header.

FIGURE 1.14

Packets that have integrity
will be processed.

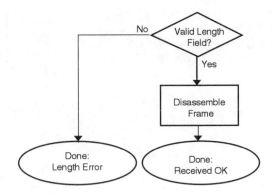

Testing a Station's Ability to Transmit and Receive

F STATIONS HAVE proper network connections, have no malfunctioning cards or transceivers, and follow the rules set forth by the CSMA/CD specifications, they should be able to transmit and receive properly formed frames.

If users are complaining that they cannot communicate on the network segment, you can use a protocol analyzer to test the station's ability to receive and transmit packets.

The NCC LANalyzer's NODEVIEW application checks the connectivity of NetWare IPX client stations. (A separate application, SERVERVU, tests the connectivity of NetWare file servers.)

The NODEVIEW application broadcasts a diagnostic packet, often referred to as a *ping packet,* as illustrated in Figure 1.15. Stations that have the Diagnostic Responder loaded must reply. Responding stations are listed in the Station Monitor screen, as you can see in Figure 1.16.

FIGURE 1.15

NODEVIEW broadcasts
a diagnostic packet on the
segment.

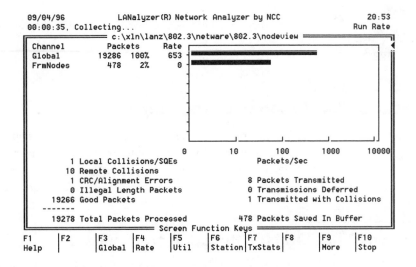

FIGURE 1.16

The Station Monitor
screen displays
responding stations.

The Diagnostic Responder is covered in detail in Chapter 19.

Stations That Respond to the Ping

If a station passes the IPX ping test but still has trouble communicating, perhaps the problem is an intermittent, or "flaky," connector. Check the connection. There might also be a problem with an upper-layer protocol, such as IPX, SPX, or NCP. (These protocols are defined and tested in Part III of this book.)

Stations That Do Not Respond to the Test

If a station does not respond, it could indicate a problem with the station's configuration or its transmit or receive function.

Is the Correct Frame Type Used?

Check the frame type being used by the station. If required, change the frame type used by the NODEVIEW application to match the frame used by the station, as defined in the station's NET.CFG file.

Is IPX Loaded?

Before assuming the station has a bad card, transceiver, or connection, make certain that IPX is loaded. If IPX is not loaded, the client cannot respond to the test. Also make sure the client has loaded either IPX.COM or IPXODI.COM. To make this determination easily, try loading IPX at the client's station. If IPX is already loaded, you will receive the message "IPX already loaded."

Is the Diagnostic Responder Loaded?

Make certain that the Diagnostic Responder is loaded on the station. NetWare's Diagnostic Responder replies to the IPX ping packet that is transmitted by the NODEVIEW application.

To be certain that the Responder is loaded, unload IPX and reload without using any parameters. When you load IPX.COM or IPXODI.COM, the Diagnostic Responder is automatically loaded unless otherwise specified using parameters. To view available IPX load parameters, type **IPX?** at the workstation. These options include

IPXODI

Installs IPX, SPX, and the Responder

IPXODI D

Installs IPX and SPX but not the Responder

IPXODI A

Installs IPX but not SPX or the Responder

If you have verified that IPX and the Diagnostic Responder are loaded, check the following:

- The transceiver's transmit/receive LEDs, if any

- The transceiver cable (if using an external transceiver)

- The connection to the cable (transceiver attachment point)

If the transceiver, transceiver cable, and connection seem to be secure and functioning properly, replace the network interface card and run NODEVIEW again.

If the station responds after the card is replaced, the original card was most likely at fault. Verify that the card settings match the configuration in the NET.CFG file. If the station still does not respond, alternately swap out the transceiver, transceiver cable, and transceiver attachment point.

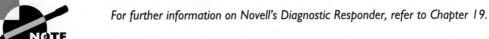
For further information on Novell's Diagnostic Responder, refer to Chapter 19.

This chapter has introduced three access methods: CSMA/CD, token-passing ring, and token-passing bus. By stepping through the procedures for transmitting and receiving data on a CSMA/CD network, you have examined the five steps for transmitting and the four steps for receiving packets on an Ethernet network.

You've tested a workstation's ability to transmit and receive packets on the Ethernet segment by using the NCC LANalyzer NODEVIEW application and learned how to determine whether a station will respond to an IPX diagnostic ping.

Chapter 2 analyzes the traffic on an Ethernet cable segment.

Performance Considerations for CSMA/CD

2

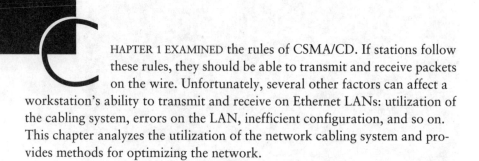

HAPTER 1 EXAMINED the rules of CSMA/CD. If stations follow these rules, they should be able to transmit and receive packets on the wire. Unfortunately, several other factors can affect a workstation's ability to transmit and receive on Ethernet LANs: utilization of the cabling system, errors on the LAN, inefficient configuration, and so on. This chapter analyzes the utilization of the network cabling system and provides methods for optimizing the network.

Defining Bandwidth Utilization

ONSIDER THE ETHERNET cable segment as a freeway, as shown in Figure 2.1. During rush hour, the commute is slow because traffic is heavy and because a higher number of accidents may be blocking the road. Also, since many freeways control access by installing timed lights at the entrance ramps, a car may enter the freeway only when the light turns green.

Rush hour on an Ethernet cable may occur at 8:00 A.M. and 5:00 P.M., when people are logging in or logging out. It may also occur when backup is performed across the network. During rush hour, you may find the network slower than normal. In an extreme case, you may not get access to the cable; it may always be busy.

If there is a lot of activity on the cable segment, you will experience collisions, as shown in Figure 2.2, as multiple stations attempt to transmit at the same time. Although collisions are considered normal for an Ethernet LAN, excessive collisions reduce the effectiveness of the network.

Generally, network personnel can tell when the network is extremely busy, based on the response time observed at a workstation. However, this does not

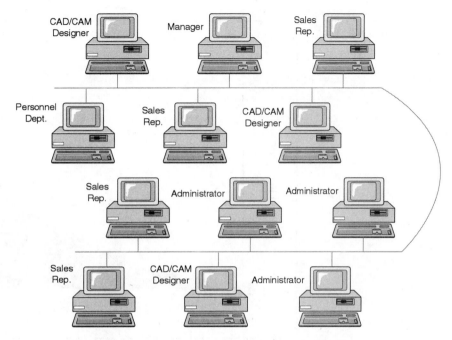

FIGURE 2.1

Ethernet freeway

identify the cause of a sudden excessive network load. Protocol analyzers allow you to monitor your network usage, so you can identify the times when the network is most active, determine typical network usage levels, and detect when the network traffic levels are unusually high.

Determining Current Bandwidth Utilization

On a freeway, the available bandwidth would be determined by the maximum number of vehicles that could use the freeway. The *current* bandwidth utilization is the amount of traffic the freeway is supporting at this time.

The maximum bandwidth available on an Ethernet LAN is 10 megabits per second. The bandwidth utilization is the amount of cable bandwidth currently in use. For example, a busy segment may be experiencing 60% utilization of the bandwidth, or 60% of 10Mb/s. To determine bandwidth utilization, analyzers look at the kilobytes per second in use as a percentage of the maximum possible. (One thousand kilobytes equal 1 megabyte.)

FIGURE 2.2

When utilization goes up, so do collisions

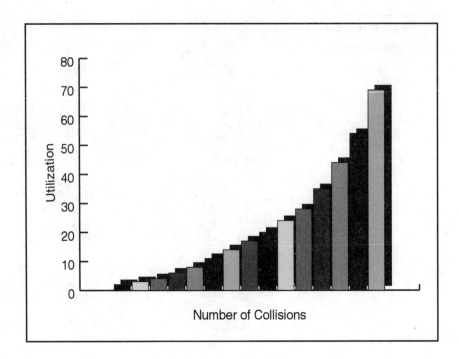

FIGURE 2.2

When utilization goes up, so do collisions

What Is Normal Utilization?

To determine if a condition is unusual, you need to understand what "usual," or "normal," is. All NetWare LANs have unique configurations and usage. "Normal" for one network may not be considered "normal" for another.

A *baseline* defines normal activity for a network. Baseline information that relates to the network bandwidth utilization should be documented and referred to often. With this information, you can answer these questions:

- Is your network load increasing?

- Are unusual peaks in utilization occurring?

- When is the cabling bandwidth at high peak and low peak?

- What types of protocols are using the bandwidth?

- Which users are taking up most of the bandwidth?

Chapter 21 provides a comprehensive list of network characteristics that should be included in your baseline. This chapter looks specifically at the bandwidth utilization.

Gathering and Interpreting Baseline Information

Running a protocol analyzer on the network segment for at least 24 hours creates a baseline against which you can compare future network activity.

In Figure 2.3, bandwidth information has been gathered for 24 hours using LANalyzer for Windows. You are viewing the time period beginning at 10:30 P.M. (22:30). You can see that the peak utilization of the bandwidth occurs at 8:30 A.M.—a time when people are logging in to the network. This morning peak is typical of most LANs.

FIGURE 2.3

Network bandwidth trend graph

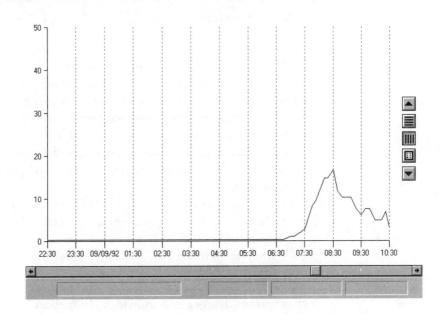

In Figure 2.4, you are viewing the bandwidth utilization graph beginning at 11:30 A.M. Two time periods show increased network utilization: 5:00 P.M. and 9:00 P.M. The first peak occurs as users log out of the network. The second occurs during a network backup of all servers to a centralized location.

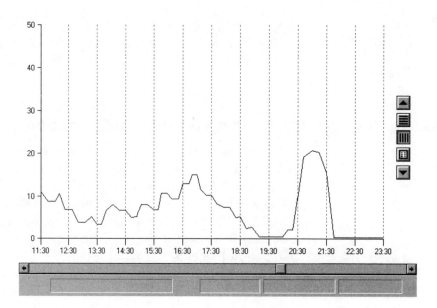

Monitoring network utilization throughout the day would be a tedious, time-consuming process unless you automated it. The NCC LANalyzer and LANalyzer for Windows allow an unattended collection of network statistics that can be imported into common spreadsheets for later graphing and analysis. The NCC LANalyzer and LANalyzer for Windows also allow you to set utilization thresholds that will trigger an alarm if exceeded, as shown in Figure 2.5. These alarms are time stamped and can be kept in an alarm report for later viewing.

For example, the typical utilization of the network during the day ranges from 5% to 15%. During peak times, however, utilization can jump to 18%. You can set an alarm at 20% utilization; when the 20% threshold is exceeded, the alarm is triggered.

Monitoring Changes in Bandwidth Utilization

If users begin to complain about performance, the baseline information you created will serve as a reference point for normal activity while you examine the current network performance.

In Figure 2.6, you can see that the network is experiencing some unusual activity. The utilization alarm has been triggered, as well. If the utilization

Thresholds		
Alarm Name	**Alarm Threshold**	
Packets/s	1000	OK
Utilization%	30	Cancel
Broadcasts/s	100	Defaults
Fragments/s	5	Advanced...
CRC Errors/s	5	Help
Server Overloads/min	15	

climbs high enough, users may begin to complain that the network is slow. In Figure 2.7, LANalyzer for Windows was used to sort station activity by the number of kilobytes transmitted to determine who was using most of the bandwidth.

You can call Fred, who is using most of the bandwidth, to find out what type of activity he is performing on the network. Perhaps he is copying the contents of his local drive up to the server or performing intense database queries. If he can perform this activity (such as backing up local drives) during low-peak utilization times, you may eliminate the additional load during work hours. If Fred must perform this activity (such as database queries) during work hours, you may need to place him on a segment that has more bandwidth available.

If, however, you notice that the network bandwidth is higher overall for each time period of the day and no single user is responsible for overloading the bandwidth, you can assume the network has become busier because more kilobytes per second are being transmitted on the cable segment; the cable has become the performance bottleneck. Or perhaps you added a database server on the local segment that each user is accessing; the communications to the new server could cause additional traffic on the local segment.

If you wish to increase performance on the network, consider splitting the network cabling system into separate segments by using a bridge or router. In this way, you are "load balancing" across two segments. Figure 2.8 illustrates

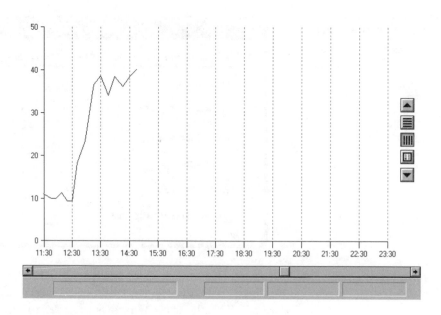

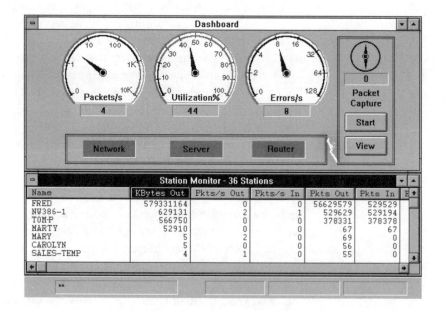

utilization before splitting the segment, and Figure 2.9 illustrates utilization after splitting the segment. (Since a repeater transmits all traffic between segments, it would not relieve this type of situation.)

FIGURE 2.8

Utilization before splitting the segment

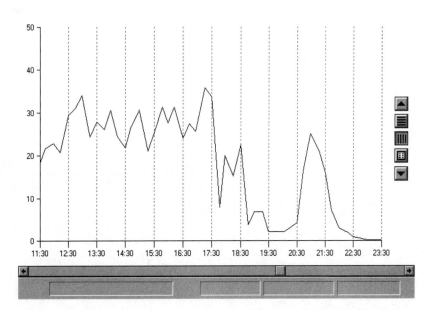

After splitting the segment, you should monitor the utilization of each segment. If you have placed most of the power users on a single segment, performance may not be acceptable. You may wish to balance these users across two segments.

Using Bridges to Load Balance

Bridges connect network segments, as shown in Figure 2.10, and do not allow traffic across that is destined for a station on the local segment. A bridge maintains a list of hardware addresses for each of its network interfaces. The bridge creates this list by examining each packet's source address and adding the station to the appropriate interface table.

For example, when station ABC transmits a packet, the bridge will see the packet on interface 1 and place station ABC in its table for interface 1. Station DEF transmits a packet, and its station address is placed in the bridge's

FIGURE 2.9

Utilization on segments
after splitting the LAN

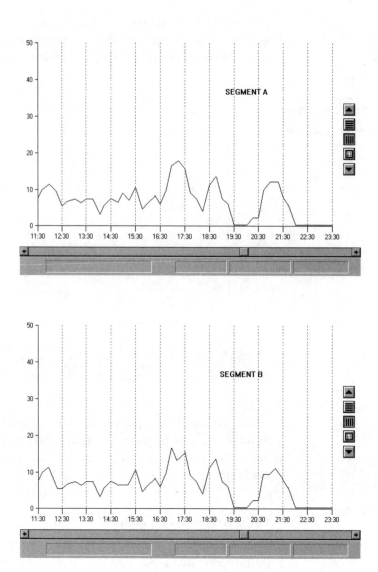

interface 1 table as well. Stations GHI and JKL, however, will be added to
the bridge's interface 2 table since their packets are received by interface 2.

The bridge will use this table to determine whether or not packets should
be forwarded to another segment. If station ABC transmits a packet destined
for station DEF, the bridge will look up the address in its tables. Since the

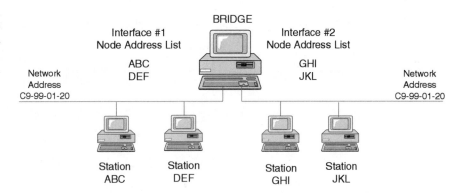

destination station is located on the interface 1 side of the bridge, the packet will not be forwarded. If, however, station ABC transmits a packet to station GHI, the packet will be forwarded to the segment attached to interface 2.

Using Routers for Load Balancing

Routers separate network traffic based on a "software" address (network address). If you separate a large network into two distinct networks using a router, traffic is not passed on to another segment unless it is destined for a station on the other network.

Routers maintain information regarding the networks to which they are connected. For example, in Figure 2.11, the router is configured to connect two NetWare networks, AB-01-01-01 and CD- 02-02-02. When a station on network AB-01-01-01 transmits a packet destined for a server on network CD-02-02-02, the router examines the destination network address contained in the packet being transmitted and forwards the packet to the other network. If, however, the packet is destined for the local address network, it will not be forwarded.

Chapter 20 examines the routing information gathered from packets on the network.

Users must consider several factors when they decide whether to use a bridge or a router. Bridges are generally quicker than routers; however, not many bridge manufacturers can connect to two unlike networks (such as Ethernet and Token Ring). Routers, though generally slower, permit connectivity between

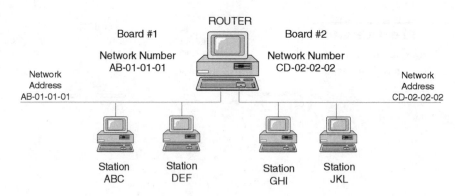

FIGURE 2.11

Routers forward packets based on network addresses.

unlike network types. Also, whereas bridges simply forward on packets not destined for the local segment, routers maintain tables of information about end-to-end connectivity, such as the next router to send a packet to for the shortest path.

Next you will look at individual bandwidth utilization and determine whether or not a network will support additional workstations on a single segment.

Monitoring Individual Use of the Bandwidth

To determine whether a segment can support additional users, you must first determine how much bandwidth each network user is consuming. You can provide an approximate percentage of bandwidth in use by each station with a simple formula:

total bandwidth used × number of nodes on segment

For example, if current overall bandwidth utilization is at 20% and you have 20 users, you can estimate that each user is using 1% of the bandwidth. Adding 20 more users at 1% each would increase overall bandwidth to 40%. This increase in utilization might create an unacceptable response time on the network because the cabling system would be overloaded.

Although simple to use, this formula is not very accurate. If you need to gather more exact statistics, you may wish to "filter" traffic from one or more users on the segment and average their utilization over time. For example, perhaps you currently have three graphic designers working on a segment, as shown in Figure 2.12. They are heavy bandwidth users because they are transferring a large number of graphics files to and from the server. You need to know the average bandwidth each designer is using so you can estimate the effect of adding another graphic designer to the local segment.

FIGURE 2.12

Graphic designers on segment

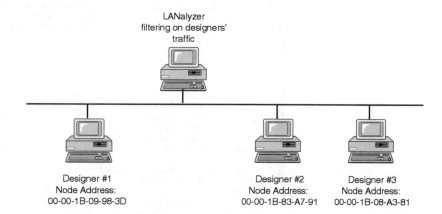

To determine the approximate load that another designer will place on the network, you can first use the NCC LANalyzer to determine how much of the bandwidth is presently being used by each of the existing designers.

By defining one receive channel for the traffic of each designer, you can determine each designer's average bandwidth utilization.

As shown in Figure 2.13, tracking the designers over twenty-four hours will define the typical bandwidth utilization of each. Once this data has been gathered, it can be exported to a spreadsheet and plotted for comparative purposes.

From the information presented in Figure 2.14, you can see that each designer's average bandwidth during working hours (8:00 A.M. to 6:00 P.M.) is in the range from 8% to 10%. We can assume, therefore, that a new designer would average 9%.

Now that you know the approximate load per designer, you can use this information to simulate a 9% load on the network and record how often the new designer will have access to the medium on the first attempt to transmit. This simulation is called a *load test*. Because you will not be transmitting the load to a specific device on the network, it is considered a *dumb load test*.

In Chapter 22, you will see how to transmit an intelligent load to test a particular device on the network.

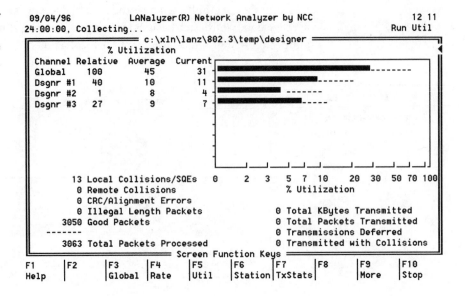

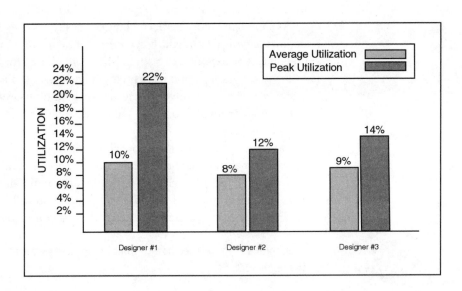

Testing Access to the Medium (Load Test)

YOU HAVE NOW determined that the designers use an average of 9% of the bandwidth. Using the NCC LANalyzer, you can transmit the same load and monitor network performance.

The NCC LANalyzer's GENLOAD application permits you to generate a dumb load on the segment. In Figure 2.15, it is specified that a 9% load of NetWare IPX packets is to be sent to node address 00-00-00-00-00-00.

FIGURE 2.15

Setting up GENLOAD to transmit a 9% load

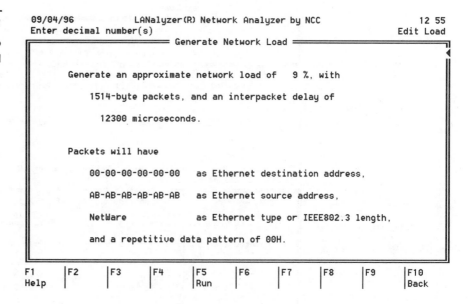

```
09/04/96              LANalyzer(R) Network Analyzer by NCC              12 55
Enter decimal number(s)                                             Edit Load
═══════════════════════ Generate Network Load ═══════════════════════
                                                                         ◀

      Generate an approximate network load of   9 %, with

         1514-byte packets, and an interpacket delay of

            12300 microseconds.


      Packets will have

            00-00-00-00-00-00     as Ethernet destination address,

            AB-AB-AB-AB-AB-AB     as Ethernet source address,

            NetWare              as Ethernet type or IEEE802.3 length,

            and a repetitive data pattern of 00H.


 F1     F2     F3     F4     F5     F6     F7     F8     F9     F10
 Help                         Run                                   Back
```

After starting the application, you can view the TxStats statistics, shown in Figure 2.16, to see that 74% of the time packets are transmitted successfully on the first attempt. This percentage seems reasonable.

Now let's perform the same test generating a 27% load on the segment to simulate the addition of three designers. The TxStats statistics show that the number of successful first attempts to transmit has decreased to 62% (Figure 2.16, screen 2). As utilization has increased, so has the number of collisions on the local segment. This additional load may not be acceptable for the network. Users will notice slowness when accessing servers or routers on the segment. (From our earlier analogy, this is like driving in rush-hour traffic.)

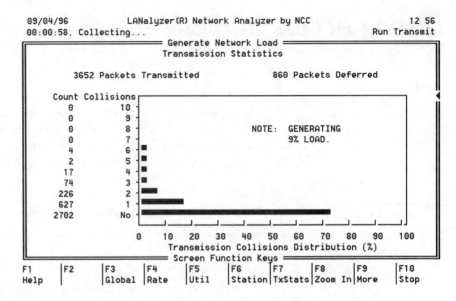

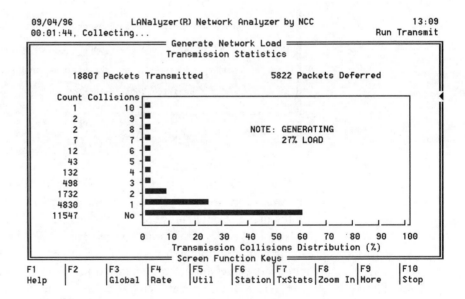

Stress-Testing the Network Cabling System

YOU HAVE SIMULATED a load on the network based on one type of user. You do not, however, know the exact impact the load has placed on the other users accessing the cable system. How much has performance degraded because of the added load?

The next example sets up a performance test measuring file transfer time under varying loads, as shown in Figure 2.17. First you will transfer a file while generating a 10% load and record the transfer time. Then you will increase the load and record the impact on the file transfer time.

FIGURE 2.17

Setting up the performance test

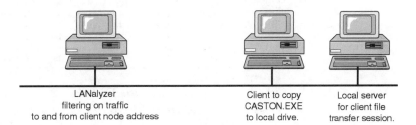

LANalyzer
filtering on traffic
to and from client node address

Client to copy
CASTON.EXE
to local drive.

Local server
for client file
transfer session.

For this test, you will need to use the NCC LANalyzer and one client workstation (for the file transfer). To perform the test, follow these steps:

1. Edit the NCC LANalyzer's default application.

2. Set up a receive channel.

3. Perform a file transfer.

4. Record the file transfer time.

5. Increase the load; repeat the file transfer.

6. Record the results.

STEP 1: Edit the NCC LANalyzer's Default Application

In order to transmit varying loads, you will use the DEFAULT application, which is already configured for load testing. Figure 2.18 illustrates the DEFAULT application transmit channels. If your NCC LANalyzer DEFAULT application is still configured as it was when installed, you can skip this step and continue with step 2.

FIGURE 2.18

DEFAULT application transmit channels

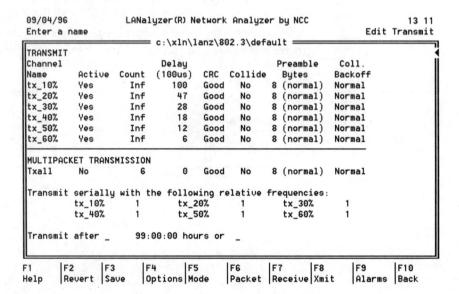

```
09/04/96          LANalyzer(R) Network Analyzer by NCC              13 11
Enter a name                                               Edit Transmit
══════════════════════════ c:\xln\lanz\802.3\default ═══════════════════╗
TRANSMIT
Channel                Delay                    Preamble    Coll.
Name      Active  Count (100us)  CRC  Collide   Bytes      Backoff
tx_10%    Yes     Inf    100     Good  No       8 (normal)  Normal
tx_20%    Yes     Inf     47     Good  No       8 (normal)  Normal
tx_30%    Yes     Inf     28     Good  No       8 (normal)  Normal
tx_40%    Yes     Inf     18     Good  No       8 (normal)  Normal
tx_50%    Yes     Inf     12     Good  No       8 (normal)  Normal
tx_60%    Yes     Inf      6     Good  No       8 (normal)  Normal

MULTIPACKET TRANSMISSION
Txall     No         6      0    Good  No       8 (normal)  Normal

Transmit serially with the following relative frequencies:
          tx_10%     1        tx_20%    1        tx_30%    1
          tx_40%     1        tx_50%    1        tx_60%    1

Transmit after _      99:00:00 hours or  _

F1      |F2     |F3    |F4      |F5    |F6     |F7      |F8    |F9     |F10
Help    |Revert |Save  |Options |Mode  |Packet |Receive |Xmit  |Alarms |Back
```

This application is configured to transmit the following loads:

Channel 1—10% load	1518-byte packets every 100 microseconds
Channel 2—20% load	1518-byte packets every 47 microseconds
Channel 3—30% load	1518-byte packets every 28 microseconds
Channel 4—40% load	1518-byte packets every 18 microseconds
Channel 5—50% load	1518-byte packets every 12 microseconds
Channel 6—60% load	1518-byte packets every 6 microseconds

STEP 2: Set Up a Receive Channel

As shown in Figure 2.19, define one receive channel that will filter on packets to and from your client station. You will use this receive channel to capture and time-stamp packets while the station transfers files.

Run the application and begin transmitting a 10% load on the network.

FIGURE 2.19

Set up one receive channel to filter on traffic to and from your client station.

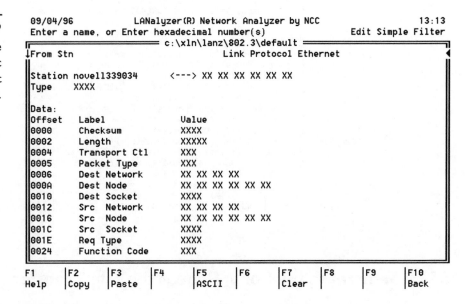

```
09/04/96          LANalyzer(R) Network Analyzer by NCC                    13:13
Enter a name, or Enter hexadecimal number(s)              Edit Simple Filter
╒═══════════════════════════ c:\xln\lanz\802.3\default ═══════════════════════╕
│↓From Stn                              Link Protocol Ethernet                 │
│                                                                              │
│Station novell339034        <---> XX XX XX XX XX XX                           │
│Type     XXXX                                                                 │
│                                                                              │
│Data:                                                                         │
│Offset    Label                Value                                          │
│0000      Checksum             XXXX                                           │
│0002      Length               XXXXX                                          │
│0004      Transport Ctl        XXX                                            │
│0005      Packet Type          XXX                                            │
│0006      Dest Network         XX XX XX XX                                    │
│000A      Dest Node            XX XX XX XX XX XX                              │
│0010      Dest Socket          XXXX                                           │
│0012      Src  Network         XX XX XX XX                                    │
│0016      Src  Node            XX XX XX XX XX XX                              │
│001C      Src  Socket          XXXX                                           │
│001E      Req Type             XXXX                                           │
│0024      Function Code        XXX                                            │
╘══════════════════════════════════════════════════════════════════════════════╛
F1     |F2    |F3     |F4    |F5     |F6    |F7     |F8    |F9    |F10
Help   |Copy  |Paste  |      |ASCII  |      |Clear  |      |      |Back
```

STEP 3: Perform a File Transfer

In this example, you are copying the CASTON.EXE file from the PUBLIC directory to the local C drive. For this file transfer, you can use the DOS COPY command.

STEP 4: Record the File Transfer Time

Since the application captured only packets to and from the client workstation, all packets in the trace buffer are from the file transfer. To calculate the total required time for the file transfer, you can select the *relative time-stamp* viewing option. Figure 2.20 depicts all packet arrival times required for the file transfer.

FIGURE 2.20

Calculating the file transfer time

```
09/04/96              LANalyzer(R) Network Analyzer by NCC                18 03
Press ALT-T to toggle between summary modes                    Trace Summary
=========================== Trace Buffer ===========================
Created On 09/05/92 18:02:21   Elapsed Time 00:00:02   Total Packets      999

  Pkt#  Source        Destination  Protocol   Size  Error  Channels   Rel Time
     1  exosC14126    novell33E9BD NetWare    348          .......8    0.000 ms
     2  cisco021602   exosC14126   NetWare    308          .......8    8.264 ms
     3  exosC14126    cisco021602  NetWare     64          .......8    9.267 ms
     4  novell33E9BD  exosC14126   NetWare    464          .......8   19.857 ms
     5  exosC14126    novell33E9BD NetWare    182          .......8   30.271 ms
     6  exosC14126    SJF-JUPITER  NetWare     64          .......8   31.018 ms
     7  novell33E9BD  exosC14126   NetWare     64          .......8   35.576 ms
     8  novell33E9BD  exosC14126   NetWare    308          .......8   43.520 ms
     9  exosC14126    novell33E9BD NetWare     64          .......8   44.516 ms
    10  novell33E9BD  exosC14126   NetWare    308          .......8   47.345 ms
    11  exosC14126    novell33E9BD NetWare     64          .......8   48.342 ms
    12  novell33E9BD  exosC14126   NetWare    308          .......8   56.723 ms
    13  exosC14126    novell33E9BD NetWare     64          .......8   57.710 ms
    14  novell1E5188  SJF-EARTH    NetWare    102          .......8   67.222 ms
    15  SJF-EARTH     novell1E5188 NetWare     64          .......8   68.360 ms
    16  SJF-EARTH     novell1E5188 NetWare    308          .......8   72.116 ms

F1     F2     F3     F4       F5    F6      F7       F8    F9     F10
Help   Load   Print  Options  Save  Decode  Compare  Find  Go To  Back
```

STEP 5: Increase the Load; Repeat the File Transfer

Repeat steps 2 through 4 for each load and record the file transfer times.

STEP 6: Record the Results

As shown in Figure 2.21, file transfer time has increased dramatically under a load of greater than 30%.

You have now experienced the delay that users are subjected to when trying to work on a network segment that is heavily used.

This chapter has examined bandwidth utilization and its effect on network efficiency. Using the NCC LANalyzer, you have generated a load on the network and analyzed the responses. When you performed a load test and examined your transmit statistics, you determined how often packets were

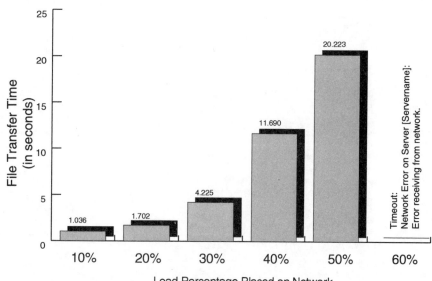

FIGURE 2.21

Network performance
during load test

transmitted successfully on the first attempt. By timing a file transfer under various load conditions, you examined network performance degradation under higher utilization.

The next chapter deals with the wiring specifications and performance of Ethernet networks, including 10Base5, 10Base2, and 10BaseT. The chapter, which presents analysis and troubleshooting techniques using various cabling tests, also explains how you can watch for specific network errors.

Wiring
Specifications
and
Performance

CHAPTER

3

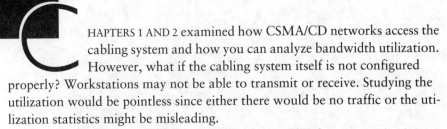

HAPTERS 1 AND 2 examined how CSMA/CD networks access the cabling system and how you can analyze bandwidth utilization. However, what if the cabling system itself is not configured properly? Workstations may not be able to transmit or receive. Studying the utilization would be pointless since either there would be no traffic or the utilization statistics might be misleading.

The wiring system of an Ethernet network provides the communication medium upon which packets travel. The 802.3 specification includes various CSMA/CD wiring configurations. This chapter begins with an overview of the most common wiring configurations for NetWare Ethernet LANs:

- 10Base5 (thicknet)

- 10Base2 (thinnet)

- 10BaseT (unshielded twisted-pair, or UTP)

You will use the NCC LANalyzer to track and determine the causes of various errors that may be related to faulty wiring or wiring that does not use recommended specifications and limitations.

10Base5

THE 10BASE5 NETWORK uses thick Ethernet cable for the primary trunk and drop cables to the individual workstations, as shown in Figure 3.1. Although bulky and difficult to install, this cabling system allows greater distance on cable segments and better shielding of electronic signals.

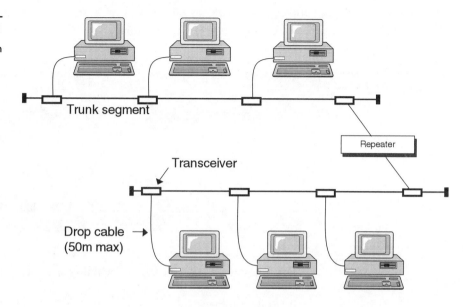

FIGURE 3.1

Thicknet cabling system

The following table lists 10Base5 cabling specifications:

Taps per segment	100
Maximum node separation	5 segments/4 repeaters
Maximum segment length	500 meters
Network span	2500 meters
Minimum length between transceivers	2.5 meters
Maximum transceiver cable length	50 meters

10Base2

THE 10BASE2 NETWORK uses thin coaxial cable, as shown in Figure 3.2. These systems are often referred to as "thinnet" or "cheapernet." This specification does not allow the use of drop cables to the workstation. Instead, workstations are attached directly to the primary trunk, using T-connectors.

FIGURE 3.2

Thinnet cabling system

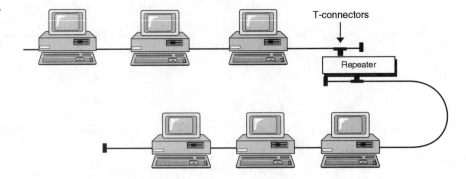

The following table lists 10Base2 cabling specifications:

Taps per segment	30
Maximum node separation	5 segments/4 repeaters
Maximum segment length	185 meters
Network span	925 meters
Minimum between workstations	.5 meters

10BaseT

THE 10BASET specification was added to 802.3 in late 1991. It defines a CSMA/CD network that uses unshielded twisted-pair (a common type of telephone wire) wiring in a star configuration, as shown in Figure 3.3. Because of its potentially low cabling costs and modular style, 10BaseT networks are extremely popular for NetWare LANs.

The 10BaseT specification defines only unshielded twisted-pair wiring. It does not include shielded twisted-pair cabling. Proper operation is dependent upon an acceptable number of twists per foot. These twists prevent crosstalk.

FIGURE 3.3

10BaseT cabling system

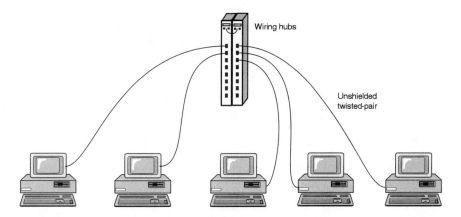

Crosstalk occurs when signals stray from one wiring pair to another, corrupting the signal.

There are some important differences between 10BaseT network specifications and 10Base2 and 10Base5. A 10BaseT segment is between a workstation and the concentrator; therefore, only two devices can be on each segment (the station and the wire center, often called a hub or concentrator).

The following table lists 10BaseT cabling specifications:

Maximum nodes per segment	2
Concentrators in sequence	4 maximum
Maximum node separation	5 segments/4 repeaters
Maximum workstation-to-concentrator length	100 meters

Improper Cabling Problems

MPROPER CABLING OF networks can cause a variety of problems on NetWare LANs. Symptoms include slow performance, inability to establish or maintain a workstation connection, and corrupted transmissions.

Many of the symptoms presented in this chapter, such as CRC errors and collisions, are covered in detail in Chapter 5. Cabling problems that can affect network performance include:

- Opens or shorts in the cable

- Noise or electromagnetic interference (EMI)

- Inadequate interspacing (spacing between taps or workstations)

- Improper termination

- Improper ground

- Segment too long

Using a protocol analyzer, you can determine whether or not a network has a possible cabling problem.

Testing for Shorts and Opens

The NCC LANalyzer and many other protocol analyzers provide a cable-checking mechanism much like a TDR (time domain reflectometer). These mechanisms transmit a series of bits down the cable, time the response, and examine the return signal (if there is one).

This function is also used to determine if the cable problem is a short or an open. Figure 3.4 shows how the NCC LANalyzer indicates a short in the cable. A short may be caused by a slight break in the cable or poor connectors. Often, a short causes only intermittent network problems. To simulate a short, unfold a metal paper clip and touch one end to the cable's center conductor and the other to the shield.

An open, however, causes the entire network segment to be unavailable for transmission. Figure 3.5 shows how the NCC LANalyzer indicates an open cable segment. A segment that has only local collisions occurring on it must be open at one end. Removing the terminator from one end of a segment will simulate an open.

FIGURE 3.4

The NCC LANalyzer indicates a short in the cable.

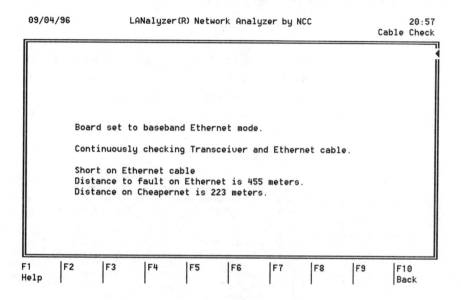

```
09/04/96              LANalyzer(R) Network Analyzer by NCC                    20:57
                                                                         Cable Check
 ┌────────────────────────────────────────────────────────────────────────────────┐
 │                                                                                  │
 │                                                                                  │
 │                                                                                  │
 │                                                                                  │
 │                                                                                  │
 │                                                                                  │
 │          Board set to baseband Ethernet mode.                                    │
 │                                                                                  │
 │          Continuously checking Transceiver and Ethernet cable.                   │
 │                                                                                  │
 │          Short on Ethernet cable                                                 │
 │          Distance to fault on Ethernet is 455 meters.                            │
 │          Distance on Cheapernet is 223 meters.                                   │
 │                                                                                  │
 │                                                                                  │
 │                                                                                  │
 │                                                                                  │
 │                                                                                  │
 └────────────────────────────────────────────────────────────────────────────────┘
 F1     │F2    │F3    │F4    │F5    │F6    │F7    │F8    │F9    │F10
 Help   │      │      │      │      │      │      │      │      │Back
```

FIGURE 3.5

The NCC LANalyzer indicates an open cable segment.

```
09/04/96              LANalyzer(R) Network Analyzer by NCC                    20:57
                                                                         Cable Check
 ┌────────────────────────────────────────────────────────────────────────────────┐
 │                                                                                  │
 │                                                                                  │
 │                                                                                  │
 │                                                                                  │
 │                                                                                  │
 │                                                                                  │
 │          Board set to baseband Ethernet mode.                                    │
 │                                                                                  │
 │          Continuously checking Transceiver and Ethernet cable.                   │
 │                                                                                  │
 │          Open on Ethernet cable                                                  │
 │          Distance to fault on Ethernet is 455 meters.                            │
 │          Distance on Cheapernet is 223 meters.                                   │
 │                                                                                  │
 │                                                                                  │
 │                                                                                  │
 │                                                                                  │
 │                                                                                  │
 └────────────────────────────────────────────────────────────────────────────────┘
 F1     │F2    │F3    │F4    │F5    │F6    │F7    │F8    │F9    │F10
 Help   │      │      │      │      │      │      │      │      │Back
```

Indications of Improper Grounding

An excessive number of CRC errors, as shown in Figure 3.6, may indicate a network that has been improperly grounded and contains a distributed fault. A *distributed fault* is one that cannot be attributed to a single component on the network. If CRC errors are coming from multiple stations, check cable grounding. However, if you can attribute CRC errors to a single network device, replace the card, connectors, or cable of that device.

Late collisions may also be caused by a deaf node, as covered in Chapter 5.

FIGURE 3.6

CRC errors from multiple stations indicate a cable grounding problem.

```
09/04/96          LANalyzer(R) Network Analyzer by NCC              21 24
Press ALT-T to toggle between summary modes              Trace Summary
                          === b:\crc ===
Created On 09/05/92 20:15:32   Elapsed Time 00:00:19   Total Packets    2600

 Pkt# Source        Destination  Protocol    Size  Error   Channels  IntPkt Time
↕ 344 novell1EF22C  SJF-SALSA    NetWare      74   CRC     12......  0.403 ms◄
↕ 345 novell1EF22C  SJF-SALSA    NetWare      74           1.......  0.403 ms◄
  346 novell187450  MKTG         NetWare      64   CRC     12......  0.475 ms
  347 MKTG          novell1EF22C NetWare     184   CRC     12......  0.770 ms
  348 MKTG          novell1EF22C NetWare     184           1.......  0.770 ms
  349 exos8e4501    SALES        NetWare      64   CRC     12......  0.561 ms
  350 SJF-SALSA     novell1EF22C NetWare      64           1.......  0.671 ms
  351 3com90d0b5    SALES        NetWare      64   CRC     12......  0.412 ms
  352 SALES         novell1EF22C NetWare     184           1.......  0.756 ms
  353 novell897612  ADMIN1       NetWare      64   CRC     12......  0.559 ms
  354 novell897612  ADMIN1       NetWare      64   CRC     12......  0.559 ms
  355 novell1EF22C  SALES        NetWare      64           1.......  0.392 ms
  356 SALES         novell1EF22C NetWare      64           1.......  0.545 ms
  357 novell1EF22C  BLDG4        NetWare     568           1.......  1.002 ms
  358 BLDG4         novell1EF22C NetWare     390           1.......  1.343 ms
  359 novell674590  BLDG4        NetWare      64   CRC     12......  0.521 ms
  360 SJF-SALSA     novell1EF22C NetWare     184           1.......  0.733 ms

F1    F2    F3    F4      F5     F6     F7      F8   F9    F10
Help  Load  Print Options Buffer Decode Compare Find Go To Back
```

Detecting Illegal Segment Lengths with Late Collisions

Late collisions, illustrated in Figure 3.7, may also be a symptom of a cabling problem. A *late collision* is a collision that has occurred 64 bytes or more into the packet. It indicates that a segment may be longer than allowed by the wiring specifications.

A station will believe it has control of the cable segment if it has already transmitted 64 bytes. If another node at the far end of the segment has not yet

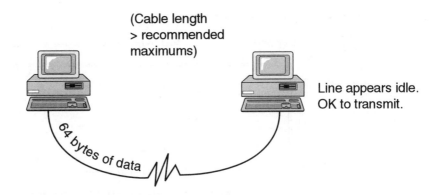

FIGURE 3.7

Late collisions may indicate that a segment is longer than specifications allow.

(Cable length > recommended maximums)

Line appears idle. OK to transmit.

64 bytes of data

seen the packet and the node transmits, this packet will collide with the first transmission after the first 64 bytes have been sent.

Testing Station Connectivity

Using the NCC LANalyzer, you can test a workstation's transceiver cable (the wire connecting a workstation to an external transceiver), as shown in Figure 3.8. Placing the NCC LANalyzer on the transceiver cable that is in question, load the NCC LANalyzer software and transmit a single packet on the network. (Try the NODEVIEW application.) An error message is displayed at the top of the screen if the NCC LANalyzer cannot transmit.

Detecting the location of cabling problems can be very difficult on an Ethernet network. When the network is down, how can one localize a fault? Many technicians recommend "shortening" an Ethernet segment until the problems are no longer seen and then beginning to expand the network until the problem recurs. Using NCC LANalyzer and LANalyzer for Windows, you can detect errors that result from poor wiring, grounding, and not following defined specifications for Ethernet cabling systems.

This chapter has listed the specifications for the three most common Ethernet cabling systems: 10Base5, 10Base2, and 10BaseT. Using the specifications and analysis procedures defined, you should now be confident in testing and solving typical cabling problems such as cabling shorts, opens, and improper grounding.

FIGURE 3.8

Testing the transceiver
cable connection

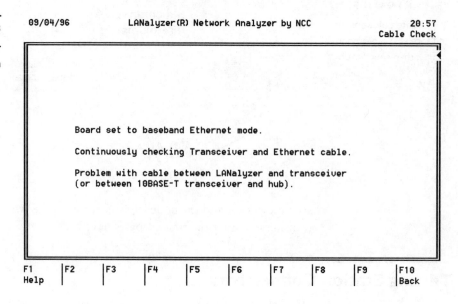

09/04/96   LANalyzer(R) Network Analyzer by NCC   20:57
                                                                      Cable Check

Board set to baseband Ethernet mode.

Continuously checking Transceiver and Ethernet cable.

Problem with cable between LANalyzer and transceiver
(or between 10BASE-T transceiver and hub).

F1   F2   F3   F4   F5   F6   F7   F8   F9   F10
Help   Back

FIGURE 3.8

Testing the transceiver
cable connection

The next chapter defines the four Ethernet frame types that can be found in
the NetWare environment.

NetWare's Ethernet Frame Structures

4

I N CHAPTERS 1 THROUGH 3, you examined the media access method (CSMA/CD), cabling utilization, and cabling specifications for 802.3/Ethernet LANs. When stations access the transmission medium, however, data must be encapsulated in a frame. *Frames* provide a method for synchronizing receiving stations, defining the sender and receiver, and defining the upper-layer protocol using the frame (such as NetWare's IPX Protocol or IP, the Internet Protocol).

Since the release of NetWare v3.0, the use of multiple frame types and multiple protocols has become quite common. This multiple-frame and multiprotocol ability allows the interconnection of a variety of protocols, such as NetWare, AppleTalk Phase I and II, TCP/IP, and FTAM. But this flexibility has caused some confusion regarding frames, protocols, and their interoperability.

This chapter first examines the NetWare operating system support for Ethernet frames, as well as the protocols that can be used with each frame type. Later in this chapter, you will view the structure of the four frame types that can be found on NetWare Ethernet LANs. Finally, you will use the frame structure information to analyze a LAN to determine which frames are in use by servers and clients and why a workstation may receive a "File server not found" message.

Frame Types on NetWare LANs

N ETWARE 3.X AND 4.X support four different frame structures for Ethernet network cards. In the NetWare environment, they are called

Ethernet_802.3

Ethernet_II

Ethernet_802.2

Ethernet_SNAP

This book uses the frame type names defined by Novell and used within the AUTOEXEC.NCF and NET.CFG files.

When NETX.COM or VLM.EXE is used, frame types are specified in the NET.CFG file for Open Data-Link Interface (ODI) workstation drivers. At the file server, the frame type is specified at the server console prompt or within the AUTOEXEC.NCF file. ODI support for NetWare v3.x and later allows multiple protocols and multiple frame types to use a single board, as you can see in Figure 4.1.

Ethernet_802.3 is the default frame type for NetWare v2.x and v3.x networks. Ethernet_802.2 is the default frame type for NetWare 4.x.

FIGURE 4.1

NetWare LANs can use multiple frames and protocols.

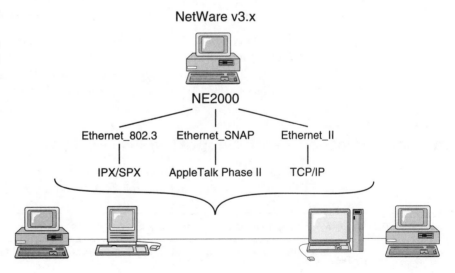

NetWare v2.x, non-ODI drivers, and external routers (BRIDGE.EXE or ROUTER.EXE) may use only the Ethernet_802.3 and Ethernet_II frame types. You can specify these frame types using the ECONFIG utility. This utility is covered later in this chapter.

Novell's MultiProtocol Router is an external router that supports multiple frame types and multiple protocols.

Table 4.1 lists the NetWare operating systems and the Ethernet frame types they support.

TABLE 4.1	NETWARE VERSION	FRAME TYPES SUPPORTED
NetWare Operating System Frame Support	NetWare v2.x	Ethernet_802.3 (802.3 raw)
		Ethernet_II
	NetWare v3.x and NetWare v4.x	Ethernet_802.3 (802.3 raw)
		Ethernet_II
		Ethernet_802.2
		Ethernet_SNAP

With the release of NetWare v3.x, you could have up to four frame types used by a single card in the server. For example, an NE2000 driver can be loaded using all four frame types listed in Table 4.1. This allows a single network interface card to support protocols that do not use the same frame type.

Matching Protocols with Supported Frame Types

Not all protocols can be used with each frame type available. Refer to Table 4.2 for a quick reference listing of frames and protocols.

TABLE 4.2	PROTOCOL	FRAME TYPES
Protocols and Assorted Frame Types	Ethernet_II	IPX/SPX, TCP/IP, and AppleTalk Phase I
	Ethernet_802.2	IPX/SPX and FTAM<$!B28>
	Ethernet_802.3	IPX/SPX
	Ethernet_SNAP	IPX/SPX, TCP/IP, and AppleTalk Phase II

The Ethernet_802.3 frame type is used only by NetWare's IPX/SPX Protocol. If you attempt to bind Ethernet_802.3 to another frame type, you will receive this error message: "Warning: [PROTOCOL] does not recognize the media 'ETHERNET_802.3'. Using defaults. Attempt to bind [PROTOCOL] LAN protocol to [LAN DRIVER/version/date] failed."

If this command was in an AUTOEXEC.NCF file, the error message may scroll past on the console screen when you boot the server. To check the protocols bound to the frame types, type **CONFIG** at the server. Figure 4.2 shows a situation in which LAN card (NE3200) is supporting two frame types but only one of the frames has a protocol bound to it.

Chapter 5 examines various Ethernet frame errors and their causes.

FIGURE 4.2

Typing CONFIG shows no protocol bound to an Ethernet_802.2 frame.

```
:CONFIG

File server name: SALES1
IPX internal network number: A9990001

NetWare NE3200 v3.18 (920115)
      Hardware setting: Slot 5, I/O Port 5C80h to 5CAFh, Interrupt 5h
      Node address: 00001B0945D4
      Frame type: ETHERNET_802.3
      Board name: IPXNET
      LAN protocol: IPX network B4440101

NetWare NE3200 v3.18 (920115)
      Hardware setting: Slot 5, I/O Port 5C80h to 5CAFh, Interrupt 5h
      Node address: 00001B0945D4
      Frame type: ETHERNET_802.2
      Board name: TEMP
      No LAN protocols are bound to this LAN board.
```

We highly recommend that you acquire CONLOG, a utility that has been released on NetWire, Novell's 24-hour technical support forum on CompuServe. CONLOG is an NLM that writes all system messages of a NetWare 3.x or 4.x server to a .LOG file. If your boot sequence scrolls messages too quickly to view, you can reference the CONLOG file to view any error messages that were displayed during bootup. You can obtain a CompuServe account by calling 1-800-848-8990.

The following sections review the structure of each Ethernet frame type. By understanding a properly formed frame, you should be able to determine when a frame is corrupted or malformed.

Ethernet_802.3

WITH NETWARE VERSIONS up to and including v3.12, Ethernet_802.3 is the default frame type. This frame type is often referred to as "802.3 raw." (NetWare 4.x defaults to the Ethernet_802.2 frame type.)

Protocols Supported

The Ethernet_802.3 frame type, shown in Figure 4.3, is exclusively for Novell's IPX/SPX Protocol. Only Novell's IPX/SPX Protocol can be bound to this frame type.

FIGURE 4.3

Ethernet_802.3 frame

Preamble/SFD (8 bytes)

Destination Address (6 bytes)

Source Address (6 bytes)

Length (2 bytes)

Data (46-1500 bytes)

FCS (4 bytes)

"802.3 raw" is similar to a true 802.3-compliant frame but does not contain the LLC (Logical Link Control) information in the packet (hence, the "raw" designator).

Ethernet_802.3 Frame Structure

The following sections define the fields shown in Figure 4.3.

Preamble and Start Frame Delimiter

The preamble is a 7-byte field used to synchronize the receiving stations. It contains alternating 1's and 0's. The start frame delimiter (SFD) is 1 byte and trails the preamble. The SFD also contains alternating 1's and 0's. The SFD, however, ends with two consecutive 1's. The two 1's signify the beginning of the frame.

The preamble and start frame delimiters are shown in Figure 4.4.

FIGURE 4.4

Preamble and start frame delimiters

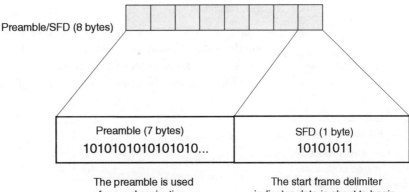

Preamble/SFD (8 bytes)

Preamble (7 bytes)	SFD (1 byte)
1010101010101010...	10101011

The preamble is used for synchronization.

The start frame delimiter indicates data is about to begin.

Destination Address

The destination address, shown in Figure 4.5, is a 6-byte field that contains the hardware (or node) address of the station on the local segment to which the packet is addressed. The address FF-FF-FF-FF-FF-FF denotes a broadcast address.

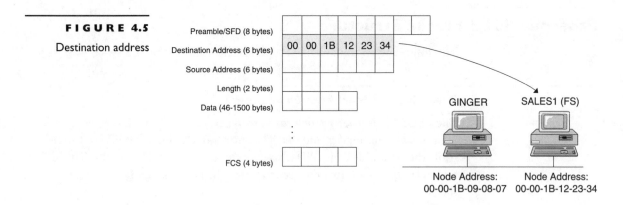

FIGURE 4.5

Destination address

Source Address

The source address, shown in Figure 4.6, contains the node address of the station on the local segment that sent the packet. The source address contains the hardware (or node) address of a local workstation, server, or router. The source address cannot be broadcast (FF-FF-FF-FF-FF-FF).

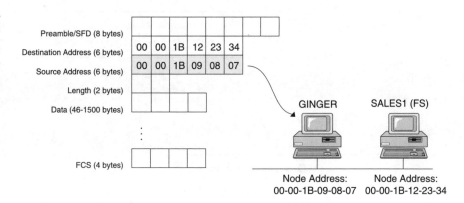

FIGURE 4.6

The source address contains the node number of the transmitting station on the local segment.

Length Field

The length field, shown in Figure 4.7, is a 2-byte field that defines the length of upper-layer data contained in the data portion of the frame. This value must be 1500 (decimal) or less in a valid Ethernet_802.3 frame.

If the frame is valid and the length value is greater than 1500 (decimal), it is an Ethernet_II frame and this is a type field.

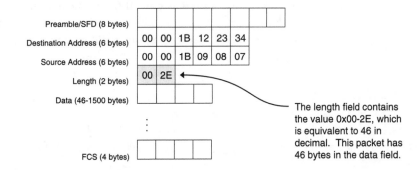

FIGURE 4.7

The length field denotes the length of the data portion of the frame.

Data Field

The data field, shown in Figure 4.8, is where NetWare's IPX header will begin. The length of the data field must be between 46 and 1500 bytes.

The IPX header format is defined in Chapter 14.

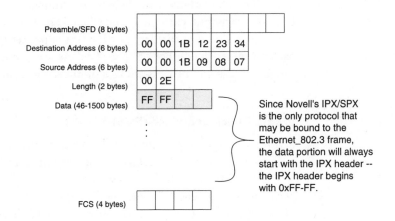

FIGURE 4.8

The data portion of the packet must be 46 to 1500 bytes long.

Padding

In order to achieve the Ethernet minimum of 64 bytes for a frame, the data field must be a minimum of 46 bytes. The 46-byte data field, added to the 18-byte frame fields, totals the required 64-byte frame size. (The preamble and SFD are not counted as part of the frame length.)

However, if the data to be transmitted in the packet does not meet the 46-byte minimum length, it will be padded with bytes, as shown in Figure 4.9, to ensure that the data portion of the frame is at least 46 bytes in length.

FIGURE 4.9

Padding can be added to the data portion to ensure that the minimum frame length requirement is met.

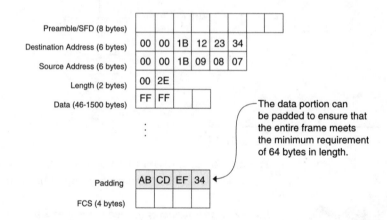

Interestingly, you may see a frame with a data portion greater than 46 bytes that still contains a single byte of padding. Novell has requested that all LAN driver manufacturers "evenize" packets. Evenizing simply means adding 1 byte of padding to the data portion of the packet to ensure that the total packet is an even number of bytes. Packets are evenized because some routers cannot handle and process packets of uneven length.

Frame Check Sequence (FCS)

Error-checking is built into each Ethernet frame to ensure that only valid frames are processed by the receiving station. The FCS field contains a 4-byte CRC (Cyclic Redundancy Check) value. The transmitting station performs a CRC check before sending the packet. The CRC value is placed in the FCS field, as you can see in Figure 4.10. The receiving station will perform the same CRC check and compare the resulting value with the contents of the FCS field. If the numbers match, the frame is assumed to be valid. The Ethernet chipset checks this field and determines whether or not a packet is valid. As shown in Chapter 1, an alignment test will also be performed on any packet with an invalid CRC value.

FIGURE 4.10

CRC values are placed in the FCS field.

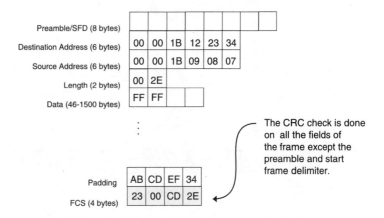

The CRC value is calculated based upon the contents of the destination address, source address, length, data, and pad.

Total Ethernet_802.3 Frame Length

When the total frame length is defined, the preamble and start frame delimiter are not counted. Based on the preceding information, minimum and maximum lengths are defined by adding all the frame field lengths:

Destination address	6 bytes
Source address	6 bytes
Length	2 bytes
Data and padding	46–1500 bytes
FCS	4 bytes
Minimum frame size	64 bytes
Maximum frame size	1518 bytes

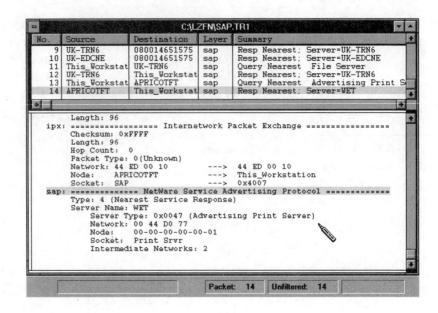

FIGURE 4.11

Decode of
Ethernet_802.3

Ethernet_802.2

THE ETHERNET_802.2 frame type is considered IEEE-compliant because it contains both the 802.3 fields and the 802.2 fields. The 802.2 fields are also referred to as the LLC (Logical Link Control) layer within the frame.

Protocols Supported

The Ethernet_802.2 frame, shown in Figure 4.12, can be linked with Novell's IPX/SPX Protocol and the FTAM (File Transfer, Access, and Management) Protocol.

FIGURE 4.12

802.2 frame structure

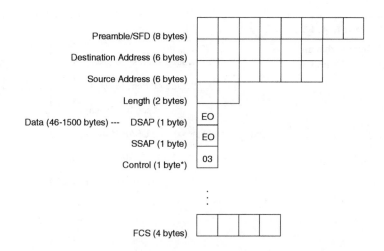

Preamble/SFD (8 bytes)
Destination Address (6 bytes)
Source Address (6 bytes)
Length (2 bytes)
Data (46-1500 bytes) --- DSAP (1 byte)   EO
SSAP (1 byte)   EO
Control (1 byte*)   03

FCS (4 bytes)

* NetWare's IPX/SPX will always use a 1-byte control field containing
the value 0x03, which denotes an unnumbered format for the Ethernet_802.2 layer.

Ethernet_802.2 Frame Structure

The Ethernet_802.2 frame structure is the default frame type for Net-Ware 4.x. The Ethernet_802.2 frame contains common fields with the Ethernet_802.3 frame. Both Ethernet_802.2 and Ethernet_802.3 frames contain

- The preamble and start frame delimiter (8 bytes)

- The destination address (6 bytes)

- The source address (6 bytes)

- The length (2 bytes)

- The data and padding (46–1500 bytes)

- The FCS field (4 bytes)

In the Ethernet_802.2 frame, the 802.2 (or LLC) fields begin immediately after the length field of the 802.3 header. Figure 4.13 details the 802.2 (LLC) fields.

FIGURE 4.13

802.2 fields within an
Ethernet_802.3 frame

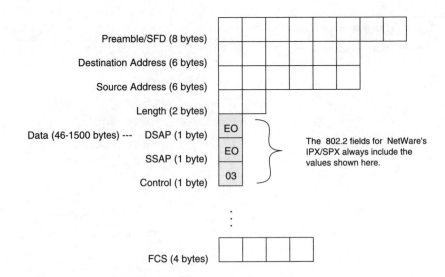

FIGURE 4.13

802.2 fields within an
Ethernet_802.3 frame

Preamble/SFD (8 bytes)

Destination Address (6 bytes)

Source Address (6 bytes)

Length (2 bytes)

Data (46-1500 bytes) --- DSAP (1 byte)   EO

SSAP (1 byte)   EO

Control (1 byte)   03

The 802.2 fields for NetWare's
IPX/SPX always include the
values shown here.

FCS (4 bytes)

Destination Service Access Point

The Destination Service Access Point (DSAP) field denotes the destination
upper-layer (or network-layer) protocol type of the packet. NetWare IPX/SPX
packets will contain the hexadecimal value 0xE0 in the DSAP field.

Values represented by hexadecimal format are generally preceded by "0x" in this book.

Source Service Access Point

The Source Service Access Point (SSAP) field (1 byte) denotes the upper-layer
(or network-layer) protocol type of the packet, as does the DSAP. NetWare
IPX/SPX packets will contain the hexadecimal value 0xE0 in the SSAP field.

Control Field

When NetWare's IPX/SPX is used, the control field will contain the value
0x03, which denotes the 802.2 unnumbered format. The unnumbered format
indicates that the LLC layer will provide connectionless services. Currently,

NetWare's IPX/SPX Protocols do not rely on the LLC layer for connection-oriented services. Figure 4.14 shows a NetWare IPX/SPX packet using the Ethernet_802.2 frame format.

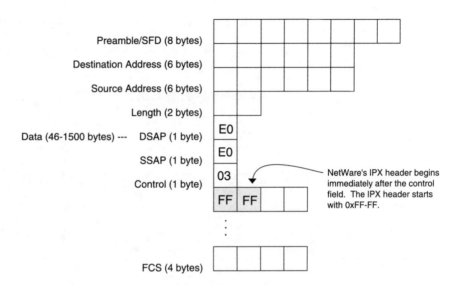

FIGURE 4.14

NetWare IPX using the Ethernet_802.2 frame

Total Ethernet_802.2 Frame Length

When the total frame length is defined, the preamble and start frame delimiter are not counted. Based on the preceding information, minimum and maximum lengths are defined by adding all the frame field lengths:

Destination address	6 bytes
Source address	6 bytes
Length	2 bytes
Data and padding	46–1500 bytes
LLC fields include	
DSAP	1 byte
SSAP	1 byte

Control	1 byte
FCS	4 bytes
Minimum frame size	64 bytes
Maximum frame size	1518 bytes

Figure 4.15 shows a decode of the Ethernet_802.2 frame.

FIGURE 4.15

Decode of the
Ethernet_802.2 frame

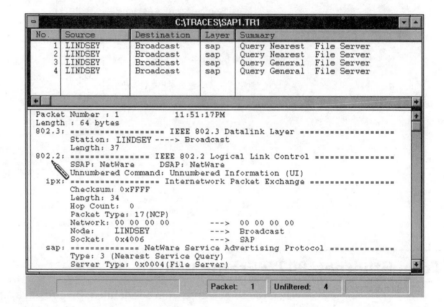

```
                          C:\TRACES\SAP1.TR1
No.   Source          Destination    Layer   Summary
   1  LINDSEY         Broadcast      sap     Query Nearest  File Server
   2  LINDSEY         Broadcast      sap     Query Nearest  File Server
   3  LINDSEY         Broadcast      sap     Query General  File Server
   4  LINDSEY         Broadcast      sap     Query General  File Server

  Packet Number : 1                11:51:17PM
  Length : 64 bytes
  802.3: ================== IEEE 802.3 Datalink Layer ==================
          Station: LINDSEY ----> Broadcast
          Length: 37
  802.2: ================ IEEE 802.2 Logical Link Control ================
          SSAP: NetWare      DSAP: NetWare
          Unnumbered Command: Unnumbered Information (UI)
   ipx: ================== Internetwork Packet Exchange ==================
          Checksum: 0xFFFF
          Length: 34
          Hop Count: 0
          Packet Type: 17(NCP)
          Network: 00 00 00 00       ---> 00 00 00 00
          Node:   LINDSEY            ---> Broadcast
          Socket: 0x4006             ---> SAP
   sap: ============== NetWare Service Advertising Protocol ==============
          Type: 3 (Nearest Service Query)
          Server Type: 0x0004(File Server)

                               Packet:  1    Unfiltered:  4
```

Ethernet_SNAP

S NAP STANDS FOR Sub-Network Access Protocol. This frame type is derived from the Ethernet_802.2 structure. It is illustrated in Figure 4.16.

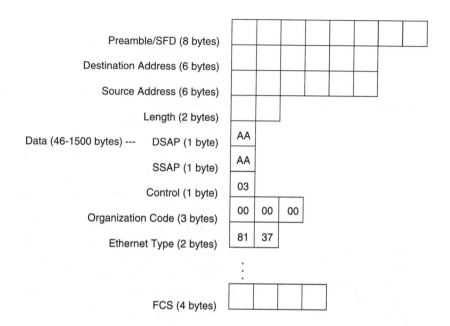

FIGURE 4.16

Ethernet_SNAP frame structure

Protocols Supported

Protocols that can use the Ethernet_SNAP frame type include IPX/SPX, TCP/IP, and AppleTalk Phase II.

Ethernet_SNAP Frame Structure

The fields for the Ethernet_SNAP frame are the same as for the Ethernet_802.2 frame:

- Preamble and start frame delimiter (8 bytes)

- Destination address (6 bytes)

- Source address (6 bytes)

- Length (2 bytes)

- Data and padding (46–1500 bytes)

- LLC 802.2 (DSAP, SSAP, and control fields)

- FCS (4 bytes)

DSAP, SSAP, and Control Fields

In Ethernet_SNAP frames, the value of the DSAP and SSAP fields will always be 0xAA. The value 0xAA indicates that the frame is a SNAP format frame.

The control field of SNAP frames is always 1 byte in length and contains the value 0x03 (unnumbered). It is followed by the organization code and Ethernet type fields, as shown in Figure 4.17.

FIGURE 4.17

Ethernet_SNAP organization code and Ethernet type fields

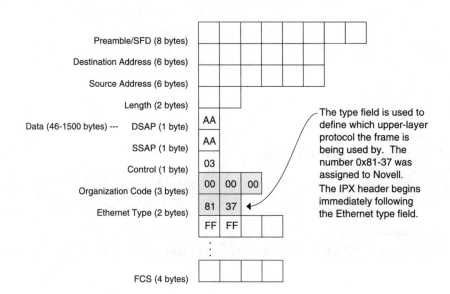

Organization Code

The organization code field denotes the organization that assigned the Ethernet type field to follow. NetWare's IPX/SPX packets contain 0x00-00-00 in the organization code field.

Ethernet Type Field

The Ethernet type field defines the upper-layer protocol. NetWare's Ethernet type number is 0x8137. (Although not currently in use, Novell has reserved type number 0x8138.)

The following is a list of values for the Ethernet type field for various network protocols:

IP (Internet Protocol)	0x0800
ARP (Address Resolution Protocol)	0x0806
Reverse ARP	0x8035
AppleTalk	0x809B
AppleTalk ARP	0x80F3
NetWare IPX/SPX	0x8137

Total Frame Length

When the total frame length is defined, the preamble and start frame delimiter are not counted. Based on the preceding information, minimum and maximum lengths are defined by adding all the frame field lengths:

Destination address	6 bytes
Source address	6 bytes
Length	2 bytes
Data and padding	46–1500 bytes

The data field includes	
DSAP	1 byte
SSAP	1 byte
Control	1 byte

Organization code	3 bytes
Ethernet type	2 bytes
FCS field	4 bytes
Minimum frame size	64 bytes
Maximum frame size	1518 bytes

Figure 4.18 shows a sample of an IPX/SPX packet using the Ethernet_SNAP frame format.

FIGURE 4.18

Decode of Ethernet_SNAP frame

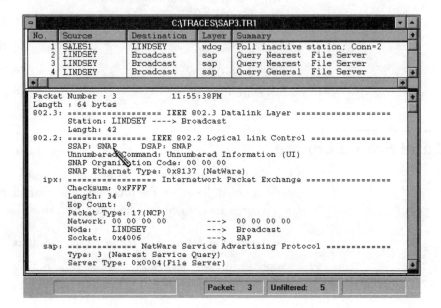

Ethernet_II

ETHERNET_II FRAMES are distinctive because of the type field that follows the source address. Ethernet_802.3, Ethernet_802.2, and Ethernet_SNAP frames contain a length field after the source address. The Ethernet_II frame structure is shown in Figure 4.19.

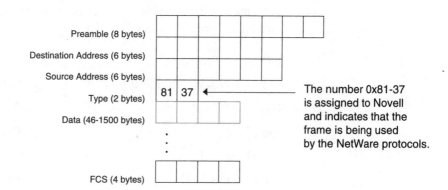

FIGURE 4.19

Ethernet_II frame
structure

Protocols Supported

The Ethernet_II frame can be used with IPX/SPX, TCP/IP, and AppleTalk Phase I.

Ethernet_II Frame Structure

Two areas distinguish the Ethernet_II frame from the others listed previously: the preamble/start frame delimiter and the type field.

Preamble

The 8-byte preamble field contains alternating 1's and 0's just as the 7-byte preamble of the other frame structures; however, in an Ethernet_II frame the 1-byte start frame delimiter (10101011) is considered part of the preamble.

Type Field

Unlike all the other frames, Ethernet_II frames contain a type field instead of a length field. This field denotes the upper-layer protocol that is using the packet.

Following is a list of values that can be contained in the type field to identify the various protcols using the frame:

IP (Internet Protocol)	0x0800
ARP (Address Resolution Protocol)	0x0806
Reverse ARP	0x8035
AppleTalk	0x809B
AppleTalk ARP	0x80F3
NetWare IPX/SPX	0x8137

Note that these are the same as the values that can be used in the Ethernet_SNAP type field.

Total Frame Length

When total frame length is defined, the preamble is not counted. Based on the preceding information, minimum and maximum lengths are defined by adding all the frame field lengths:

Destination address	6 bytes
Source address	6 bytes
Type	2 bytes
Data and padding	46–1500 bytes
FCS	4 bytes
Minimum frame size	64 bytes
Maximum frame size	1518 bytes

Figure 4.20 shows a decode of the Ethernet_II frame.

The ECONFIG Utility

NetWare 2.x operating systems, non-ODI drivers, and the NetWare external router programs (BRIDGE.EXE and ROUTER.EXE) do not permit the

FIGURE 4.20

Decode of the Ethernet_II frame

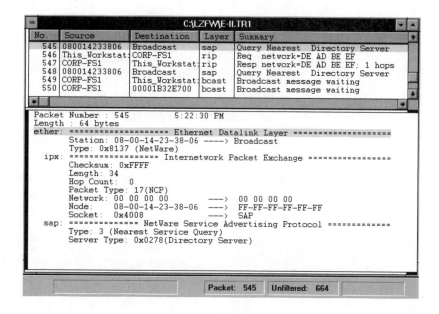

```
=                          C:\LZFW\E-II.TR1                          ▼ ▲
No. │ Source          │ Destination    │ Layer │ Summary                      ▲
545 │ 080014233806    │ Broadcast      │ sap   │ Query Nearest  Directory Server
546 │ This_Workstat:  │ CORP-FS1       │ rip   │ Req  network=DE AD BE EF
547 │ CORP-FS1        │ This_Workstat: │ rip   │ Resp network=DE AD BE EF; 1 hops
548 │ 080014233806    │ Broadcast      │ sap   │ Query Nearest  Directory Server
549 │ CORP-FS1        │ This_Workstat: │ bcast │ Broadcast message waiting
550 │ CORP-FS1        │ 00001B32E700   │ bcast │ Broadcast message waiting      ▼
◄                                                                              ►

Packet Number : 545              5:22:30 PM
Length  : 64 bytes
ether: ================== Ethernet Datalink Layer ==================
       Station: 08-00-14-23-38-06 ----> Broadcast
       Type: 0x8137 (NetWare)
  ipx: ================= Internetwork Packet Exchange =================
       Checksum: 0xFFFF
       Length: 34
       Hop Count:  0
       Packet Type: 17(NCP)
       Network: 00 00 00 00        ---> 00 00 00 00
       Node:    08-00-14-23-38-06  --->  FF-FF-FF-FF-FF-FF
       Socket:  0x4008             --->  SAP
  sap: ============== NetWare Service Advertising Protocol =============
       Type: 3 (Nearest Service Query)
       Server Type: 0x0278(Directory Server)


                                    Packet:  545   Unfiltered:  664
```

dynamic linking and unlinking of protocols with frame types. They can support only the frame types Ethernet_802.3 and Ethernet_II.

Novell's MultiProtocol Router (MPR) permits dynamic linking and unlinking of protocols and frame types.

If you wish to use the Ethernet_II frame type with NetWare 2.x servers, non-ODI client drivers, or the NetWare external router program, you must use the ECONFIG utility.

You can run the ECONFIG utility on the following files to configure them to use the Ethernet_II frame type:

- IPX.COM (non-ODI client IPX driver)

- NET$OS.EXE (NetWare OS)

- BRIDGE.EXE (external router program—old)

- ROUTER.EXE (external router program)

Ethernet_802.3 to Ethernet_II Frame Type

In order to configure the files listed above to use the Ethernet_II frame format, you must use the defined ECONFIG command syntax.

For IPX.COM, at the DOS prompt, type

```
ECONFIG IPX.COM SHELL:E 8137
```

For NET$OS.EXE, log in to the server with supervisory privileges. You may ECONFIG the operating system, but the new configuration will not take effect until you reboot the server. From within the SYSTEM directory, flag NET$OS.EXE as shareable, read/write, and type

```
ECONFIG NET$OS.EXE [LAN Designator]:E 8137
```

For the NetWare external router programs BRIDGE.EXE and ROUTER.EXE, access the directory containing BRIDGE.EXE or ROUTER.EXE and type

```
ECONFIG BRIDGE.EXE [LAN Designator]:E 8137
```

or

```
ECONFIG ROUTER.EXE [LAN Designator]:E 8137
```

Ethernet_II to Ethernet_802.3 Frame Type

In order to configure a non-ODI client IPX driver, a NetWare 2.x operating system, or an external router program to use the default Ethernet_802.3 frame format again, you may use the ECONFIG utility, specifying the type as "N." The "N" denotes that you are using the NetWare default frame type, Ethernet_802.3.

The following table shows you how to configure these programs back to the Ethernet_802 frame:

IPX.COM	Type **ECONFIG IPX.COM SHELL:N**
NET$OS.EXE	Type **ECONFIG NET$OS.EXE [LAN Designator]:N**
BRIDGE.EXE	Type **ECONFIG NET$OS.EXE [LAN Designator]:N**
ROUTER.EXE	Type **ECONFIG ROUTER.EXE [LAN Designator]:N**

Multiple Protocols/Multiple Frames

W ITH THE ODI capabilities of NetWare v3.x, it became possible to use a variety of frame types with server and workstation drivers. However, a server and a workstation must use the same frame type to communicate, as you can see in Figure 4.21.

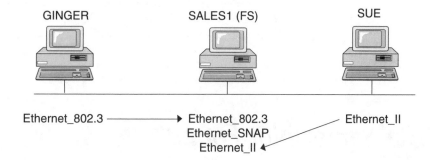

For example, if a NetWare v3.x server is using the Ethernet_802.3 frame type, workstations must use the Ethernet_802.3 frame in order to communicate with the server.

Differentiating between Frame Types

T HE SIMPLE FLOWCHART presented in Figure 4.22 defines how to tell which frame type a packet is using.

FIGURE 4.22

Frame type flowchart

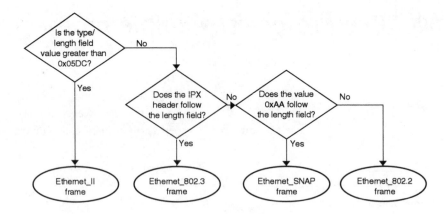

"File Server Not Found"

 ANY TIMES, THE "File server not found" message is caused when the same frame type is not used at the server and client. With a protocol analyzer, you can spot this situation easily.

Determining Which Frame Type the Server Is Running

By capturing a file server's Service Advertising Process (SAP) packets, you can tell which frame types the server is configured to use. NetWare servers will broadcast SAP packets every 60 seconds to announce the services that are available (file services, print services, remote console services, and so on).

A NetWare server will broadcast one SAP packet for each frame type loaded. If a server is using all four frame types defined, it will send out four SAP packets in a row—one for each frame type. View the packets to see the frame types in use by the server.

For more information on the function and structure of SAP packets, refer to Chapter 17.

Determining Which Frame Type the Client Is Running

By simply capturing and viewing packets from the workstation, you can view the frame type the client is using. In Figure 4.23, the client is using the Ethernet_SNAP frame format.

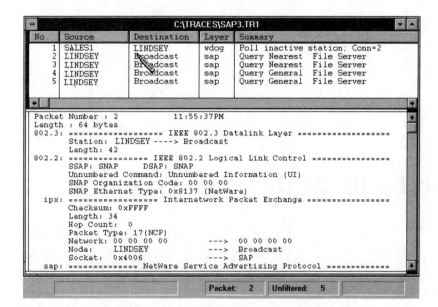

Configuring NetWare v3.x to Use Multiple Frame Types

F YOU ARE running multiple protocols from your NetWare server, you can also configure it to use multiple frame types.

For example, on a NetWare LAN with 100 workstations, if you load the TCP/IP stack at the server, you must load your LAN driver with either the

Ethernet_II or Ethernet_SNAP frame type. The default frame type of Ethernet_802.3 does not support the TCP/IP Protocol.

You can use the following commands in the AUTOEXEC.NCF to bind NetWare's IPX/SPX to the default frame type and TCP/IP to the Ethernet_II frame type:

```
load NE2000 port=300 int=3 frame=ETHERNET_802.3

bind IPX to NE2000 net=BA5EBA11

load tcpip

load ne2000 port=300 int=3 frame=Ethernet_II

bind IP to NE2000 addr=130.50.20.31
```

Filtering on a Frame Type

USING THE PROPER values in the correct fields, you can set up an analyzer to capture NetWare packets using various frame types. Figure 4.24 highlights the fields that are unique to each of the frame types.

Understanding the structures of the various frame types and how to use each one will help you troubleshoot the "File server not found" message and various configuration errors. Learning the difference between a properly formatted frame (as presented in this chapter) and an illegal or malformed frame will also assist you in network troubleshooting.

FIGURE 4.24

Fields unique to each frame type

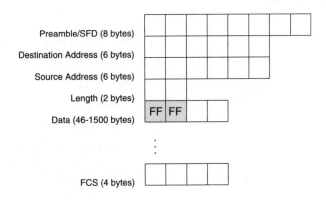

ETHERNET_802.3

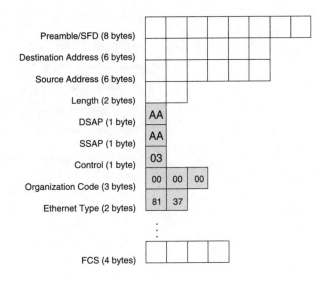

ETHERNET_SNAP

FIGURE 4.24

Fields unique to each
frame type (continued)

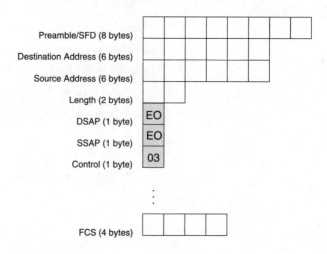

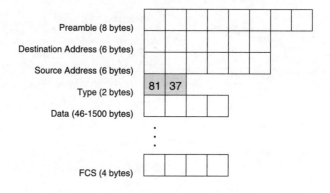

In this chapter you have viewed the proper structure of the four frame types supported by Novell: Ethernet_II, Ethernet_802.2, Ethernet_802.3, and Ethernet_SNAP. You have also learned how to determine which frame types are in use by the servers and clients and how to use the ECONFIG utility and AUTOEXEC.CFG file to configure a system to use other frame types.

The next chapter examines the types and causes of Ethernet frame errors.

Troubleshooting at the Data Link Layer

5

F A STATION transmits a properly formed frame, as defined in Chapter 4, and the wiring system does not cause corruption of the frame, the receiving station should detect a legal frame and process the data contained therein. Unfortunately, not all stations transmit properly formed frames; faulty transceivers, network interface cards, and LAN drivers may cause malformed frames to be transmitted. The cabling system, as well, may cause the corruption of frames on the wire.

In this chapter you will use the NCC LANalyzer and LANalyzer for Windows to track, capture, and view illegal or corrupt frames. The chapter focuses on frames that do not meet the defined frame specifications. By analyzing and interpreting these frame errors, you can determine whether a network is overloaded or whether the cabling system, network interface card, LAN driver, or transceiver is faulty.

Four types of errors are examined in this chapter:

- Local and remote collisions

- CRC/alignment errors and late collisions

- Frame size errors

- Jabber

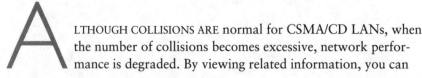

Monitoring Local and Remote Collisions

LTHOUGH COLLISIONS ARE normal for CSMA/CD LANs, when the number of collisions becomes excessive, network performance is degraded. By viewing related information, you can determine whether a collision is due to an overloaded network segment or a faulty component. Network administrators should monitor their network to observe what a typical number of local and remote collisions is for their installation. Figure 5.1 illustrates local and remote collisions. The following table compares local and remote collision statistics:

Collision Type	< 64 Bytes	Bad CRC	CD Pair Triggered
Local	Yes	Yes	Yes
Remote	Yes	Yes	No

FIGURE 5.1

Local/remote collisions

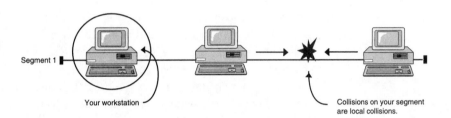

Collisions on your segment are local collisions.

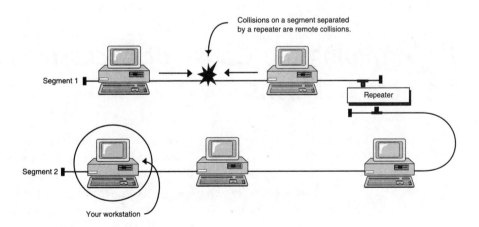

Collisions on a segment separated by a repeater are remote collisions.

Local Collisions

Local collisions are collisions that occur on the local segment. A *collision fragment* is less than 64 bytes in length, with a bad CRC. Local collisions are detected by the collision-detection circuitry on the network interface card or transceiver. The detection of a collision by the collision detection circuitry differentiates local collisions from remote collisions, which are not noticed by the receive pair.

Remote Collisions

Remote collisions occur on the other side of a repeater separating network segments. A remote collision is assumed when a packet that is less than 64 bytes and has an invalid CRC is observed. Repeaters will pass on collision fragments to all connected segments, whereas bridges and routers will not. If you are experiencing excessive remote collisions, you may wish to install a bridge between the segments to filter out collisions. Ideally, however, you would reduce the load on the segment where the excessive collisions occur by reconfiguring the cabling system or fixing a problem component.

Determining the Cause of Excessive Local and Remote Collisions

HOW MANY COLLISIONS are too many? Each network can withstand different numbers of collisions before noticeable performance degradation. When the collisions affect your network to the extent that users begin complaining about performance, the collisions are excessive.

When you view collision statistics, it is also important to view the utilization statistics. This information will help you determine whether excessive collisions are due to an overloaded segment or a faulty component. Whether caused by hardware problems or excessive traffic, this increase in collisions is generally rapid and easily identified when compared to historical collision statistics.

Overloaded Segment

If utilization has increased because of the addition of nodes or new applications and the number of collisions is high, it is likely that the collisions result from increased traffic on the network segment.

In Figure 5.2, on the first screen you are viewing a network segment that is experiencing high utilization. On the second screen, you can see the number of fragments displayed. Fragments are the result of collisions. The number of fragments displayed in the errors table has also increased dramatically.

One possible solution for overloaded segments involves reconfiguring (load balancing) the network cabling system using bridges and/or routers. (Repeaters do not filter traffic.) Bridges and routers filter out remote collisions and keep locally addressed traffic on a single segment.

As defined in Chapter 3, when a bridge connecting two or more segments sees a packet, it records the source hardware (or physical) address and the interface number from which the packet arrived. This information is maintained and used by the bridge to determine which packets are destined for another segment (forwarded) and which are not (filtered). True bridges examine the Ethernet address only—not the network (IPX) information or addressing.

Routers will forward only packets that are destined to another network address. Packets destined for the local network will not be forwarded by the routers.

Figure 5.3 illustrates segment utilization before and after installing a bridge to filter traffic.

Cable Segment Too Long

If a cable segment exceeds the maximum allowed by specification (as defined in Chapter 3), nodes at the far end of the cable may believe the cable is free when, in fact, a packet is on the wire. Since the packet on the wire may not have propagated throughout the cabling system, nodes at the far end may transmit, thereby causing a collision. In this case, since the local collisions are not due to an extremely busy network, utilization will not be higher than normal. Check the segment cable length to ensure that it does not exceed the maximum length allowed.

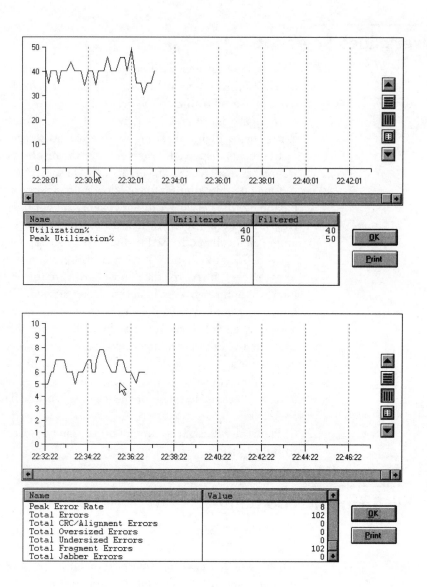

Remote Segment Overloaded

If a segment is experiencing a high number of remote collisions, the segment attached via the repeater is encountering a high number of local collisions.

FIGURE 5.3

Before and after installing
a bridge/router

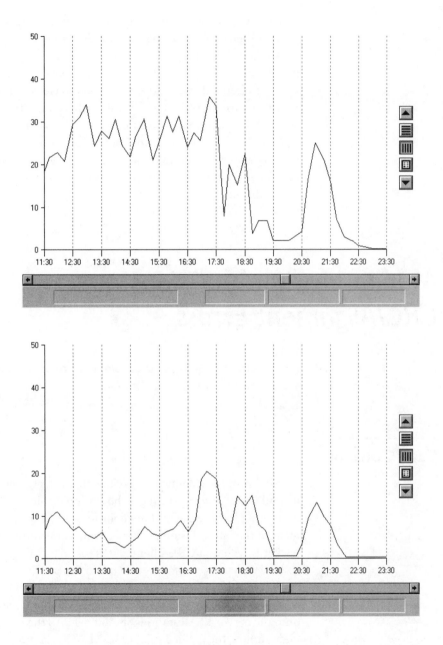

FIGURE 5.3

Before and after installing
a bridge/router

Determine the cause of the local collisions on the attached segment. To reduce
the number of remote collisions crossing onto the local segment, replace the

repeater with a bridge or router. Bridges and routers filter out collisions to prevent them from crossing onto other segments.

A network with segments connected by repeaters should have approximately the same traffic (load) on all segments since all traffic is "repeated" and not filtered. If one segment seems to have significantly more collisions, it may be the result of bad hardware, such as a faulty network board or transceiver. Since stations involved in a collision will try to retransmit right away (within the backoff constraints), monitor several collisions and see if you can identify a single station that always seems to be transmitting soon after the collisions. That station is likely to have bad hardware, which may also cause late collisions.

Monitoring Late Collisions and CRC/Alignment Errors

LATE COLLISIONS AND CRC/alignment errors indicate problems with the network cabling or components.

Late Collisions

Late collisions are defined as packets that are greater than 64 bytes with an invalid CRC. They also trigger the station's collision-detection pair if they occur on a local segment. Late collisions are counted only for the local segment; if the late collision packet is being transmitted from across a router, the packet is seen as a CRC/alignment error.

Late collisions are not normal on an Ethernet network. A late collision indicates that although a station transmitted a sufficient number of bytes (64) to be considered in control of the transmission medium, another station transmitted onto the network. All stations should defer to the packet on the wire. If all nodes follow the defined rules of CSMA/CD, late collisions should never occur.

CRC/Alignment Errors

Packets that do not contain the proper CRC (Cyclical Redundancy Check) value in the frame check sequence field are considered "errored." Upon transmitting a frame on the medium, a station will append a CRC value to the end of the frame. This value is the remainder of a mathematical equation that the source station performs on the contents of the frame. The destination station must perform the same equation and compare the results to the value in the FCS field. If the values do not match, the frame is counted as a CRC error.

If the frame does not end on an 8-bit boundary, it is considered an alignment error. Both types of errors are grouped and counted as CRC/alignment errors. The following table compares late collision and CRC/alignment errors:

Error Type	< 64 Bytes	Bad CRC	CD Pair Triggered
Late collision	No	Yes	Yes
CRC/alignment	No	Yes	No

Determining the Cause of Late Collisions and CRC/Alignment Errors

L ATE COLLISIONS AND CRC/alignment errors are not considered "normal" for an Ethernet LAN. These types of errors should be tracked and resolved to ensure that they do not affect network performance. There are two primary causes of these errors: cabling problems and component problems.

Cabling Problems

Cabling problems such as shorts or noise caused by electromagnetic interference are most likely to blame for CRC/alignment errors. Improper cabling (not following specifications) or a deaf mode (bad carrier sensing) is the most likely cause of late collisions. If a network is experiencing an increasing number of late collisions or CRC/alignment errors, check the following potential cabling problems:

- **Segment too long:** Nodes at the far end of the cabling system transmit, unaware that a station at the other end has already gained control of the medium by transmitting the first 64 bytes of a frame.

- **Failing cable:** Packet data traveling through shorted or damaged cabling may become corrupt before reaching the destination station.

- **Segment not grounded properly:** Improper grounding of a segment may allow ground-induced noise to corrupt data flow.

- **Improper termination:** If a cable segment is not properly terminated, allowing the signal to be absorbed upon reaching the end of the segment, a partial signal will bounce back and collide with existing signals.

- **Taps too close:** Follow the minimum recommended spacing between cable taps to ensure minimal reflection buildup and data distortion.

- **Noisy cable:** Interference or noise (electromagnetic interference produced by motors or other devices) can distort the signals and cause CRC/alignment errors.

Component Problems

Faulty components can cause either late collisions or CRC/alignment errors. The following is a list of some common component problems:

- **Deaf/partially deaf node:** A faulty station that cannot hear the activity is considered a *deaf node*. If a station is suspected of being a deaf node, the network interface card or transceiver should be replaced.

- **Failing repeater, transceiver, or controller card:** Repeaters, transceivers, and controller cards can disrupt the network signal, transmit erroneous signals on the wire, or ignore incoming packets. The malfunctioning component should be replaced.

Monitoring Frame-Length Errors

As DEFINED IN Chapter 4, Ethernet frames must be between 64 and 1518 bytes in length (including the header and FCS). Frames that are less than 64 bytes or more than 1518 bytes but have a valid CRC field are considered frame-length errors.

Short Frames

Short frames (also called "runts" or "shorts") are less than 64 bytes in length but have a valid CRC value.

Long Frames

Frames that are longer than 1518 bytes yet have a valid CRC value are *long frames*.

Determining the Cause of Illegal-Length Frames

ILLEGAL-LENGTH FRAMES are credited to the transmitting station. Finding the node responsible for sending illegal-length frames is easy since the frame is well formed and contains the source address in the header.

Generally, illegal-length frames are caused by a faulty LAN driver. Check the revision of the LAN driver and replace it if it is old. If the LAN driver is current, the file may be corrupt. Reload it from the original disk or copy a LAN driver file from another station that is transmitting properly sized frames.

Routers may also cause illegal-length frames. If a router connects two dissimilar network types and does not enforce the proper frame size restrictions on either side, it may transmit illegal-length frames. For example, the ATM (Asynchronous Transfer Mode) environment uses 53-byte packets called *cells*.

When information is routed from the ATM environment to the Ethernet environment, the router should pad all 53-byte packets to the minimum 64-byte minimum Ethernet size. If a router is continuously transmitting illegal-length frames, notify the manufacturer.

Monitoring Jabber

*J*ABBER IS DEFINED as a frame that is greater than 1518 bytes and has a bad CRC. Jabber is associated with a malfunctioning transceiver. By specification, a transceiver may transmit for only 150 milliseconds. This is sufficient time to transmit 1518 bytes. If a transceiver does not halt transmission after 1518 bytes, it is called a *jabbering transceiver*. If you suspect that a transceiver is jabbering, check the transmit light on the outside to see whether it is continuously transmitting. Replace a jabbering transceiver to ensure that network performance is not affected.

This chapter has defined numerous frame errors that can occur on an Ethernet segment. Monitoring your network and setting alarms will help catch errors before they affect your network communications. Table 5.1 summarizes the characteristics of each error condition.

TABLE 5.1
Error Conditions

ERROR	TRIGGERING CONDITION	POSSIBLE CAUSE
Local collisions	Less than 64 bytes	Overloaded segment
	Bad CRC	Cable segment too long
	CD triggered	
Remote collisions	Less than 64 bytes	Remote segment overload
	Bad CRC	Remote cable segment too long
Late collisions	Equal to or greater than 64 bytes	Deaf node

TABLE 5.1
Error Conditions
(continued)

ERROR	TRIGGERING CONDITION	POSSIBLE CAUSE
	Bad CRC	Segment too long
	CD triggered	Component problem
CRC/alignment	From 64 to 1518 bytes long	Failing cable
	Bad CRC	Noisy cable
	Doesn't end on 8-bit boundary	Component problem
Short frames	Less than 64 bytes	Faulty LAN driver
	Good CRC	
Long frames	Greater than 1518 bytes	Faulty LAN driver
	Good CRC	
Jabber	Greater than 1518 bytes	Faulty transceiver
	Bad CRC	

Now that you've completed Part I of this book, you should have a good feel for the Ethernet access method, cabling system, and errors associated with improper cabling, faulty components, and high utilization.

Part II focuses on the Token Ring access method, frame types, management, and wiring specifications. Part II also provides an overview of source routing and the spanning tree protocol.

Token Ring/802.5 LANs

P A R T

Overview of Token Ring LANs

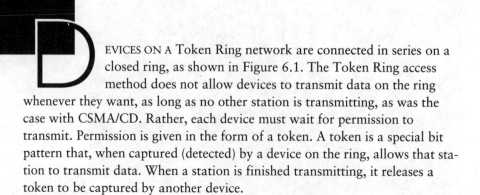

EVICES ON A Token Ring network are connected in series on a closed ring, as shown in Figure 6.1. The Token Ring access method does not allow devices to transmit data on the ring whenever they want, as long as no other station is transmitting, as was the case with CSMA/CD. Rather, each device must wait for permission to transmit. Permission is given in the form of a token. A token is a special bit pattern that, when captured (detected) by a device on the ring, allows that station to transmit data. When a station is finished transmitting, it releases a token to be captured by another device.

FIGURE 6.1

Token Ring devices are connected serially in a ring.

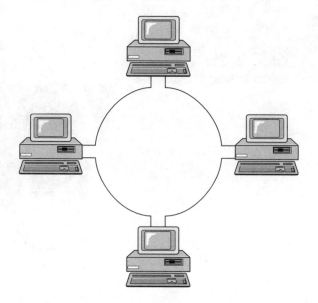

Advantages and Disadvantages of Token Ring

THE TOKEN-PASSING access method and built-in media access management gives Token Ring a number of advantages, including:

- **High throughput:** All devices take turns. This eliminates contention, and thus collisions, and allows Token Ring to use a high percentage of available bandwidth without throughput degradation (80%+), even on rings with many transmitting devices.

- **Deterministic access:** Every device on a Token Ring network can be assured of an opportunity to transmit. This feature gives stations access to the network at regular intervals. It is ideal for mission-critical applications that require deterministic access.

- **Troubleshooting and management:** Token Ring has a great deal of built-in management, which can provide information helpful in troubleshooting and managing the ring and its devices.

- **Fault tolerance:** Token Ring can dynamically isolate and recover from most hardware-related problems.

The main disadvantages of Token Ring include:

- **Cost:** Token Ring requires special hardware, and although costs are coming down, this can be expensive.

- **Complex installation:** Token Ring requires extensive planning, using complex formulas, prior to the purchase and installation of cable and equipment. Installations that are out of specification (especially rings using unshielded twisted-pair) may run poorly or not at all.

- **Recovery and management overhead:** Fault tolerance can be a disadvantage if network managers do not have the diagnostic equipment and training to recognize and repair ongoing, intermittent hardware problems. Instead of bringing the ring down and demanding attention to solve the problem, Token Ring will keep recovering from the error and continue to run, but at a much lower throughput. This can cause network sluggishness.

How Token Ring Works

AS NOTED EARLIER, all Token Ring stations are connected in serial on a closed ring. All signals pass through, and are repeated by, each station, as illustrated in Figure 6.2. This means that each station acts as a repeater and requires a two-pair cable connection to the ring. One pair is an input for receive and one an output for transmit. A ring station connected to a ring station's receive cable is known as its *upstream neighbor*. The station connected to a ring station's transmit cable is its *downstream neighbor*. In Figure 6.2, station A is B's upstream neighbor and station C is B's downstream neighbor.

FIGURE 6.2

Each ring station acts as a
repeater with an input
(receive) and an output
(transmit).

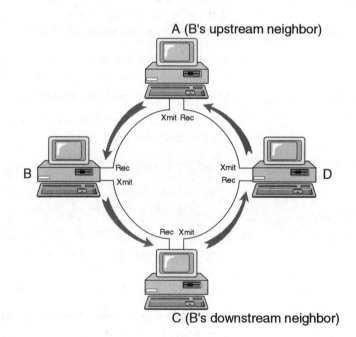

In order to transmit data, each station must perform four basic steps. These four steps make up, and will be termed in this book as, the *token protocol*.

The token protocol states that to transmit data, a ring station must

1. Capture a token

2. Transmit queued data

3. Strip transmitted frame(s)

4. Transmit a free token

Step 1: Capture a Token

To transmit data, a ring station must first capture a free token. For example, in Figure 6.3, ring station B's Token Ring adapter receives data to be transmitted from an upper-layer protocol. After queuing the data for transmission, the adapter monitors the ring for a token. Only one station at a time may transmit data on a Token Ring. In our example, when ring station B recognizes a token bit pattern, it captures the token. The adapter then changes the token into a frame in which it will transmit the queued data.

FIGURE 6.3

Ring station B captures a free token.

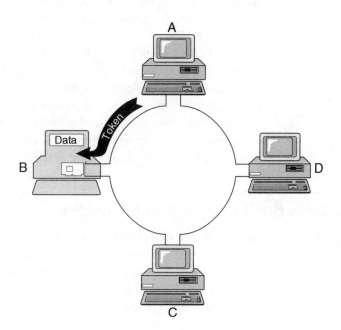

Tokens are described in detail in Chapter 13.

Step 2: Transmit Queued Data

Once the ring station's adapter has captured the token, it may transmit queued data until it is finished or until its token-holding timer expires (10 milliseconds by default), whichever comes first. The transmitted frames are repeated by every station on the ring until they reach the transmitting station.

Token Ring protocol timers (and there are many) are listed in Appendix D.

As each station repeats the frame, it checks it for errors. If a station detects an error in the frame, it sets a bit in the frame, called the Error Detected Indicator, telling other stations to ignore the error. This prevents the error from being reported multiple times for one frame.

In the example, station B has transmitted a frame containing the queued data, and stations C, D, and A repeat the frame, as shown in Figure 6.4.

The station to which the transmitted frame is addressed also repeats the frame. However, when the station recognizes that the frame contains its address in the Destination Address field, it sets a bit called the Address Recognized Indicator (ARI). If sufficient incoming buffers are available on the adapter, it makes a copy of the frame and sets the Frame Copied Indicator (FCI).

Station D is the target station in the example. As shown in Figure 6.5, station D makes a copy of the frame as it repeats it.

Step 3: Strip the Transmitted Frame(s)

It is the responsibility of the transmitting station to strip its transmissions from the wire. The station does this by not repeating its own frame(s). It checks the frame for errors and to determine whether the target station was attached to the ring (ARI bit) and whether it copied the frame (FCI bit).

In Figure 6.6, station B effectively strips its transmissions from the ring by not repeating them.

FIGURE 6.4

Every station on the ring repeats a frame until it is received by the transmitting station.

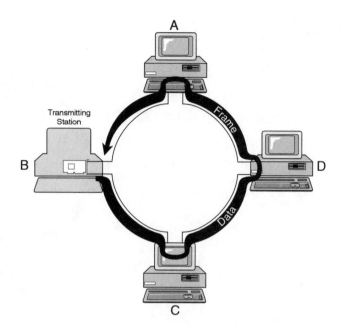

FIGURE 6.4

Every station on the ring repeats a frame until it is received by the transmitting station.

Even though the transmitting station's adapter may be alerted to a target station that is not attached to the ring (ARI not set), a target station that did not copy the frame (FCI not set), or a frame containing an error, this information is typically not passed to the upper-layer protocols, and the adapter will not retransmit the data. Retransmission of lost or damaged frames is the responsibility of upper-layer protocols (NCP, SPX II, Packet Burst, and so on). However, the adapter reports the ARI and FCI information to management stations on the ring. This information is most important for finding those adapters with insufficient frame-buffering capabilities for their particular task. For example, servers and routers would have to buffer more incoming frames than, say, a workstation.

An error to a frame may occur after the target station has copied it. Thus, it is possible for the transmitting station to receive a frame that has both the error-detected and FCI bits set.

FIGURE 6.5

The target station copies
the frame as it repeats it.

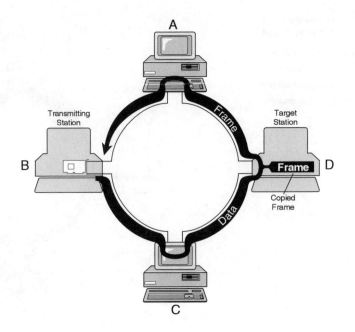

Step 4: Transmit a Free Token

After its queued data has been transmitted or when its token-holding timer
has expired, and after it has stripped all frames from the ring, the ring station
adapter must release, or transmit, a free token, as shown in Figure 6.7.

Token Ring Topology and Hardware Overview

T DOESN'T TAKE a rocket scientist to see that if Token Ring were physically wired as a true ring (as illustrated in Figures 6.1 through 6.7) and
an adapter failed or a cable broke, the entire ring would become inoper-
ative. All data transfer would stop, alarms would go off, and somewhere a red

FIGURE 6.6

The transmitting station
strips its transmissions
from the ring.

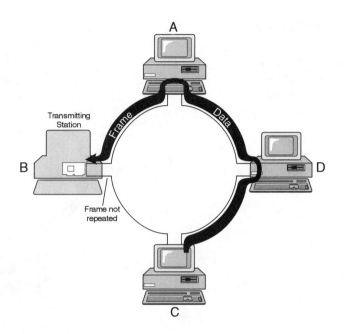

FIGURE 6.6

The transmitting station
strips its transmissions
from the ring.

light would flash a fatal error message. This would hardly be consistent with
the fault-tolerant media access method described earlier in this chapter.

Token Ring Topology

The designers of Token Ring, in their wisdom, designed Token Ring topology
not as a true ring but rather as a star. Electrically it is still a ring, but physically it is a star, as shown in Figure 6.8.

Wiring Token Rings in a star topology provides two advantages:

- Equipment and cabling can be consolidated and centralized for ease of
  access and repair.

- Token Ring hubs provide fault tolerance and maintain the integrity of
  the ring in case of most hardware failures and cable breaks.

FIGURE 6.7

The transmitting station releases a free token when it has finished transmitting.

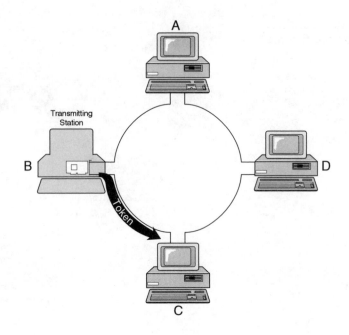

FIGURE 6.8

Token Ring is implemented as a star topology.

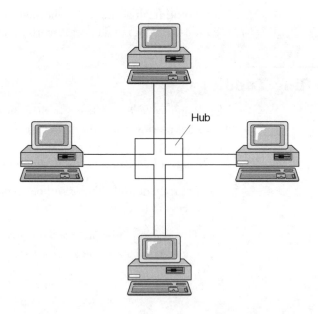

Centralized hardware and wiring make installation and repairs of cable and equipment easier. All the Token Ring hardware is typically mounted in a small room called a *wiring closet*. All cabling is terminated there as well.

Before we discuss how Token Ring hubs provide fault tolerance for the ring, let's briefly examine typical Token Ring hardware and its terminology.

Token Ring Hardware

Of all the media access methods, Token Ring is probably number one in the race for most available hardware specifications, components, and options. Thus, take care to design and implement Token Ring hardware and cabling according to the specifications in the *IBM Introduction and Planning Guide*. A Token Ring network that is out of tolerance will not provide stable, fault-tolerant data transfer—if it works at all—and will be the source of great frustration for the network users, administrators, and technicians. Conversely, if it is designed and installed properly, Token Ring will provide a worry-free, efficient, fault-tolerant network. Following is a brief overview of the hardware components associated with Token Ring.

Figure 6.9 shows the minimum hardware for a Token Ring. They are:

- **Multistation access unit (MSAU):** This hub provides fault tolerance for the ring. Each MSAU typically supports eight connections, although 4- and 16-port MSAUs are not uncommon. The IBM model 8228 is a typical 8-port, passive MSAU.

- **Token Ring network adapter:** This adapter provides the interface between the ring station and the ring. It executes the Token Ring protocol by way of the Token Ring chipset. IBM adapters use the IBM Tropic or LANStreamer chipset. Third-party adapters typically use Texas Instruments' TMS380 chipset.

- **Lobe:** The lobe is the total cable run between the ring station and the MSAU. This is a two-pair (one receive, one transmit), shielded or unshielded twisted-pair cable.

- **Connectors:** Shielded twisted-pair (STP) cable (type 1 cable) connects to adapters with a nine-pin DB-style connector and to MSAUs and intermediate connections with an IBM-style data connector. Unshielded twisted-pair (UTP) cable (type 3 cable) connects to adapters, intermediate connections, and MSAUs with RJ45 jacks.

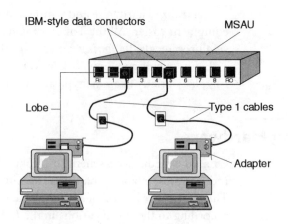

*IBM-style data connectors are both male and female connectors and provide a loopback
between the transmit and receive pairs when they are not connected.*

You may chain together MSAUs to increase the number of ring stations
attached to the ring. You connect MSAUs using special cables called *patch
cables*. As Figure 6.10 shows, patch cables connect the ring-in (RI) and ring-out
(RO) ports.

FIGURE 6.10

Token Ring with multiple
MSAUs

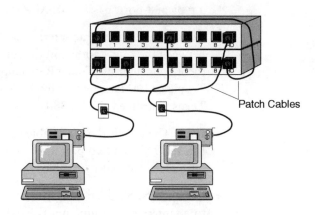

Ring-in and ring-out port relays do not require phantom current to operate. As soon as a patch cable's connector is plugged into an RI or RO port, the ring is routed through the patch cable. (See Figure 6.14 a little later in this chapter.)

MSAUs are typically passive devices with little management capability (vendor specific). Smart MSAUs are called controlled access units (CAUs). Along with lobe attachment modules (LAMs), CAUs provide managed access to the ring. A single CAU can support up to 4 LAMs, and each LAM provides 20 connections. CAUs have RI and RO ports, which allow them and their associated LAMs to be chained in the same manner as MSAUs. The IBM CAU is the model 8230. Third-party CAU/LAMs include Madge Networks' SmartCAU and SmartLAM.

CAUs include management agents that provide LAM port information and control to administrators from a management console on the ring. Some can even be managed with communications over the network or by way of an asynchronous (RS232 typical) connection. In addition, CAUs typically provide automatic bypass of failed patch cables in a chained series. Figure 6.11 shows a picture of a rack-mounted CAU manufactured by Madge Networks, Inc.

Vendors manufacture a variety of LAM configurations. Figure 6.12 shows a Madge Networks' rack-mounted SmartLAM that connects to the rack-mounted CAU pictured in Figure 6.11.

Operations of MSAUs and LAMs

Contained inside CAUs and LAMs are relays associated with every port. These relays provide a bypass around a ring station connector, if the ring station is not attached to the ring, and a loopback path on the lobe cable for ring station self tests. Figure 6.13 shows how relays in the MSAU bypass ring station B when it is not attached to the ring. (The special three-port MSAU was designed specifically for this writing and is not available from any vendor.) The fact that a ring station's lobe cable is physically connected to the MSAU does not necessarily mean it is attached, electrically, to the ring.

FIGURE 6.11

Madge Networks' CAU

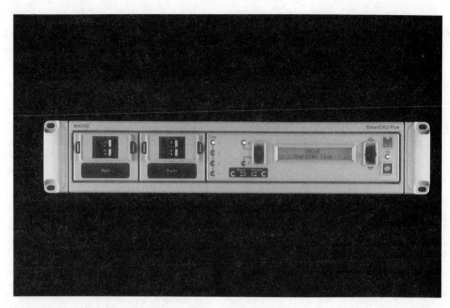

FIGURE 6.12

Madge Networks'
SmartLAM

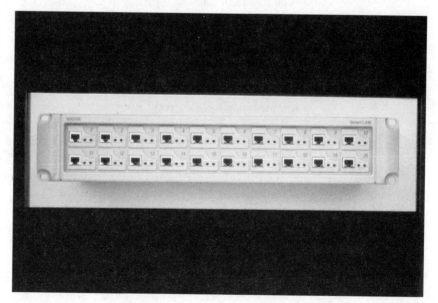

As Figure 6.13 illustrates, the Token Ring signal travels counterclockwise around the ring, or from left ports to right ports as you are standing in front of an MSAU or a LAM. The electrical ring is completed by a wiring loop inside the MSAU or CAU/LAM.

FIGURE 6.13

Relays in MSUAs and LAMs bypass ring stations that are not attached to the ring.

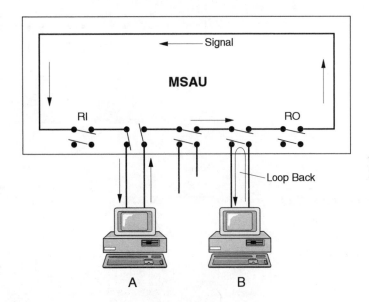

When the ring station attaches to the ring (see the section "Station Initialization" in Chapter 8 for details on the initialization process), it puts a phantom current on the lobe. This DC current activates the relay, physically connecting the station to the ring, as shown in Figure 6.14. Ring station initialization occurs when the adapter's driver is loaded.

The cabling of multiple MSAUs (shown earlier Figure 6.10) is the recommended method. This method actually provides patch cable redundancy. In other words, you could remove any one of the patch cables, and the ring would recover by using the extra cable pair in the other patch cable and the internal loopbacks in the MSAUs, as shown in Figure 6.15. In the top illustration, both patch cables are operational and the signal travels through one pair of each cable. The signal does not use the internal loopback in the MSAUs. In the bottom illustration, one patch cable has failed and has been removed. The extra pair in the other patch cable and the internal loopback in both MSAUs are now used to complete the ring.

FIGURE 6.14

The adapter applies a
phantom current to the
lobe cable, and the ring
station is attached to
the ring.

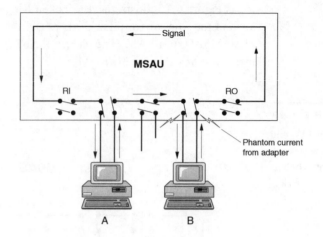

FIGURE 6.15

Recommended cabling of
MSAUs provides patch
cable redundancy.

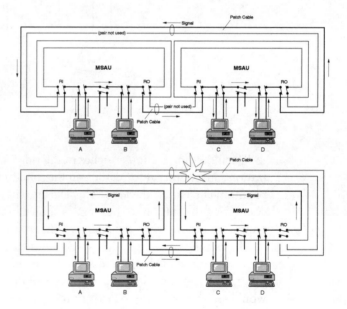

Now that you have a basic understanding of the Token Ring media access
protocol and have learned some of the fundamental hardware and terminology,
we can begin to examine the details of the somewhat elaborate (to put it mildly)
token protocol access and management protocols. Chapter 7 discusses the functional stations, and Chapter 8 examines the functional processes.

Functional Management Stations/Addresses

7

HE TOKEN RING protocol provides for a great deal of management. As part of this management, the Token Ring protocol has specified five functional stations. Some of these functions are built into the Token Ring chipset, and some are provided by software created by management software developers and installed on ring stations. You will discover in this section that some of the functional stations are required, while others are optional. In addition, even though some of the optional functional stations are not employed on the ring, you can still use information sent to them by the ring stations (provided you have a protocol analyzer) to manage and troubleshoot the ring. Figure 7.1 illustrates the five Token Ring functional stations.

FIGURE 7.1

Token Ring functional stations

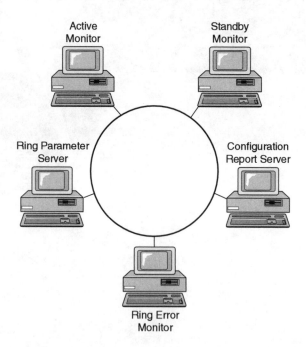

Functional stations are addressed by way of a special address called a *functional address*. Functional addresses are logical addresses, and stations designated as functional stations will respond to the functional address as well as their burned-in address (hardware address).

Functional addresses are discussed in detail in Chapter 9.

The following list indicates the functional stations specified for Token Ring management:

Functional Station	Functional Address
Active Monitor	C0 00 00 00 00 01
Standby Monitor	N/A
Ring Parameter Server	C0 00 00 00 00 02
Ring Error Monitor	C0 00 00 00 00 08
Configuration Report Server	C0 00 00 00 00 10

Following are descriptions of each functional station and its role in ring management.

Active Monitor (Required)

THE ACTIVE MONITOR (AM) is by far the most important functional station. The AM function is built into the Token Ring chipset and is mandatory. The AM is dynamically "elected" from all the stations on the ring, using a procedure known as *Monitor Contention*. Once elected, the AM becomes king of the ring and guardian of the token protocol. Without an AM, there can be no token protocol. Without the operation of the token protocol, there can be no data transfer and thus no network. Period. And there can only be one, and only one, AM per Token Ring. Figure 7.2 illustrates the functions of the Active Monitor.

FIGURE 7.2

Functions of the Active
Monitor

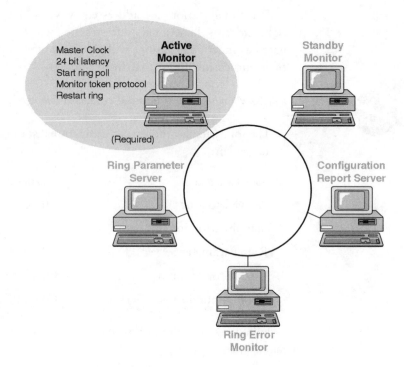

Monitor Contention is discussed in detail in Chapter 8.

The responsibilities of the AM are as follows:

- To provide the master clock for the ring

- To induce a 24-bit latency delay

- To start the Ring Poll process

- To monitor for token protocol operation

- To restart the ring after interruption of the token protocol

Master Clock

The first job of an Active Monitor is to provide the master clock for the ring. Token Ring is a closed loop, and there is always a clock signal on the ring. Because the clock is always on the ring, the ring stations are always synchronized. Thus, there is no need for long synch patterns at the front of a Token Ring frame (see Chapter 4), as was the case with Ethernet. Any period with no tokens or frames will contain an idle signal (all 0's). This is rare because a token or frame must always exist on the ring; and a token (the smallest at 24 bits), to be physically larger than a 16Mbps ring, would have to be about 2.5 kilometers in circumference! This brings us to the next responsibility of the AM, the latency buffer.

Latency Buffer

To make sure an entire token fits on the ring, the AM induces a 24 bit-latency, or delay, in the ring, using a special buffer on the Token Ring adapter. But why is this latency needed?

A basic law of token protocol is that a token or frame must always exist on the ring. If no station is transmitting, a token is passed around and around the ring until it is captured by a station waiting to transmit data. In Chapter 6 you learned that a frame is stripped from the wire by a transmitting station. This means that the station could be receiving the front of the frame at the same time it is transmitting the same frame.

The problem arises because ring stations do not strip off tokens. An entire token must fit on a ring to prevent the front of the token from being received by a station before it has completed transmission of that same token. If the token did not fit, it would be corrupted as it ran into the back of itself within a repeating ring station, as shown in Figure 7.3.

Start Poll Sequence

Every 7 seconds of every minute, hour, day, week, and year for the life of a Token Ring network, a Token Ring runs through a process known as *Ring Poll* or *Neighbor Notification*. Through this process, ring stations learn the identity of their upstream neighbor. Newly attached stations become "of the ring" after participating in Ring Poll. Upstream neighbor information is

FIGURE 7.3

A token must fit on the ring to prevent it from running into itself.

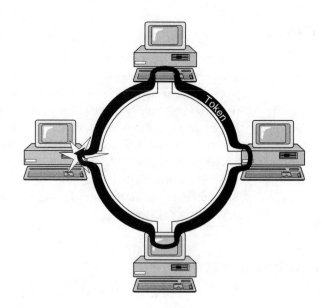

essential in isolating problems on the Token Ring. It is the responsibility of the AM to initiate this process (every 7 seconds).

Monitor Token Protocol Operation

The AM is the guardian of the ring. It constantly monitors the ring to ensure that the token protocol does not fail. This basically means ensuring that a valid (uncorrupted) token or frame is detected within the time specified by the T(any_token) timer (10 milliseconds).

A complete list of Token Ring protocol timers can be found in Appendix D.

Restart the Ring

If a token or frame is corrupted or lost, the token protocol will be interrupted and the T(any_token) timer in the AM will expire. If this happens, it is the responsibility of the AM to restart the ring. To restart the ring, the AM first attempts to purge the ring. If the AM can successfully purge the ring, it releases a new token, and the token protocol is restored. Purging is the first step in Token Ring error recovery when the error is detected by the AM.

See Chapter 9 for details about purging.

Standby Monitor(s) (Required)

EVERY STATION ON the ring that is not an Active Monitor is a Standby Monitor (SM). SM functionality is built into the Token Ring chipset, and it is required on rings with more than one ring station. The job of every SM is to monitor the AM. If the token protocol is interrupted for a longer period of time than the AM's T(any_token) time, the SM assumes the AM has died and initiates the Monitor Contention process in order to find another AM. Once a new AM is appointed, the ring can recover, and normal token protocol resumes. Monitor Contention is the first step of error recovery when the error is discovered by the SM. Figure 7.4 illustrates the function of the Standby Monitor.

The Token Ring error recovery process and time line are explained in detail in Chapter 11.

Ring Parameter Server (Optional)

THE RING PARAMETER Server (RPS) function provides a method for distributing parameters to ring stations as they attach to the ring. The RPS must be implemented as software on a ring station attached to the ring. Network managers enter the desired parameter settings for all ring stations.

FIGURE 7.4

Function of the Standby
Monitor

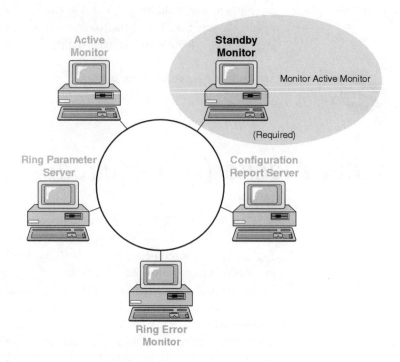

The following list indicates the parameters that can be set by the RPS during station initialization:

- Physical drop number

- Local ring number

- Allowed access priority

- Soft error report timer

- Authorized environment

Figure 7.5 illustrates the function of the Ring Parameter Server.

Every ring station queries the RPS for parameters during station initialization, regardless of whether the RPS exists. If ring stations do not receive a reply to their queries, they accept the default value for all parameters.

FIGURE 7.5

Function of the Ring
Parameter Server

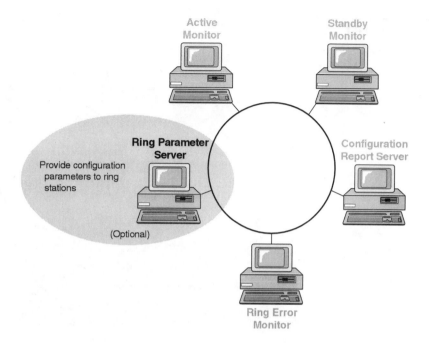

For details on station parameters, see the section "Station Initialization" in Chapter 8.

Ring Error Monitor (Optional)

THE RING ERROR Monitor (REM) has a tough job. It does
nothing. It just sets on the ring and waits for ring stations to
report errors they have detected. Network managers can then
go to the REM and view the error information collected. To be an REM, a
station must have software installed that supports that function. Figure 7.6
describes the function of a REM.

FIGURE 7.6

Function of the Ring Error
Monitor

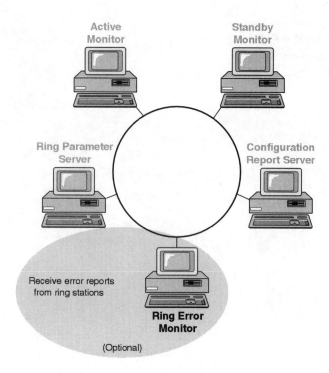

What you need to know about the REM concerns the frames from the ring stations that contain the errors they have discovered. (Actually, the REM has nothing to do with these frames except that they are addressed to its functional address.)

What these reported errors are and how you can use them to troubleshoot are discussed in Chapters 10 and 11, respectively.

Configuration Report Server (Optional)

THE CONFIGURATION REPORT Server (CRS) function manages ring stations and reports ring events. To be a CRS, a ring station requires software installed that supports those functions. Figure 7.7 describes the functions of the CRS.

FIGURE 7.7

Functions of the
Configuration Report
Server

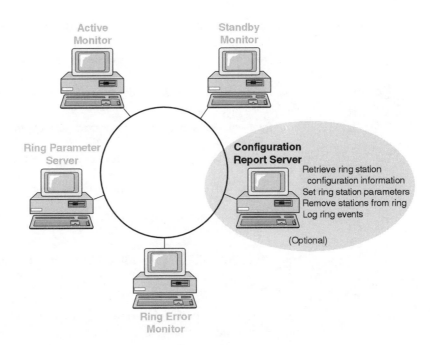

The CRS function is designated CRS by the IBM and IEEE specifications. Texas Instruments terms this function the Network Manager.

The CRS can retrieve and set information in ring stations. Any parameter that can be set by the RPS, during station initialization, can be set by the CRS at any time. In addition, the CRS can retrieve the following information from ring stations on demand:

- Station address

- Station state

- Station attachments

The CRS also has the capability of removing a ring station from the ring. This is an on-demand function executed by a network manager. The CRS sends a special frame to a ring station's adapter. The adapter will immediately exit the ring (remove phantom current from the lobe). The station cannot re-enter the ring until the adapter's driver is reloaded.

When a ring station is removed using the CRS "remove ring station" function, users are not notified that their station has been removed. Their only indication will be a network error from whatever network operating system software they are using.

Ring events reported by ring stations to the CRS include the following:

- New Active Monitor (Monitor Contention process has been executed)

- Changes in upstream neighbor addresses (ring station has entered or exited the ring)

- Ring Poll failure (Ring Poll process did not complete)

- Active Monitor error

The optional functional stations depend on a vendor's software implementation. Each vendor's implementation will differ in features and functionality. Following are some products that implement the Token Ring functional stations:

- IBM LAN Server

- IBM 8209 Bridge

- Madge's Smartbridge

This chapter has briefly described the Token Ring functional stations. The AM and SM are required functions and are built into the Token Ring hardware (chipset). The REM, RPS, and CRS are optional management functions that require software installed on a ring station.

To fully understand the token protocol and Token Ring management and how they and the capabilities of the functional stations can help you trouble-shoot your NetWare Token Ring LAN, you need to examine the details of the token protocol processes and the Token Ring management frames. These subjects are discussed in Chapters 8 and 9.

Token Ring
Functional
Processes

CHAPTER

8

TOKEN RING USES a number of processes in order to initialize and maintain operation of the token protocol. The following list indicates the processes of most concern to you, as the Token Ring manager and/or troubleshooter:

- Monitor Contention (token claiming)

- Ring Poll

- Station initialization

- Ring Purge

- Beacon

All of these process protocols are built into the Token Ring chipset.

Monitor Contention (Token Claiming)

AS EXPLAINED IN Chapter 6, operation of the token protocol, and thus transfer of data on the Token Ring, cannot begin without an Active Monitor (AM) functional station. When a ring is brought up for the first time (even if there is only a single station on the ring), an AM must be appointed before any data can be exchanged. In addition, if the AM disappears or begins to fail on a functioning ring, a new AM must be appointed before the ring can be restarted.

Token Ring uses a process called Monitor Contention, sometimes referred to as token claiming, to appoint an AM. The process is initiated by the first station to notice that the AM has disappeared. On a ring starting for the first time, this is generally the first station to connect to the ring. On a functioning ring, it is usually the station immediately downstream from the old AM.

A ring station starts the Monitor Contention process when it either detects the absence of an AM or detects an AM that is not operating properly. When it detects one of these conditions, the ring station immediately starts to transmit a special media access control (MAC) frame called a Claim Token MAC frame. It does this without waiting for a free token.

The structure of MAC frames is discussed in detail in Chapter 12.

The station that discovered the absence or failure of the AM transmits a Claim Token MAC frame every 20 milliseconds. All other stations join the contention process or go into Claim Token repeat mode as soon as they detect a Claim Token frame. During Monitor Contention, all data transmission is suspended on the ring. The new AM is the participating station with the highest Token Ring (universal or local) address.

The station that started the Monitor Contention process continues to transmit Claim Token frames until one of the following occurs:

- The station receives a Claim Token frame with a source address higher than its own, in which case the ring station discontinues transmitting Claim Token frames and enters Contention repeat mode.

- The station receives three of its own Claim Token MAC frames, in which case the ring station has won the contention process and becomes the new AM.

In order for a ring station to be a participant in the Monitor Contention process, it must be designated as a participant. By default, a ring station is *not* a participant. To be a participant, a ring station must meet either of the following two criteria:

- It is the station that discovered the absence or failure of the AM.

- It was designated a participant when the adapter driver was loaded.

Example of Monitor Contention

Let's say the AM, station A, fails or leaves the ring, as shown in Figure 8.1. Station A's downstream neighbor, Standby Monitor (SM) B, detects the absence of the AM. Because station B detected the AM failure, it automatically becomes a participant in the Monitor Contention process. Station D is another participant in contention because it was so designated when its driver was loaded. Station B starts to transmit Claim Token MAC frames without waiting for a token.

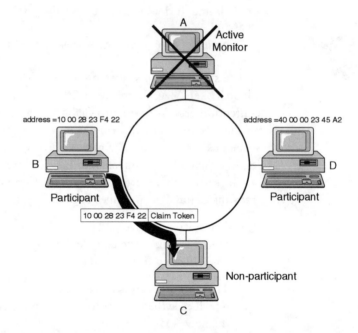

Station C detects B's Claim Token MAC frame, as shown in Figure 8.2. Since C is not a participant, it immediately goes into Contention repeat mode.

Station D starts to repeat B's Claim Token frame, as illustrated in Figure 8.3. D is a participant, so it checks the Source Address field of the frame. Because station D's address is greater than the address received, it replaces the address with its own.

Station B, as it repeats the Claim Token frame, notices that its address has been replaced by station D's address, as you can see in Figure 8.4. This address is higher than its own, so it takes itself out of contention and goes into Monitor Contention repeat mode.

Station D eventually receives three Claim Token frames in a row with a source address equal to its own, "winning" Monitor Contention and becoming the new AM, as shown in Figure 8.5.

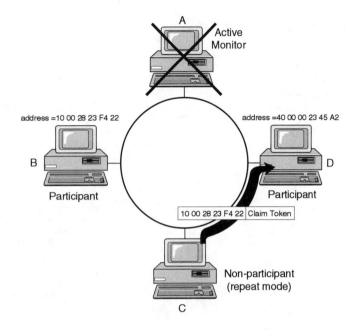

FIGURE 8.2

Station C goes into Contention repeat mode.

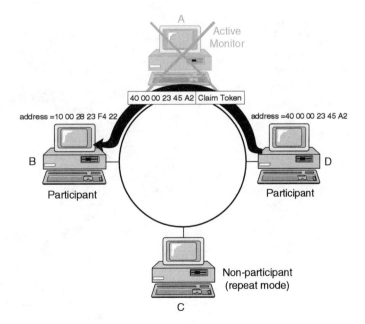

FIGURE 8.3

Participating station D changes the Claim Token frame address.

FIGURE 8.4

Station B, on detecting a higher source address, goes into Monitor Contention repeat mode.

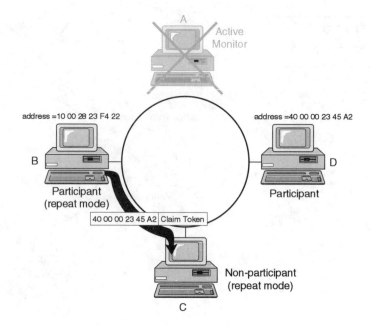

FIGURE 8.5

Station D receives three Claim Token frames with its address and becomes the Active Monitor.

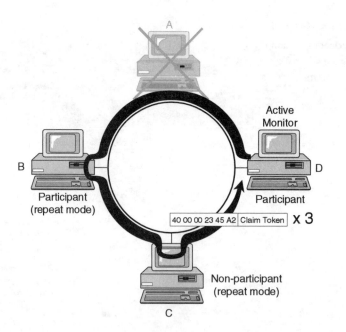

Viewing Monitor Contention with the LANalyzer

Viewed by LANalyzer for Windows, the Monitor Contention process appears as shown in Figure 8.6. Set up the packet capture filter for "MAC Frames Only." As you can see, on a normally functioning ring this takes very little time, creates very little traffic, and is totally transparent to users on the ring.

FIGURE 8.6

LANalyzer for Windows trace of the Monitor Contention process

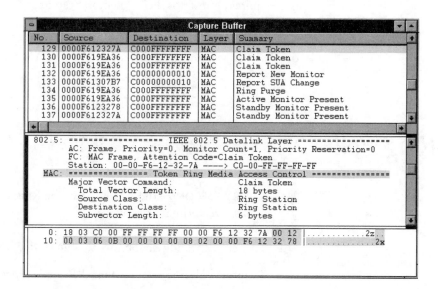

The Monitor Contention process is the first step in the hardware error-recovery process when it is detected by a Standby Monitor, but it is the second step when discovered by an Active Monitor. The LANalyzer trace file is quite different in that case (see Chapter 14).

On the LANalyzer by NCC, an indicator called Ring Recovery appears on the Run Rate and Run Util screens. Every time the LANalyzer detects the Monitor Contention process, it increments this counter by 1.

Chapter 14 explains how to use the Ring Recover indicator to troubleshoot and baseline your Token Ring network.

In the real world, virtually no one sets up ring stations to be participants in Monitor Contention. The first station to detect the absence of the AM and start Monitor Contention is more often than not the only participant on the ring, in which case it becomes the AM. A ring station that is on all the time (server, bridge, router, and so on) will eventually become the AM and remain so until it is brought down.

As a network manager, you have more important things to do than set up stations with locally assigned addresses so you can control which stations will be AMs. (See Chapter 9 for details on Token Ring addressing.) The AM function requires almost no CPU or memory resources of a host station, so assigning stations to be AMs is basically a wasted effort. All AM processing occurs on the adapter as a front-end process. The host, be it a workstation, a server, a router, or whatever, is not measurably affected by the AM function.

Ring Poll

EVERY 7 SECONDS, the AM initiates the Ring Poll process. This process has three primary purposes:

- To alert all Standby Monitors that an Active Monitor is present

- To inform all ring stations that the ring is functioning properly

- To allow all ring stations to learn the identity of their upstream neighbor (useful when troubleshooting Token Ring problems)

Two different MAC frames are used in the Ring Poll process. They are the Active Monitor Present (AMP) and Standby Monitor Present (SMP) MAC frames. These frames are addressed to the Token Ring broadcast address (C0 00 FF FF FF FF).

The best way to demonstrate how the Ring Poll process works is to walk through an example.

Ring Poll Example

When the AM's T(neighbor_notification) timer expires, the AM (station A) waits for a free token and then transmits an AMP frame, as shown in Figure 8.7.

The AM's downstream neighbor, Standby Monitor station B, is the first station to see the AMP frame.

FIGURE 8.7

The Active Monitor starts Ring Poll by transmitting an Active Monitor Present MAC frame.

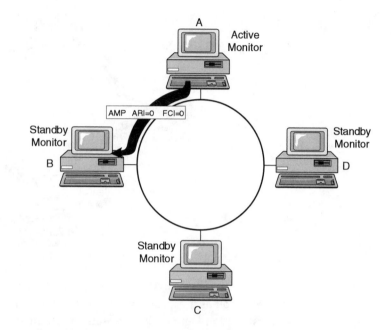

Station B knows it is the first station because the Address Recognized Indicator (ARI) and Frame Copied Indicator (FCI) bits are set to 0 in the AMP frame. The fact that the ARI/FCI bits are not set also indicates to station B that station A is its *nearest active upstream neighbor (NAUN)*. Station B stores this information on its Token Ring adapter. The stored address is known as the *saved upstream address,* or *SUA*.

Station B resets its T(receive_notification) timer and sets the ARI and FCI bits to 1 as it repeats the frame, as shown in Figure 8.8.

Every other station (and SM) on the ring repeats the AMP. Because the ARI and FCI bits are set to 1, the stations know they are not the first to see the frame, so they do not save the source address as their NAUN. However, because it is an AMP frame, they reset their T(receive_notification) timer.

The T(receive_notification) timer is really the AM watchdog timer maintained by every SM. If that timer goes off before the Ring Poll process has been detected by an SM, the SM starts the Monitor Contention process.

FIGURE 8.8

Station B resets its
T(receive_notification)
timer, stores A as its SUA,
and sets the ARI and FCI
bits to 1.

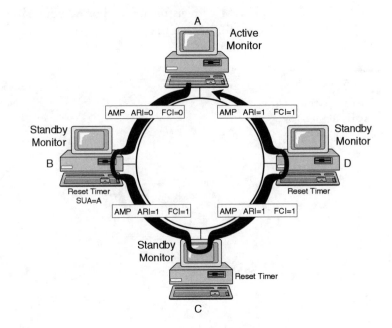

As soon as it captures a free token, station B transmits an SMP frame, as illustrated in Figure 8.9. The Standby Monitor, station C, checks the ARI/FCI bits to determine whether it is the first to see the frame. The ARI/FCI bits are 0, so station C sets them to 1 and stores station B's address as its NAUN. All other stations simply repeat the frame because they detect that the ARI/FCI bits are set to 1.

This process—each station, in turn, transmitting an SMP frame, and the station's downstream neighbor saving its address and setting the ARI/FCI bits so other stations know they are not the immediate downstream neighbor—continues until the AM receives an SMP with the ARI/FCI bits set to 0, as shown in Figure 8.10. The SMP frame with the ARI/FCI bits set to 0 gives the AM its NAUN and also indicates that the Ring Poll is complete (at least for 7 seconds).

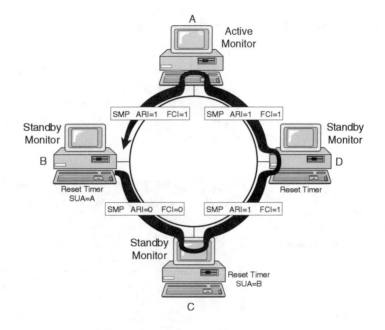

FIGURE 8.9

Station B transmits a
Standby Monitor Present
frame.

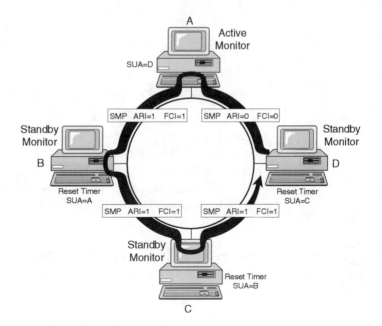

FIGURE 8.10

The Ring Poll process
is complete when the
AM receives a Standby
Monitor Present frame
with the ARI/FCI bits
set to 0.

Viewing Ring Poll with the LANalyzer

Capturing a Ring Poll with a LANalyzer, as shown in Figure 8.11, gives you a quick view of all the active stations on the network in order from the AM. (Again, set the packet filter to capture MAC packets only.) This view is useful when you need to know which stations are active on the network. In a situation where you don't have any wiring diagrams, this can give you a clue to where a station is, relative to the LANalyzer, on the ring.

FIGURE 8.11

The Ring Poll process as captured by LANalyzer for Windows

```
                              Capture Buffer
No.   Source        Destination    Layer  Summary
   5  0000F6123279  C0000FFFFFFFF  MAC    Active Monitor Present
   6  0000F61307B7  C0000FFFFFFFF  MAC    Standby Monitor Present
   7  This_Workstat: C0000FFFFFFFF  MAC    Standby Monitor Present
   8  100028A4A8E4  C0000FFFFFFFF  MAC    Standby Monitor Present
   9  0000F618E8EF  C0000FFFFFFFF  MAC    Standby Monitor Present
  10  0000F619EA36  C0000FFFFFFFF  MAC    Standby Monitor Present

MAC: =============== Token Ring Media Access Control ================
      Major Vector Command:              Active Monitor Present
        Total Vector Length:             18 bytes
        Source Class:                    Ring Station
        Destination Class:               Ring Station
        Subvector Length:                6 bytes
        Physical Drop Number:            00000000
        Subvector Length:                8 bytes
        Upstream Neighbor's Address:     00-00-F6-12-32-7A

   0: 10 05 C0 00 FF FF FF FF 00 00 F6 12 32 79 00 12  |...........2y..
  10: 00 05 06 0B 00 00 00 00 08 02 00 00 F6 12 32 7A  |..........2z
```

The LANalyzer by NCC LANalyzer has an application in the [Physical] group called MAP. This application has two channel filters, one for AMP and one for SMP frames, and it has a trigger set for the AMP frames. Running this application automatically captures only the Ring Poll process starting from the Active Monitor, and it displays them on the Run Station screen, as shown in Figure 8.12.

Be aware that the stations displayed by a LANalyzer are active stations. Any number of inactive stations may be physically connected between any of the active stations.

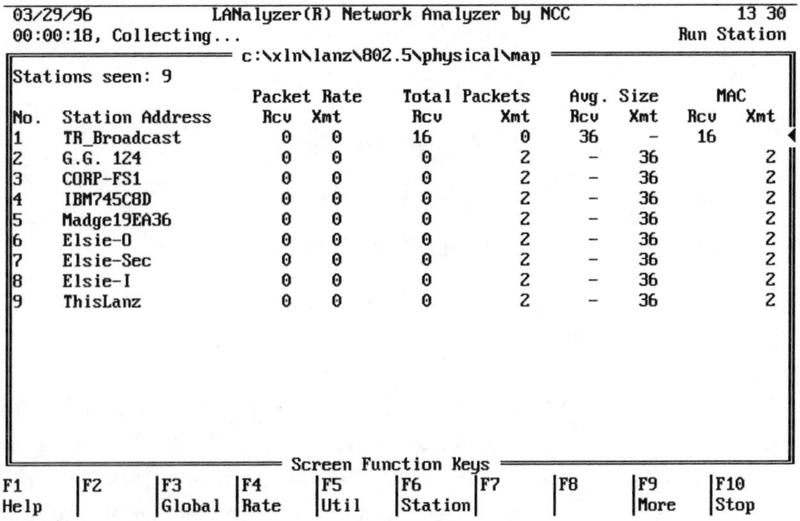

FIGURE 8.12

The Ring Poll process
as captured by the
LANalyzer by NCC MAP
application

```
03/29/96              LANalyzer(R) Network Analyzer by NCC                13 30
00:00:18, Collecting...                                                Run Station
                        c:\xln\lanz\802.5\physical\map
Stations seen: 9
                     Packet Rate    Total Packets    Avg. Size      MAC
No.  Station Address   Rcv  Xmt      Rcv     Xmt     Rcv   Xmt   Rcv   Xmt
1    TR_Broadcast       0    0       16       0      36     -    16
2    G.G. 124           0    0        0       2       -    36          2
3    CORP-FS1           0    0        0       2       -    36          2
4    IBM745C8D          0    0        0       2       -    36          2
5    Madge19EA36        0    0        0       2       -    36          2
6    Elsie-0            0    0        0       2       -    36          2
7    Elsie-Sec          0    0        0       2       -    36          2
8    Elsie-I            0    0        0       2       -    36          2
9    ThisLanz           0    0        0       2       -    36          2




                        Screen Function Keys
F1      F2      F3      F4      F5      F6      F7      F8      F9      F10
Help            Global  Rate    Util    Station                 More    Stop
```

Station Initialization Process

ATTACHING A RING station to the ring is not as simple as applying the phantom current to the relays in the MSAU or LAM. Rather, a ring station must go through a regimented set of six procedures, or phases, in order to attach to and become "of the ring." The phases executed when the adapter's driver is loaded must be completed in the following order:

Phase 1: Set adapter defaults

Phase 2: Lobe media check

Phase 3: Monitor check

Phase 4: Address verification

Phase 5: Participate in Ring Poll

Phase 6: Request initialization

PHASE 1 The adapter sets its configurable parameters to their defaults. The defaults are

- Physical drop number = 0

- Local ring number = 0

- Soft error report timer = 2 seconds

- Enable function class mask

- Allowed access priority = 3

- All error counters = 0

PHASE 2 The ring station performs a test of the lobe cable (via the loopback connection at the MSAU) and the Token Ring adapter, as shown in Figure 8.13. To pass this test, the adapter must successfully transmit and receive 2047 Lobe Media Check MAC frames and one Duplicate Address Test MAC frame on the lobe loopback path.

FIGURE 8.13

The ring station tests its lobe cable and adapter.

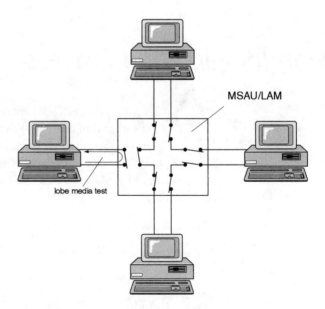

MSAU/LAM

lobe media test

PHASE 3 If the loopback test is successful, the adapter puts the phantom current on the lobe and activates the bypass relay in the MSAU, as illustrated in

Figure 8.14. Then the adapter waits for one of the following frames on the ring in order to verify that an AM is present on the ring and, thus, that it has entered a functioning ring:

- Active Monitor Present MAC frame

- Standby Monitor Present MAC frame

- Ring Purge MAC frame

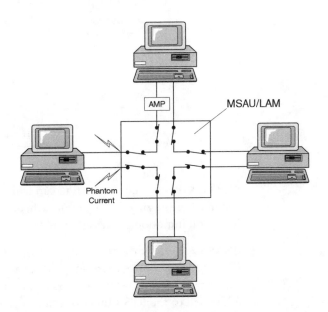

If the station does not detect one of the frames listed above within 18 seconds, it assumes there is no AM on the ring and so goes into Monitor Contention. If no other participating stations are on the ring, it becomes the AM.

PHASE 4 The station next checks to make sure its hardware address is unique to the ring, as shown in Figure 8.15. It does this by transmitting a series of Duplicate Address Test MAC frames on the ring. If the adapter receives two frames in row with the ARI and FCI bits set to 1, it assumes there is another ring station that shares its address and removes itself from the ring by removing the phantom current from the lobe. If the ring station receives any two frames in a row with the ARI and FCI bits set to 0, it assumes that its address is unique and proceeds to phase 5.

FIGURE 8.15

The ring station verifies
that its address is unique
to the ring.

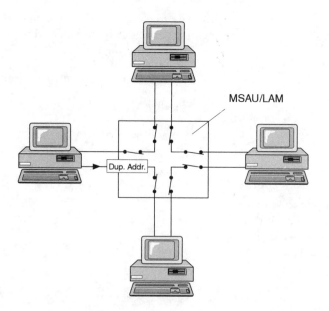

PHASE 5 Before the ring station can truly be a part of the ring family, it must become "of the ring." This occurs when the ring station participates in the Ring Poll initiation process (Figure 8.16) and receives its NAUN's address.

PHASE 6 Finally, the ring station must query the Ring Parameter Server (RPS) for any change to its adapter's parameters, as illustrated in Figure 8.17. The ring station transmits a series of Request Initialization MAC frames addressed to the RPS's functional address. (For details about functional addresses, see Chapters 7 and 12.) The adapter will wait a finite amount of time for an Initialize Ring Station MAC frame from the RPS or a Change Parameters MAC frame from the Configuration Report Server (CRS). If the ring station does not receive a reply from either the RPS or CRS (after trying and timing out four times), it accepts its adapter default parameters and starts normal token protocol.

A ring station will query a Ring Parameter Server, regardless of whether one exists on the ring.

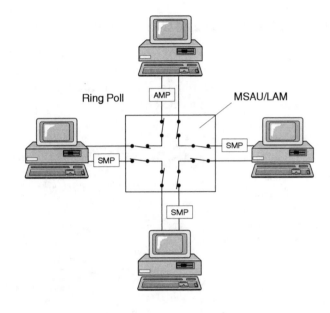

FIGURE 8.16

The ring station participates in Ring Poll and becomes "of the ring."

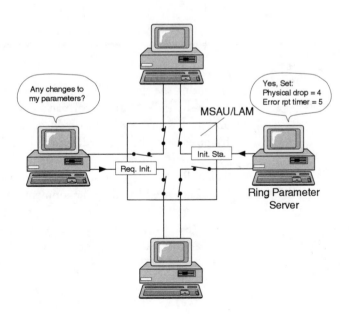

FIGURE 8.17

The ring station queries the Ring Parameter Server for changes to adapter parameters.

View Station Initialization Process with the LANalyzer

With a LANalyzer, you can see the last three phases on the ring, as shown in Figure 8.18. You will see Address Verification MAC frames, the station participating in Ring Poll, and the request-for-parameters exchange with RPS and/or CRS.

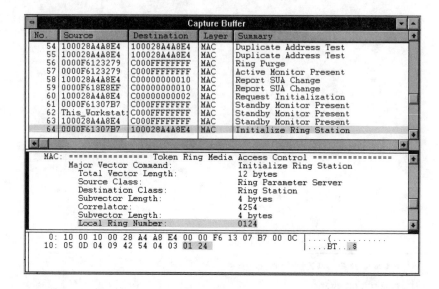

During the ring station initialization process, you will see a number of Ring Purges by the AM and error packets sent to the Ring Error Monitor (REM) and the CRS. The Ring Error Monitor will receive burst and possibly line or frame errors. The CRS will receive two Change of Saved Upstream Neighbor (SUA) MAC frames. These purges by the AM and errors are a normal part of Token Ring during the station initialization process and should not alarm you. They are caused by the momentary opening of the ring when the bypass relays switch in the attaching ring station. The two Change of SUAs sent to the CRS are from the station entering the ring and its downstream neighbor, whose SUA address changed when the new station entered the ring.

Errors are discussed in detail in Chapters 9 and 14.

Ring Purge Process

L ET'S SAY THE AM uses the Ring Purge process to "kickstart" the ring after a break in the token protocol. The Ring Purge process is done by a ring station when it first becomes the AM, after winning Monitor Contention, and when it detects a lost or corrupted token or frame.

Ring Purge Example

The AM detects a break in token protocol when its T(good_token) timer goes off before it has seen a valid (uncorrupted) token or frame on the ring. When the timer expires, the AM starts transmitting Ring Purge MAC frames every 4 milliseconds without waiting for a free token, as shown in Figure 8.19.

The AM continues to transmit Ring Purge MAC frames until it receives one uncorrupted Ring Purge frame. It then stops transmitting purge frames and releases a new token, thus reestablishing the token protocol, as you can see in Figure 8.20.

Ring Purge is the first step in the hardware error recovery process when the problem is detected by the AM (see Chapter 12).

View Ring Purge with the LANalyzer

Ring Purge frames viewed by a LANalyzer will vary based on the position of the LANalyzer relative to the AM and the hardware error causing the purging. On a normally operating ring, this hardware error is usually the bypass relays in the MSAU as stations attach to the ring. If the LANalyzer is downstream from the AM and upstream from the hardware problem, it will see a great many Ring Purge frames before the ring recovers. This is because it is capturing every Ring Purge frame the AM is transmitting, as shown in Figure 8.21.

FIGURE 8.19

The AM starts transmitting Ring Purge frames when it detects a break in the token protocol.

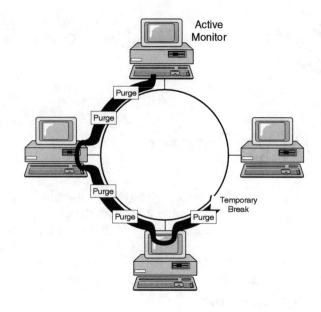

FIGURE 8.20

The AM releases a new token when it receives one valid Ring Purge frame.

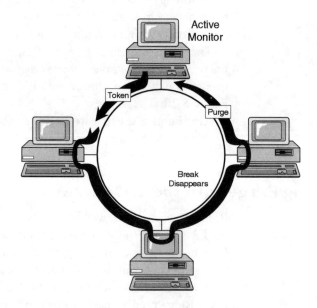

FIGURE 8.21

Ring Purge frames as seen
by a LANalyzer upstream
from the hardware
problem

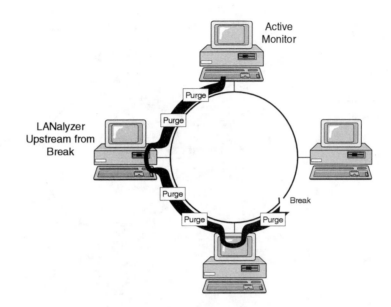

If the LANalyzer is upstream from the AM and downstream from the hardware problem, it will see very few Ring Purge frames. This is because it captures only the Ring Purge frames that it repeats after the hardware problem has been resolved and before the AM sees a valid one and stops transmitting, as illustrated in Figure 8.22.

Purge frames are always followed by error reports to the REM or CRS. Under normal operation, purge frames occur when stations enter or leave the ring and operate the bypass relays in the MSAU, breaking the ring for an instant. They also occur rarely when a station loses a frame or transmits an abort sequence.

Normally, purge frames should happen sporadically as stations enter and leave the ring (a good baseline). If the NCC LANalyzer detects a steady stream of Ring Purge events but no Ring Recoveries (Monitor Contention processes), the ring is not healthy. For details on how to improve this situation, see Chapter 11.

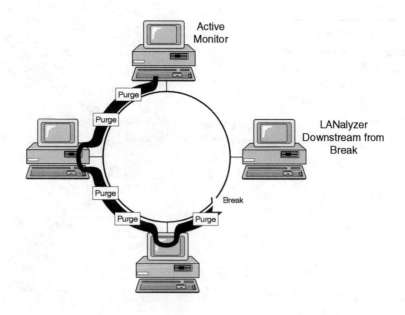

Beacon Process

THE BEACON PROCESS is the last desperate attempt by the ring to recover from a permanent hardware problem. If the Beacon process is successful, the ring will isolate the problem and recover. If it is not successful, the network technicians must manually intervene to fix the problem so the ring can recover. On a positive note, if you have a LANalyzer, you can capture a Beacon frame, and the ring will tell you where the trouble is located.

The best way to describe the Beacon process is to step through an example.

Beacon Example

Let's say station A detects a hardware failure on its receive cable. Station A assumes the problem is not with itself and blames its upstream neighbor, station

D. Station A starts transmitting Beacon MAC frames every 20 milliseconds without waiting for a token, as illustrated in Figure 8.23. Inside the Beacon frame, station A lists station D, its upstream neighbor, as the likely problem. All stations on the ring stop normal token protocol and enter Beacon repeat mode as soon as they detect a Beacon frame.

FIGURE 8.23

Station A detects a hardware error and starts transmitting Beacon frames.

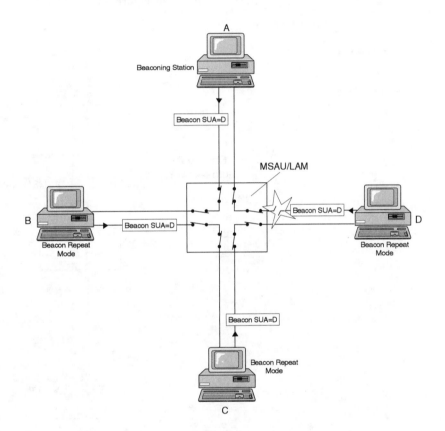

Station D starts receiving Beacon frames from station A. The Beacon frame lists station D as the upstream neighbor. When station D has received eight Beacon frames, it removes itself from the ring and runs the lobe media test described in the section "Station Initialization Process" earlier in this chapter. The mystery as to whether or not the ring will recover is always the same up to this point. However, there are three possible endings to this Beacon mystery.

ENDING #1 (GOOD ENDING) Station D's media test fails, and it remains off the ring. Because the hardware error was in station D's lobe or adapter, station A starts to receive its own Beacon frames as soon as station D exits the ring. When station A receives its own Beacon frames, it stops transmitting Beacon frames and goes into Monitor Contention. An AM is elected and the ring recovers, as shown in Figure 8.24.

FIGURE 8.24

Station D's lobe media test fails and the ring recovers.

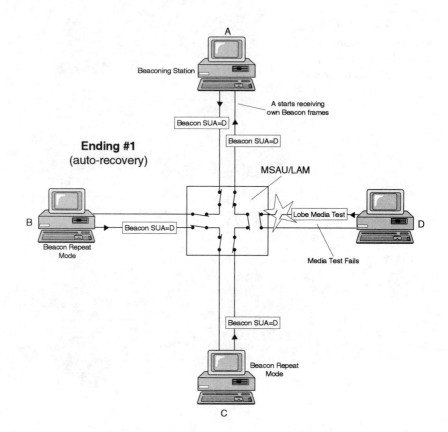

ENDING #2 (GOOD ENDING) Station D passes its media lobe test, reinserts itself into the ring, and enters Beacon repeat mode. Station A has not received one of its Beacon frames for 16 seconds (enough time for its upstream neighbor to run its lobe media test and reenter the ring). After 16 seconds, station A exits the ring and runs a lobe media check. It fails and station A remains off the ring. Station A's downstream neighbor, station B, took over transmitting Beacon frames when station A left the ring, but at a lower priority. (Beacon priorities are discussed in Chapter 14.) Because the hardware problem was in station A's lobe or adapter, station B starts to receive its own Beacon frames and goes into Monitor Contention, and the ring recovers, as shown in Figure 8.25.

FIGURE 8.25

Station A's lobe media test fails and the ring recovers.

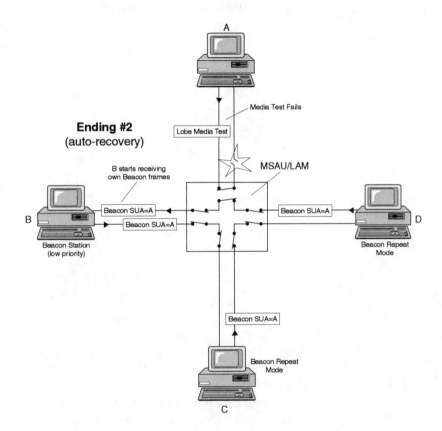

ENDING #3 (BAD ENDING) Station A passes its lobe media test and reenters the ring. Station A resumes Beaconing and station B goes into Beacon repeat mode because station A has a higher priority Beacon. Station A continues to beacon forever or until a technician fixes the problem, whichever comes first, as illustrated in Figure 8.26.

To save the ring, you, the network technician, need to capture and decode just one Beacon frame with a LANalyer. In this case, the source address of the

FIGURE 8.26

Both stations pass the
lobe media test, and the
ring continues to beacon
until there is manual
intervention.

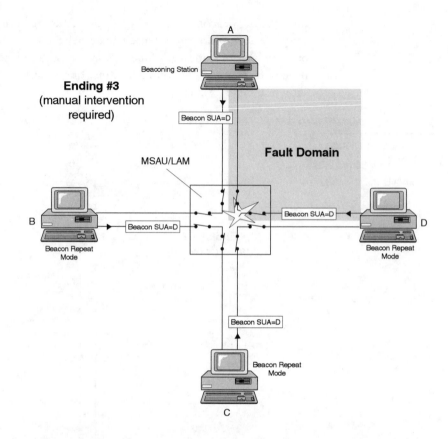

Beacon frame is station A. Inside the decoded frame is station A's upstream neighbor's address. Between these two addresses is the area known as the *fault domain*.

If a ring continues beaconing for more than about 26 seconds, it is not going to recover on its own. You know that the lobe and adapter of both stations in the fault domain have been checked and approved. That leaves whatever hardware is between them (typically an MSAU, but it could be a patch cable, a repeater, and so on).

For more details on troubleshooting a Beaconing ring, see Chapter 12.

Viewing the Beacon Process with a LANalyzer

Unless you plan it, you probably will never see the complete Beacon process with a LANalyzer—it lasts for only around 26 seconds, and either the ring recovers or it doesn't within that time span. If it doesn't recover, you will see the same Beacon frame over and over and over until you fix the problem. The screen in Figure 8.27 is a decoded Beacon frame showing the fault domain.

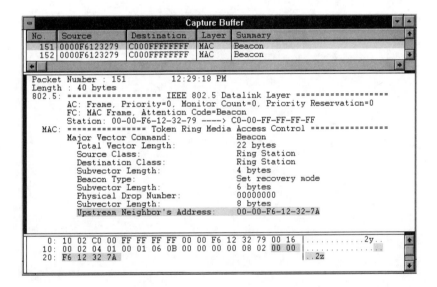

In this chapter you have gotten a glimpse of the complexity of Token Ring self management. In later chapters you will learn how to use this management ability to your advantage.

Now that you understand Token Ring protocol and processes, the next chapter examines the Token Ring token and frame formats. (If you're not interested in bits and bytes, you may want to skip the next chapter.)

Token Ring
Frame
Structures

U P TO NOW we have looked at the processes and procedures associated with Token Ring. Now is a good time to look at the Token Ring bit patterns and frame formats and how they relate to the Token Ring protocols and processes. We will take a look at bits and bytes because, if you use a protocol analyzer, information about them will give you a greater understanding of the Token Ring mechanism. You will then be better able to analyze the activities, good and bad, of your Token Ring networks.

Token Ring has two frame formats: MAC frames and Non-MAC frames. MAC frames are used for ring and station management, and Non-MAC frames carry user data. In addition to frames, Token Ring uses two other bit patterns. These are tokens and abort sequences. We'll examine tokens and abort sequences first and then break down the MAC and Non-MAC frames.

Special Token Ring Bit Patterns

T HE TWO BIT patterns Token Ring uses are not really frames as you typically think of frames, but more like frame "wanna-be's." These special bit patterns are tokens and abort sequences.

Tokens, as the name suggests, are an integral part of Token Ring. They consist of three 8-bit fields, as shown here:

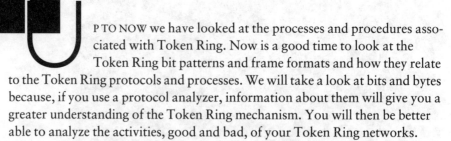

SDEL (1 byte)
AC (1 byte)
EDEL (1 byte)

These fields are also part of Token Ring frames. As a station captures a free token, it actually adds fields to the token bit pattern, thus making it a frame. (We will discuss each field in the token in detail when we discuss frames, later in this chapter.)

Tokens cannot be captured by protocol analyzers, but analyzers, like the LANalyzer by NCC, that use specialized hardware can measure the token rotation time.

Token rotation time is a good measure of Token Ring congestion. It is described in detail in Chapter 10.

An *abort sequence* consists of Start Delimiter (SDEL) and End Delimiter (EDEL) fields, back to back, as shown here:

SDEL (1 byte)

EDEL (1 byte)

Abort sequences are rarely used by ring stations; they are basically the ring station's way of saying, "Oops, I didn't really mean to transmit right now." Adapters transmit abort sequences for two reasons:

- The adapter detects a non-fatal error within itself during transmission of a frame that is severe enough to require the transmission to be aborted.

- The host PC directs the adapter to abort current transmission of frame(s). This request is usually from the upper-layer protocols or the application.

When an adapter transmits an abort sequence, it doesn't complete the token protocol by transmitting a free token. It just stops, leaving the ring suddenly without a token or frame. This situation generates a couple of soft-error reports to the Ring Error Monitor (REM). The Active Monitor (AM) purges the ring and then reports a Token error for a lost token/frame. The ring station that transmitted the abort sequence reports an Abort Delimiter Transmitted error.

For details on soft errors and what they mean, see Chapter 10.

Token Ring Frames

T HERE ARE TWO types of Token Ring frames. Media Access Control (MAC) frames are used by the ring to carry management information between ring stations. It is with MAC frames that all processes like Ring Poll, Monitor Contention, and Beaconing are accomplished. Non-MAC frames carry user data and are the reason Token Ring networks exist.

Non-MAC Frame Structure

Non-MAC frames carry user data inside Logical Link Control (LLC) Protocol Data Units (LPDUs). Figure 9.1 shows the Non-MAC frame structure.

FIGURE 9.1

Token Ring Non-MAC
frame structure

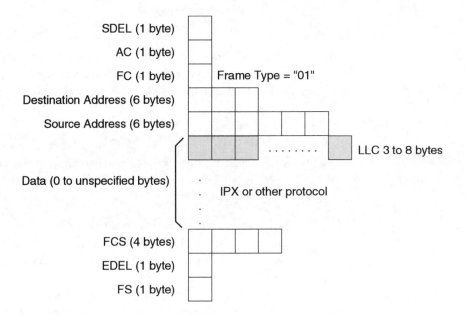

SDEL (1 byte)
AC (1 byte)
FC (1 byte)   Frame Type = "01"
Destination Address (6 bytes)
Source Address (6 bytes)

LLC 3 to 8 bytes

Data (0 to unspecified bytes)   IPX or other protocol

FCS (4 bytes)
EDEL (1 byte)
FS (1 byte)

For details on LLC format, see the section "Ethernet_802.2 Frame Structure" in Chapter 4.

Unlike Ethernet, Token Ring requires only two ODI frame formats, one for standard LLC and another for the SNAP LLC. They are named as follows:

- TOKEN-RING (for Unnumbered (U) or Information/Supervisory (I/S) LLC format)

- TOKEN-RING_SNAP (for SNAP LLC format)

MAC Frame Structure

MAC frames carry only Token Ring management information. They are specific to a ring; in other words, they are not passed by bridges and routers to other rings. For example, you wouldn't want Beacon MAC frames from one ring passing over to another ring. Figure 9.2 shows the MAC frame format.

FIGURE 9.2

Token Ring MAC frame structure

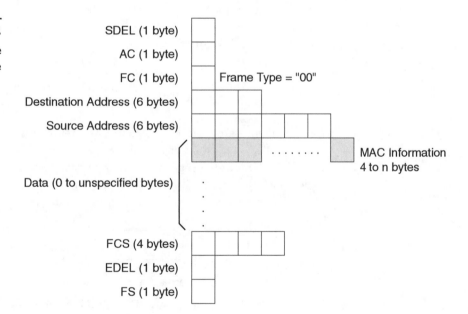

MAC frames and the information they carry are discussed in detail in Chapter 10.

The Token Ring frame format is basically the same for both MAC and Non-MAC frames. The frame itself is the same, as you have seen, the only difference being the information carried in the data field. Now let's look at the format of the frame itself.

Start Delimiter (SDEL) and End Delimiter (EDEL)

Token Ring is a closed loop with a continuous clock signal (phase locked loop). Because of this, all stations are constantly in synch with each other. All, then, that is needed is a method of designating the beginning and end of a token and/or frame.

The beginning and end of a Token Ring frame were determined by purposely violating the Differential Manchester Encoding (the method Token Ring uses to encode data) of 1's and 0's in specific patterns in combination with valid 1's and 0's to designate the beginning and end of tokens and frames.

The SDEL is shown here:

Violations are typically designated as J and K; J is the encoding violation of a 1, and K is the violation of a 0.

The EDEL uses a slightly different pattern of violations and valid bits to designate the end. However, the EDEL contains two additional bits: the Intermediate Frame bit and the Error Detected Indicator bit, as shown here:

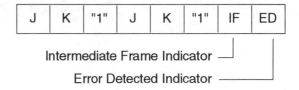

Intermediate Frame Bit

The Intermediate Frame bit is set to 0 by the transmitting station if the frame is the last or only frame transmitted in this set. It is set to 1 if there are more frames to follow.

Error Detected Indicator Bit

The Error Detected Indicator bit is set by the first station to detect a CRC error in a frame. (In Token Ring terminology, CRC errors are known as *line errors*.) Every station on the ring performs a CRC check on every frame as it is repeated. A station sets the Error Detected Indicator bit to 1 when it detects a line error so other stations downstream do not report the same error.

For more details on line errors, see Chapter 10.

Access Control (AC) Field

The access control (AC) field has three functions:

- To signify whether the following fields constitute a frame or a token

- To indicate the priority of the token or frame and provide a place for ring stations to reserve a priority token

- To give the Active Monitor a method of determining whether a frame or priority token has circled the ring more than once

Figure 9.3 shows the bit assignments of the AC field. The following sections provide detailed descriptions of these bits.

FIGURE 9.3

Access Control field bit assignments

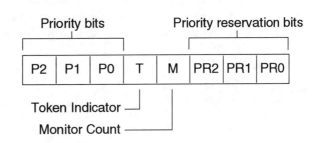

Priority Bits

The three priority bits determine the priority of the token or frame. These three bits provide eight levels of priority: bit 000 (0) through bit 111 (7).

Token Indicator

The Token Indicator bit lets the ring station know what follows, whether it be a token or a frame. A bit set to 1 indicates that what follows is a frame. A bit set to 0 indicates that the ring station has obtained a token.

Monitor Count Bit

The Monitor Count bit is initially set to 0 by the transmitting station. When the Active Monitor repeats a frame or token with a priority greater than 0, it sets this bit to 1. If the Active Monitor detects this frame or priority token again, it assumes that the station responsible for stripping it has failed to do so, for whatever reason, and strips the frame or priority token and then purges the ring.

For details on Ring Purge, see Chapter 8.

Priority Reservation Bits

Priority Reservation bits are used by ring stations to reserve a token with the priority indication they set with these bits in a token or frame. Priority reservation values are identical to the priority bit values.

Frame Control Field

The Frame Control field determines whether a frame is a MAC or Non-MAC frame. For MAC frames, it also provides an early indication of one of the media management MAC frames (Purge, Claim Token, Beacon, and so on). Figure 9.4 shows bit assignments for the Frame Control field.

FIGURE 9.4

Frame Control bit
assignments

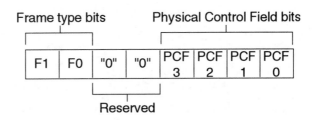

Frame Type Bits

The Frame Type bits determine whether the frame is MAC or Non-MAC, as follows:

00 = MAC frame

01 = Non-MAC frame

1x = Reserved

Physical Control Field (PCF) Bits

Valid only for MAC frames (frame type = 00), the Physical Control Field (PCF) bits give early warning to the ring station of media management MAC frames. They also give priority to adapter buffer–to–host frame transfer. A normal buffer indicates to the ring station that the data in the MAC frame can be buffered and transferred to the host in a normal fashion. An Express buffer indicates that the MAC data should be immediately forwarded to the host for processing.

The following table shows the PCF bit assignment values:

PCF Indication	Binary	Decimal
Normal buffer	0000	0
Express buffer	0001	1
Purge	0010	2

PCF Indication	Binary	Decimal
Claim Token	0011	3
Beacon	0100	4
Active Monitor Present	0101	5
Standby Monitor Present	0110	6

Token Ring Addresses

Token Ring and Ethernet both use the IEEE 32-bit (6 byte) universal MAC address standard (the one burned into ROMs on network adapters). Namely, the first 3 bytes are assigned to the manufacturer by IEEE, and the last 3 bytes are assigned by the manufacturer. FF FF FF FF FF FF is used to address frames to all devices (broadcast). However, Token Ring destination and source addresses have a number of format variations, not used by Ethernet. In addition, Token Ring implementations commonly use some of the IEEE standard formats not typically found in Ethernet implementations. These format variations are explained in the following sections.

Destination Address

Figure 9.5 shows the destination address and the important format bits. It is the use of the these bits in different combinations that determines the various destination address types. For this reason we will abandon our pattern of discussing bits individually and discuss the different address formats instead.

FIGURE 9.5

Token Ring destination address

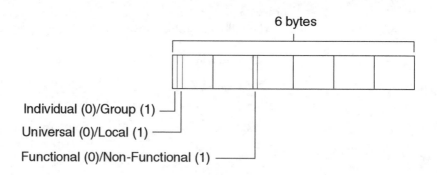

GROUP ADDRESSES Destination addresses can be to a specific station, or they can be addresses to a group of devices. If the Group/Specific bit is set to 1, the destination address is a group address.

Two types of group addresses are broadcast addresses and multicast addresses. *Broadcast addresses* are addressed to and copied by every device on the network. For example, when a NetWare client looks for a server to attach to, it sends a frame addressed to broadcast in hopes of locating a server somewhere on the network. *Multicast addresses* are addressed to a specific group of devices. For example, a router manufacturer may use a multicast address to provide communication to only its routers.

The universal broadcast address is forwarded by bridges (both source-routing and transparent) but not by routers. Routers act as broadcast firewalls and so contain broadcast traffic to the local network.

Token Ring implements two broadcast addresses. One is the standard universal broadcast address shown here:

FF FF FF FF FF FF

This broadcast address broadcasts user data and is forwarded across bridges to other rings on the local network.

The other broadcast address is the Token Ring broadcast, shown here:

C0 00 FF FF FF FF

This broadcast address is used for Token Ring–specific MAC management functions and is ring specific. This means that frames addressed to this broadcast address are not forwarded by bridges to other rings. For example, many of the MAC frames used in the Token Ring processes described in Chapter 8, such as Beacon and Claim Token MAC frames, are addressed to Token Ring broadcast.

FUNCTIONAL/NONFUNCTIONAL ADDRESSES Token Ring multicast addresses are further divided into two categories, functional and nonfunctional.

Functional multicast addresses are Token Ring specific. They are assigned by IBM to different Token Ring functional devices, such as the Configuration Report Server, Ring Error Monitor, and source-route bridges, and are indicated by the Functional/Nonfunctional bit set to 0. The following table lists common Token Ring functional addresses:

Functional Device	Functional Address
Active Monitor	C0 00 00 00 00 01
Ring Parameter Server	C0 00 00 00 00 02
Ring Error Monitor	C0 00 00 00 00 08
Configuration Report Server	C0 00 00 00 00 10
Source-Route Bridge	C0 00 00 00 01 00

Nonfunctional addresses are multicast addresses that are not Token Ring specific—in other words, all the addresses assigned to vendors for their particular devices. The Functional/Nonfunctional bit is set to 1 to indicate a nonfunctional address.

UNIVERSAL/LOCALLY ASSIGNED ADDRESSES The address assigned by IEEE and the adapter manufacturer that comes burned into a ROM on the Token Ring adapter is the *universal address*. Universal addresses have the Universal/Local bit set to 0. If you decide to override the universal address on the board with your own address, by convention you must set the Universal/Local bit to 1.

To override the universal address of an ODI-compliant adapter, add the following parameter to the appropriate LINK DRIVER section of the NET.CFG file:

NODE ADDRESS *hex_address*

The *hex_address* is the 6-byte local address in hexadecimal.

Source Address

Figure 9.6 shows the Token Ring source address format. Source addresses can only be specific addresses. (You will never see a frame *from* broadcast.) Thus, the same rules apply for source addresses as for specific/locally assigned destination addresses.

The Group/Specific bit for destination addresses is used as the Route Information Indicator (RII) bit in source addresses. If the RII bit is set to 1, it indicates that routing information follows immediately after the source address in

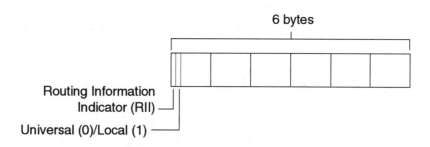

6 bytes

Routing Information
Indicator (RII)

Universal (0)/Local (1)

the data field. Source-route bridges check this bit to determine whether they should copy the frame.

See Chapter 13 for details on source routing.

Data Field

The Token Ring Data field contains MAC information for MAC frames and user data for Non-MAC frames. User data may include routing information (RII set to 1). It will always include a Logical Link Control (LLC) header.

See Chapter 4 for specifics about Logical Link Control.

The Token Ring Data field, by specification, can be from 0 to an unlimited number of bytes in length. The upper limit of data in the data field is determined by:

The token holding timer (10 ms by default): This Token Ring timer determines the time a ring station has to transmit data.

The limit of the adapter driver: For example, the ODI TOKEN driver has an upper limit of 17K, with a default of 4K. The limit the driver uses is configured in the MLID driver section of the NET.CFG file, using the MAX FRAME SIZE *number* parameter.

The size of the packet as negotiated by the transport layer: In NetWare, the Large Internet Packet (LIP) will determine the maximum packet size during client server negotiation when the NetWare shell (requester) is loaded (see

Chapter 16). This negotiation takes the maximum-packet-size driver setting into account, but the negotiated packet size takes precedence if it is smaller.

Frame Check Sequence

The Frame Check Sequence is exactly the same CRC check made by Ethernet/ IEEE 802.3. Again, remember that every station on the ring performs a CRC test on frames as they are repeated. The only fields that are protected by the FCS are the Frame Control through Data fields, as shown in Figure 9.7. The other fields have data that changes as the frame travels around the ring (the monitor count bit in the Access Control field, for example) and, obviously, fields that have bits that change would cause a CRC or line error when recalculated by another station.

FIGURE 9.7

FCS and code violation–
protected areas of the
Token Ring frame

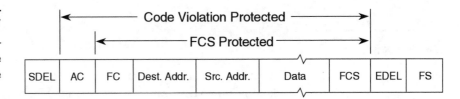

Frame Status Field

The Frame Status field contains duplicate information, as shown here:

ARI	FCI	"0"	"0"	ARI	FCI	"0"	"0"

The first 4 bits are identical to the last 4 bits. The reason for this is that the Frame Status field is not FCS- or code violation–protected.

The data contained in the Frame Status field consists of the Address Recognized Indicator (ARI) and Frame Copied Indicator (FCI).

See Chapter 11 for details on troubleshooting stations with chronic congestion problems and Chapter 12 for hints on how to configure Token Ring adapters and drivers to optimize the adapter's packet receive capability.

Address Recognized Indicator (ARI)

If a station recognizes its address in the Destination Address field as it repeats the frame, it sets the ARI bits to 1.

Frame Copied Indicator (FCI)

If a station recognizes its address in the Destination Address field and has sufficient buffer to copy the frame, it sets the FCI bits to 1.

If a target station does not copy a frame destined for it, the transmitting station's Token Ring adapter will not automatically retransmit the frame on its own. It is up to upper-layer protocols (transport layer, for example) to determine that the frame was lost and request a retransmission. The ARI and FCI bits are more important to Token Ring for use with the Ring Poll process (see Chapter 8) and in providing information to management stations than for alerting a source if a destination has recognized and/or copied a frame.

In this chapter, you have learned about the Token Ring frame in its entirety. You don't need to memorize everything about the frame; you can use Appendix D of this book as a reference for all the frame formats. In the next chapter, you'll learn how the information contained in a MAC frame is formatted, and you can reference this material as well in Appendix D.

MAC Frame
Information

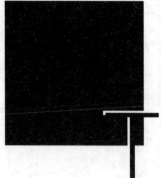

OKEN RING MAC frames hold the key to Token Ring trouble-shooting and management. There are 25 different MAC frames, divided into the following four functional categories:

- Station initialization

- Media management

- Error reporting

- Station management

This chapter examines the format of the MAC frame data and provides a reference for interpreting the information contained inside. Table 10.1 names and categorizes all 25 MAC frames.

Chapter 8 discusses how to use the Station Initialization and Media Control MAC frames. Chapter 11 provides details on using the Error Reporting MAC frames.

TABLE 10.1 MAC Frames and Functional Categories	STATION INITIALIZATION	MEDIA CONTROL	ERROR REPORTING	STATION MANAGEMENT
	Lobe Media Test	Beacon	Report Error	Report New Monitor
	Duplicate Address Test	Claim Token	Report Monitor Errors	Report SUA Change
	Request Initialization	Ring Purge	Report Ring Poll Failure	Remove Ring Station
	Initialize Ring Station	Active Monitor Present		Transmit Forward

TABLE 10.1 MAC Frames and Functional Categories (continued)	STATION INITIALIZATION	MEDIA CONTROL	ERROR REPORTING	STATION MANAGEMENT
	Change Parameters	Standby Monitor Present		Report Transmit Forward
				Response
				Request Station State
				Request Station Attachment
				Request Station Address
				Report Station State
				Report Station Attachment
				Report Station Address

MAC Information Format

O NLY MAC INFORMATION is carried in the data area of MAC frames (frame type bits in the Frame Control field = "00"). MAC data consists of a major vector and a variable number of supporting subvectors, as shown in Figure 10.1. The *major vector* determines the type, or command, of the MAC frame (Beacon, Purge, Remove Station, and so on) and the source and destination station type, or class (Ring Station, Ring Error Monitor, and so on). *Subvectors* provide supporting information for the major vector (upstream neighbor's address, physical drop number, and so on).

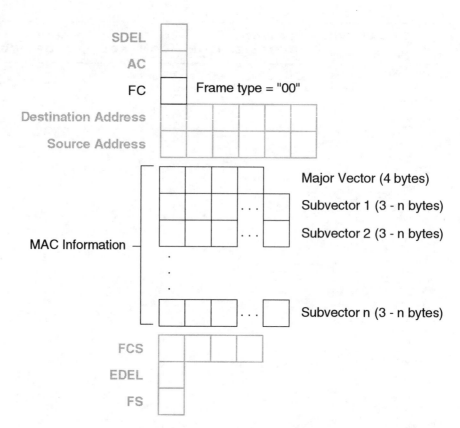

Major Vector ID Format

The major vector (MV) determines the command of the MAC frame and thus the action the ring stations must take when the MAC frame is detected. For example, when a ring station detects an Active Monitor Present MAC frame (MV=05h), it knows that the Ring Poll process has started and that it must prepare to participate.

The following diagram illustrates the format of the MV, which consists of the Length, Class, and Command fields:

Major Vector ID

Length 2 bytes	Class - 1 byte		Command 1 byte
	Dest.	Source	

LENGTH The Length field contains the total length of the MAC information, including the MV and all subvectors.

CLASS The Class field describes the destination and source stations. It is split into two 4-bit subfields: Destination Class and Source Class. This is really a description of the station function, and you will recognize the common functional stations. The following table lists the class values and their associated functional classes.

Class Value	Functional Class
0h	Ring Station
1h	LLC Manager (IEEE) or DLC.LAN.MGR (IBM)
4h	Configuration Report Server/Network Manager
5h	Ring Parameter Server
6h	Ring Error Monitor

COMMAND The Command field contains the assigned hexadecimal value of the MAC frame command. This value determines the MAC frame type. Table 10.2 includes the MV command value for all 25 MAC frames. Figure 10.2 shows a decoded MV.

The command value for the Media Control group of MAC frames is redundantly posted in the PCF bits of the FC field (see Chapter 9). This is because ring stations need advanced warning of these types of frames and the processes associated with them (see Chapter 8).

FIGURE 10.2

Decoded Beacon MAC
frame with MV highlighted

```
Packet Number : 248            6:32:18 PM
Length  : 40 bytes
802.5: =================== IEEE 802.5 Datalink Layer ===================
       AC: Frame, Priority=0, Monitor Count=0, Priority Reservation=0
       FC: MAC Frame, Attention Code=Beacon
       Station: Bridge_2 ----> C0-00-FF-FF-FF-FF
MAC:   =============== Token Ring Media Access Control ===============
       Major Vector Command:          Beacon
         Total Vector Length:         22 bytes
         Source Class:                Ring Station
         Destination Class:           Ring Station
         Subvector Length:            4 bytes
         Beacon Type:                 Set recovery mode
         Subvector Length:            6 bytes
         Physical Drop Number:        00000000
         Subvector Length:            8 bytes
         Upstream Neighbor's Address: Holli's_PC
```

TABLE 10.2

MAC Frames and Their
Associated Subvectors

CMD	NAME	DEST CLASS	SRC CLASS	SUBVECTORS
00h	Response	Request SrcClass	Ring Stn	[O] Correlator
				[R] Response Code
02h	Beacon	Ring Stn	Ring Stn	[R] Beacon Type
				[R] NAUN
				[O] Physical Drop No.
03h	Claim Token	Ring Stn	Ring Stn	[R] NAUN
				[O] Physical Drop No.
04h	Ring Purge	Ring Stn	Ring Stn	[R] NAUN
				[O] Physical Drop No.
05h	Active Monitor Present	Ring Stn	Ring Stn	[R] NAUN
				[O] Physical Drop No.

	CMD	NAME	DEST CLASS	SRC CLASS	SUBVECTORS
TABLE 10.2 MAC Frames and Their Associated Subvectors (continued)	06h	Stdby Monitor Present	Ring Stn	Ring Stn	[R] NAUN
					[O] Physical Drop No.
	07h	Duplicate Address Test	Ring Stn	Ring Stn	None
	08h	Lobe Test	Ring Stn	Ring Stn	[R] Wrap data
	09h	Transmit Forward	Ring Stn	CRS	[R] Frame Forward
	0Bh	Remove Ring Station	Ring Stn	CRS	None
	0Ch	Change Parameters	Ring Stn	CRS	[O] Local Ring No.
					[O] Assign Physical Location
					[O] Soft Error Rpt Timer
					[O] Enabled Function Class
					[O] Allowed Access Priority
					[O] Correlator
	0Dh	Initialize Ring Station	Ring Stn	RPS	[O] Local Ring No.
					Assign Physical Location
					Soft Error Rpt Timer

TABLE 10.2
MAC Frames and Their
Associated Subvectors
(continued)

CMD	NAME	DEST CLASS	SRC CLASS	SUBVECTORS
				Correlator
0Eh	Req Ring Station Address	Ring Stn	CRS	[O] Correlator
0Fh	Req Ring Station Address	Ring Stn	CRS	[O] Correlator
10h	Req Ring Station Attachments	Ring Stn	CRS	[O] Correlator
20h	Request Initialization	RPS	Ring Stn	[R] NAUN
				[R] Product Instance ID
				[R] Ring Stn Microcode Lvl
22h	Rpt Ring Stn Address	CRS	Ring Stn	[R] NAUN
				[R] Correlator
				[R] Physical Drop No.
				[R] Group Address
				[R] Functional Address(s)
23h	Rpt Ring Stn State	CRS	Ring Stn	[R] Correlator
				[R] Ring Stn Microcode Lvl

	CMD	NAME	DEST CLASS	SRC CLASS	SUBVECTORS
TABLE 10.2 MAC Frames and Their Associated Subvectors (continued)					[R] Station ID
					[R] Ring Sta Status Vector
	24h	Rpt Ring Stn Attachments	CRS	Ring Stn	[R] Enabled Func. Class
					[R] Allowed Access Priority
					[R] Correlator
					[R] Product Instance ID
					Functional Address(es)
	25h	Report New Active Monitor	CRS	Ring Stn	[R] NAUN
					[R] Physical Drop No.
					[R] Product Instance ID
	26h	Report NAUN Change	CRS	Ring Stn	[R] NAUN
					[R] Physical Drop No.
	27h	Report Poll Error	REM	Ring Stn	[R] Address of Last Neighbor Notification
	28h	Report Monitor Errors	REM	Ring Stn	[R] NAUN
					[R] Physical Drop No.

	CMD	NAME	DEST CLASS	SRC CLASS	SUBVECTORS
TABLE 10.2 MAC Frames and Their Associated Subvectors (continued)					[R] Error Code
	29h	Report Error	REM	Ring Stn	[R] NAUN
					[R] Physical Drop No.
					[R] Isolating Error Counts
					[R] Nonisolating Error Counts
	2Ah	Rpt Transmit Forward	CRS	Ring Stn	[R] Transmit Status Code

Subvector Format

Every MAC frame can contain 0, 1, or more subvectors (SVs). Some SVs are required by specification and some are optional. Table 10.2 lists the required SVs, and common optional ones, associated with each MAC frame.

SVs, contrary to the status implied by the name, actually provide the most important information in the MAC frame. For example, using decoded SV information, Token Ring can tell you the location of an intermittent hard error that is consuming the ring's bandwidth. (For details, see Chapter 11.)

SVs all have the same format, with Length, Type, and Value fields, as shown here:

Length 1 byte	Type 1 byte	Value variable

LENGTH The Length field contains the total length of the SV.

TYPE The Type field contains a hexadecimal value that names the SV. For example, 02h is the value for the Nearest Active Upstream Neighbor (NAUN) SV.

VALUE The Value field contains the subvector data. For example, the value of the NAUN subvector is the 6-byte hardware address of the upstream neighbor.

Figure 10.3 shows subvectors in a decoded Beacon MAC frame.

FIGURE 10.3

Decoded Beacon MAC frame with highlighted subvectors

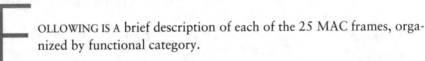

```
Packet Number : 248           6:32:18 PM
Length : 40 bytes
802.5: ==================== IEEE 802.5 Datalink Layer ==================
       AC: Frame, Priority=0, Monitor Count=0, Priority Reservation=0
       FC: MAC Frame, Attention Code=Beacon
       Station: Bridge_2 ----> C0-00-FF-FF-FF-FF
MAC:   ================ Token Ring Media Access Control ================
       Major Vector Command:           Beacon
         Total Vector Length:          22 bytes
         Source Class:                 Ring Station
         Destination Class:            Ring Station
         Subvector Length:             4 bytes
         Beacon Type:                  Set recovery mode
         Subvector Length:             6 bytes
         Physical Drop Number:         00000000
         Subvector Length:             8 bytes
         Upstream Neighbor's Address:  Holli's_PC
```

MAC Frames Described

FOLLOWING IS A brief description of each of the 25 MAC frames, organized by functional category.

Station Initialization MAC Frames

You use station initialization when a station inserts itself into the ring.

For details on the station initialization process, see Chapter 8.

LOBE MEDIA TEST (COMMAND=08H) The Lobe Media Test frame tests the integrity of a ring station's adapter and lobe. The destination address used during the test is null (00 00 00 00 00 00). You also use this MAC frame for the Lobe Media test in the Beacon process.

DUPLICATE ADDRESS TEST (COMMAND=07H) The Duplicate Address Test frame is sent from the ring station, addressed to itself, after physically attaching to the ring. It ensures that the address is unique on the ring.

REQUEST INITIALIZATION (COMMAND=20H) The ring station uses the Request Initialization frame to request adapter parameters from the Ring Parameter Server (RPS) function.

INITIALIZE RING STATION (COMMAND=0DH) The Ring Parameter Server uses the Initialize Ring Station frame to send parameters to a ring station's adapter after a request for initialization from the ring station.

CHANGE PARAMETERS (COMMAND=0CH) The Configuration Report Server uses the Change Parameter frame to send adapter parameter updates to a ring station. This may occur in response to an initialization request from the ring station, or an administrator from a Configuration Report Server functional station may initiate it.

Media Control MAC Frames

Token Ring stations use Media Control MAC frames to maintain token protocol on the ring. Media Control MAC frames are identified in the Frame Control field, as well as in the Major Vector Command field. This provides the ring station with quicker notification of a token protocol event.

For details on the Token Ring processes that use Media Control MAC frames, see Chapter 8. Media Control MAC frames are also an important part of troubleshooting and baselining your Token Ring network, as described in Chapter 11.

BEACON (COMMAND=02H) Ring stations use Beacon frames to recover from a hard error. Information provided in the Beacon frame indicates the source of the error (fault domain). Beaconing is the last stage of the hard-error recovery process.

CLAIM TOKEN (COMMAND=03H) Claim Token MAC frames are used to "elect" an Active Monitor during the monitor contention process. Monitor contention is also the second step for Active Monitors, and the first step for Standby Monitors, in the hard-error recovery process.

RING PURGE (COMMAND=04H) The Ring Purge frame is transmitted only by the Active Monitor to restart the token protocol after the loss or corruption of a token or frame (type 2 or above soft error).

ACTIVE MONITOR PRESENT (COMMAND=05H) The Active Monitor Present frame is used only by the Active Monitor to start the Ring Poll process.

STANDBY MONITOR PRESENT (COMMAND=06H) Standby Monitors use the Standby Monitor Present frame during the Ring Poll process, as explained in Chapter 8.

Error Reporting MAC Frames

As the name indicates, Error Reporting MAC frames report errors to the Ring Error Monitor (REM). Ring stations will report errors to the REM function regardless of whether or not an REM exists on the ring. With a protocol analyzer that will monitor and capture these error-reporting frames, you have a big advantage in maintaining your Token Ring network.

REPORT ERROR (COMMAND=29H) Ring stations use the Report Error frame to report their soft-error counts to the Ring Error Monitor. Ring stations report soft errors every time their T(_soft_error_report) timer expires (2 seconds by default), if there are errors to report.

REPORT MONITOR ERRORS (COMMAND=28H) The Report Monitor Errors frame is sent by ring stations to the Ring Error Monitor to report problems with the Active Monitor.

REPORT RING POLL FAILURE (COMMAND=27H) The Active Monitor sends the Report Ring Poll Failure to the Ring Error Monitor when the Ring Poll process fails. The frame includes the address of the last ring station that responded before the failure.

Station Management MAC Frames

The majority of MAC frames fall into the category of Station Management MAC frames, but they are the least valuable for troubleshooting and monitoring the Token Ring network. This is mainly because most of them deal with managing ring stations, not the Token Ring access protocols. Following is a brief description of each.

REPORT NEW MONITOR (COMMAND=25H) After winning monitor contention, the new Active Monitor reports its new role to the Configuration Report Server using the Report New Monitor frame.

REPORT SUA CHANGE (COMMAND=26H) The Report SUA (saved upstream neighbor's address) Change frame reports the change in a ring station's upstream neighbor to the Configuration Report Server. These frames appear when a station enters or leaves the ring.

REMOVE RING STATION (COMMAND=0BH) The Remove Ring Station MAC frame is the most interesting, if not the most useful, of the Station Management MAC frames. A station that detects this frame with its address as the destination *must* remove itself from the ring. The only way to get it back on the ring is to reload the adapter's driver.

The Remove Ring Station frame is a Configuration Report Server (CRS) function. If you don't have a CRS but happen to have a protocol analyzer that can transmit frames—the LANalyzer by NCC, for example—you can create one and transmit it to remove a ring station.

TRANSMIT FORWARD (COMMAND=09H) The Transmit Forward frame tests a path between ring stations. The frame is sent from the Configuration Report Server (CRS) to a ring station. A subvector in the frame contains an embedded Transmit Forward frame that is to be stripped out and transmitted to another specified station. Both stations—the one that received the frame from the CRS and the one that receives the embedded frame—must report to the CRS with a Report Transmit Forward frame.

REPORT TRANSMIT FORWARD (COMMAND=2AH) A ring station transmits the Report Transmit Forward frame to the Configuration Report Server when it receives a Transmit Forward MAC frame.

RESPONSE (COMMAND=00H) The Response MAC frame is sent from one ring station to another to acknowledge receipt of, and to respond to, a MAC frame that requires a response.

REQUEST STATION STATE (COMMAND=23H) The Request Station State frame is sent to a ring station by the Configuration Report Server to request the state of the station.

REQUEST STATION ATTACHMENT (COMMAND=24H) The Request Statement Attachment frame is sent to a ring station by the Configuration Report Server to request information about the station's adapter.

REQUEST STATION ADDRESS (COMMAND=22H) The Configuration Report Server sends the Request Station Address frame to a ring station to request the station's MAC address.

REPORT STATION STATE (COMMAND=0FH) The Report Station State frame is sent to the Configuration Report Server in response to a Request Station State MAC frame.

REPORT STATION ATTACHMENT (COMMAND=10H) The Report Station Attachment frame is sent to the Configuration Report Server in response to a Request Station Attachment MAC frame.

REPORT STATION ADDRESS (COMMAND=0EH) The Report Station Address frame is sent to the Configuration Report Server in response to a Request Station Address MAC frame.

In this chapter you learned about the different types of MAC frames and the kinds of management information they carry. The next chapter discusses how to use MAC frames and the information they contain to troubleshoot and monitor your Token Ring networks.

Troubleshooting at the Data Link Layer

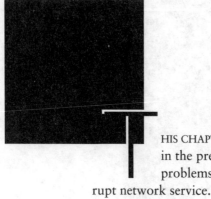

HIS CHAPTER SHOWS you how to use the information you learned in the preceding chapters in Part II to troubleshoot hardware problems on Token Ring and even to detect them before they disrupt network service.

Token Ring Errors

OKEN RING ERRORS come in two categories: *hard errors* (the most serious errors) and *soft errors* (ranging from simply informative to extremely serious).

Hard Errors

Hard errors tend to be catastrophic. This means that the ring most often will need to Beacon if it is to recover automatically, and you will have to manually intervene if Beaconing does not isolate the error. During Beaconing, the ring is not operational. This makes hard errors Token Ring's worst enemy. As demonstrated in Figure 11.1, hard errors are most often associated with Token Ring adapters, hubs (MASUs, LAMs, and so on), patch cables, and the cable plant (all other cabling).

Of all this hardware, the cable plant is the most critical. Technology and modern manufacturing techniques have made adapters and hubs very reliable. Cabling, on the other hand, is pretty much left to you, the consumer, to install and maintain. The bottom line is, do not compromise the integrity of your Token Ring cable plant. The cable plant is the foundation of a Token Ring network. If it is not installed properly, within specification, you can expect

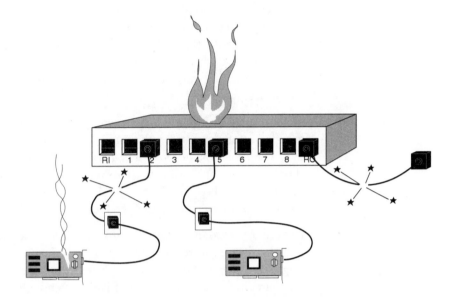

FIGURE 11.1

Hard errors are
associated with Token
Ring hardware.

nothing but troubleshooting nightmares and poor performance for the life of
your Token Ring. Conversely, if the cable plant is solid, you can expect years
of high-performance, worry-free operation. If your company is looking to cut
costs on a network installation and you have any say in the decision, do not
let them cut costs on the cable or its installation.

Installing Token Ring cable involves a complex set of formulas based on
the number of stations, hubs, wiring closets, and so on. It should be done by
experienced cable installers. If you do not have the expertise in house, consider hiring experienced outside contractors.

Following is a description of common Token Ring hard errors.

STREAMING ERRORS Two forms of streaming errors are Bit Streaming and
Frame Streaming. *Bit Streaming* involves destroying frames or tokens by over-
writing or replacing ring data. This situation is typically associated with a bad
adapter that is transmitting out of turn. Because modern adapters are
extremely reliable, this type of error is rare.

Frame Streaming is analogous to Ethernet jabber. An adapter starts continuously transmitting tokens, abort sequences, frames, or garbage. Again, this
hard error is rare.

FREQUENCY ERRORS Every ring station compares the frequency of the incoming signal to its own on-board clock. If the frequency of the incoming signal varies more than 0.6%, it is considered a *Frequency error*. A bad master clock from the Active Monitor (AM) or bad transmitting circuitry on any device on the ring might cause this type of error. Frequency errors are relatively rare.

SIGNAL LOSS ERRORS If the incoming signal has insufficient energy or is grossly out of phase, it is considered a *Signal Loss error*. This is by far the most common type of error. It is usually associated with cabling that is open, shorted, or out of specification or that has excessive noise (electromagnetic interference and so on). To a lesser degree, signal loss can be caused by bad adapters, hubs, repeaters, and patch cables.

INTERNAL ERRORS *Internal errors* occur when an adapter detects an error in its hardware severe enough to cause the adapter to remove itself from the ring. Token Ring adapters are constantly running error checks on key areas of their circuitry. If a hardware error is severe enough to cause ring failure, the adapter withdraws from the ring.

Hard-Error Recovery Timeline

When Token Ring stations detect a hard error, they take a set sequence of steps in an attempt to resolve the error. This set of steps is known as the *hard-error recovery timeline*. Figure 11.2 shows a diagram of the timeline. How the error is detected—whether by an AM or by a Standby Monitor—(SM) determines where a station starts the sequence of steps.

FIGURE 11.2

Error recovery timeline

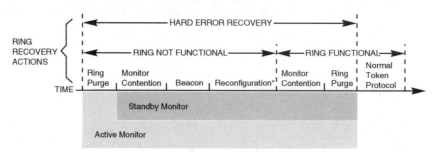

*Automatic or manual reconfiguration

If the hard error is detected by the AM, the AM steps through the following events of the hard-error recovery timeline (see Figure 11.2):

1. The AM tries to resolve the problem by purging the ring.

2. If the AM fails to receive back one of its Purge frames in 1 second, it tries to recover using the Monitor Contention process.

3. If the Monitor Contention process does not resolve the problem within 1 second, the AM starts the Beaconing process.

4. At this point, the problem must be resolved either automatically, through the Beaconing process, or manually, by technician intervention.

5. Once the hard error has been resolved, the AM starts the Monitor Contention process, and a new AM is elected.

6. The new AM purges the ring and releases a new token, the token protocol is restored, and the ring recovers.

When a hard error is detected by an SM, the process is exactly the same except that the SM starts the error-recovery process from the Monitor Contention step. (Remember, only AMs purge.)

Soft Errors

Soft errors require zero, one, or more steps of the hard-error recovery timeline to recover. Every station maintains a soft-error counter. Detected errors are reported to the Ring Error Monitor every 2 seconds, by default.

The four categories of soft errors, depending on the number of steps required to resolve them, are

Type 1	No recovery steps needed
Type 2	Ring Purge step required
Type 3	Steps up to Monitor Contention required
Type 4	Steps up to Beaconing required

Table 11.1 shows all soft errors by category.

TABLE 11.1 Soft Errors and Their Categories	**TYPE 1**	**TYPE 2**	**TYPE 3**	**TYPE 4**
	Line	Burst 5	Lost Monitor	All hard errors
	Internal	Abort Delimiter Transmitted	Frequency	
	Multiple Monitor	Lost Frame		
	ARI/FCI Set	Corrupted Token		
	Receive Congestion	Lost Token		
	Frame Copied	Circulating Frame or Priority Token		

The following are descriptions of all the soft errors.

Type 1 Soft Errors

Because type 1 soft errors do not disrupt the token protocol, they do not require any recovery procedures.

LINE ERRORS *Line errors* are Token Ring's name for CRC errors. Every station does a CRC check on the Frame Control through Data fields. When a ring station detects a CRC error, it increments its Line error counter and then sets the Error Detected bit in the EDEL so no other stations will report the same error.

One station's frequent reporting Line errors usually indicates a bad adapter in the station's upstream neighbor. If a number of stations on the ring are intermittently reporting Line errors, look for other error conditions, such as Burst errors or induced noise, on the ring. (See the section "Burst 5 Errors" later in this chapter.)

INTERNAL ERRORS The Internal error counter is incremented when a ring station's adapter discovers a minor recoverable error in its hardware.

If a ring station starts to consistently report this error, chances are the adapter is starting to fail.

MULTIPLE MONITOR ERRORS If an AM detects a Purge or Active Monitor Present MAC frame not its own, it immediately terminates all AM functions and increments the Multiple Monitors counter. This soft error is rare.

ARI/FCI SET ERRORS A ring station reports an ARI/FCI Set error when it detects two Standby Monitor Present (SMP) MAC frames with the ARI/FCI bits set to 0 without an intervening Active Monitor Present (AMP) MAC frame during one Ring Poll process. (See the section "Ring Poll Process" in Chapter 8.) A ring station should see only one SMP with the ARI/FCI bit set to 0 during a single Ring Poll process. If this error occurs, the error-detecting ring station terminates the Ring Poll process. This soft error is very rare.

RECEIVE CONGESTION ERRORS A ring station increments the Receive Congestion error counter when it detects a frame addressed to it but has insufficient buffer to copy the frame.

This error is caused by a ring station that cannot copy frames from the ring because of congestion in the ring station's Frame Copy pipeline.

What the Frame Copy pipeline is and how you can optimize it are discussed in Chapter 12.

FRAME COPIED ERRORS A ring station reports a Frame Copied error when it detects a frame with its address as the destination but the ARI/FCI bits are already set.

Because of the duplicate-address test during station initialization (see Chapter 8), this error is very rare. It can occur on bridged multi-ring networks, usually those using locally assigned addresses. The frame with the duplicate assigned address is passed to another ring through a bridge. Depending on where the bridge is, relative to the target station, the ARI/FCI bits may be set.

Type 2 Errors

Type 2 errors reflect a momentary breakdown in the token protocol. A Ring Purge by the Active Monitor is all that is required to recover from a type 2 soft error.

BURST 5 ERRORS Ring stations report a Burst 5 error when they detect signal loss for at least five half-bit cycles. This indicates a temporary interruption in the signal caused by an intermittent hardware error.

Next to Token errors, Burst errors are probably the most common soft errors on a ring. This is because they result from normal Token Ring operation. Every time a station enters or leaves the ring, Burst errors will result from the operation of relays in the MASU or LAM. Burst errors are the most useful soft errors for troubleshooting intermittent hardware problems. (The section "Troubleshooting" later in this chapter discusses these errors in more detail.)

ABORT DELIMITER TRANSMITTED ERRORS Whenever a station transmits an abort delimiter for any reason it reports an Abort Delimiter Transmitted error. After transmitting an abort delimiter, a ring station does not transmit a token. It is then up to the AM to detect the interruption in token protocol and purge the ring.

LOST FRAME ERRORS When a station transmits the trailer of a frame, it sets a timer [T(physical_trailer)]. If the station has not stripped off the same trailer before the timer goes off, the station aborts all transmissions without transmitting a token and increments its Lost Frame counter. Burst 5 errors that destroy the frame typically cause lost frames. (See the section "Burst 5 Errors" later in this chapter.)

TOKEN ERRORS The AM is the only station that reports Token errors. The AM reports a Token error for every error type 2 or above. In other words, every time the AM has to purge the ring, it reports a Token error. The following interruptions in token protocol cause the AM to report a Token error:

Corrupted token or frame: If a ring station detects a corrupted token or frame, it transmits an abort sequence. The Active Monitor detects this and purges the ring.

Lost token: The AM must detect a valid (good) token or frame on the ring at least every 10ms to ensure the proper operation of the token protocol. If a valid token or frame is not detected in this period of time, the AM purges the ring.

Circulating Frame or Priority token: When the AM detects a frame or token with a priority greater than 0 that has the Monitor Count bit in the Access Control field set to 1, it strips the frame or token and purges the ring.

Type 3 Soft Errors

Type 3 soft errors require the Monitor Contention process, and thus a new Active Monitor, to recover.

LOST MONITOR ERRORS If the AM leaves the ring or becomes inoperable, the SMs enter Monitor Contention to elect a new one. The SM that discovered the AM missing reports the Lost Monitor error.

FREQUENCY ERRORS Most Frequency errors result from an AM's clock gone bad. Monitor Contention usually resolves this problem. The SM that detected the frequency error starts the Monitor Contention process and reports the error.

Type 4 Soft Errors

Type 4 soft errors are all hard errors that cannot be resolved by the Monitor Contention process. Don't let this confuse you. The difference between a type 4 soft error and a hard error is this: if a hard error is resolved automatically by the Beacon process, it is a type 4 soft error. If it requires manual intervention, it is a hard error.

Troubleshooting

ARMED WITH A protocol analyzer and an understanding of Token Ring protocols, you can quickly determine whether a network problem is a Token Ring problem or an upper-layer problem. And if it is a Token Ring problem, Token Ring, by reviewing MAC frames and decoding a packet or two, can tell you not only what the problem is but where it is located.

Determining the Health of a Token Ring

The secret to determining the health of your Token Ring is Purge frames, which result from a breakdown in token protocol. The only time Purge frames should be on a ring (ideally) is when a ring station enters or leaves the ring and causes the relays in the MSAU or LAM to activate/deactivate.

Figure 11.3 shows the trace of the MAC frames—Purge, SUA Change, Station Initialization, and Report Error—that accompany a station entering the ring. The Purge and Report Error MAC frames result from Burst errors caused by the relay action in the MSAU or LAM.

FIGURE 11.3

Trace file of ring station entering the ring

No.	Source	Destination	Layer	Summary
71	Holli's_PC	C000FFFFFFFF	MAC	Standby Monitor Present
72	Bridge_2	C000FFFFFFFF	MAC	Standby Monitor Present
73	Roger's_PC	C000FFFFFFFF	MAC	Standby Monitor Present
74	LANZ	C000FFFFFFFF	MAC	Ring Purge
75	LaRae's_PC	LaRae's_PC	MAC	Duplicate Address Test
76	LANZ	C000FFFFFFFF	MAC	Active Monitor Present
77	LaRae's_PC	LaRae's_PC	MAC	Duplicate Address Test
78	LaRae's_PC	C00000000010	MAC	Report SUA Change
79	LaRae's_PC	C000FFFFFFFF	MAC	Standby Monitor Present
80	CORP_SERV	C00000000010	MAC	Report SUA Change
81	LaRae's_PC	C00000000002	MAC	Request Initialization
82	Taylor's_MAC	Holli's_PC	MAC	Request Station Address
83	Holli's_PC	Taylor's_MAC	MAC	Report Station Address
84	CORP_SERV	C000FFFFFFFF	MAC	Standby Monitor Present
85	Taylor's_MAC	C000FFFFFFFF	MAC	Standby Monitor Present
86	Roger's_PC	LaRae's_PC	MAC	Initialize Ring Station
87	LaRae's_PC	Roger's_PC	MAC	Response
88	Holli's_PC	C000FFFFFFFF	MAC	Standby Monitor Present
89	Bridge_2	C000FFFFFFFF	MAC	Standby Monitor Present
90	Roger's_PC	C000FFFFFFFF	MAC	Standby Monitor Present
91	Taylor's_MAC	Taylor's_MAC	MAC	Request Station Address
92	Taylor's_MAC	Taylor's_MAC	MAC	Report Station Address
93	Taylor's_MAC	CORP_SERV	MAC	Request Station Address
94	CORP_SERV	Taylor's_MAC	MAC	Report Station Address
95	Taylor's_MAC	LaRae's_PC	MAC	Request Station Address
96	LaRae's_PC	Taylor's_MAC	MAC	Report Station Address
97	LANZ	Taylor's_MAC	MAC	Report Station Address
98	Taylor's_MAC	Roger's_PC	MAC	Request Station Address
99	Roger's_PC	Taylor's_MAC	MAC	Report Station Address
100	Taylor's_MAC	Holli's_PC	MAC	Request Station Address
101	Holli's_PC	Taylor's_MAC	MAC	Report Station Address
102	CORP_SERV	C00000000008	MAC	Report Error
103	LANZ	C00000000008	MAC	Report Error
104	Taylor's_MAC	Holli's_PC	MAC	Request Station Address
105	Holli's_PC	Taylor's_MAC	MAC	Report Station Address

Figure 11.4 shows a trace of MAC frames captured as a ring station left the ring. In this case, Purge frames are accompanied only by SUA Change and

Report Error frames. Again, Purge and Report Error frames result from relay action.

FIGURE 11.4

Trace file of ring station exiting the ring

No.	Source	Destination	Layer	Summary
17	LANZ	C000FFFFFFFF	MAC	Ring Purge
18	LANZ	C00000000010	MAC	Report Station State
19	LANZ	C000FFFFFFFF	MAC	Active Monitor Present
20	CORP_SERV	C00000000010	MAC	Report SUA Change
21	CORP_SERV	C000FFFFFFFF	MAC	Standby Monitor Present
22	Taylor's_MAC	C000FFFFFFFF	MAC	Standby Monitor Present
23	Holli's_PC	C000FFFFFFFF	MAC	Standby Monitor Present
24	Bridge_2	C000FFFFFFFF	MAC	Standby Monitor Present
25	Roger's_PC	C000FFFFFFFF	MAC	Standby Monitor Present
26	Taylor's_MAC	Holli's_PC	MAC	Request Station Address
27	Holli's_PC	Taylor's_MAC	MAC	Report Station Address
28	Taylor's_MAC	Taylor's_MAC	MAC	Request Station Address
29	Taylor's_MAC	Taylor's_MAC	MAC	Report Station Address
30	Taylor's_MAC	CORP_SERV	MAC	Request Station Address
31	CORP_SERV	Taylor's_MAC	MAC	Report Station Address
32	LANZ	Taylor's_MAC	MAC	Report Station Address
33	Taylor's_MAC	Roger's_PC	MAC	Request Station Address
34	Roger's_PC	Taylor's_MAC	MAC	Report Station Address
35	Taylor's_MAC	Holli's_PC	MAC	Request Station Address
36	Holli's_PC	Taylor's_MAC	MAC	Report Station Address
37	CORP_SERV	C00000000008	MAC	Report Error
38	Taylor's_MAC	Holli's_PC	MAC	Request Station Address
39	Holli's_PC	Taylor's_MAC	MAC	Report Station Address
40	Taylor's_MAC	Holli's_PC	MAC	Request Station Address
41	Holli's_PC	Taylor's_MAC	MAC	Report Station Address
42	Taylor's_MAC	Holli's_PC	MAC	Request Station Address
43	Holli's_PC	Taylor's_MAC	MAC	Report Station Address
44	Taylor's_MAC	Holli's_PC	MAC	Request Station Address
45	Holli's_PC	Taylor's_MAC	MAC	Report Station Address
46	Taylor's_MAC	Holli's_PC	MAC	Request Station Address
47	Holli's_PC	Taylor's_MAC	MAC	Report Station Address
48	LANZ	C000FFFFFFFF	MAC	Active Monitor Present
49	CORP_SERV	C000FFFFFFFF	MAC	Standby Monitor Present
50	Taylor's_MAC	C000FFFFFFFF	MAC	Standby Monitor Present
51	Holli's_PC	C000FFFFFFFF	MAC	Standby Monitor Present

Purge and the resultant Report Error MAC frames are normal only when a station enters or leaves the ring. If you connect your protocol analyzer to the ring, filter for MAC frames only, and see Purge frames being transmitted consistently without accompanying SUA Change MAC frames, the Token Ring has a problem. Figure 11.5 shows a LANalyzer for Windows trace of such a ring. Notice the number and consistency of the Purge frames.

Figure 11.6 shows an NCC LANalyzer trace captured by filtering for Purge frames only. In the low-level decode, shown in Figure 11.7, notice the interpacket arrival time between the frames. An excessive number of Purge frames on a ring like the one shown in Figure 11.7—which was averaging about one

FIGURE 11.5

LANalyzer for Windows
trace of a ring with
excessive Purge MAC
frames

No.	Source	Destination	Layer	Summary
1	Bridge_2	C000FFFFFFFF	MAC	Ring Purge
2	Bridge_2	C000FFFFFFFF	MAC	Active Monitor Present
3	Roger's_PC	C000FFFFFFFF	MAC	Standby Monitor Present
4	LANZ	C000FFFFFFFF	MAC	Standby Monitor Present
5	LaRae's_PC	C000FFFFFFFF	MAC	Standby Monitor Present
6	CORP_SERV	C000FFFFFFFF	MAC	Standby Monitor Present
7	Taylor's_MAC	C000FFFFFFFF	MAC	Standby Monitor Present
8	Holli's_PC	C000FFFFFFFF	MAC	Standby Monitor Present
9	Taylor's_MAC	Holli's_PC	MAC	Request Station Address
10	Holli's_PC	Taylor's_MAC	MAC	Report Station Address
11	Holli's_PC	C00000000008	MAC	Report Error
12	Bridge_2	C00000000008	MAC	Report Error
13	Bridge_2	C000FFFFFFFF	MAC	Ring Purge
14	Bridge_2	C000FFFFFFFF	MAC	Active Monitor Present
15	Roger's_PC	C000FFFFFFFF	MAC	Standby Monitor Present
16	LANZ	C000FFFFFFFF	MAC	Standby Monitor Present
17	LaRae's_PC	C000FFFFFFFF	MAC	Standby Monitor Present
18	CORP_SERV	C000FFFFFFFF	MAC	Standby Monitor Present
19	Taylor's_MAC	C000FFFFFFFF	MAC	Standby Monitor Present
20	Holli's_PC	C000FFFFFFFF	MAC	Standby Monitor Present
21	Taylor's_MAC	Holli's_PC	MAC	Request Station Address
22	Holli's_PC	Taylor's_MAC	MAC	Report Station Address
23	Bridge_2	C000FFFFFFFF	MAC	Ring Purge
24	Bridge_2	C000FFFFFFFF	MAC	Active Monitor Present
25	Roger's_PC	C000FFFFFFFF	MAC	Standby Monitor Present
26	LANZ	C000FFFFFFFF	MAC	Standby Monitor Present
27	Taylor's_MAC	Holli's_PC	MAC	Request Station Address
28	Holli's_PC	Taylor's_MAC	MAC	Report Station Address
29	LaRae's_PC	C000FFFFFFFF	MAC	Standby Monitor Present
30	CORP_SERV	C000FFFFFFFF	MAC	Standby Monitor Present
31	Taylor's_MAC	C000FFFFFFFF	MAC	Standby Monitor Present
32	Holli's_PC	C000FFFFFFFF	MAC	Standby Monitor Present
33	Holli's_PC	C00000000008	MAC	Report Error
34	Bridge_2	C00000000008	MAC	Report Error
35	Taylor's_MAC	Holli's_PC	MAC	Request Station Address

Purge frame per second—indicates an intermittent ring problem. The more frequent and consistent the Purge frames, the more severe the problem.

Determining the Severity of an Error

If the problem indicated by the excessive number of Purge frames on the ring progresses, the ring moves past simple purging to the next step of the hard-error recovery timeline, Monitor Contention.

A ring with constant purging is running less than optimally, but it is still operational. In the Purge state, users may notice a degradation in network performance, depending on the number of and interval between Purge frames. But you need to isolate and resolve the intermittent problem before it becomes Monitor Contention.

FIGURE 11.6

NCC LANalyzer trace summary of a ring with excessive Purge MAC frames

```
04/01/95              LANalyzer(R) Network Analyzer by NCC                10:26
Press ALT-T to toggle between summary modes           Filter Trace Summary
========================= c:\traces\tr\purge =========================
Created On 12/14/95 18:29:38   Filtered Packets  182    Total Packets    500
  Pkt# Source        Destination  Layer   Highest Layer
‡  180 Elsie-I       TR_Broadcast 802.5:  Ring Purge                          ◄
   182 Elsie-I       TR_Broadcast 802.5:  Ring Purge
   184 Elsie-I       TR_Broadcast 802.5:  Ring Purge
   186 Elsie-I       TR_Broadcast 802.5:  Ring Purge
   188 Elsie-I       TR_Broadcast 802.5:  Ring Purge
   190 Elsie-I       TR_Broadcast 802.5:  Ring Purge
   192 Elsie-I       TR_Broadcast 802.5:  Ring Purge
   194 Elsie-I       TR_Broadcast 802.5:  Ring Purge
   196 Elsie-I       TR_Broadcast 802.5:  Ring Purge
   198 Elsie-I       TR_Broadcast 802.5:  Ring Purge
   200 Elsie-I       TR_Broadcast 802.5:  Ring Purge
   202 Elsie-I       TR_Broadcast 802.5:  Ring Purge
   204 Elsie-I       TR_Broadcast 802.5:  Ring Purge
   206 Elsie-I       TR_Broadcast 802.5:  Ring Purge
   208 Elsie-I       TR_Broadcast 802.5:  Ring Purge
   210 Elsie-I       TR_Broadcast 802.5:  Ring Purge

F1      |F2    |F3    |F4      |F5   |F6     |F7     |F8    |F9   |F10
Help    |Load  |Print |Options|      |Decode |Compare|Filter|Find |Back
```

FIGURE 11.7

Trace summary from Figure 11.6, showing interpacket arrival times

```
04/01/95              LANalyzer(R) Network Analyzer by NCC                10:29
Press ALT-T to toggle between summary modes           Filter Trace Summary
========================= c:\traces\tr\purge =========================
Created On 12/14/95 18:29:38   Filtered Packets  182    Total Packets    500
  Pkt# Source        Destination  Protocol   Size      Channels IntPkt Time
‡  180 Elsie-I       TR_Broadcast MACFrame    36       ...4....  0.922 ms◄
   182 Elsie-I       TR_Broadcast MACFrame    36       ...4....  1.648 ms
   184 Elsie-I       TR_Broadcast MACFrame    36       ...4....  0.572 ms
   186 Elsie-I       TR_Broadcast MACFrame    36       ...4....  0.784 ms
   188 Elsie-I       TR_Broadcast MACFrame    36       ...4....  1.462 ms
   190 Elsie-I       TR_Broadcast MACFrame    36       ...4....  1.650 ms
   192 Elsie-I       TR_Broadcast MACFrame    36       ...4....  0.571 ms
   194 Elsie-I       TR_Broadcast MACFrame    36       ...4....  0.773 ms
   196 Elsie-I       TR_Broadcast MACFrame    36       ...4....  1.446 ms
   198 Elsie-I       TR_Broadcast MACFrame    36       ...4....  0.773 ms
   200 Elsie-I       TR_Broadcast MACFrame    36       ...4....  1.450 ms
   202 Elsie-I       TR_Broadcast MACFrame    36       ...4....  0.783 ms
   204 Elsie-I       TR_Broadcast MACFrame    36       ...4....  1.436 ms
   206 Elsie-I       TR_Broadcast MACFrame    36       ...4....  0.768 ms
   208 Elsie-I       TR_Broadcast MACFrame    36       ...4....  1.154 ms
   210 Elsie-I       TR_Broadcast MACFrame    36       ...4....  1.475 ms

F1      |F2    |F3    |F4      |F5   |F6     |F7     |F8    |F9   |F10
Help    |Load  |Print |Options|      |Decode |Compare|Filter|Find |Back
```

When rings start consistently experiencing Monitor Contention, users definitely notice degraded performance. Network errors and shell/redirector timeouts become common. Some protocol analyzers, like the LANalyzer by NCC, give you a Ring Recovery indicator; every time the ring goes into ring recovery, the counter increments by 1. Figure 11.8 shows the Ring Recovery counter on the NCC LANalyzer. On a ring containing an error serious enough to cause it to regularly experience ring recovery, the counter increments consistently.

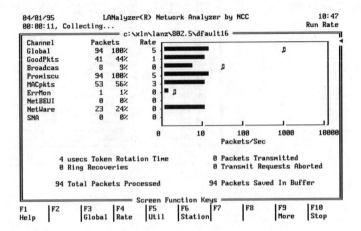

FIGURE 11.8

Ring Recovery counter on the NCC LANalyzer

If the ring moves past Monitor Contention to Beaconing, it is the last desperate attempt of the ring to recover from a catastrophic error. A Token Ring is not operational during Beaconing.

Locating the Source of the Error

Once you have determined that there is a problem on the ring, how can you tell what it is and where it is? Token Ring provides this information. You need only capture Report Error MAC frames, for Purge or Monitor Contention problems or, in a Beacon condition, a single Beacon frame.

Ring stations transmit Error MAC frames to the Ring Error Monitor every 2 seconds if there are soft errors to report. By decoding the Report Error MAC frames, you can determine the nature of the fault and its location.

You can discover the nature of the fault by examining the isolating and nonisolating error counter subvectors found in the Report Error MAC frame. The location of the fault, or the *fault domain,* is between the sending station (source address) and its upstream neighbor. We'll examine a troubleshooting scenario to see how to find and isolate an intermittent error, but first, let's examine isolating and nonisolating errors.

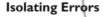

Isolating Errors

An *isolating error* is one whose fault domain can be determined by the information found in the Report Error MAC frame. Figure 11.9 shows a decoded Report Error MAC frame and the isolating error counter subvector. The following sections describe the isolating errors.

FIGURE 11.9

Decoded Report Error
MAC frame showing the
isolating error counters

```
802.5: =================== IEEE 802.5 Datalink Layer ==================
       AC: Frame, Priority=0, Monitor Count=1, Priority Reservation=0
       FC: MAC Frame, Attention Code=0
       Station: Holli's_PC ----> C0-00-00-00-00-08
  MAC: =============== Token Ring Media Access Control ================
       Major Vector Command:              Report Error
         Total Vector Length:             34 bytes
         Source Class:                    Ring Station
         Destination Class:               Ring Error Monitor
         Subvector Length:                8 bytes
         Isolating Error Counts:          Line Error:          1
                                          Internal Error:      0
                                          Burst Error:         0
                                          ARI/FCI Error:       0
                                          Abort Delimiter:     0
         Subvector Length:                8 bytes
         Non-isolating Error Counts:      Lost Frame:          0
                                          Receive Congestion:  0
                                          Frame Copied Error:  0
                                          Frequency Error:     0
                                          Token Error:         0
         Subvector Length:                6 bytes
         Physical Drop Number:            00000000
         Subvector Length:                8 bytes
         Upstream Neighbor's Address:     Taylor's_MAC
```

LINE ERRORS Line errors are generally reported by a single station and indicate the failure of the reporting station's upstream neighbor. Since all Report Error MAC frames must contain the NAUN address, it is possible to determine the location of this error. If Line errors are being randomly reported by ring stations as a result of Burst errors, you can ignore them until the Burst errors are resolved.

INTERNAL ERRORS If an adapter is consistently reporting internal errors, you can probably conclude that the adapter is failing.

BURST 5 ERRORS If an adapter detects an intermittent loss of signal for five consecutive half-bit cycles at its receive side, it does not propagate that signal loss on its transmit side, but rather converts every missing half-bit cycle after number 4 to an idle (0). Therefore, the ring stations downstream will not detect a Burst 5 error. (They will, however, report Line, Lost Frame, and Token errors resulting from the corruption of the frame or token.) A ring station will not propagate a burst 5 error, which allows the error to be isolated between the reporting station and its upstream neighbor. Burst errors cause other soft errors—most notably, Line, Lost Frame, and Token errors.

ARI/FCI ERRORS If a ring station consistently reports an ARI/FCI error, its upstream neighbor's adapter is failing.

ABORT DELIMITER TRANSMITTED ERRORS If a ring station consistently reports an Abort Delimiter Transmitted error, its adapter or adapter driver is bad or it has a misbehaving upper-layer protocol or application.

Nonisolating Errors

A *nonisolating error* is one that cannot be isolated based on the information provided in the Report Error MAC frame. These errors are reported in the Nonisolating Error Counter subvector. Figure 11.10 shows the decoded Nonisolating Error Counter subvector in a Report Error MAC frame. The following sections list the nonisolating errors and explain why they are so categorized.

FIGURE 11.10

Decoded Report Error MAC frame showing the nonisolating error counters

```
802.5: =================== IEEE 802.5 Datalink Layer ===================
       AC: Frame, Priority=0, Monitor Count=1, Priority Reservation=0
       FC: MAC Frame, Attention Code=0
       Station: Holli's_PC ----> C0-00-00-00-00-08
  MAC: ================ Token Ring Media Access Control ================
       Major Vector Command:              Report Error
         Total Vector Length:             34 bytes
         Source Class:                    Ring Station
         Destination Class:               Ring Error Monitor
         Subvector Length:                8 bytes
         Isolating Error Counts:          Line Error:          1
                                          Internal Error:      0
                                          Burst Error:         0
                                          ARI/FCI Error:       0
                                          Abort Delimiter:     0
         Subvector Length:                8 bytes
         Non-isolating Error Counts:      Lost Frame:          0
                                          Receive Congestion:  0
                                          Frame Copied Error:  0
                                          Frequency Error:     0
                                          Token Error:         0
         Subvector Length:                6 bytes
         Physical Drop Number:            00000000
         Subvector Length:                8 bytes
         Upstream Neighbor's Address:     Taylor's_MAC
```

LOST FRAME ERRORS A ring station knows if it has lost a frame, but it doesn't know where on the ring the frame was lost. However, in rare cases, a single ring station may consistently report lost frames, and you will detect no Burst 5 or other errors on the ring to justify them. In these cases the adapter is probably starting to fail.

RECEIVE CONGESTION ERRORS IBM, IEEE, and Texas Instruments all list the Receive Congestion error as nonisolating. Logically, though, if a ring station is consistently reporting that it cannot copy frames because it is congested, it is easy to figure out which station is having the problem. Many technicians have solved this type of problem by assuming that this is an *isolating* error.

FRAME COPIED ERRORS If a station detects a frame addressed to it with the ARI/FCI bits already set, it has no idea which station set the bits.

FREQUENCY ERRORS When a station detects a Frequency error, it doesn't know whether the error is the result of a bad AM (although it probably is), a bad ring station upstream, or noise on the line.

TOKEN ERRORS A Token error is reported only by the AM, which knows only that the token protocol was interrupted for some reason and that it had to purge the ring. The AM has no idea where the error occurred.

The next section presents a typical troubleshooting scenario involving an intermittent hardware error on the ring.

Troubleshooting Scenario: Isolating an Intermittent Error

Let's say users on Ring #010 are complaining of sluggish response. Using LANalyzer for Windows, you start capturing MAC frames only from the ring. You let the capture run for about one minute.

As you view the trace summary, shown in Figure 11.11, you immediately notice a large number of Purge and Report Error MAC frames. You also notice that ring stations Bridge_2 and Holli's_PC are reporting most of the errors, and they seem to be always in pairs. A number of other random stations are also reporting errors (not shown in the Figure 11.11 trace).

The number and consistency of Purge and Report Error MAC frames indicate a definite problem on this ring. To locate the problem, you look at the decoded Report Error MAC frame from ring station Bridge_2, as shown in Figure 11.12. You first examine the isolating and nonisolating error counts; there are no isolating errors and 24 nonisolating Token errors. Once you see the Token errors, you know that Bridge_2 is the AM. (Actually, you already knew this, because Bridge_2 was the station transmitting Purge and AMP frames.) This is no help in locating the problem, because Token errors are nonisolating.

Having no luck with Bridge_2's packet, you decode the Report Error frame from Holli's_PC, as shown in Figure 11.13. You see one Line error and 25

FIGURE 11.11

Trace file from suspect ring, showing excessive Purge and Report Error frames

No	Source	Destination	Layer	Summary
1	Bridge_2	C000FFFFFFFF	MAC	Ring Purge
2	Bridge_2	C000FFFFFFFF	MAC	Active Monitor Present
3	Roger's_PC	C000FFFFFFFF	MAC	Standby Monitor Present
4	LANZ	C000FFFFFFFF	MAC	Standby Monitor Present
5	LaRae's_PC	C000FFFFFFFF	MAC	Standby Monitor Present
6	CORP_SERV	C000FFFFFFFF	MAC	Standby Monitor Present
7	Taylor's_MAC	C000FFFFFFFF	MAC	Standby Monitor Present
8	Holli's_PC	C000FFFFFFFF	MAC	Standby Monitor Present
9	Taylor's_MAC	Holli's_PC	MAC	Request Station Address
10	Holli's_PC	Taylor's_MAC	MAC	Report Station Address
11	Holli's_PC	C00000000008	MAC	Report Error
12	Bridge_2	C00000000008	MAC	Report Error
13	Bridge_2	C000FFFFFFFF	MAC	Ring Purge
14	Bridge_2	C000FFFFFFFF	MAC	Active Monitor Present
15	Roger's_PC	C000FFFFFFFF	MAC	Standby Monitor Present
16	LANZ	C000FFFFFFFF	MAC	Standby Monitor Present
17	LaRae's_PC	C000FFFFFFFF	MAC	Standby Monitor Present
18	CORP_SERV	C000FFFFFFFF	MAC	Standby Monitor Present
19	Taylor's_MAC	C000FFFFFFFF	MAC	Standby Monitor Present
20	Holli's_PC	C000FFFFFFFF	MAC	Standby Monitor Present
21	Taylor's_MAC	Holli's_PC	MAC	Request Station Address
22	Holli's_PC	Taylor's_MAC	MAC	Report Station Address
23	Bridge_2	C000FFFFFFFF	MAC	Ring Purge
24	Bridge_2	C000FFFFFFFF	MAC	Active Monitor Present
25	Roger's_PC	C000FFFFFFFF	MAC	Standby Monitor Present
26	LANZ	C000FFFFFFFF	MAC	Standby Monitor Present
27	Taylor's_MAC	Holli's_PC	MAC	Request Station Address
28	Holli's_PC	Taylor's_MAC	MAC	Report Station Address
29	LaRae's_PC	C000FFFFFFFF	MAC	Standby Monitor Present
30	CORP_SERV	C000FFFFFFFF	MAC	Standby Monitor Present
31	Taylor's_MAC	C000FFFFFFFF	MAC	Standby Monitor Present
32	Holli's_PC	C000FFFFFFFF	MAC	Standby Monitor Present
33	Holli's_PC	C00000000008	MAC	Report Error
34	Bridge_2	C00000000008	MAC	Report Error
35	Taylor's_MAC	Holli's_PC	MAC	Request Station Address

Burst errors. You ignore the Line error because you know that Burst errors cause Line and other errors. The 25 Burst errors are what you are looking for.

You know that the Report Error frame was transmitted by Holli's_PC. The Upstream Neighbor Address subvector lists Taylor's_MAC as Holli's_PC's upstream neighbor. These two addresses give you the location of the fault domain—specifically, all the hardware from Taylor's_MAC adapter transmitter to Holli's_PC adapter receiver, as shown in Figure 11.14.

In a situation like the one just described, you will see a number of random stations transmitting Report Error MAC frames. You should discount them, however, for two reasons:

- They were not consistently reported by the same station.

- When decoded, the error counters declared Line and Lost Frame errors, as shown in Figure 11.15.

FIGURE 11.12

Decoded Report Error
MAC frame, showing
excessive Token errors

```
802.5: =================== IEEE 802.5 Datalink Layer ===================
       AC: Frame, Priority=0, Monitor Count=0, Priority Reservation=0
       FC: MAC Frame, Attention Code=0
       Station: Bridge_2 ----> C0-00-00-00-00-08
  MAC: ================ Token Ring Media Access Control ================
       Major Vector Command:              Report Error
         Total Vector Length:             34 bytes
         Source Class:                    Ring Station
         Destination Class:               Ring Error Monitor
         Subvector Length:                8 bytes
         Isolating Error Counts:          Line Error:          0
                                          Internal Error:      0
                                          Burst Error:         0
                                          ARI/FCI Error:       0
                                          Abort Delimiter:     0
         Subvector Length:                8 bytes
         Non-isolating Error Counts:      Lost Frame:          0
                                          Receive Congestion:  0
                                          Frame Copied Error:  0
                                          Frequency Error:     0
                                          Token Error:        24
         Subvector Length:                6 bytes
         Physical Drop Number:            00000000
         Subvector Length:                8 bytes
         Upstream Neighbor's Address:     Holli's_PC
```

FIGURE 11.13

Decode Report Error
MAC frame, showing Line
and excessive Burst
errors

```
802.5: =================== IEEE 802.5 Datalink Layer ===================
       AC: Frame, Priority=0, Monitor Count=1, Priority Reservation=0
       FC: MAC Frame, Attention Code=0
       Station: Holli's_PC ----> C0-00-00-00-00-08
  MAC: ================ Token Ring Media Access Control ================
       Major Vector Command:              Report Error
         Total Vector Length:             34 bytes
         Source Class:                    Ring Station
         Destination Class:               Ring Error Monitor
         Subvector Length:                8 bytes
         Isolating Error Counts:          Line Error:          1
                                          Internal Error:      0
                                          Burst Error:        25
                                          ARI/FCI Error:       0
                                          Abort Delimiter:     0
         Subvector Length:                8 bytes
         Non-isolating Error Counts:      Lost Frame:          0
                                          Receive Congestion:  0
                                          Frame Copied Error:  0
                                          Frequency Error:     0
                                          Token Error:         0
         Subvector Length:                6 bytes
         Physical Drop Number:            00000000
         Subvector Length:                8 bytes
         Upstream Neighbor's Address:     Taylor's_MAC
```

Always discount Line and Lost Frame errors as long as unaccounted-for Burst errors (no stations entering or leaving the ring) are present on the ring.

You should troubleshoot rings that have problems severe enough to cause them to move to the Ring Recovery stage exactly the same way as in the scenario. The only difference is that you will see a very high number of Burst

FIGURE 11.14

Fault domain between
Holli's_PC and
Taylor's_MAC

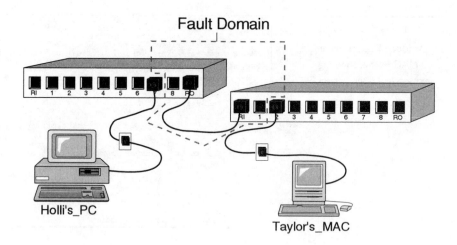

Fault Domain

Holli's_PC

Taylor's_MAC

FIGURE 11.15

Random Report Error
MAC frame, reporting a
Lost Frame error.

```
802.5: =================== IEEE 802.5 Datalink Layer ==================
       AC: Frame, Priority=0, Monitor Count=0, Priority Reservation=0
       FC: MAC Frame, Attention Code=0
       Station: CORP_SERV ---> C0-00-00-00-00-08
  MAC: ================ Token Ring Media Access Control ================
       Major Vector Command:              Report Error
          Total Vector Length:            34 bytes
          Source Class:                   Ring Station
          Destination Class:              Ring Error Monitor
          Subvector Length:               8 bytes
          Isolating Error Counts:         Line Error:         0
                                          Internal Error:     0
                                          Burst Error:        0
                                          ARI/FCI Error:      0
                                          Abort Delimiter:    0
          Subvector Length:               8 bytes
          Non-isolating Error Counts:     Lost Frame:         1
                                          Receive Congestion: 0
                                          Frame Copied Error: 0
                                          Frequency Error:    0
                                          Token Error:        0
          Subvector Length:               6 bytes
          Physical Drop Number:           00000000
          Subvector Length:               8 bytes
          Upstream Neighbor's Address:    LaRae's_PC
```

errors (perhaps as many as 54 Burst errors during one 2-second error report
cycle on rings in this condition) and Claim Token MAC frames (frames used
in Monitor Contention).

Once you have found the fault domain, you need to isolate the problem to
a cable, adapter, MSAU, or some other hardware component within the
domain. One good way to isolate the problem even more is to remove the two

stations, one at a time. If they are both out and the problem persists, it must be in the intervening hardware (MSAU/LAM, patch cables, and so on).

Troubleshooting the Beacon Condition

When a ring starts Beaconing, it immediately becomes nonfunctional—an extremely serious situation. Typically, you will become aware of the Beaconing ring if it doesn't recover automatically.

If the ring does recover automatically, it means that a station somewhere has been stripped from the ring. Fortunately, it's usually easy to locate devices once they're removed from the ring.

For further details on the Beaconing process, see Chapter 8.

Time is of the essence if the ring does not recover automatically and you have to find and resolve the problem manually. Here's a simple four-step process for locating the Beacon fault domain using only a protocol analyzer:

1. Insert your analyzer into the ring. This may not always be easy, since a ring station will not, by protocol, insert itself into a Beaconing ring. Most protocol analyzers, however, will override the protocol and insert themselves into the ring, anyway.

2. Capture and decode one Beacon MAC frame. The fault domain is between the transmitting station and its upstream neighbor.

3. With good wiring diagrams, locate the ports of the two ring stations in step 2. The fault is between those two ports. Idle stations that were not on the ring at the time may exist physically between them. Remember that the Beacon process has already checked the lobe cables of both stations all the way to the connectors at the MSAU/LAM.

4. Fix the problem: check patch cables, MSAU/LAMs, or cabling between wiring closets (if you have the two stations in different closets). It is a good idea to keep extra hardware in each wiring closet to facilitate the rapid swapping of equipment, as well as a cable scanner to test cable between wiring stations.

Some CAUs automatically bypass a LAM with Beaconing stations. Check with your equipment documentation or vendor for specifics.

NetWare servers send an error message to the console screen when a ring goes into a Beacon state. The server also prints a message when the Beacon condition has cleared.

As you can see, troubleshooting Token Ring is not difficult. But it's not pleasant to be surprised by a sudden desperate call about the network not operating properly. Being proactive in your approach to network management can save you much anxiety. By observing your network under normal conditions, setting baselines for critical Token Ring vital signs, and monitoring your ring segments with any of a number of monitoring agents available on the market, you can stay a couple of steps ahead of trouble and plan for future growth. In Chapter 12 we will discuss baselining, monitoring, and optimization of the Token Ring.

Performance Considerations for Token-Passing Rings

12

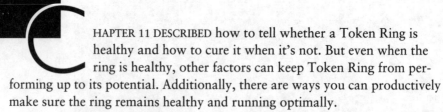

CHAPTER 11 DESCRIBED how to tell whether a Token Ring is healthy and how to cure it when it's not. But even when the ring is healthy, other factors can keep Token Ring from performing up to its potential. Additionally, there are ways you can productively make sure the ring remains healthy and running optimally.

This chapter explains how to optimize your Token Ring network and keep it running up to its potential. You will learn how to determine baselines for vital Token Ring characteristics and set thresholds for monitoring those characteristics of Token Ring that affect its health and performance.

Optimizing Token Ring

OKEN RING OPTIMIZATION is based on two fundamental factors:

- Throughput (how much data can be moved, and how quickly)
- Ability of ring stations to copy frames

Optimizing Throughput

You know that errors and the resulting Ring Purges use bandwidth that could otherwise be carrying good frames. In Chapter 11, you learned that some errors are a normal part of Token Ring and you learned how to troubleshoot and resolve abnormal errors. The following discussion of optimizing throughput assumes the rings are clean, or free of all but normal errors caused by stations entering and leaving the ring.

Minimizing Broadcast Traffic

Some of the optimization challenges for Token Ring are the same as for Ethernet. Most notable is broadcast traffic. On networks, broadcast traffic is a necessary evil. Broadcast frames provide a service but do not directly contribute to meaningful work on the network.

Broadcast traffic can also contribute to congestion errors in adapters that are bordering on congestion, anyway. This is because broadcast packets must be copied by all adapters, whether or not the data inside is meant for them.

For these reasons, broadcast traffic should be kept to a minimum—usually by tuning upper-layer protocols, because they are the ones that most often use broadcast services. But how much broadcast is too much? The amount varies, depending on your particular environment, but generally if broadcast traffic on your network exceeds 3% of the available bandwidth on a consistent basis (you will have spikes higher than that from time to time), you probably want to find out why it is so high.

For information on controlling NetWare broadcasts, see Chapters 17 and 18.

To view the amount of broadcast traffic on your network, set up a filter in LANalyzer for Windows for all frames addressed to broadcast, as shown in Figure 12.1. Let the LANalyzer run for about a day and then view the Utilization Trends graph by selecting Monitor ➤ Trends ➤ Utilization from the main menu bar. As shown in Figure 12.2, the Trend graph will display broadcast and total utilization. In this case, the broadcast traffic is generally running at about 2% of the total bandwidth.

Early Token Release

When Token Ring was first introduced, it had a data rate of 4Mb/s. The protocol at the time dictated that there could be only one token or frame on the ring at once. In other words, a ring station had to completely strip off a transmitted frame before it could transmit another frame or free token. With a 4Mb/s data rate, this did not result in much wasted bandwidth, as demonstrated in Figure 12.3. (Idles, or 0's, were transmitted as a filler between the end of a frame or token until the station could transmit another frame or

Capture Filter

Stations:

Broadcast   ○ <----> <ANY>

○ ---->

◉ <-----

OK

Cancel

Protocol:

Available

NetWare
AppleTalk
TCP/IP
SNA
DECnet
NetBEUI

Add ->

Remove <-

Selected

Clear

Help

☐ Apply filter to Station Monitor

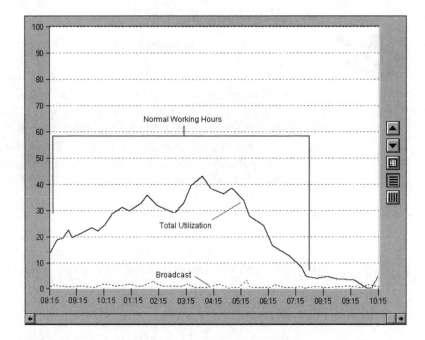

token.) With the introduction of the 16Mb/s data rate, things happened more quickly, but the protocol remained the same. This resulted in much more wasted bandwidth.

The Early Token Release (ETR) protocol allowed ring stations to start transmitting a token or frame at the tail-end of a previously transmitted frame without waiting for the frame to be completely stripped. As illustrated in Figure 12.3, this resulted in a more efficient use of the 16Mb/s bandwidth.

FIGURE 12.3

Original Token Release protocol versus early Token Release

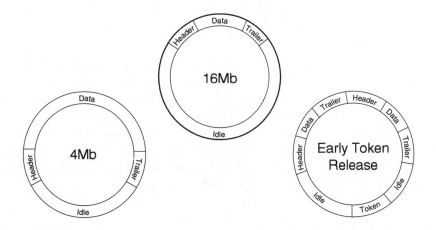

16Mb/s ETR adapters and 16Mb/s adapters running the old protocol can coexist on the same ring. The only disadvantage is that those adapters running the old protocol are wasting bandwidth.

Most manufacturers of Token Ring adapters support both protocols, with ETR being the default. Check with the adapter documentation for details. If you have old 16Mb/s adapters that do not support ETR, replace them to increase the overall throughput of the ring. The larger the ring, the more nodes, and the higher the utilization, the more the ring will benefit from 16Mb/s ETR.

Preventing Congestion in Ring Stations

Ring stations with no available on-board frame receive buffers will not copy the frame. This results in bandwidth wasted to retransmit the frame. If a chronically congested ring station is a critical device, such as a server, bridge, or router, this wasted bandwidth can adversely affect other areas of network performance—for example, by slowing server response time and delaying inter-ring or internetwork communications.

There are a number ways to prevent congestion on a ring station. They are associated with three aspects of a ring station that directly affect the ring station's ability to copy frames from the ring:

- On-board receive buffers

- Data bus transfer rate

- Host receive buffers

These three items make up what we'll call the packet transfer pipeline. The ability to move frames along this pipeline from the adapter's on-board buffer to the host's memory will determine whether or not the ring station can keep up with all the frames transmitted to it.

Figure 12.4 illustrates an adapter with too few on-board buffers. There is plenty of buffer space in the host and the bus could accommodate the frames being received; however, the adapter just does not have enough on-board buffer, so packets are not copied.

FIGURE 12.4

Token Ring adapter with insufficient on-board buffers to copy frames sent to it

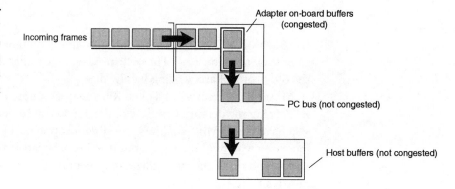

The more on-board receive buffers an adapter has, the more frames it can buffer and the less likely it is to have congestion errors. Check the specifications of Token Ring adapters to determine the amount of on-board memory available for frame buffering. The amount of memory an adapter has is usually an indication of its performance rating and of its relative expense. Be aware that a workstation may not require as high a frame-copy rate as, for example, a file server. Therefore, performance considerations are a factor in choosing the proper adapter for the job.

Figure 12.5 shows an adapter with plenty of on-board buffer and a host with plenty of available frame buffer space, but the data bus is too slow to provide a fast enough transfer rate between the adapter and the host memory to prevent the adapter's buffers from backing up.

FIGURE 12.5

Frames not being copied as a result of a slow data bus

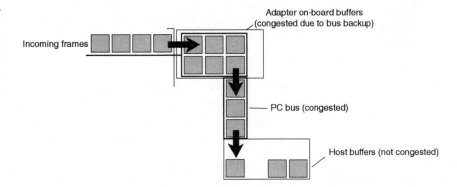

You know that the more lanes a freeway has, the more traffic it can carry. The same is true of a PC data bus. Eight-bit buses have very few lanes; 16-bit buses have a few more; and 32-bit buses have the most. If you install an 8-bit Token Ring adapter in a server, it won't matter how fast the processor is; you will probably experience congestion errors because there are too few lanes to move data quickly enough into host memory to keep up with incoming frame traffic. Using a 16-bit or 32-bit bus and adapter is highly recommended for devices that must handle a large number of incoming frames. PCs with ISA bus architecture support 8- or 16-bit adapters. EISA, Microchannel, and Local Bus architectures support 32-bit adapters.

Another factor in moving data between the card and the host memory is how the data is copied into memory once it has been moved across the bus. The two basic methods of getting the data into memory are direct memory access (DMA) and shared memory. Shared memory is preferred because it allows the adapter to write data directly to memory without having to go through the DMA controller, which would induce a number of extra steps and, thus, introduce added latency into the transfer.

For some adapters (IBM 16/4 and Novell NTR2000, for example), you can optimize the shared memory transfer even more by setting the adapter to use a 64K memory page window as opposed to an 8K or 16K page. Make sure you have enough room in the C0000-to-D0000 area of upper memory to support a page transfer that large before setting the adapter parameters. If the PC is using EMS memory or if there are other boards that use this area for shared memory, use the 16K page, which is the default on most adapters. This capability of choosing a larger page size is vendor implementation specific.

Having more on-board buffers on an adapter is more important than whether or not you can set the page size to 64K, so make it a higher priority when choosing a Token Ring adapter.

Finally, the amount of buffer available in the host and how the host forwards data to the application for which it is destined can ultimately affect how quickly the data is moved off the adapter. As illustrated in Figure 12.6, insufficient buffer in the host can cause a backup in the adapter's on-board buffer.

FIGURE 12.6

Insufficient host buffering can cause congestion errors

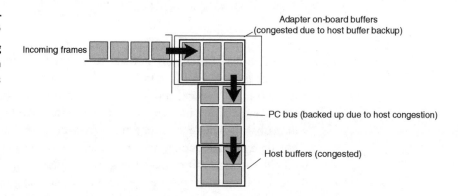

Many drivers, and the transport protocol stacks associated with them, require receive buffers for packets received from the Token Ring adapter. If those buffers are configurable, simply increase the number of them. For example, let's say you are running an ODI-compatible protocol stack that requires receive buffers. The following line appears in the Link Support section of the NET.CFG file:

BUFFERS 6 4096

This line indicates that there are six 4096-byte buffers available to receive frames from the adapter. To increase the number of receive buffers, simply change the "6" to a higher value. Be aware that these additional buffers come out of the lower 640K of PC memory on a workstation.

IPXODI.COM does not use receive buffers but, rather, forwards the frame data directly to the application. This further speeds up the data transfer process by not injecting another memory transfer step. If you are using MS Windows, be sure to load the VIPX.386 driver, because then IPXODI will transfer data directly to the MS Windows application in extended memory.

Receive buffers on NetWare servers are a little more involved. The Set Minimum Packet Receive Buffers and Set Maximum Packet Receive Buffers settings on a NetWare server specify how the server allocates buffers to incoming packets.

The Set Minimum Packet Receive Buffer setting allocates a fixed number of receive buffers as soon as the server is brought up. If you do not specify a minimum amount, the server will allocate buffers gradually as it determines an average amount required over a period of time. This may result in poor performance and congestion errors for a period of time before the number of buffers is brought up to an optimal level. View the number of receive buffers allocated by the server by loading MONITOR and viewing the server information window, as shown in Figure 12.7.

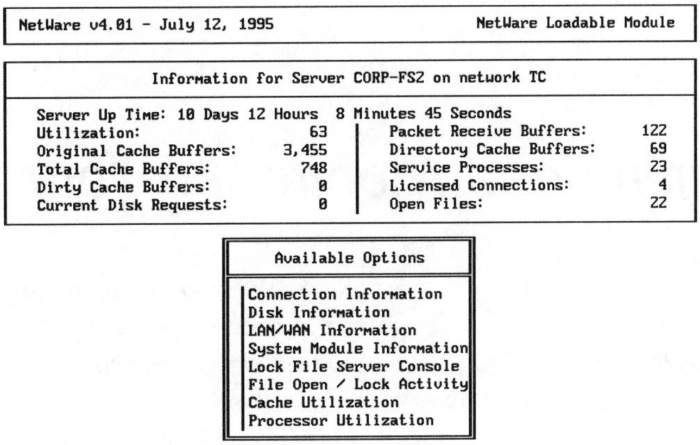

FIGURE 12.7

NetWare Server information window

```
┌──────────────────────────────────────────────────────────────────┐
│ NetWare v4.01 - July 12, 1995            NetWare Loadable Module   │
└──────────────────────────────────────────────────────────────────┘
┌──────────────────────────────────────────────────────────────────┐
│            Information for Server CORP-FS2 on network TC           │
├──────────────────────────────────────────────────────────────────┤
│ Server Up Time: 10 Days 12 Hours  8 Minutes 45 Seconds            │
│ Utilization:                63    Packet Receive Buffers:    122   │
│ Original Cache Buffers:   3,455    Directory Cache Buffers:   69   │
│ Total Cache Buffers:       748    Service Processes:          23   │
│ Dirty Cache Buffers:         0    Licensed Connections:        4   │
│ Current Disk Requests:       0    Open Files:                 22   │
└──────────────────────────────────────────────────────────────────┘
            ┌────────────────────────────────┐
            │        Available Options        │
            ├────────────────────────────────┤
            │ Connection Information          │
            │ Disk Information                │
            │ LAN/WAN Information             │
            │ System Module Information       │
            │ Lock File Server Console        │
            │ File Open / Lock Activity       │
            │ Cache Utilization               │
            │ Processor Utilization           │
            └────────────────────────────────┘
```

If you have a Minimum Receive Buffer setting and are still experiencing congestion errors, monitor the number of receive buffers allocated by the server in the server information window. If the number is more than the minimum you set and rising, you may want to increase the Minimum Receive Buffer setting.

The Maximum Packet Receive Buffer setting prevents the server from allocating too much memory to receive buffers. This feature was put in place because once receive buffers are allocated from the general cache, they are not returned until the server is downed and brought back up. The Maximum Receive Buffer setting is usually not a problem unless it is set too low. For example, suppose you set the minimum receive buffer to 100 and the maximum to 200 and, because of incoming traffic to the server, the server starts allocating buffers above 100. If traffic to the server is such that it needs more than 200 buffers to handle incoming traffic, you may start seeing congestion errors because the server cannot allocate more than 200 buffers. In this case, you would probably raise the Maximum and Minimum Receive Buffer settings.

Setting a Network Maximum Frame Size

One other way to improve ring station throughput is to set a maximum frame size that every transmitting station will use when possible. Novell recommends a maximum frame size of 4096 bytes. Optimization tests by Novell engineers have shown that a 4096 frame is an optimum size for buffering and transferring frames using ODI technology. Most of the ODI defaults for the workstation and server ODI drivers reflect this optimum size.

Baselining and Monitoring Your Token Ring

ONCE YOUR TOKEN Ring is running optimally, it is a good practice to become proactive about keeping it that way. Probably the best way to be proactive is to gather trend data to establish the network baseline. Baselining can tell you how the Token Ring behaves during normal operation. Once you know this, you can set alarm thresholds to monitor those aspects of the Token Ring condition that will give you early warning of impending trouble. Those aspects of Token Ring that can be trended, baselined, and monitored are known as the *Token Ring vital signs*.

Token Ring Vital Signs

Token Ring has a couple of characteristics that directly relate to how it is operating. Just as your pulse and body temperature are vital signs for how you are feeling, so are the following indicative of how a Token Ring is performing:

- Utilization/token rotation time

- Purge/Error Report MAC frames

Utilization and Token Rotation Time

Utilization is the universal measure of how busy a network is, regardless of the media access type. Utilization typically determines when network traffic has reached a point such that the network can no longer supply users with the network access to which they have become accustomed. Token Ring, because of its collision-avoidance nature, can function well at a higher percentage of maximum utilization than Ethernet, before throughput starts to degrade.

A better measurement of Token Ring access is the *token rotation time*. This is a measure, in microseconds, of how often a free token is available to a ring station. Looking at utilization may tell you that a ring's bandwidth is consistently being used at a high rate, but remember that only one station at a time has full use of the Token Ring's bandwidth. This means you might have only two stations on the ring, transmitting large volumes of data. The utilization will appear high, but the token rotation time will be low because so few transmitting stations have to give up and recapture a token every time their token-holding timer expires.

If, however, there are many stations trying to transmit on the ring, the utilization will still appear high. However, now the token rotation time will be high, as well. This is because there are more stations trying to transmit and, therefore, more of them capturing tokens, which causes the token to take more time to circle the network.

Unfortunately, you need a Token Ring adapter with special hardware to measure token rotation time. Protocol analyzers that use off-the-shelf adapters cannot measure token rotation time; Analyzers with special adapters, like NCC's LANalyzer, can. Figure 12.8 shows the NCC LANalyzer Run Rate screen with the Token Rotation Time counter. Most remote monitoring agents do not measure token rotation time.

FIGURE 12.8

NCC LANalyzer screen
with the Token Rotation
Time counter.

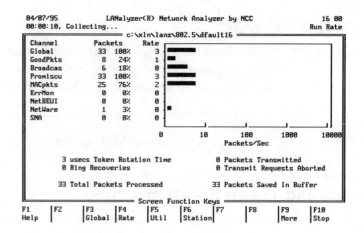

```
04/07/95              LANalyzer(R) Network Analyzer by NCC          16 00
00:00:10, Collecting...                                         Run Rate
                        c:\xln\lanz\802.5\dfault16
Channel       Packets    Rate
Global         33  100%    3  ▐████
GoodPkts        8   24%    1  ▐███
Broadcas        6   18%    0  ▐██
Promiscu       33  100%    3  ▐████
MACpkts        25   76%    2  ▐████
ErrMon          0    0%    0  ▐
NetBEUI         0    0%    0  ▐
NetWare         1    3%    0  ▐■
SNA             0    0%    0  ▐
                           0      10      100     1000    10000
                                     Packets/Sec

        3 usecs Token Rotation Time      0 Packets Transmitted
        0 Ring Recoveries                0 Transmit Requests Aborted

       33 Total Packets Processed       33 Packets Saved In Buffer
                        Screen Function Keys
F1      F2      F3      F4      F5      F6      F7      F8      F9      F10
Help            Global  Rate    Util    Station                 More    Stop
```

Ring Purge/Report Error MAC Frames

In Chapter 11 you learned that the appearance of Purge and the resulting
Report Error MAC frames on a ring, at any time other than when a station is
entering or leaving the ring, is a sure sign of Token Ring problems. By monitoring these frames, you can detect minor cabling and adapter errors and
resolve them before they become major problems. Intermittent hardware
problems on a Token Ring network use a great deal of bandwidth that would
otherwise be available to frames doing real work. This substantially lowers
performance.

Determining Utilization Baselines and Thresholds

Chapter 2 discusses baselining Ethernet utilization. The concepts described
there hold true for Token Ring, except that Token Ring uses a much higher
percentage of the available bandwidth than does Ethernet. For example, your
network utilization baseline may run between 20% to 65% of the theoretical
4Mb/s or 16Mb/s during normal work hours. Ethernet seldom operates well
above the 40% range. But, like Ethernet, the range in Token Ring will vary,
depending on the sensitivity of your network applications for response timeouts and users as to how long they will wait for a response. It is up to you to
decide what is optimal for your network.

To find what your utilization baseline is, you have to gather utilization trend data on each ring to determine what is normal for your network. Figure 12.9 shows utilization for one day on a ring.

FIGURE 12.9

Utilization trend graph
(one day)

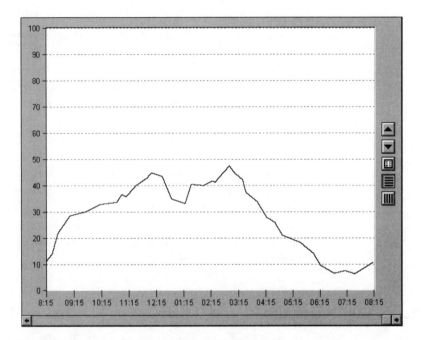

Once you have determined a baseline for utilization on your network, you need to look at the upper range of that baseline and decide what percentage of average utilization would indicate an unusual condition on the ring.

Your threshold should allow for spikes in network utilization. You want to be alerted to a sustained rise in network utilization, not to momentary spikes. Many monitoring agents, such as the NetWare LANalyzer agent, allow you to set a sampling interval. The longer the interval, the less likely you are to have momentary spikes set off your alarm. This is because spikes are averaged into the utilization over that period. Sampling intervals of 15 to 30 minutes are usually good enough to average out momentary spikes.

Using Bridges and Routers to Load-Balance Token Ring

What do you do when the normal utilization on a ring starts to reach unacceptable levels? The same thing you do for Ethernet networks, as described in Chapter 2: split the ring into two rings separated by a source-route or transparent bridge or a router. What you use depends upon your environment and your personal administrative preferences.

Use source-route bridges if you are in an IBM environment. IBM hosts, such as AS400, require source routing in order to communicate with workstations running PC Support. You may use transparent bridges in environments where source routing is not a requirement.

If all ring stations are using routable protocols (for example, IP and IPX are routable; SNA is not) you may wish to use routers to segment traffic. Routers should especially be considered if your network contains a mix of Ethernet and Token Ring segments. Bridging these two media access methods is a nontrivial solution that is best accomplished via routers. If you have routable and nonroutable protocols, a brouter (combination bridge and router) may be a good solution. A brouter will route routable protocols that it supports and bridge all other traffic.

Determining Baselines and Thresholds for Token Ring Errors

It may seem strange to consider setting baselines for errors. Because you instinctively do not want any errors, your impulse will be to set a very low threshold. With Token Ring, however, you have seen that errors occur normally when stations enter or leave a ring. Most of these errors will happen at the beginning and end of the work day, as users power their workstations on and off. You need to determine a normal rate of legitimate errors for your rings and, from that, determine a threshold for errors.

Figure 12.10 shows a burst errors trend graph from a Novell NetWare Management System console. The graph, which shows packets per second, was gathered by a NetWare LANalyzer agent on a server connected to an error-free Token Ring. Notice the large number of burst errors in the morning and evening, times when users are powering their machines on and off. There are almost no errors during the middle of the work day. To perform a complete baselining, you would need to get trends of all the critical errors (line, congestion, and so on).

FIGURE 12.10

Trend graph of Token
Ring errors

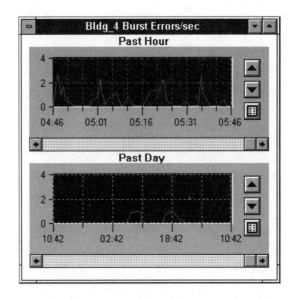

Agents that monitor Token Ring networks (including the RMON agent) typically break down the Report Error MAC frames into individual isolating and nonisolating errors and allow you to set thresholds for each individual error. This provides great flexibility as to which errors you monitor and which you don't. For example, you probably want to monitor burst, line, and congestion errors, whereas token and ARI/FCI are less critical.

In this chapter you have learned how to optimize your Token Rings and ring stations, both workstations and servers. You have been given hints on how to gather trends, determine baselines, and set thresholds so you can productively maintain your Token Ring networks. In the next chapter, you will learn the secrets of source-route bridging and the Spanning Tree protocol and how to implement them to create and manage multi-ring networks.

Source-Route Bridging and the Spanning Tree Protocol

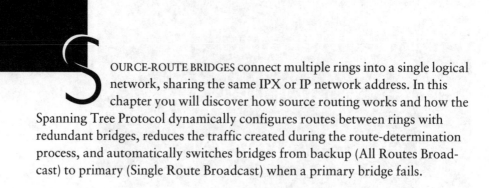

SOURCE-ROUTE BRIDGES connect multiple rings into a single logical network, sharing the same IPX or IP network address. In this chapter you will discover how source routing works and how the Spanning Tree Protocol dynamically configures routes between rings with redundant bridges, reduces the traffic created during the route-determination process, and automatically switches bridges from backup (All Routes Broadcast) to primary (Single Route Broadcast) when a primary bridge fails.

Source-Route versus Transparent Bridges

BRIDGES EXIST TO overcome the limitations of a media access method. For Token Ring this includes, among other things, maximum number of stations (260/IBM or 255/IEEE), MSAUs, wiring closets, and bandwidth (throughput). If you have two rings (or media access segments) connected by a bridge, each ring can support the maximum number of stations and throughput, yet a ring station on one ring can communicate to a ring station on the other ring.

There are two types of bridges: transparent and source routing. *Transparent bridges* are specified in the IEEE 802.1D standard and can connect any IEEE-compatible media access method (802.3, 802.4, 802.5, and so on). They are so named because devices on connected segments are not aware that the frames they are transmitting are crossing a bridge to reach the target station. Stations require no software in addition to the network adapter driver and shell/requester.

A transparent bridge copies every frame on each connected segment. It takes all the responsibility for determining which frames should be forwarded and which should be filtered, based on the hardware address and the port on which the frames were received. With this information, the transparent bridge builds and maintains a database of hardware addresses and their location, as shown in Figure 13.1.

FIGURE 13.1

Transparent bridges build and maintain a filter/ forward database.

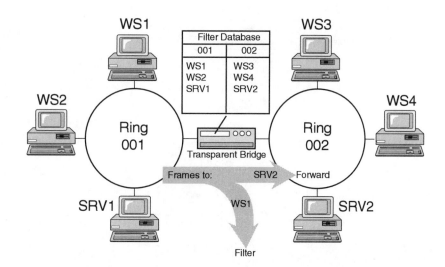

Source-route bridges, developed by IBM, differ in two ways: they connect only Token Rings, and each device on the network is responsible for creating and maintaining the route to a target device, as shown in Figure 13.2. This means that each device must have software installed that enables it to support source routing. Source-routing bridges copy only frames with the Route Information Indicator (RII) set to 1. They do not maintain a forwarding database, and they forward a frame only if they are instructed to do so by the routing information supplied by the sending station.

Source-Route Bridging

N A SOURCE-ROUTE environment, the route, or forwarding, database, is distributed among all devices on the network. Ring stations must therefore create and maintain their own route table.

FIGURE 13.2

Stations on a source-route network are responsible for creating and maintaining route tables.

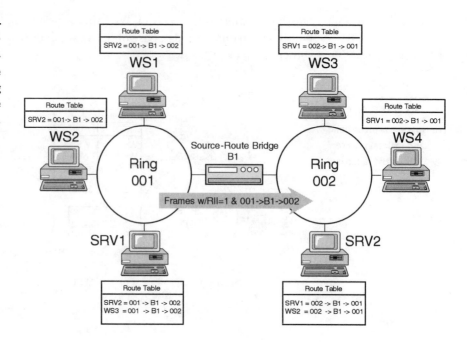

FIGURE 13.2

Stations on a source-route network are responsible for creating and maintaining route tables.

To participate in source routing, a ring station must have source-routing software loaded. In terms of NetWare, this means loading ROUTE.COM on workstations and ROUTE.NLM on 3.x and above servers. Both must be loaded after the Token Ring adapter's ODI driver has been loaded. (See the section "Configuring NetWare Servers and Workstations for Source Routing" later in this chapter.)

Source-route bridges check all frames they repeat to see whether the Routing Information Indicator (RII) is set. Those frames for which the RII bit = 1 are copied, and the routing information is examined to determine whether the frame is to be forwarded or filtered. Source-route bridges can be configured as All Routes Broadcast or Single Route Broadcast. (The differences between these configurations are discussed later in this chapter.)

Routing Information Format

The routing information format is shown in Figure 13.3. Following is a brief description the format of each of the fields.

FIGURE 13.3

Source-route information
format

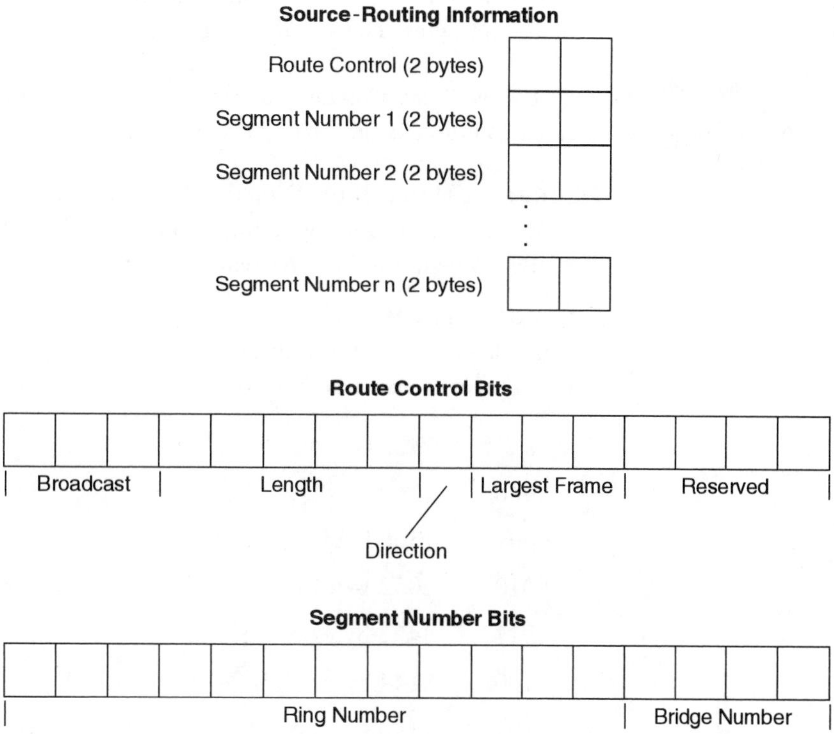

Source-Routing Information

Route Control (2 bytes)

Segment Number 1 (2 bytes)

Segment Number 2 (2 bytes)

.
.
.

Segment Number n (2 bytes)

Route Control Bits

| Broadcast | Length | | Largest Frame | Reserved |

Direction

Segment Number Bits

| Ring Number | Bridge Number |

Route Control Field

The Route Control Field contains information telling source-route bridges
how to process and interpret the route information. Following are descriptions of bit responsibilities in the Route Control field.

BROADCAST BITS The Broadcast bits determine whether the frame is an All
Route Broadcast, a Single Route Broadcast Route Determination frame, or a
Specific Route frame. The bit configurations are as follows:

Bit	Description
0xx	Non-Broadcast (Specific Route)
10x	All Routes Broadcast
11x	Single Route Broadcast

LENGTH BITS The Length bits contain the total length of the routing information in bytes. The specified range is 2 to 16 bytes.

By IBM specification, a frame can cross a maximum of seven bridges (hence the maximum 16 bytes of source-routing information).

DIRECTION BIT If the Direction bit = 0, source-route bridges read the segment numbers as sending to target station (SN1 –> SNx). If the Direction bit is 1, the segment numbers are read as target to sending station (SNx –> SN1).

LARGEST FRAME BITS The Largest Frame bits are set by bridges during route determination to indicate the largest frame they can forward. A bridge may decrease the value but not increase it. Values are as follows:

Bit	Value
000	516 bytes
001	1500 bytes
010	2052 bytes
011	4472 bytes
100	8144 bytes
101	11407 bytes
110	17800 bytes

Segment Number Fields

By IBM specification, the routing information can contain up to seven Segment Number fields. This limits to seven the number of bridges a frame can cross and to eight the number of rings it can appear on. Following are brief descriptions of the Segment Number fields bit responsibilities.

RING NUMBER The 12 Ring Number bits contain the ring numbers, as assigned by the network administrator.

BRIDGE NUMBER The 4 Bridge Number bits contain the bridge numbers assigned to the bridges by the network administrator.

Building the Route Table

The process of discovering the route to a target station is called *Route Determination*. The discovered route information is then stored in a *route table*. Route tables are most often implemented as volatile dynamic tables in the ring station's memory. To discover a route, the ring station can use any "ping" type communication protocol that requires a response from the target station.

The best way to describe the Route Determination process is to step through an example. As shown in Figure 13.4, ring station WS1, on ring 001, has data queued for transmission to SRV1 on ring 003.

FIGURE 13.4

WS1 transmits a Route Determination frame.

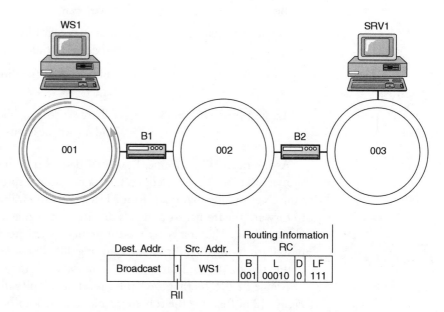

WS1, as a NetWare workstation, uses the Service Advertising Protocol (SAP) Request Nearest Server to illicit a response from the target station, server SRV1. SNA nodes use the LLC eXchange ID (XID) protocol. Any protocol that requires a response from the target is acceptable, and the choice of protocols is implementation specific.

In this example, WS1 transmits a SAP request for the nearest NetWare file server that uses a broadcast (FF FF FF FF FF FF) destination address. However, a specific address can be used just as well with other protocols.

WS1 has no entry for SRV1 in its route table (in fact, WS1's NetWare shell/requester doesn't even know that SRV1 exists; see Chapter 19), so it sets the RII bit to 1 and includes only the RII Control field in the data area, with the following configuration:

Bits	Description
Broadcast bits = 100	Indicates that this is an All Routes Broadcast Route Determination frame
Direction bit = 0	Indicates that the direction is source to target
Largest frame bits = 111	All are set to 1 as filler because only bridges set these bits

As it repeats WS1's frame, Bridge B1 detects that the RII bit is set to 1, as shown in Figure 13.5. B1 copies the frame and interprets the routing information. Determining that it is a Route Determination frame and that it is the first to forward the frame, B1 appends the first two segment numbers to the Route Control field. The first two segment numbers indicate that the frame has passed from ring 001, through B1, to ring 002. In addition, B1 sets the Largest Frame bits to 100, indicating that it can forward frames up to 8144K.

Bridge B2 detects that the RII bit is set and copies the frame, as shown in Figure 13.6. Reading the route information, B2 knows that this is a Route Determination frame and that it is not the first bridge to forward the frame. Bridge B2 appends a single segment number to the routing information. The routing information now indicates that the route is ring 001, through bridge B1 to ring 002, and through bridge B2 to ring 003. Bridge B2 sets the Largest Frame bits to 011, indicating that it can forward frames up to 4472K, and then forwards the frame to ring 003.

Server SRV1 copies the frame, as shown in Figure 13.7. The SAP stack on the NetWare server responds with a SAP reply. Server SRV1 copies the route information from the SAP request packet into the SAP Reply frame.

FIGURE 13.5

FIGURE 13.5

Bridge B1 adds the first
two segment numbers and
forwards the frame
to ring 002.

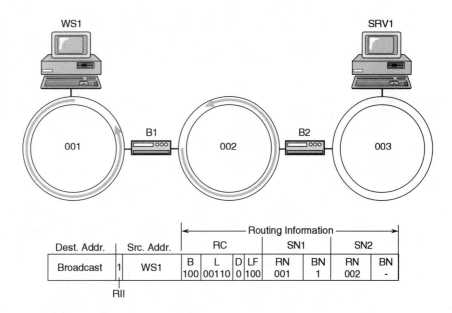

Dest. Addr.		Src. Addr.	RC				SN1		SN2	
						Routing Information				
Broadcast	1	WS1	B 100	L 00110	D 0	LF 100	RN 001	BN 1	RN 002	BN -

RII

FIGURE 13.6

FIGURE 13.6

Bridge B2 appends a
segment number and
forwards the frame
to ring 003.

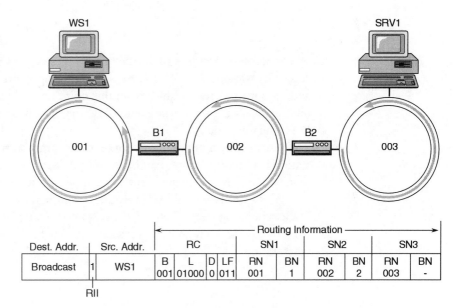

Dest. Addr.		Src. Addr.	RC				SN1		SN2		SN3	
						Routing Information						
Broadcast	1	WS1	B 001	L 01000	D 0	LF 011	RN 001	BN 1	RN 002	BN 2	RN 003	BN -

RII

However, it changes the Broadcast bits to 000 to indicate that the frame should follow the route specified by the routing information. SRV1 also sets the Direction bit to 1. This tells bridges to read the route information from SN3 to SN1. The Response frame is addressed specifically to station WS1.

FIGURE 13.7

The Route Determination frame is returned to the sender with route information to target.

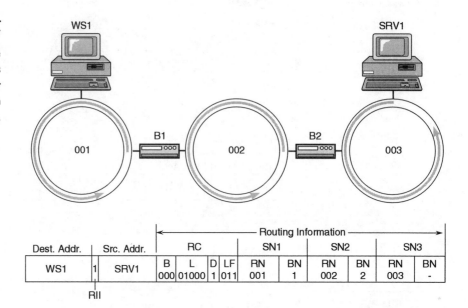

The response frame is forwarded by bridges B2 and B1 to ring 001 and copied by station WS1. WS1 extracts the routing information from the frame and adds it to its route table. From this point on, as long as WS1 is not rebutted, it can communicate with SRV1 without having to perform Route Determination again.

There may be more than one route to the target station, and the sending station may receive more than one response. Most implementations take the first response as the entry for the route table and ignore the rest.

Figure 13.8 shows a decoded Route Determination packet from a NetWare workstation. Figure 13.9 shows the Response Route Determination packet from the server. Note that the server is only one bridge, or hop, away from the workstation.

FIGURE 13.8

Decoded Route
Determination frame

```
04/04/95              LANalyzer(R) Network Analyzer by NCC              08:31
Packet #: 1                                                      Trace Decode
           ============== c:\traces\tr\vlmtoken ==============
┌──────────────────────────────────────────────────────────────────────────┐
│Frame: Number: 1            Length:    57 bytes                             │
│       Frame Status: Address not recognized, frame not copied               │
│       Receive Channels: rtedet                                             │
│802.5: ============== IEEE 802.5 Datalink Layer ==============              │
│       AC: Frame Priority=0  Monitor Count=0  Priority Reservation=0        │
│       FC: Non-MAC Frame     Attention Code=0                               │
│       Station: IBM745C8D          ----> Broadcast                          │
│       Source Routing Information:                                          │
│         Length:         2 bytes                                            │
│         Broadcast:      Single-route broadcast, all routes broadcast return│
│         Direction:      From originating station                           │
│         Largest Frames: 65535 bytes, initial value                         │
│802.2: ============== IEEE 802.2 Logical Link Control ==============        │
│       SSAP: NetWare     DSAP: NetWare                                      │
│       Unnumbered Command: Unnumbered Information (UI)                       │
│  ipx: ============== NetWare Internetwork Packet Exchange Protocol ======= │
│       Checksum: 0xFFFF          Length: 34                                 │
│       Hop Count:  0             Packet Type: 17 (NCP)                      │
│       Network: 00 00 00 00      ---> 00 00 00 00                           │
└──────────────────────────────────────────────────────────────────────────┘
F1    │F2    │F3    │F4     │F5    │F6     │F7    │F8    │F9    │F10
Help  │Copy  │Print │Options│EBCDIC│AltDisp│Prev  │Next  │Goto  │Back
```

FIGURE 13.9

Decoded Route
Determination Response
frame

```
04/04/95              LANalyzer(R) Network Analyzer by NCC              08:33
Packet #: 2                                                      Trace Decode
           ============== c:\traces\tr\vlmtoken ==============
┌──────────────────────────────────────────────────────────────────────────┐
│Frame: Number: 2            Length:   123 bytes                             │
│       Frame Status: Address recognized, frame copied                       │
│       Receive Channels: rtedet                                             │
│802.5: ============== IEEE 802.5 Datalink Layer ==============              │
│       AC: Frame Priority=0  Monitor Count=1  Priority Reservation=0        │
│       FC: Non-MAC Frame     Attention Code=0                               │
│       Station: Madge19EA36        ----> IBM745C8D                          │
│       Source Routing Information:                                          │
│         Length:         6 bytes                                            │
│         Broadcast:      Non-broadcast                                      │
│         Direction:      From responding station                            │
│         Largest Frames: 17800 bytes (LF=6)                                 │
│           Ring Number   123    124                                         │
│                                ^                                           │
│           Bridge Number    └─1─┘                                           │
│802.2: ============== IEEE 802.2 Logical Link Control ==============        │
│       SSAP: NetWare     DSAP: NetWare                                      │
│       Unnumbered Command: Unnumbered Information (UI)                       │
│  ipx: ============== NetWare Internetwork Packet Exchange Protocol ======= │
└──────────────────────────────────────────────────────────────────────────┘
F1    │F2    │F3    │F4     │F5    │F6     │F7    │F8    │F9    │F10
Help  │Copy  │Print │Options│EBCDIC│AltDisp│Prev  │Next  │Goto  │Back
```

All Routes Broadcast versus Single Route Broadcast

Route determination has a side effect that can adversely affect large source-routing networks that have redundant bridges and routes. Figure 13.10 shows a six-ring network connected by redundant bridges. Redundancy is used as fault tolerance between rings in case a bridge fails. But look what happens when WS1 transmits a Route Determination frame on ring 001.

FIGURE 13.10

Excessive Route Determination traffic on a multi-ring network

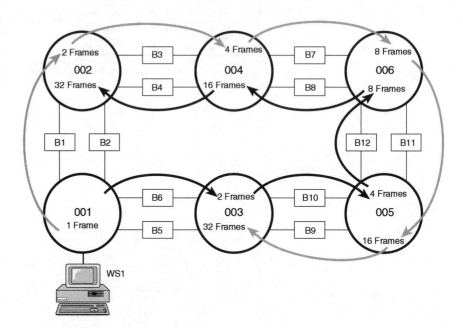

The Route Determination frame transmitted on ring 001 by WS1 is forwarded by bridges B1 and B2 to ring 002, resulting in two frames on ring 002. At the same time, bridges B5 and B6 are each forwarding the frame to ring 003, resulting in 2 frames on ring 003. As you can see in Figure 13.10, frames are forwarded and replicated in both directions to all rings on the network by powers of 2. As many as 34 frames appear on rings 002 and 003.

Because source-route bridges will not forward a frame to a ring it has already been on, as indicated by the route information, source routing does not experience bridging loops. Thus, in this example frames are never forwarded back to ring 001.

Redundancy of bridges between rings is good, but the resultant Route Determination can cause an undesirable amount of network traffic. There needs to be a way to put the redundant bridge in a backup mode so that it doesn't forward frames until the primary bridge fails. In source routing, you do this by running bridges in Single Route Broadcast or All Route Broadcast mode.

Bridges configured as All Routes Broadcast are the backup bridges. All Routes Broadcast bridges forward only two types of frames:

- All Route Broadcast Route Determination

- Specific Route

Bridges configured as Single Route Broadcast are considered primary or designated bridges. Single Route Broadcast bridges forward the following types of frames:

- Single Route Broadcast Route Determination

- All Route Broadcast Route Determination

- Specific Route

To make this traffic reduction scheme work, you configure one of the bridges between each ring as a Single Route Broadcast and the other as All Route Broadcast. Then you configure each device on all of the rings so that, when they do a Route Determination, they transmit the Route Determination frame with the Broadcast bits set to Single Route Broadcast.

In our example, we have configured all even-numbered bridges as Single Route Broadcast and all odd-numbered bridges as All Route Broadcast. WS1 is configured to transmit Single Route Broadcast Route Determination frames (Broadcast bits = 110). Now only the even-numbered bridges will forward the Route Determination frames between rings. As shown in Figure 13.11, this significantly reduces the Route Determination traffic on the network.

Once the level of Route Determination traffic is reasonable, and since we still have redundant bridges, almost everything is taken care of. But let's say that each ring is in a different building. You are in building 1 and the primary bridge in building 6 fails. You could avoid having to physically go to the backup bridge and reconfigure it as a Single Route Broadcast (some bridge management systems will let you do this from a management console, but what if you're away from your desk?) if the backup bridge were able to detect

FIGURE 13.11

Using a Single Route
Broadcast configuration
to reduce Route
Determination traffic

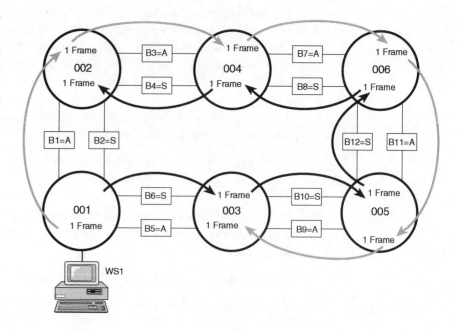

FIGURE 13.11

Using a Single Route Broadcast configuration to reduce Route Determination traffic

the failure of the primary bridge and automatically reconfigure itself. The Spanning Tree Protocol, described in the next section, does just that.

Spanning Tree Protocol

HE SPANNING TREE Protocol (STP) is a bridge hierarchy protocol that dynamically organizes the routes between rings with redundant bridges or paths, in order to minimize the amount of traffic on connecting rings.

Originally defined by the IEEE 802.1D specification for use with transparent bridges, the Spanning Tree Protocol has been adapted by IBM for Token Ring. The STP provides a communication between source-route bridges that allows them to automatically reconfigure the bridging routes when a bridge fails or is removed from service. A special type of data packet, called the Bridge Protocol Data Unit, enables this communication between bridges.

Bridge Protocol Data Units

Bridge Protocol Data Units (BPDUs) contain the information that bridges use to constantly communicate with each other about the status of bridge routes and any required reconfiguration of the network resulting from failure or removal of a bridge. BPDUs are addressed to the source-route bridge functional address (C0 00 FF FF FF FF). The two types of BPDUs are

- Configuration BPDUs

- Topology Change Notification BPDUs

Figure 13.12 shows the format of the two BPDU types. Following is a brief description of each BPDU field.

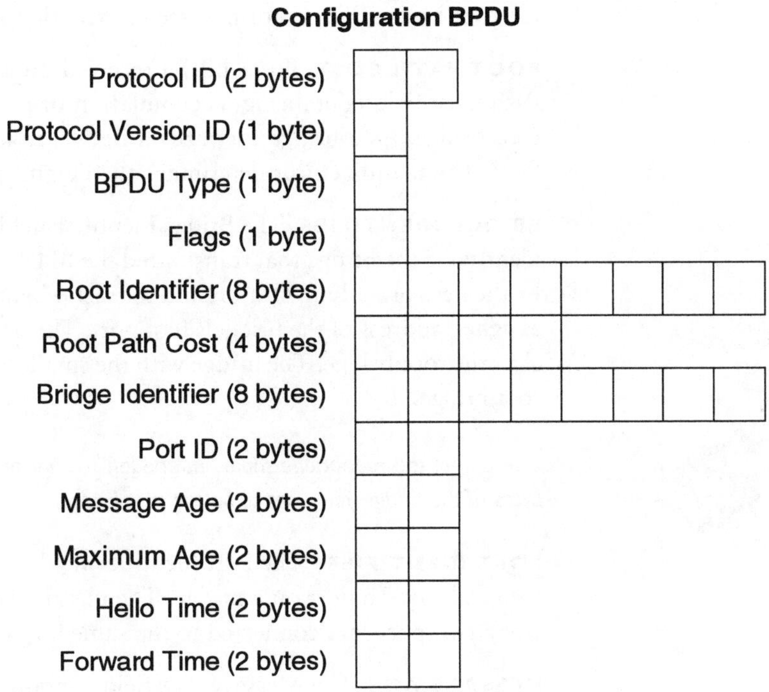

FIGURE 13.12

Bridge Protocol Data Unit format

Configuration BPDU

Protocol ID (2 bytes)
Protocol Version ID (1 byte)
BPDU Type (1 byte)
Flags (1 byte)
Root Identifier (8 bytes)
Root Path Cost (4 bytes)
Bridge Identifier (8 bytes)
Port ID (2 bytes)
Message Age (2 bytes)
Maximum Age (2 bytes)
Hello Time (2 bytes)
Forward Time (2 bytes)

PROTOCOL IDENTIFIER The Protocol Identifier field identifies the bridge protocol being used—00 00h for the STP.

PROTOCOL VERSION The Protocol Version field contains the current version of the bridge protocol. The current version of the STP is 00h.

BPDU TYPE The BPDU Type field identifies the BPDU as a configuration or topology change BPDU. The value for each is as follows:

00h = Configuration BPDU

80h = Topology Change BPDU

FLAGS The following are the only two flags currently defined for the STP.

0000 0001 (01h) = Topology Change Flag

1000 0000 (80h) = Topology Change Acknowledgment Flag

ROOT IDENTIFIER The Root Identifier field contains the bridge identifier of the root bridge. For its format, see the section "Bridge Identifier."

ROOT PATH COST For a BPDU received on a bridge's root port, the Root Path Cost field contains an accumulation of root port path costs from the root bridge. As a bridge forwards a BPDU, it adds its root port cost to this field. The manufacturer determines the default port cost.

BRIDGE IDENTIFIER The Bridge Identifier field contains an 8-byte value identifying the bridge that transmitted the BPDU. The first 2 bytes are assigned by the network administrator, and the last 6 bytes are the universal or locally assigned address of the bridge's first port. The STP uses the bridge identifier to elect the root bridge. The bridge with the smallest bridge identifier becomes the root bridge.

Selection of the root bridge should not be left to chance. Assign a low value to the first 2 bytes of the bridge you want to be the root bridge.

PORT IDENTIFIER The Port Identifier field contains a 2-byte identifier assigned to each port on a bridge. The identifier selects a designated port when two ports are connected to the same link.

MESSAGE AGE The Message Age field contains the age of the configuration message, in seconds, since it was generated by the root bridge. This field ensures the aging of configuration information. Upon retransmission of the

Configuration BPDU, each bridge increments this number by a value set by management. Bridges use this information to discard information that exceeds Max Age. The Message Age field is not applicable to source routing.

MAX AGE The value in the Max Age field is set by the root bridge so that all bridges have a consistent value for testing the age of configuration information (in seconds). The Max Age field is not applicable to source routing.

HELLO TIME The Hello Time field contains the time (in seconds) between transmissions of Configuration BPDUs from the root bridge. It is set by management in the root bridge. The STP does not use it, but the management protocol may use it for bridge performance testing.

FORWARD DELAY The Forward Delay field contains the time (in seconds), set by the root bridge, that a port waits before forwarding frames after a network reconfiguration. This field is not applicable for source routing.

How Spanning Tree Works

To establish a hierarchy of bridge routes through primary bridges (Single Route Broadcast) and provide automatic reconfiguration of the backup bridge (All Routes Broadcast) to the primary bridge after primary bridge failure, the STP executes the series of events described in the following sections to establish designated routes and inter-bridge communication.

Electing a Root Bridge

The STP must first elect a bridge as the root bridge. Initially, all bridges try to elect themselves as the root bridge by transmitting Configuration BPDUs with the bridge's Bridge Identifier (BID) as the Root Identifier (RID) on all ports, as shown in Figure 13.13. A *port* is a bridge's physical connection to a ring or segment.

When a bridge receives a BPDU on any port that has an RID of lesser value than its own BID, it ceases to contest root bridge status. (For illustration purposes, only the first 2 bytes of the BID are used in Figure 13.13.) At that point the bridge starts transmitting BPDUs, with the RID set to the lesser BID, on all its ports except the port on which the BPDU with the lesser BID was received (the *root port*).

FIGURE 13.13

Bridges elect a root
bridge.

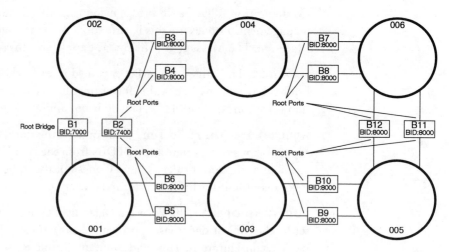

In Figure 13.13, bridge B1 eventually becomes the root bridge, since it has the lowest BID. Do not leave the root bridge selection to chance. You can set the first 2 bytes of a bridge ID to control root bridge selection and its backup. Place root bridges as close as possible to the center of the network.

Bridge B2 immediately detects root bridge B1's BPDUs on both of its ports. This tells B2 that it is in parallel with the root bridge. B2 immediately enters backup mode as an All Routes Broadcast bridge. In case of root bridge failure, B2 would become the root bridge because its BID is second lowest on the network.

Determining Designated Routes

After the root bridge is elected, its task is to initiate BPDU transmissions. Approximately every two seconds, the root bridge transmits a BPDU on all its ports, as shown in Figure 13.14. Other bridges receive the BPDUs on their root ports, update the information in the BPDU, and then forward the frame.

Single Route Broadcast (primary) and All Route Broadcast (backup) bridges, and thus the designated routes, are determined using port costs. The network administrator assigns port costs to the root port of all bridges. This means you can control the designated routes of your Token Ring network.

FIGURE 13.14

Designated routes and
primary and backup
bridges are determined by
port costs.

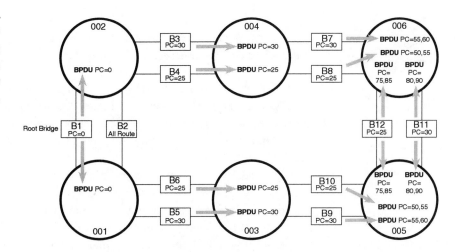

Port costs determine the state of each bridge connected to a ring. BPDUs transmitted by the root bridge start with a port cost of 0. As each bridge receives and retransmits the BPDU, it adds its port cost to the port cost received in the BPDU. When two bridges are transmitting BPDUs on the same ring, they copy each other's BPDU. When a bridge detects a BPDU with a port cost lower than its own, it automatically configures itself as All Routes Broadcast (backup). The bridge with the lowest port cost becomes the primary or Single Route Broadcast bridge. Figure 13.15 shows an STP configuration screen.

FIGURE 13.15

Source-route bridge
Spanning Tree
configuration screen
(Courtesy Madge
Networks)

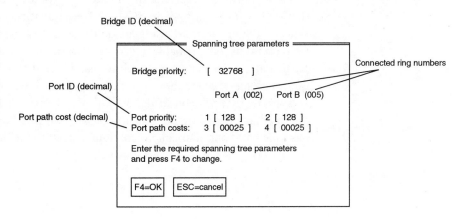

If a tie in total port cost occurs between two bridges on a ring, the port adapter's address is the tiebreaker. The lowest address becomes the primary bridge.

Bridges 4, 6, 8 and 10 become the primary bridges because their accumulated port costs are the lowest (see Figure 13.14). Bridges 11 and 12 both become backup bridges since they lose the port-cost contest in both directions. In a source-routing environment, bridges 11 and 12 could probably be considered overkill.

Figure 13.16 shows the network in a Spanning Tree diagram after the STP route configuration. Note that ring stations that could at one time communicate directly between rings 5 and 6 now have to go all the way around. This is the trade-off for having automatic configuration/reconfiguration with STP. However, if you have the luxury of planning an STP network from scratch, you can minimize the distance a frame must travel. Figure 13.17 shows one ideal layout for an STP network. In this example, regardless of the route configuration, a frame will never have to cross more than two bridges.

Reconfiguring the Network after a Bridge Failure

The root bridge has been transmitting BPDUs on all its ports approximately every two seconds. The primary bridges receive the BPDUs on their root ports and forward them on all other ports. In this way, BPDUs will eventually appear on all rings, as shown in Figure 13.18.

Backup bridges are in standby mode (All Routes Broadcast). This means that they will not participate in Route Determination (assuming all ring stations on the network are using Single Route Broadcast for Route Determination) and thus will probably never forward frames. However, they do still participate in the STP: they watch to make sure that a BPDU is transmitted onto the ring opposite their root port at regular intervals.

Suppose that primary bridge B8 fails (see Figure 13.18). Backup bridge B7 detects that BPDUs are no longer appearing on ring 006. B7 assumes that B8 has failed and automatically reconfigures itself to Single Route Broadcast. A route to ring 006 is now reestablished.

FIGURE 13.16

Spanning Tree diagram of
the network after route
configuration is complete

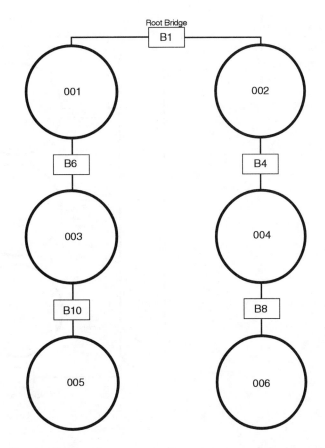

Once B7 has reconfigured itself, all stations with entries in their routing tables that used the path bridge B8 to ring 006 will have to rediscover the route. You can accomplish this by reloading ROUTE.COM (workstation) or ROUTE.NLM (server) with the CLEAR option or by rebooting a workstation.

FIGURE 13.17

Example of an ideal
network configuration
for STP

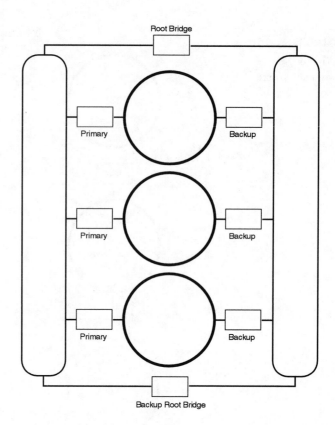

FIGURE 13.18

BPDUs from the root
bridge eventually reach all
segments.

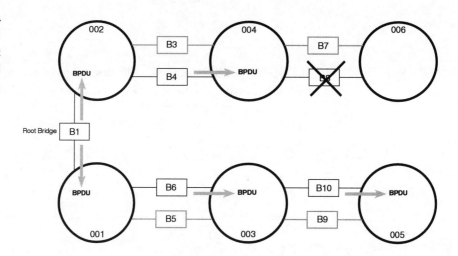

Configuring NetWare Servers and Workstations for Source Routing

F OR NETWARE SERVERS and workstations to participate in a source-routing environment, you have to load ROUTE.NLM on servers and ROUTE.COM on workstations. The following sections provide information on loading the ROUTE modules and configuring them for All Route or Single Route Broadcast.

Loading ROUTE.NLM

Load ROUTE.NLM after loading the LAN driver for the server's Token Ring adapter, using the following syntax:

LOAD ROUTE [parameter…]

Use the parameter options in Table 13.1 to configure the way the server handles Route Determination.

TABLE 13.1 ROUTE.NLM Parameters	PARAMETER	SYNTAX	EXPLANATION
	Default	DEF	Add this parameter if you do not want to transmit Route Determination frames as Single Route Broadcast. When the Default parameter is used, all Route Determination frames are sent All Routes Broadcast.
	General Broadcast Frames	GBR	Add this parameter if you want General Broadcast frames (frames addressed to FF FF FF FF FF FF) sent as All Routes Broadcast. By default, they are sent Single Route Broadcast.
	Clear	CLEAR	Reload ROUTE.NLM with this parameter to clear the server's source-route table. Do this if a bridge goes down and bridging routes are reconfigured on the network.

For complete parameter options, see Novell's Utilities Reference manual for 4.x servers or the System Administration Guide for 3.x servers.

Configuring ROUTE.COM on a Workstation

Execute ROUTE.COM after loading the Token Ring adapter ODI driver but before the protocol stack (IPXODI.COM, for example). Use the following syntax:

ROUTE *parameter…*

Use the parameter options presented in Table 13.2 to configure the way the workstation handles Route Determination.

TABLE 13.2 ROUTE.COM Parameters	PARAMETER	SYNTAX	EXPLANATION
	Default	DEF	Add this parameter if you do not want to transmit Route Determination frames as Single Route Broadcast. When you use this parameter, all Route Determination frames are sent All Routes Broadcast.
	General Broadcast Frames	GBR	Add this parameter if you want General Broadcast frames (frames addressed to FF FF FF FF FF FF) sent All Routes Broadcast. By default, they are sent Single Route Broadcast.
	Clear	CLEAR	Reexecute ROUTE.COM with this parameter to clear the workstation's source-route table. Do this if a bridge goes down and bridging routes are reconfigured on the network.

For complete parameter options, see the DOS and Windows Workstation manual in 4.x documentation or Utilities manual in 3.x documentation.

In this chapter you have learned about IBM's source-route bridging protocol and how they have implemented the Spanning Tree Protocol. Be aware that the IBM implementation of Spanning Tree is not IEEE 802.1D compatible—mainly because the IEEE specification was created for transparent bridges, not source-route bridges, and these totally different types of bridges are not compatible. Thus, if you have a mixed environment of source-route and transparent bridges, you cannot implement Spanning Tree across all bridges, with one exception. You can do so if you implement source-route/transparent bridges (both bridges in one box) all from the same vendor.

Part III of this book has given you some insights into how Token Ring operates, how to detect whether the Token Ring is operating properly, how to use the information in MAC frames to isolate errors, how to optimize your Token Ring networks, and how source routing and the Spanning Tree Protocol operate. Now it is time to move away from the data-link layer CSMA/CD and Token Ring access methods and begin learning about upper-layer NetWare protocols.

NetWare
Protocols

PART

NetWare's IPX, SPX, and SPX II Protocols

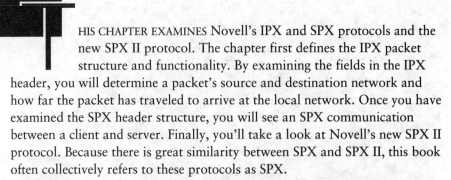

HIS CHAPTER EXAMINES Novell's IPX and SPX protocols and the new SPX II protocol. The chapter first defines the IPX packet structure and functionality. By examining the fields in the IPX header, you will determine a packet's source and destination network and how far the packet has traveled to arrive at the local network. Once you have examined the SPX header structure, you will see an SPX communication between a client and server. Finally, you'll take a look at Novell's new SPX II protocol. Because there is great similarity between SPX and SPX II, this book often collectively refers to these protocols as SPX.

When stations transmit data, they place a frame around the data (*encapsulation*) to determine where the data should be sent, who sent the data, and what the upper-layer protocol is. The upper-layer protocols examined in this book are NetWare specific.

When a NetWare client and server communicate, they may be using either connection-oriented or connectionless services. Connection-oriented communications use Novell's Sequenced Packet Exchange (SPX and SPX II) protocols. Connectionless communications use Novell's Internetwork Packet Exchange (IPX) protocol.

IPX and SPX communications require an additional header to be placed in front of the data, before the frame, as shown in Figure 14.1. These headers include routing data, sequencing information, and upper-layer protocol identification (such as NCP, SAP, and RIP).

Most of NetWare's client/server communications use the IPX protocol for transport. Developers must compare the advantages and disadvantages of each protocol to determine if their application requires IPX, SPX, or SPX II.

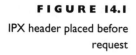

FIGURE 14.1

IPX header placed before request

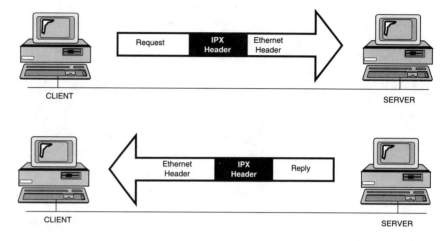

Advantages and Disadvantages of IPX, SPX, and SPX II

NETWARE'S IPX, SPX, and SPX II offer three distinctly different network communications protocols. IPX is connectionless. SPX and SPX II are connection oriented. Many application programmers need to weigh the low overhead of IPX against the guaranteed delivery of SPX and SPX II.

Because IPX is a connectionless (or datagram) protocol, no connection "handshake" is required prior to communicating with an IPX partner. There is no guarantee of delivery, however, and packets can arrive in any sequence. (Connectionless protocols are often compared to regular mail. You drop a letter in the mailbox and trust that it will be delivered.) IPX supports broadcast of packets, whereas SPX and SPX II communications must be established with each station individually before data can be sent.

Because SPX and SPX II are connection oriented, they require the SPX/SPX II partner to be available before data can be sent. (Connection-oriented protocols are often compared to sending a registered letter. Information regarding the delivery, such as acceptance of the letter, is returned to the sender.) SPX and SPX II packets are sequenced, so they arrive in proper order, whereas IPX packets can arrive in any order. SPX and SPX II are slower communication protocols because of the packet overhead (12 bytes per packet for SPX, and even more for SPX II), the acknowledgment required for each packet of data sent, and the connection setup and termination packets.

This chapter discusses the following topics:

- The IPX packet structure, how to interpret field values, and how to optimize the network configuration based on the information contained in the IPX header

- The functionality and structure of Novell's SPX protocol

- Why the SPX II protocol was developed and its unique functionality

The IPX Header

THE IPX HEADER is always 30 bytes in length and begins with the hexadecimal value 0xFFFF. IPX headers are transmitted after the media access control frame but before the packet data. Figure 14.2 defines the IPX header format.

CHECKSUM By default, the Checksum field in the IPX header is not used. The value 0xFFFF is placed in the Checksum field, which is 2 bytes long. Novell intentionally did not use the Checksum field in the IPX header because a CRC check is already done on the entire frame and data.

NetWare 4.01, however, in conjunction with the NetWare DOS Requester, allows you to use checksums, if desired. The NetWare DOS Requester uses VLMs (Virtual Loadable Modules) and is available with NetWare 4.01 and on CompuServe.

You cannot use IPX checksums with Novell's Ethernet_802.3 frame type because the Checksum field is the only indicator that the frame is a NetWare packet. Ethernet_II, Ethernet_802.2, and Ethernet_SNAP frames contain a Protocol Identification field that indicates the frame as a NetWare packet.

FIGURE 14.2

IPX header format

Checksum (2 bytes)

Length (2 bytes)

Transport Control (1 byte)

Packet Type (1 byte)

Destination Node Address (6 bytes)

Destination Network Address (4 bytes)

Destination Socket (2 bytes)

Source Node Address (6 bytes)

Source Network Address (4 bytes)

Source Socket (2 bytes)

FF FF

Many analyzers, such as LANalyzer for Windows, display the source and destination information (network, node, and socket information) in reverse order of the actual packet order. This is done to present a more appealing, logical look (source on the left; destination on the right).

The IPX checksum is simply a check of the validity of the IPX header only, not the data or frame.

To enable the IPX checksums on a NetWare 4.01 server, type **SET ENABLE IPX CHECKSUMS**=*number,* where *number* indicates whether the IPX checksum is enabled, as shown in Figure 14.3. This command should be placed in the STARTUP.NCF file to ensure that it is always loaded when the NetWare OS is loaded.

You can enable the IPX Checksum field only when you use Ethernet_802.2, Ethernet_II, or Ethernet_SNAP frame types—not the Ethernet_802.3 frame type.

To enable checksums at the client, place CHECKSUM=number in the NET.CFG file. You must be using the NetWare DOS Requester software at

FIGURE 14.3

Checksums must be enabled at the client and server.

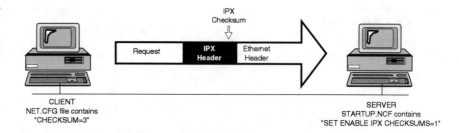

the client to use checksums. The following tables detail the settings available for enabling checksums:

Server Setting	Description
0	Checksums are disabled
1	Checksums are used if enabled at the client (default)
2	Checksums are required

Client Setting	Description
0	Checksums are disabled (default)
1	Checksums are enabled but not preferred
2	Checksums are enabled and preferred
3	Checksums are required

Enabling IPX checksums decreases the performance of network communications slightly because the client and server must complete an IPX checksum calculation before passing the packet up to the next layer (NCP, for example). The following table compares the performance of various tasks with and without checksums (s = seconds; ms = microseconds):

Task	Without Checksums	With Checksums
Launch NWTOOLS	116.023ms	117.902ms
Open the Concepts Manual	3.796s	3.883s
Capture a port	148.388ms	150.203ms
Launch NETADMIN	3.649s	3.739s

The decision to use checksums is entirely up to you—are you willing to accept the slight performance degradation for the additional error checking offered by IPX checksums? Most people do not use the checksum feature because frames include error checking on the entire contents of the packet, as shown in Chapter 5.

> Contrary to popular belief, the maximum length of an IPX header and data on Ethernet is currently 1518 bytes. If, however, an IPX packet will cross a router without using the Large Internet Packet (LIP) protocol, the maximum of 576 bytes is applicable. Novell has created the LIP protocol to allow stations to transmit larger frame sizes across IPX routers. LIP is covered in Chapter 16.

LENGTH The Length field contains the length of the internetwork packet. This includes the IPX header and the valid data that follows. It does not include the Ethernet frame fields.

On an Ethernet network, Ethernet_802.3 and Ethernet_II packets that contain an uneven number of bytes in the data portion will have 1 additional byte of random data placed at the end in order to "evenize" the packet. A few years ago, companies found that some routers generate errors as the result of an uneven amount of data. Novell's LAN Driver division drafted a memorandum requiring that all drivers evenize Ethernet_802.3 and Ethernet_II packets by adding a single extra byte of data. As shown in Figure 14.4, the IPX header's Length field indicates that there are 37 bytes of valid data (including the IPX header itself), while the Ethernet header indicates that there are 38 bytes of valid data. Neither Length field takes into account the 14 bytes required for the Ethernet_802.3 header (Destination, Source, and Length fields). This packet has been "evenized" by the LAN driver. The Length field shown at the top of the screen indicates the total length of the frame, including the Ethernet_802.3 header. The entire frame size has jumped to 64 bytes because of the 64-byte minimum frame size requirement on Ethernet networks.

TRANSPORT CONTROL The Transport Control field is used by IPX routers and denotes the number of routers an IPX packet has crossed (hops used). The originating station sets this field to 0. Packets may cross up to 15 routers. The packet will be discarded by the 16th router.

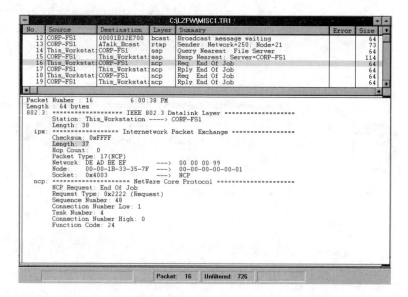

```
                              C:\LZFW\MISC1.TR1
No.  Source          Destination     Layer  Summary                              Error  Size
 12 CORP-FS1         00001B32E700    bcast  Broadcast message waiting                     64
 13 CORP-FS1         ATalk_Bcast     rtmp   Sender: Network=250; Node=21                  73
 14 This_Workstat:   CORP-FS1        sap    Query Nearest  File Server                    64
 15 CORP-FS1         This_Workstat:  sap    Resp Nearest; Server=CORP-FS1                 114
 16 This_Workstat:   CORP-FS1        ncp    Req End Of Job                                64
 17 CORP-FS1         This_Workstat:  ncp    Rply End Of Job                               64
 18 This_Workstat:   CORP-FS1        ncp    Req  End Of Job                               64
 19 CORP-FS1         This_Workstat:  ncp    Rply End Of Job                               64

Packet Number : 16              6:00:38 PM
Length : 64 bytes
802.3: ================= IEEE 802.3 Datalink Layer ==================
      Station: This_Workstation ----> CORP-FS1
      Length: 38
  ipx: ================= Internetwork Packet Exchange =================
      Checksum: 0xFFFF
      Length: 37
      Hop Count : 0
      Packet Type: 17(NCP)
      Network: DE AD BE EF         ---> 00 00 00 99
      Node:    00-00-1B-33-35-7F   ---> 00-00-00-00-00-01
      Socket:  0x4003              ---> NCP
  ncp: ================= NetWare Core Protocol ====================
      NCP Request: End Of Job
      Request Type: 0x2222 (Request)
      Sequence Number: 48
      Connection Number Low: 1
      Task Number: 4
      Connection Number High: 0
      Function Code: 24

                         Packet:  16    Unfiltered:  726
```

PACKET TYPE The Packet Type field indicates the type of service a packet will use, as shown in the following list. For IPX-based communications, this value will be 0, 4, 5, or 17.

IPX-based communications	0 or 4
SPX-based communications	5
NCP communications	17

NetWare's IPX header structure is similar to the XNS (Xerox Networking System) IDP (Internet Datagram Packet) header structures. An IPX header, however, generally contains the value 0xFF-FF in the Checksum field (unless checksums are turned on, as discussed earlier in this chapter). XNS packets always contain a checksum value in the Checksum field.

DESTINATION NETWORK The Destination Network field contains the 4-byte network address on which the destination node resides. If this field contains 0x-00-00-00-00, the packet is destined for the same network as the source station. It will not be passed on by a router. If a packet is addressed to a NetWare 3.x or NetWare 4.x server, the packet is addressed to the internal IPX address.

DESTINATION NODE Destination Node is a 6-byte field that contains the node address of the destination station or 0xFF-FF-FF-FF-FF-FF (broadcast).

Packets addressed to a NetWare 3.x or 4.x server will contain the value 0x00-00-00-00-00-01 in the destination node address within the IPX header. This is the node address automatically assigned to the NetWare protocol stack on the internal IPX network. The Destination Address field in the Ethernet or Token Ring frame, however, shows the actual hardware address of the server's network interface card if it is on the local network, or the local router if the server is on another network.

DESTINATION SOCKET Destination Socket is a 2-byte field that contains the socket number of the intranode process to which the packet is addressed. Common socket numbers include

0x451	NetWare Core Protocol (see Chapter 15)
0x452	Service Advertising Protocol packet (see Chapter 17)
0x453	Routing Information Protocol packet (see Chapter 18)
0x455	NetBIOS packet
0x456	Diagnostic packet (see Chapter 19)
0x457	Serialization packet (see Chapter 15)

At the workstation, socket numbers are dynamically assigned. These dynamic socket numbers range from 0x4000 to 0x8000. Figure 14.5 shows a packet that is destined for a NetWare routing information socket.

SOURCE NETWORK The Source Network field contains the network address to which the source node belongs. If the source node is a NetWare v3.x or 4.x server, the source network in the IPX header will be the internal IPX address.

FIGURE 14.5

IPX header addressed to
the RIP socket

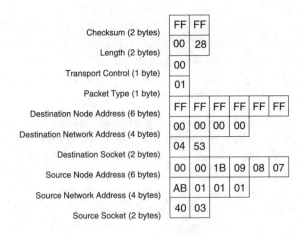

Checksum (2 bytes)	FF	FF				
Length (2 bytes)	00	28				
Transport Control (1 byte)	00					
Packet Type (1 byte)	01					
Destination Node Address (6 bytes)	FF	FF	FF	FF	FF	FF
Destination Network Address (4 bytes)	00	00	00	00		
Destination Socket (2 bytes)	04	53				
Source Node Address (6 bytes)	00	00	1B	09	08	07
Source Network Address (4 bytes)	AB	01	01	01		
Source Socket (2 bytes)	40	03				

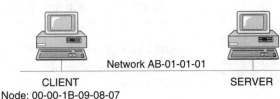

Network AB-01-01-01

CLIENT
Node: 00-00-1B-09-08-07

SERVER

SOURCE NODE The Source Node field contains the 6-byte node address of the transmitting station. If the packet is transmitted by a NetWare v3.x server, this field will contain the value 0x00-00-00-00-00-01. Unlike the Destination Address field, the Source Node field cannot contain a broadcast address (0xFF-FF-FF-FF-FF-FF).

SOURCE SOCKET The Source Socket field contains the socket number of the process that is transmitting the packet. Workstations may use dynamically assigned socket numbers ranging from 0x4000 to 0x8000, while servers reply from defined socket numbers, as described earlier in this chapter. Although not commonly done, NetWare servers can also use these socket numbers for communications.

Packets That Have Crossed Routers

M ANY LARGE INTERNETWORKS are connected with routers. When a packet crosses a router, as shown in Figure 14.6, it undergoes several changes, including the following:

- The Transport Control field will be incremented by 1.

- The existing media access frame (Ethernet, Token Ring, and so on) will be stripped off.

- A new frame will be placed on the packet.

```
Packet Number : 12              6:24:24PM
Length : 64 bytes
802.3: ==================== IEEE 802.3 Datalink Layer ==================
       Station: FS-BLDG2 ----> NW386-1
       Length: 36
  ipx: ==================== Internetwork Packet Exchange ================
       Checksum: 0xFFFF
       Length: 36
       Hop Count:  1
       Packet Type: 0(Unknown)
       Network: C9 13 86 38        --->  00 04 44 67
       Node:    00-00-00-00-00-01  --->  00-00-00-00-00-01
       Socket:  0x0000             --->  Serialize
  ser: ========= Novell Serialization (Copy Protection) Packet =========
       Serialization Data: 0 4 0 153 0 1
```

After a router strips off the frame, it places a new Ethernet (or Token Ring, ARCnet, and so on) frame on the data. The new frame contains the hardware address of the destination station (if it is on a network attached to the router) or the next router in the path to the destination network.

By examining the Transport Control field, you can determine how many routers a packet has crossed to reach the local network, as shown in Figure 14.7.

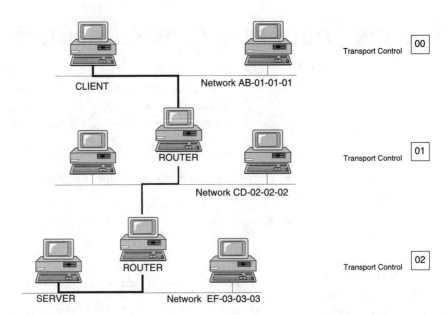

FIGURE 14.7

Transport control
increments when routers
are crossed.

CLIENT   Network AB-01-01-01   Transport Control 00

ROUTER   Network CD-02-02-02   Transport Control 01

SERVER   ROUTER   Network EF-03-03-03   Transport Control 02

Using the Transport Control Information to Optimize the LAN

YOU CAN USE the Transport Control field information to determine whether an internetwork can be reconfigured for improved performance. If a workstation communicates primarily only with servers located on another network, perhaps the workstation should be placed directly on that network rather than routing all its packets through the local network and attached router. For example, you can use a protocol analyzer to track packets that have crossed one or more routers.

The HOPCOUNT application listed in Figure 14.8 was defined with the following criteria:

Channel 1	Transport control = 0 (local network)
Channel 2	Transport control = 1
Channel 3	Transport control = 2
Channel 4	Transport control = 3
Channel 5	Transport control = 4–7
Channel 6	Transport control = 8–11
Channel 7	Transport control = 12–15

FIGURE 14.8

HOPCOUNT application

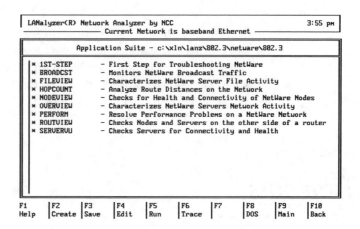

```
LANalyzer(R) Network Analyzer by NCC                              3:55 PM
                 Current Network is baseband Ethernet

            Application Suite - c:\xln\lanz\802.3\netware\802.3
  * 1ST-STEP     - First Step for Troubleshooting NetWare
  * BROADCST     - Monitors NetWare Broadcast Traffic
  * FILEVIEW     - Characterizes NetWare Server File Activity
  * HOPCOUNT     - Analyze Route Distances on the Network
  * NODEVIEW     - Checks for Health and Connectivity of NetWare Nodes
  * OVERVIEW     - Characterizes NetWare Servers Network Activity
  * PERFORM      - Resolve Performance Problems on a NetWare Network
  * ROUTVIEW     - Checks Nodes and Servers on the other side of a router
  * SERVERVU     - Checks Servers for Connectivity and Health



F1     |F2      |F3    |F4    |F5   |F6     |F7  |F8   |F9   |F10
Help   |Create  |Save  |Edit  |Run  |Trace  |    |DOS  |Main |Back
```

If most of the traffic on the local network contains a transport control value of 0, most traffic is between local stations and servers.

If, however, much of the traffic is from remote networks, as illustrated in Figure 14.9, this is an indication that perhaps the network cabling system could be optimized to reduce the amount of routed traffic.

Using the flowchart shown in Figure 14.10 for guidance, you can determine whether or not the LAN needs reconfiguration.

As shown in Figure 14.11, you can move a station to the local network to reduce the traffic on intermediate networks. However, since recabling or

FIGURE 14.9

Most traffic from remote
networks

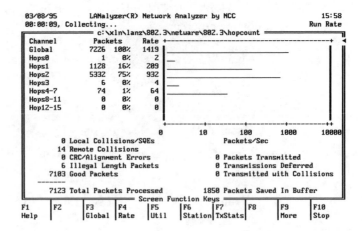

moving users between networks is not always a practical solution, you can explore moving applications and/or data from remote to local segments.

If a workstation's requests are being routed excessively, the communications are being slowed down as they pass through each router. Stations may be experiencing IPX timeouts because of poorly configured routes.

IPX Timeouts

THE NETWARE SHELL (NETX.COM) and DOS Requester (VLM.EXE) use IPX to transport requests to a file server. IPX, however, is not a connection-oriented service and does not guarantee delivery of packets. The request/response nature of NetWare's NCP and workstation shell (except Burst Mode technology, covered in Chapter 16) guarantees that packets have arrived at the destination. For example, if a workstation transmits an NCP request to open a file using IPX for transport, the NCP reply from the server is an indication that the request arrived successfully.

However, some conditions may exist on the LAN that prevent a request from arriving or the response from returning. The NetWare shell maintains a

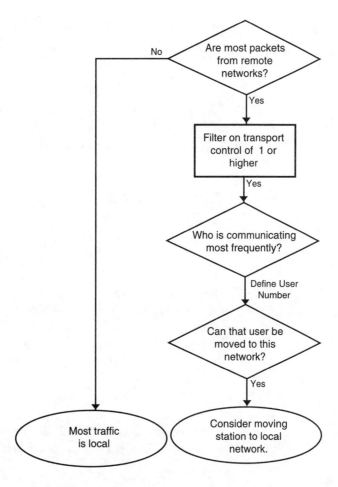

receive timeout timer. If a response is not received within the receive timeout value, the shell will use IPX again to send another NCP request, as shown in Figure 14.12.

If a station is intermittently receiving a timeout message, a problem may exist on the network. The LAN may have a cable problem (a short), or perhaps there is excessive traffic on the local segment. You can check each of these conditions by using the methods defined in Chapters 2 and 3.

Until the problem is fixed, however, you may wish to increase the number of attempts the workstation will make before displaying the timeout message

FIGURE 14.11

Move to a local segment

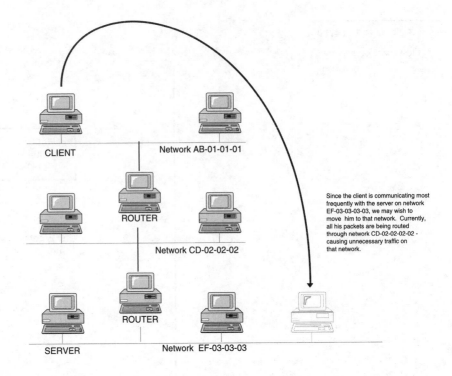

CLIENT

Network AB-01-01-01

ROUTER

Network CD-02-02-02

ROUTER

SERVER

Network EF-03-03-03

Since the client is communicating most frequently with the server on network EF-03-03-03, we may wish to move him to that network. Currently, all his packets are being routed through network CD-02-02-02 - causing unnecessary traffic on that network.

to the user. The default retry count is 20. To increase the IPX retry count, place the following line in a workstation's SHELL.CFG or NET.CFG file:

```
IPX RETRY COUNT = 30
```

NetWare v3.x and 4.x Server Considerations

 ETWARE V3.X AND 4.X servers send packets from node address 0x00-00-00-00-00-01. This is the node address automatically assigned to the NetWare protocol stack on the IPX internal network.

FIGURE 14.12

Repeat request by NCP
using IPX for transport

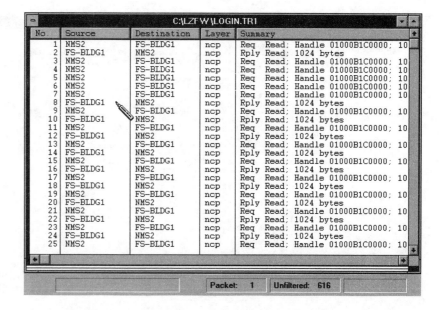

When filtering on packets being sent to a NetWare server, be certain to use this node address in the IPX header. The network address will contain the internal IPX network address assigned when the server is first brought up.

Figure 14.13 shows communication between a workstation and a NetWare v3.x server.

NetWare v2.x servers, however, do not have an internal IPX network. Communications between a workstation and a NetWare v2.x server are shown in Figure 14.14.

Sequenced Packet Exchange (SPX)

WHEN A COMMUNICATION is dependent upon receipt of each packet in sequence, Novell's IPX protocol may not be adequate since it is a connectionless, nonguaranteed-delivery protocol. Use of the SPX protocol can provide guaranteed packet delivery.

FIGURE 14.13

IPX header to NetWare
v3.x server

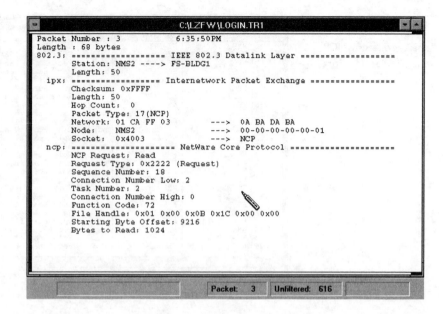

FIGURE 14.14

IPX header to NetWare
v2.x server

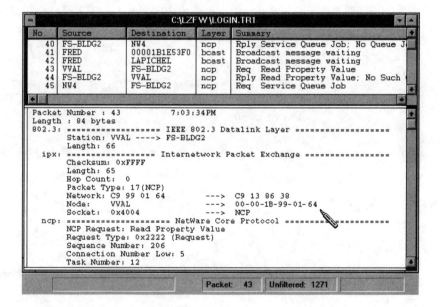

SPX provides sequenced and acknowledged communications. It does not, however, provide sliding window functionality. SPX II, an enhanced version of SPX, does offer sliding window functionality.

SPX communications are used for programs such as Novell's Print Server (PSERVER) and Remote Printer (RPRINTER), as well as Remote Console (RCONSOLE). If programmers require their application to use guaranteed packet delivery, they can design the program to use SPX. An SPX header contains all the fields defined in the IPX header and an additional 12 bytes. The additional 12 bytes provide Sequence and Acknowledgment fields.

Two versions of SPX are currently available: SPX and SPX II. SPX is included with NetWare 2.x, 3.x, and 4.x. SPX II, however, is included only with NetWare 4.x. First, let's take a look at the standard SPX protocol.

The SPX Header

N SPX HEADER, as shown in Figure 14.15, is always 42 bytes long and begins with the same initial fields as an IPX header.

FIGURE 14.15

SPX header format

| Connection Control (1 byte) |
| Datastream Type (1 byte) |
| Source Connection ID (2 bytes) |
| Destination Connection ID (2 bytes) |
| Sequence Number (2 bytes) |
| Acknowledgement Number (2 bytes) |
| Allocation Number (2 bytes) |

The Length field value includes the data field length and 42 bytes for the SPX header.

Earlier sections in this chapter provided field definitions for checksum; length; transport control; packet type; destination network; node and socket; and source network, node, and socket. In an SPX header, the Packet Type field will contain the value 0x05, indicating that the packet uses SPX for transport.

The fields described in the following sections are unique to the SPX header.

CONNECTION CONTROL The Connection Control field controls the bidirectional flow of data. Values can include the following:

Value	Name	Description
0x10	End-of-Message	Symbolizes that the client wishes to end the connection
0x20	Attention	This field is not implemented yet
0x40	Acknowledgment Required	Data has been sent, and acknowledgment is required
0x80	System Packet	Acknowledgment packet; SPX uses this internally; it is not delivered to the shell of the destination station

DATASTREAM TYPE Datastream Type is a 1-byte field that indicates the type of data contained within the packet. This field can contain a client-defined number or one of the following values:

Value	Name	Description
0xFE	End-of-Connection	Generated to indicate that a client wishes to terminate a communication
0xFF	End-of-Connection Acknowledgment	Transmitted upon receipt of an End-of-Connection request

SOURCE CONNECTION ID The Source Connection ID field contains a 2-byte number assigned by the source SPX station; it is used for demultiplexing SPX communications. Since concurrently active connections on a machine can use the same socket number, this field is necessary to distinguish each virtual connection. The number it contains will be used in the Destination Connection ID field by an SPX partner when responding to an originator.

DESTINATION CONNECTION ID Destination Connection ID is a 2-byte field that contains the connection ID number of the destination station. During the initial connection establishment, this field will be set to 0xFFFF since the sender does not yet know the destination connection ID the receiver will use.

SEQUENCE NUMBER Sequence Number is a 2-byte field that contains the count of data packets transmitted from a station. This number will increment only after receiving an acknowledgment for a data packet transmitted. A station will not increment this counter when it transmits an acknowledgment packet.

ACKNOWLEDGE NUMBER During an SPX connection, packets may be lost. The Acknowledge Number field contains the value of the sequence number expected in the next SPX packet from the SPX partner. If the sequence number is not correct, the receiving station assumes an error in communications has occurred.

ALLOCATION NUMBER The Allocation Number field indicates the number of receive buffers available at a workstation. This value begins with 0 for the first buffer available; therefore, the value 6 in this field indicates that seven packet receive buffers are available. When the receiving station's application processes information received, it frees up a buffer. If the station is busy and cannot clear the packets from the buffers, the number of available buffers will decrease each time a data packet is received by a station.

The functionality of the Allocation Number field is different for SPX and SPX II. Refer to the section "The Next Generation: SPX II" later in this chapter.

Establishing and Terminating an SPX Connection

S PX CONNECTIONS MUST be established before data packets can be exchanged. This is often referred to as an *SPX handshake*. Figure 14.16 shows the SPX headers used to establish a connection between systems.

Monitoring an SPX Connection

I N AN SPX CONNECTION, various values within the header will be used for sequencing and acknowledgment of packets. Figure 14.17 illustrates an SPX conversation progressing normally.

In the example, the client has established an SPX connection with the file server. In packet #1, the client is sending data to the server. Packet #2 shows the server acknowledging receipt of the data. Packets #3 and #5 show that the server is transmitting data to the client now. Packets #4 and #6 are the acknowledgment packets from the client. Remember that the Acknowledgment Number field increments to indicate the next sequence number expected. The Sequence Number field increments only for data that is sent.

When an SPX client has completed the communication, it transmits an SPX Close Connection request to the SPX partner. The partner, in turn, responds with an End of Connection reply with a closing acknowledgment, thereby terminating the connection. Figure 14.18 shows an SPX session being terminated by the client.

FIGURE 14.16

SPX header during
handshake

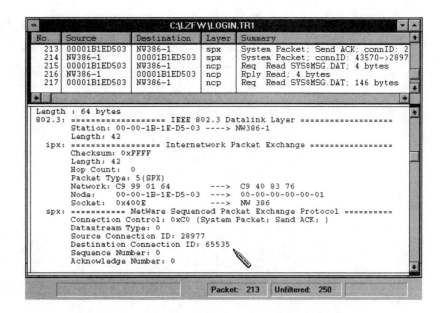

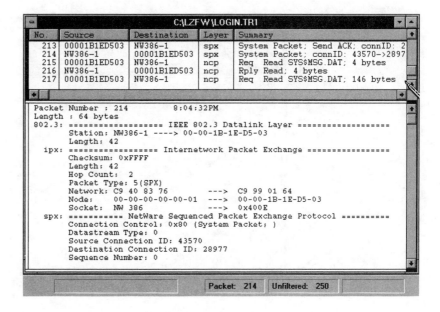

FIGURE 14.16

SPX header during
handshake
(continued)

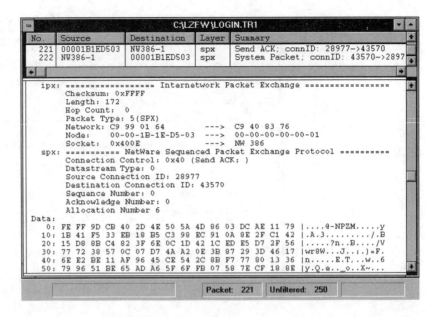

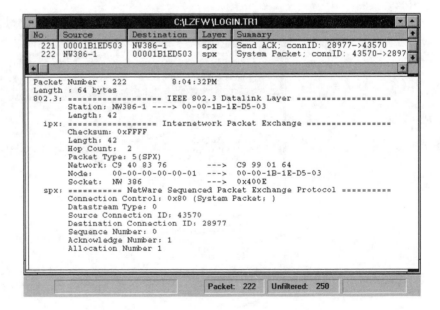

FIGURE 14.17

SPX communication

FIGURE 14.17

SPX communication

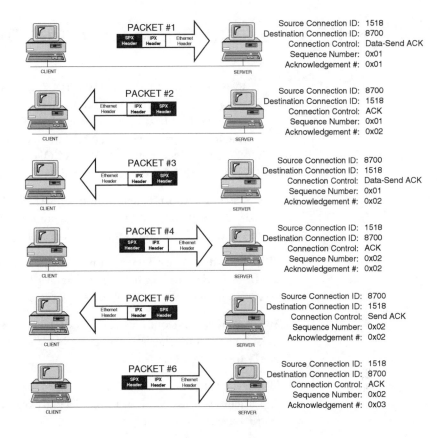

FIGURE 14.18

SPX session being
terminated

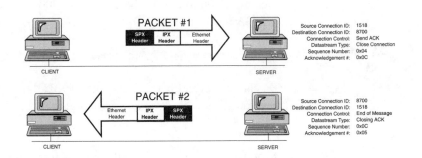

SPX Timeout Monitoring/Configuring

SEVERAL CONFIGURABLE PARAMETERS can be customized for SPX connections on NetWare 3.x and 4.x networks. If a network has a heavy bandwidth utilization or poor wiring, SPX connections may timeout. To configure SPX parameters at NetWare 3.x and 4.x file servers, use the SPXCONFG utility by typing **LOAD SPXCONFG** at the server. The following is a list of SPX parameters that are set at the server console.

SPX Watchdog Abort Timeout (in ticks): Available values for this setting are between 540 and 5400 ticks. The default is 540 ticks on NetWare 3.x servers and 1500 ticks on NetWare 4.x servers.

SPX Watchdog Verify Timeout (in ticks): Available values for this setting are from 10 ticks to 255 ticks. The default is 54 ticks on NetWare 3.x servers and 108 ticks on NetWare 4.x servers.

SPX Ack Wait Timeout (in ticks): Available values range from 10 to 3240 ticks. The default value is 108 ticks on NetWare 3.x servers and 54 ticks on NetWare 4.x servers.

SPX Default Retry Count: Available values for this setting range from 1 to 255 attempts. The default is 10 on NetWare 3.x servers and 50 on NetWare 4.x servers.

Maximum Concurrent SPX Connections: Available values for this setting range from 100 to 2000. The default is 1000 connections for both NetWare 3.x and 4.x servers.

A tick is approximately 1/18 th of a second.

You can use several parameters with SPXCONFG. To view available parameters, at the server console prompt, type

```
LOAD SPXCONFG H
```

At the workstation, specific SPX parameters can be defined in the SHELL.CFG or NET.CFG file. The following is a list of workstation SPX parameters.

SPX Abort Timeout (in ticks): This parameter defines how long an SPX partner will wait before terminating a session. The default is 540 ticks.

SPX Listen Timeout: This SPX parameter adjusts the amount of time SPX will wait before requesting the other side to verify the connection. The default is 108 ticks.

SPX Verify Timeout: This parameter adjusts the interval between SPX packets sent to the SPX partner to inform the partner that the connection is valid even though no data is being sent at this moment. The default is 54 ticks.

The Next Generation SPX: SPX II

N JULY 1991, Novell established an SPX development team to create an improved version of SPX called SPX II. At Novell's developer conference in March 1992, SPX II was introduced to developers and received a favorable response.

The primary improvements provided by SPX II include utilization of larger packet sizes and implementation of a windowing protocol. Let's review these enhancements and then take a closer look at an SPX II communication.

Larger Packet Sizes

SPX-based communications have a 576-byte maximum packet size. Since SPX has a 42-byte header, only 534 bytes remain for data. This smaller packet size causes additional overhead on the network. If a server needs to send 1500 bytes of data, it must create three separate SPX packets, send them one at a time, and ensure that an acknowledgment is sent before sending the next data packet in the sequence. This 576-byte maximum packet size is unreasonable since both Ethernet and Token Ring can support larger packet sizes.

SPX II can use the maximum packet size allowable by the network type. For example, on an Ethernet LAN, an SPX II packet can be a full 1518 bytes. As you can imagine, using larger packet sizes for SPX communications dramatically increases efficiency.

Windowing

Standard SPX permitted only one packet to be outstanding at any time. Station A would transmit a packet to the server and wait for an acknowledgment; Station A was not permitted to send another packet until it received an acknowledgment for the previous packet sent. SPX assumes the connection between sender and receiver is not reliable.

SPX II allows multiple outstanding packets and is able to transmit a negative acknowledgment (NAK) to indicate that some packets were not received, as shown in Figure 14.19.

FIGURE 14.19

A NAK indicates missing packets in an SPX II communication.

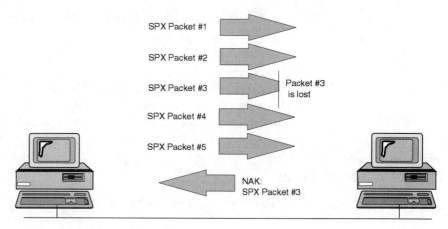

The window size is negotiated using the Allocation Number field in the SPX II header. The source SPX II station adds the calculated window size to the current sequence number. The result indicates the allowable number of outstanding packets in the SPX II session.

If desired, the number of allowable outstanding packets can be hardcoded by an application programmer. For example, a programmer could select five outstanding packets for communications on the networks that are less than five hops away and ten for all other communications.

SPX II Packet Format

LTHOUGH THE SPX II packet format appears similar to SPX, as shown in Figure 14.20, there are three main differences:

- SPX II contains additional definitions for the Connection Control field and the Datastream Type field.

- SPX II uses an extended acknowledgment header that contains an additional field.

- Packet sequencing is different, to allow for the new size negotiation and window management.

FIGURE 14.20

SPX II header format

Connection Control (1 byte)

Datastream Type (1 byte)

Source Connection ID (2 bytes)

Destination Connection ID (2 bytes)

Sequence Number (2 bytes)

Acknowledgement Number (2 bytes)

Allocation Number (2 bytes)

Extended Acknowledgment (2 bytes)

Connection Control Field Values

Two additional definitions in the Connection Control field enable SPX II clients to negotiate size and indicate that the communication is SPX II based:

Value	Name	Description
0x04	Size	Negotiate size request/response
0x08	SPX2	SPX II type packet

Datastream Type

Two additional values are supported in the datastream type field for SPX II:

0xFC	Orderly release request
0xFD	Orderly release acknowledgment

SPX II Connection Establishment

Connection establishment in SPX II differs from SPX because of the ability to negotiate packet sizes for SPX II communications. Let's examine how SPX II connections are established.

The basic flow of communications for an SPX II connection establishment is as follows:

Source	Definition
Client	SPX II Connection Request
Host	Extended SPX II ACK
Client	Negotiate Size Request
Host	Extended SPX II ACK (Negotiate Size ACK)
Host	Session Setup/Negotiate Size
Client	Extended SPX II ACK (Negotiate Size ACK)

If an application knows that all packets will be small (less than 576 bytes) or that the connection is short (less than 50 packets), the application may be able to avoid the overhead of size negotiation. The application programmer must specify that size negotiation is not used, and the Size Connection Control bit should not be set.

Initial Connection Request/Reply

Although the connection sequence indicates that special packets are used to negotiate packet sizes, the first two packets of the SPX connection also contain some packet-size information. In the first packet, SPX II Connection Request, the SYS, ACK, SIZ, and SPX2 bits of the Connection Control field are set. Just as in the SPX communications, a client assigns its Source Connection ID at this point and leaves the Connection ID field set to 65535 (0xFFFF) because the host has not yet responded with a Connection ID.

The Length field of the Connection request indicates 44 bytes because the packet contains 2 additional bytes containing size information following the header. The 2 additional bytes define the optimum size for communications. Optimum size is defined as the smaller of the client's or host's driver size. For example, if a client's Ethernet driver can support 1518 bytes, this number follows the standard Allocation Number field of an SPX header.

The host replies with the SYS, SIZ, and SPX2 bits of the Connection Control field set. The host also includes 2 additional bytes that indicate the optimum size after the standard SPX II header.

Packet Size Negotiation

Once the initial connection is established and the client and host have defined their connection IDs, the client begins the packet size negotiation process by sending a Negotiate Size Request packet.

The Negotiate Size Request packet can actually be sent at any time in the communications if packets are not getting through to the destination.

In the connection setup phase, the Negotiate Size request is sent immediately after the SPX II Connection ACK is received. The Negotiate Size Request includes an SPX II header and data, as shown in Figure 14.21.

FIGURE 14.21

Negotiate Size Request
packet

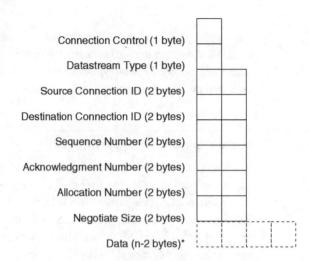

Connection Control (1 byte)

Datastream Type (1 byte)

Source Connection ID (2 bytes)

Destination Connection ID (2 bytes)

Sequence Number (2 bytes)

Acknowledgment Number (2 bytes)

Allocation Number (2 bytes)

Negotiate Size (2 bytes)

Data (n-2 bytes)*

* Where "n" = optimum packet size received by first two connection setup packets.

If the Size Negotiation ACK is not received within the SPX II timeout (a function of the driver and number of routers between the client and the host), *n* is reduced to the next logical driver size and the packet is re-sent. For example, if the packet negotiates a size of 2048 bytes but is not acknowledged, the client reduces the data portion of the packet to 1024 and retransmits the Packet Size Negotiation request. This feature is especially valuable in the case where a router that does not forward packets above 1024 in size is between the client and the host. The size is negotiated down to an acceptable level to ensure the ability to traverse the network.

When the host replies, it sends an SPX II packet that contains all fields of the Size Negotiation request except the Data field. The Negotiate Size field must match the value in the client's Size Negotiation request. This ensures that the maximum connection size is established even when the host responds too slowly, causing the client to drop down to a smaller packet size and send the request again.

The final portion of connection setup is another Size Negotiation request; once again, the extended header is used and data is tacked along with the request. The host responds with a Size Negotiation ACK (excluding the Data field). After this final exchange of packets, the basic SPX II connection is established.

SPX II to SPX Communications

What if your client supports SPX II but the host supports only SPX? The client issues a Connection request with the SPX2 and SIZ bits set. The host ignores the SPX2 and SIZ bits and sends a standard SPX connection acknowledgment. The resulting communications session relies on the standard SPX protocol, not SPX II.

What if the client supports SPX and the host supports SPX II? In this case, the client issues an SPX Connection request and the host "drops back" to SPX and replies with a standard SPX Connection ACK.

Additional Negotiable Features of SPX II

Several other communication options can be negotiated during an SPX II connection, including the following:

- **Default timeout values:** How long should SPX II partners wait before assuming a connection error and retransmit a packet?

- **Default retry counts:** How many retransmissions should an SPX II source attempt before assuming the connection is terminated?

As defined in this chapter, Novell's IPX, SPX, and SPX II headers follow the MAC frame. The IPX header is always 30 bytes long and contains information for routing and upper-layer protocol identification. The SPX header includes all the fields of the IPX header and an additional 12 bytes that contain Sequencing and Acknowledgment fields. The SPX II header can be either 12 or 14 additional bytes, depending on the function.

This chapter has also examined the additional functionality and benefits provided by Novell's SPX II protocol. Analyzing information contained in the IPX and SPX/SPX II headers, you can determine whether most communications are local or remote and whether the network is subjected to routing inefficiencies.

So far, you have looked at how packets are framed and routed and how connection-oriented services are tracked. The next chapter examines Novell's NetWare Core Protocol (NCP), which defines the structure of client requests and server responses.

NetWare Core Protocols (NCP)

S O FAR, THIS book has discussed the method for transmitting packets using frames (Ethernet and Token Ring) and network headers (IPX/SPX). You know that data transmitted across the network must have a frame for local transmission and an IPX or IPX/SPX header for routing and sequencing. Inside these packets, however, some standardized language for requests and replies must be defined.

NCP messages are prepared and sent using the formats and conventions specified by Novell's defined NCP standards. This chapter examines NCP functions and message formats, including Request and Reply header formats. This chapter also discusses miscellaneous NetWare communications that don't follow the general rules set forth by NCP. These communications include NetWare Watchdog, Serialization, and Message packets.

NCP is the language NetWare servers and clients speak. Clients make requests of servers using the NetWare Core Protocol (NCP). An NCP header follows the frame and IPX/SPX header, as you can see in Figure 15.1.

FIGURE 15.1

The NCP header follows the IPX/SPX header.

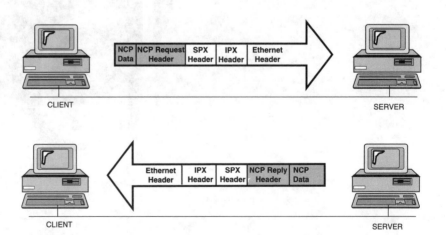

Workstations transmit NCP messages to request file reads and writes, create queue jobs, determine drive mappings, search through directories, and so on. Servers answer NCP requests with NCP replies.

By understanding NCP communications, you can determine the types of requests being made by NetWare clients. You can use this information to determine the types of operations a server is most commonly asked for (such as file reads and writes, queue requests, and so on).

Protocol analyzers that decode NetWare protocols display the NCP request or reply in plain English instead of code.

Establishing an NCP Connection

BEFORE A CLIENT is permitted to make NCP requests of a server, it must attach to a server and request an NCP connection. The server, in turn, executes the request and transmits an NCP reply, granting the connection if possible. Each client NCP request solicits a server NCP reply, as shown in Figure 15.2. This one-request/one-response communication has given NCP the nickname "ping-pong" protocol.

Chapter 16 focuses on the Burst Mode protocol, which you can use to increase the effi-ciency of NetWare file reads and writes.

The NCP Request and Reply Header Formats

NCP REQUESTS AND replies each contain a unique header that is of fixed length and followed by a variable data portion. The NCP Request header contains five fields, and the NCP Reply header contains seven fields.

FIGURE 15.2

NCP requests and replies

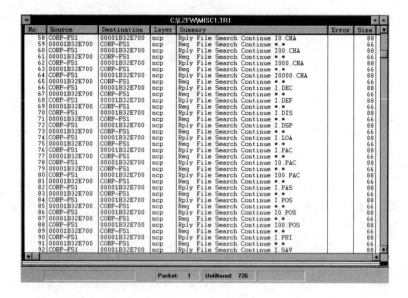

FIGURE 15.2

NCP requests and replies

NCP Request Header

Clients must identify themselves and the purpose of their NCP message to the server. The five fields of an NCP Request header contain information the receiving client or server uses to determine the type of NCP message (request, reply, establish connection, destroy connection, and so on), check to see if the client is communicating in a proper sequence, determine which client is sending the NCP message, and track the task the client has requested. The NCP Request header is shown in Figure 15.3.

The Request header format is used for all communications from the client to the server. This header is 6 bytes long and is followed by additional NCP information that defines the client's request.

FIGURE 15.3

NCP Request header

Request Type (2 bytes)		
Sequence Number (1 byte)	
Connection Number Low (1 byte)	
Task Number (1 byte)	
Connection Number High (1 byte)	

REQUEST TYPE The first field, Request Type, indicates the type of NCP request being sent from the client to the server. Request type values include the following:

Value	Description
1111	Create a service connection
2222	Service request
5555	Destroy service connection
7777	Burst Mode transfer

When a client wishes to connect to a server, it issues a Create Service Connection NCP request and specifies type 1111 in the Request Type field. When a station wishes to detach from a server, it issues a Destroy Service Connection request, specifying type 5555 in the Request Type field.

Client requests use 2222 in the Request Type field to specify a general service request. This may be a request for a file, a query of the bindery, a submission of a queue job, and so on.

The Burst Mode protocol is discussed in detail in Chapter 16.

When using the Burst Mode protocol for file reads and writes, the client will use 7777 in the Type field.

SEQUENCE NUMBER Use the sequence number to track the sequence of the communication between the server and client. Clients will place the last sequence number plus 1 in this field.

CONNECTION NUMBER LOW The Connection Number Low field contains the service connection number assigned to the client upon logging on to the server. You can observe this number in the NetWare Monitor screen under "Connection Information" and by typing **USERLIST** at a workstation.

TASK NUMBER The task number indicates which client task is making the request. The server will track these tasks and automatically deallocate resources when a task ends. Task number 0 signals to the server that all tasks have ceased execution and resources may be deallocated.

CONNECTION NUMBER HIGH The Connection Number High field is used only on the 1000-user version of NetWare. On all other versions of NetWare, the value in this field is set at 0x00.

NCP Reply Header

When the server answers a client's request, it has special considerations that must be addressed in the header format. The server must tell the client whether the request received was completed successfully and whether the NCP connection is still valid. The server will use an NCP Reply header, as shown in Figure 15.4, after the IPX/SPX header and before the additional NCP information.

FIGURE 15.4

NCP Reply header

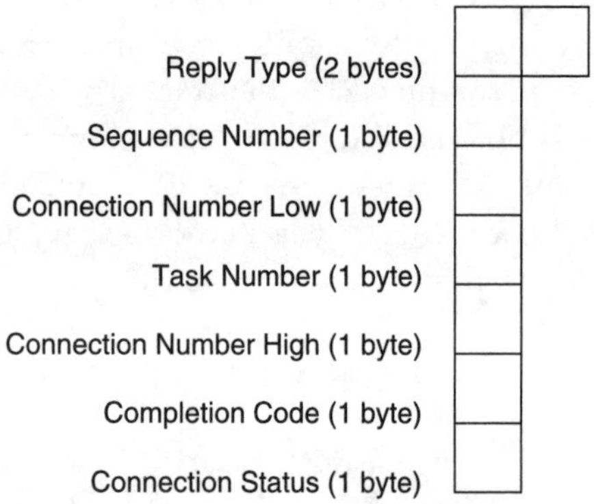

Reply Type (2 bytes)

Sequence Number (1 byte)

Connection Number Low (1 byte)

Task Number (1 byte)

Connection Number High (1 byte)

Completion Code (1 byte)

Connection Status (1 byte)

The NCP Reply header has two more fields than the Request header. These are the Completion Code and Connection Status fields.

NCP REPLY TYPES NCP reply type values include the following:

Value	Description
3333	Service reply
7777	Burst Mode Connection
9999	Request Being Processed

Servers answer most NCP requests with a service reply, specifying type 3333 in the Reply Type field. If a server has a client's request queued for execution and the client reexecutes a request because it has not received a reply from the server, the server responds with a Request Being Processed NCP reply. This causes the workstation to reset its shell timeout, increment its retry counters, and continue to wait. If the reply is not received by the client before the timeout counter expires, the client repeats the request. The default number of retries is 20; however, the client can increase this number, as described in Chapter 14.

When using Burst Mode to transfer files to and from workstations, the server uses NCP reply type 7777.

COMPLETION CODE The completion code indicates whether or not the client's request was successful. A 0 in the Completion Code field indicates that the request was successful. Any other value in this field indicates that an error occurred while the server was processing the client's request.

Connection Status Flags

NetWare clients must check the Connection Status Flags field in all incoming NCP replies from a server. If **DOWN** is typed at the console prompt to bring the server down, the fourth bit in this byte will be set to 1.

NCP Function Codes and Subfunction Codes

BESIDES THE STANDARD Request or Reply headers discussed in the preceding sections, each NCP message must contain an NCP function code identifying the service being requested or replied to.

For example, if a workstation requests to open a file, as shown in Figure 15.5, it transmits an NCP message type 2222 (request) with a function code of 76. This function code is defined by Novell as Open File. Upon receipt of an NCP message containing the type 2222 and the function code 76, the server knows the client is requesting to open a file. The file name and access level requested appear later in the NCP packet.

FIGURE 15.5

NCP request to open
a file

Many NCP function codes require a subfunction code as well. For example, many NCP messages dealing with the bindery use function code 23. To differentiate among the various types of bindery requests, NCP messages must specify a subfunction code. For example, Get Bindery Access Level is function code 23 and subfunction code 70, as you can see in Figure 15.6, while Get Internet Address is function code 23 and subfunction code 19, as shown in Figure 15.7.

FIGURE 15.6

Request for Get Bindery Access Level uses function code 23 and subfunction code 70.

FIGURE 15.7

Get Internet Address uses function code 23 and subfunction code 19.

Typical NCP function and subfunction codes seen on NetWare LANs include the ones shown in Table 15.1.

			SUBFUNC-
TABLE 15.1	**REQUEST**	**FUNCTION**	**TION**
SERVICE	**TYPE**	**CODE**	**CODE**

NCP Function Codes

SERVICE	REQUEST TYPE	FUNCTION CODE	SUBFUNCTION CODE
Accounting Services			
Get Current Account Status	2222	23	150
Submit Account Charge	2222	23	151
Submit Account Hold	2222	23	152
Submit Account Note	2222	23	153
Apple File Services			
AFP 2.0 Create Directory	2222	35	13
AFP 2.0 Create File	2222	35	14
AFP 2.0 Create Directory	2222	35	13
AFP 2.0 Scan File Information	2222	35	17
AFP 2.0 Set File Information	2222	35	16
AFP 2.0 Alloc Temporary Directory Handle	2222	35	11
AFP Create Directory	2222	35	01
AFP Create File	2222	35	02
AFP Delete	2222	35	03
AFP Get DOS Name from Entry ID	2222	35	18
AFP Get Entry ID from NetWare Handle	2222	35	06
AFP Get Entry ID from Name	2222	35	04

TABLE 15.1
NCP Function Codes
(continued)

SERVICE	REQUEST TYPE	FUNCTION CODE	SUBFUNCTION CODE
AFP Get Entry ID from Name Path	2222	35	12
AFP Get File Information	2222	35	05
AFP Get Macintosh Info on Deleted File	2222	35	19
AFP Open File Fork	2222	35	08
AFP Rename	2222	35	07
AFP Scan File Information	2222	35	10
AFP Set File Information	2222	35	09
Auditing Services			
Query Volume Audit Status	2222	88	01
Add Audit Property	2222	88	02
Add Auditor Access	2222	88	03
Change Audit Password	2222	88	04
Check Auditor Access	2222	88	05
Delete Audit Property	2222	88	06
Disable Volume Auditing	2222	88	07
Enable Volume Auditing	2222	88	08
Is User Audited	2222	88	09
Read Audit Bit Map	2222	88	10
Read Audit Config Header	2222	88	11
Read Auditing File	2222	88	12

SERVICE	REQUEST TYPE	FUNCTION CODE	SUBFUNC-TION CODE
Remove Auditor Access	2222	88	13
Reset Audit File	2222	88	14
Reset History File	2222	88	15
Write Audit Bit Map	2222	88	16
Write Audit Config Header	2222	88	17
Bindery and Rights Services			
Add Bindery Object to Set	2222	23	65
Change Bindery Object Password	2222	23	64
Change Bindery Object Security	2222	23	56
Change Property Security	2222	23	59
Close Bindery	2222	23	68
Create Bindery Object	2222	23	50
Create Property	2222	23	57
Delete Bindery Object	2222	23	51
Delete Bindery Object from Set	2222	23	66
Delete Property	2222	23	58
Get Bindery Access Level	2222	23	70
Get Bindery Object Access Level	2222	23	72
Get Bindery Object ID	2222	23	53

SERVICE	REQUEST TYPE	FUNCTION CODE	SUBFUNC- TION CODE
Get Bindery Object in Set	2222	23	54
Is Bindery Object in Set?	2222	23	67
Is Calling Station a Manager?	2222	23	73
Keyed Change Password	2222	23	75
Keyed Verify Password	2222	23	74
List Relations of an Object	2222	23	76
Open Bindery	2222	23	69
Read Property Value	2222	23	61
Rename Object	2222	23	52
Scan Bindery Object	2222	23	55
Scan Bindery Object Trustee Paths	2222	23	71
Scan Property	2222	23	60
Verify Bindery Object Password	2222	23	63
Write Property Value	2222	23	62
Connection Services			
Change Connection State	2222	23	29
Clear Connection Number List	2222	88	01
Create Service Connection	1111	—	—
Destroy Service Connection	5555	00	—
End of Job	2222	24	—

TABLE 15.1

NCP Function Codes
(continued)

SERVICE	REQUEST TYPE	FUNCTION CODE	SUBFUNC-TION CODE
Get Big Packet NCP Max Packet Size	2222	97	—
Get Connection List from Object	2222	23	31
Get Internet Address	2222	23	26
Get Login Key	2222	23	23
Get Object Connection List	2222	23	27
Get Station Number	2222	19	—
Get Station's Logged Information	2222	23	28
Keyed Object Login	2222	23	24
Login Object	2222	23	20
Logout	2222	25	—
Negotiate Buffer Size	2222	33	—
Request Being Processed	9999	—	—
Request Processed	3333	—	—
Set Watchdog Delay Interval	2222	23	30
Extended Attribute Services			
Close Extended Attribute Handle	2222	86	01
Duplicate Extended Attributes	2222	86	05
Enumerate Extended Attribute	2222	86	04

SERVICE	REQUEST TYPE	FUNCTION CODE	SUBFUNC- TION CODE
Read Extended Attribute	2222	86	03
Write Extended Attribute	2222	86	02
File/Directory Services			
Add Extended Trustee to Directory or File	2222	22	39
Add Trustee to Directory	2222	22	13
Add Trustee Set to File or Subdirectory	2222	87	10
Add User Disk Space Restriction	2222	22	33
Allocate Permanent Directory Handle	2222	22	18
Allocate Short Directory Handle	2222	87	12
Allocate Special Temporary Directory Handle	2222	22	22
Allocate Temporary Directory Handle	2222	22	19
Allow Task to Access File	2222	78	—
Close File	2222	66	—
Commit File	2222	61	—
Copy from One File to Another	2222	74	—
Create Directory	2222	22	10
Create File	2222	67	—

SERVICE	REQUEST TYPE	FUNCTION CODE	SUBFUNC- TION CODE
Create New File	2222	77	—
Deallocate Directory Handle	2222	22	20
Delete Directory	2222	22	11
Delete a File or Subdirectory	2222	87	08
Delete Trustee from Directory	2222	22	14
Delete Trustee Set from File or Subdirectory	2222	87	11
Erase File	2222	68	—
File Migration Request	2222	90	150
File Search Initialize	2222	62	—
File Search Continue	2222	63	—
Generate Directory Base and Volume Number	2222	87	22
Get Current Size of File	2222	71	—
Get Directory Disk Space Restriction	2222	22	35
Get Directory Entry	2222	22	31
Get Directory Information	2222	22	45
Get Directory Path	2222	22	01
Get Effective Directory Rights	2222	87	29
Get Effective Rights for Directory Entry	2222	22	42

TABLE 15.1
NCP Function Codes
(continued)

SERVICE	REQUEST TYPE	FUNCTION CODE	SUBFUNC-TION CODE
Get Extended Volume Information	2222	22	51
Get Full Path String	2222	87	28
Get Huge Name Space Information	2222	87	26
Get Name Space Directory Entry	2222	22	48
Get Name Space Information	2222	87	19
Get Name Spaces Loaded List from Volume Number	2222	87	24
Get Object Disk Usage and Restrictions	2222	22	41
Get Object Effective Rights for Directory Entry	2222	22	50
Get Path Name of a Volume-Directory Number Pair	2222	22	26
Get Path String from Short Directory Handle	2222	87	21
Get Sparse File Data Block Bit Map	2222	85	—
Get Volume Info with Handle	2222	22	21
Get Volume Info with Number	2222	18	—
Get Volume and Purge Information	2222	22	44
Get Volume Name	2222	22	06

SERVICE	REQUEST TYPE	FUNCTION CODE	SUBFUNC-TION CODE
Get Volume Number	2222	22	05
Map Directory Number to Path	2222	22	243
Modify File or Subdirectory DOS Information	2222	87	07
Modify Maximum Rights Mask	2222	22	04
Obtain File or Subdirectory Information	2222	87	06
Open Data Stream	2222	22	49
Open/Create File	2222	84	—
Open/Create File or Subdirectory	2222	87	01
Parse Tree	2222	90	00
Purge All Erased Files	2222	23	206
Purge Salvageable File	2222	87	18
Query Name Space Information Format	2222	87	23
Read from a File	2222	72	—
Recover Salvageable File	2222	87	17
Remove Extended Trustee from Directory or File	2222	22	43
Remove User Disk Space Restriction	2222	22	34
Rename Directory	2222	22	15
Rename File	2222	69	—

SERVICE	REQUEST TYPE	FUNCTION CODE	SUBFUNC- TION CODE
Rename or Move a File or Subdirectory	2222	87	04
Rename or Move	2222	22	46
Scan a Directory	2222	22	30
Scan Directory Disk Space	2222	22	40
Scan Directory for Trustees	2222	22	12
Scan Directory Information	2222	22	02
Scan File Information	2222	23	15
Scan File or Directory for Extended Trustees	2222	22	38
Scan File or Directory for Trustees	2222	87	05
Scan Salvageable Files	2222	87	16
Scan Volume's User Disk Restrictions	2222	22	32
Search for a File	2222	64	—
Search for a File or Subdirectory	2222	87	03
Search for a File or Subdirectory Set	2222	87	20
Set Directory Disk Space Restriction	2222	22	36
Set Directory Entry Information	2222	22	37
Set Directory Handle	2222	22	0

SERVICE	REQUEST TYPE	FUNCTION CODE	SUBFUNCTION CODE
Set Directory Information	2222	22	25
Set File Attributes	2222	70	—
Set File Extended Attribute	2222	79	—
Set File Information	2222	23	16
Set File Time Date Stamp	2222	75	—
Set Hugh Name Space Information	2222	87	27
Set Name Space Information	2222	87	25
Set Short Directory Handle	2222	87	09
Write to a File	2222	73	—
File Server Environment			
Allocate a Resource	2222	15	—
Check Console Privileges	2222	23	200
Clear Connection Number	2222	23	254
Deallocate a Resource	2222	16	—
Disable File Server Login	2222	23	203
Disable Transaction Tracking	2222	23	207
Down File Server	2222	23	211
Enable File Server Login	2222	23	204
Enable Transaction Tracking	2222	23	208
Get Connection's Open Files	2222	23	235

	SERVICE	REQUEST TYPE	FUNCTION CODE	SUBFUNC- TION CODE
TABLE 15.1 NCP Function Codes (continued)				
	Get Connection's Semaphores	2222	23	241
	Get Connection's Task Information	2222	23	234
	Get Connection Usage Statistics	2222	23	229
	Get Connections Using a File	2222	23	236
	Get Disk Channel Statistics	2222	23	217
	Get Disk Utilization	2222	23	14
	Get Drive Mapping Table	2222	23	215
	Get File Server Date and Time	2222	20	—
	Get File Server Description Strings	2222	23	201
	Get File Server Extended Misc Information	2222	23	245
	Get File Server Information	2222	23	17
	Get File Server LAN I/O Statistics	2222	23	231
	Get File Server Login Status	2222	23	205
	Get File Server Misc Information	2222	23	232
	Get File System Statistics	2222	23	212
	Get LAN Driver Configuration Information	2222	23	227

SERVICE	REQUEST TYPE	FUNCTION CODE	SUBFUNC- TION CODE
Get Logical Record Information	2222	23	240
Get Logical Records by Connection	2222	23	239
Get Network Serial Number	2222	23	18
Get Object's Remaining Disk Space	2222	23	230
Get Physical Record Locks by Connection and File	2222	23	221
Get Physical Record Locks by Connection and File	2222	23	237
Get Physical Record Locks by File	2222	23	238
Get Semaphore Information	2222	23	242
Get Transaction Tracking Statistics	2222	23	213
Get Volume Extended Miscellaneous Information	2222	23	246
Get Volume Information	2222	23	233
Read Disk Cache Statistics	2222	23	214
Read Physical Disk Statistics	2222	23	216
Send Console Broadcast	2222	23	253
Set File Server Date and Time	2222	23	202
Release a Resource	2222	23	252
Verify Serialization	2222	23	12

TABLE 15.1

NCP Function Codes
(continued)

SERVICE	REQUEST TYPE	FUNCTION CODE	SUBFUNCTION CODE
Message Services			
Broadcast to Console	2222	21	09
Check Pipe Status	2222	21	08
Close Message Pipe	2222	21	07
Disable Broadcasts	2222	21	02
Enable Broadcasts	2222	21	03
Get Broadcast Message	2222	21	01
Get Personal Message	2222	21	05
Log Network Message	2222	23	13
Open Message Pipe	2222	21	06
Send Broadcast Message	2222	21	10
Send Personal Message	2222	21	04
Print and Queue Services			
Close Spool File	2222	17	01
Create Spool File	2222	17	09
Delete Spool File	2222	17	05
Get Printer Status	2222	17	06
Get Printer's Queue	2222	17	10
Get Queue Jobs from Form List	2222	23	137
Scan Spool File Queue	2222	17	04
Set Spool File Flags	2222	17	02

	SERVICE	REQUEST TYPE	FUNCTION CODE	SUBFUNCTION CODE
TABLE 15.1 NCP Function Codes (continued)	Spool a Disk File	2222	17	03
	Write to Spool File	2222	17	00
	Queue Services			
	Abort Servicing Queue Job	2222	23	132
	Attach Queue Server to Queue	2222	23	111
	Change Job Priority	2222	23	130
	Change Queue Job Entry	2222	23	123
	Change Queue Job Position	2222	23	110
	Change to Client's Rights	2222	23	116
	Close a File and Start Queue Job	2222	23	127
	Create Queue	2222	23	100
	Create Queue Job and File	2222	23	121
	Destroy Queue	2222	23	101
	Detach Queue Server from Queue	2222	23	112
	Finish Servicing Queue Job	2222	23	131
	Get Queue Job File Size	2222	23	135
	Get Queue Job List	2222	23	129
	Read Queue Current Status	2222	23	125
	Read Queue Job Entry	2222	23	122

SERVICE	REQUEST TYPE	FUNCTION CODE	SUBFUNC- TION CODE
Read Queue Server Current Status	2222	23	134
Remove Job from Queue	2222	23	128
Restore Queue Server Rights	2222	23	117
Service Queue Job	2222	23	124
Set Queue Current Status	2222	23	126
Set Queue Server Current Status	2222	23	119
Synchronization Services			
Clear File	2222	07	—
Clear File Set	2222	08	—
Clear Logical Record	2222	11	—
Clear Logical Record Set	2222	14	—
Clear Physical Record	2222	30	—
Clear Physical Record Set	2222	31	—
Close Semaphore	2222	111	01
Examine Semaphore	2222	111	04
File Set Lock	2222	01	—
File Release Lock	2222	02	—
Lock File Set	2222	106	—
Lock Logical Record Set	2222	108	—
Lock Physical Record Set	2222	110	—

SERVICE	REQUEST TYPE	FUNCTION CODE	SUBFUNC- TION CODE
Log File	2222	105	—
Log Logical Record	2222	107	—
Log Physical Record	2222	109	—
Open/Create Semaphore	2222	111	00
Release File	2222	05	—
Release File Set	2222	06	—
Release Logical Record	2222	12	—
Release Logical Record Set	2222	13	—
Release Physical Record	2222	28	—
Release Physical Record Set	2222	29	—
Signal Semaphore	2222	111	03
Wait on Semaphore	2222	111	02
Transaction Tracking Services			
TTS Abort Transaction	2222	34	03
TTS Begin Transaction	2222	34	01
TTS End Transaction	2222	34	02
TTS Get Application Thresholds	2222	34	05
TTS Get Transaction Bits	2222	34	09
TTS Get Workstation Thresholds	2222	34	07
TTS Is Available	2222	34	00

	SERVICE	REQUEST TYPE	FUNCTION CODE	SUBFUNC-TION CODE
TABLE 15.1 NCP Function Codes (continued)	TTS Set Application Thresholds	2222	34	06
	TTS Set Transaction Bits	2222	34	10
	TTS Set Workstation Thresholds	2222	34	08
	TTS Transaction Status	2222	34	04
	NetWare Directory Services*			
	Close NDS Fragment	2222	104	03
	Return Bindery Context	2222	104	04
	Monitor NDS Connection	2222	104	05
	Ping for NDS NCP	2222	104	01
	Send NDS Fragmented Request/Reply	2222	104	02
	NetWare 4.x Statistical Information Services			
	Get Cache Information	2222	123	01
	Get File Server Information	2222	123	02
	NetWare File Systems Information	2222	123	03
	User Information	2222	123	04
	Packet Burst Information	2222	123	05
	IPX/SPX Information	2222	123	06
	Garbage Collection Information	2222	123	07

			SUBFUNC-TION
TABLE 15.1 NCP Function Codes (continued)			

SERVICE	REQUEST TYPE	FUNCTION CODE	SUBFUNC-TION CODE
CPU Information	2222	123	08
Volume Switch Information	2222	123	09
Get NLM Loaded List	2222	123	10
NLM Information	2222	123	11
Get Directory Cache Information	2222	123	12
Get Operating System Version Information	2222	123	13
Get Active Connection List by Type	2222	123	14
Get NLM Resource Tag List	2222	123	15
Active LAN Board List	2222	123	20
LAN Configuration Information	2222	123	21
LAN Common Counters Information	2222	123	22
LAN Custom Counters Information	2222	123	23
LSL Information	2222	123	25
LSL Logical Board Information	2222	123	26
Get Media Manager Object Information	2222	123	30
Get Media Manager Objects List	2222	123	31

TABLE 15.1

NCP Function Codes
(continued)

SERVICE	REQUEST TYPE	FUNCTION CODE	SUBFUNC- TION CODE
Get Media Manager Object Children's List	2222	123	32
Get Volume Segment List	2222	123	33
Active Protocol Stacks	2222	123	40
Get Protocol Stack Configuration Information	2222	123	41
Get Protocol Stack Statistics Information	2222	123	42
Get Protocol Stack Custom Information	2222	123	43
Get Protocol Stack Numbers by Media Number	2222	123	44
Get Protocol Stack Numbers by LAN Board Number	2222	123	45
Get Media Name by Media Number	2222	123	46
Get Loaded Media Number List	2222	123	47
Get General Router and SAP Information	2222	123	50
Get Network Router Information	2222	123	51
Get Network Routers Information	2222	123	52
Get Known Networks Information	2222	123	53
Get Server Information	2222	123	54

TABLE 15.1

NCP Function Codes
(continued)

SERVICE	REQUEST TYPE	FUNCTION CODE	SUBFUNC- TION CODE
Get Server Sources Information	2222	123	55
Get Known Servers Information	2222	123	56
Get Server Set Commands Information	2222	123	60
Get Server Set Categories	2222	123	61

* Refer to Chapter 20 for additional information on NDS NCP calls and a listing of NDS protocol verbs.

Sample NCP Communications

THE REMAINDER OF this chapter depicts a NetWare client and server communicating by using NCP requests and replies.

Attaching to a Netware Server

When a NetWare client loads the shell (NETX.COM), the first NCP call the client sends is a Create Service Connection, as shown in Figure 15.8. This NCP type number is 1111. The server replies, granting a connection if possible.

Packets 11 and 12 are the Negotiate Buffer Size NCP calls. In these packets, the client and server are exchanging the maximum packet size they may use. The client then issues a Logout NCP call to ensure that any previous connection it may have held open is closed. Finally, the client requests the file server information through a Get File Server Date and Time NCP.

FIGURE 15.8

The NetWare client launches NETX.COM.

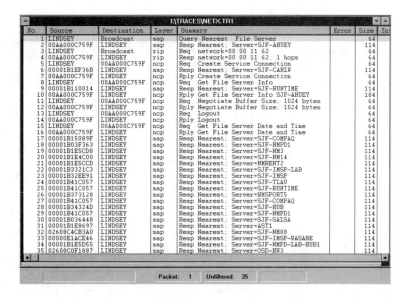

Logging Out of a Netware Server

Figure 15.9 shows a portion of the logout procedure. After typing **LOGOUT**, the server copies the contents of the LOGOUT.EXE file to the client. Packet 101 shows the Close File NCP request from the client. This indicates that the client has received the entire file.

In packets 103, 105, 107, and 111, the client issues NCPs requesting information regarding the station's bindery access level (privileges), object name (login name), and logged information. The station's logged information includes the object name (username) and the time and date the user logged on to the server.

Mapping a Network Drive Letter

When issuing the MAP command, the server downloads the entire MAP.EXE file to the local workstation's memory. In Figure 15.10 you can see a portion of the NCP calls that occur when you map a directory. Packet 176 shows the

FIGURE 15.9

The client issues the LOGOUT command.

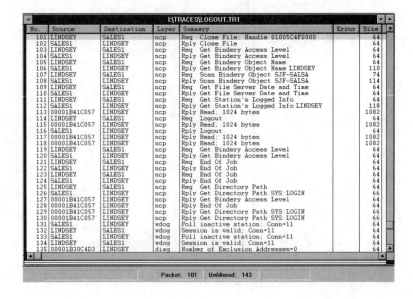

directory that is being mapped. The directory name is HOME/LCHAPPEL. When the client issues the Scan Directory Information request, the server returns information regarding the directory's creation date and time, the owner, and the access rights mask.

Launching a Program on the Server

When the client types a command to load an application that resides on the server, the communication follows three primary steps to download the application to the client:

1. Search for the file.

2. Download the file.

3. Download any supplementary files.

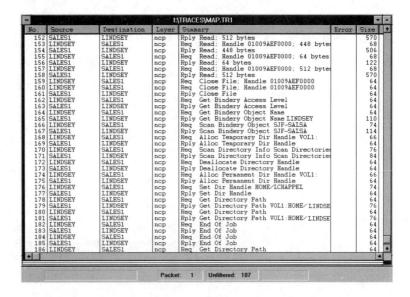

FIGURE 15.10

Mapping a NetWare
drive letter

In Figure 15.11, the client has typed **WP** to launch WordPerfect at her workstation. The Open File failures occurred because the file named WP is not located in the directory the client is presently in. As seen in packet 13, the shell next searches for the file WP.COM. Since this failed, it then searches for WP.EXE and, finally, WP.BAT. If Lindsay had executed the file by typing the entire file name, she would have made only one request—asking for the file by its full name.

Since the file is not located in the directory the user is in, the shell begins looking for the file through assigned search drives. In packet 25 you can see the shell searching in the EMAIL directory. The shell looks through all the search drives in order until it either finds the file and begins copying it to the local drive or cannot find the file and issues a "File Not Found" message.

In Figure 15.12, the shell has found the file in the HOME/LCHAPPEL/ APPS directory. Once the file has been found, the shell begins copying the file to the local workstation's memory.

In Figure 15.13 you can see supplemental files being copied to the workstation. Packets 934 and 936 depict the client reading the WPLAC}.SET file. This file contains the preferences for the user's WordPerfect environment.

FIGURE 15.11

The shell searches for the file named WP.

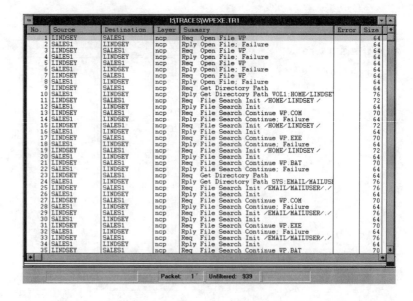

FIGURE 15.12

The file is copied to the client.

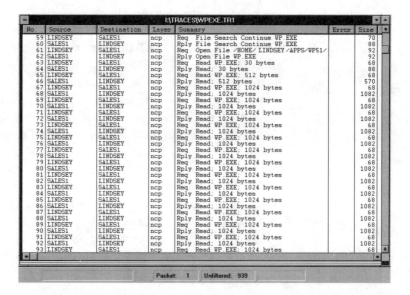

FIGURE 15.13

Any required
supplemental files are
also downloaded.

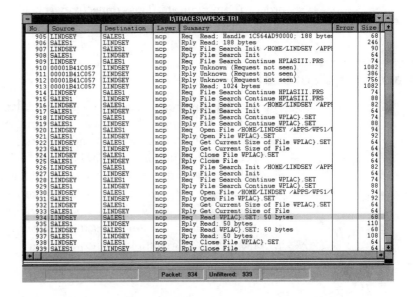

No.	Source	Destination	Layer	Summary	Error	Size
905	LINDSEY	SALES1	ncp	Req Read; Handle 1C564AD90000; 188 bytes		68
906	SALES1	LINDSEY	ncp	Rply Read; 188 bytes		246
907	LINDSEY	SALES1	ncp	Req File Search Init /HOME/LINDSEY /APPS		90
908	SALES1	LINDSEY	ncp	Rply File Search Init		64
909	LINDSEY	SALES1	ncp	Req File Search Continue HPLASIII.PRS		74
910	00001B41C057	LINDSEY	ncp	Rply Unknown (Request not seen)		1082
911	00001B41C057	LINDSEY	ncp	Rply Unknown (Request not seen)		386
912	00001B41C057	LINDSEY	ncp	Rply Unknown (Request not seen)		756
913	00001B41C057	LINDSEY	ncp	Rply Read; 1024 bytes		1082
914	LINDSEY	SALES1	ncp	Req File Search Continue HPLASIII.PRS		74
915	SALES1	LINDSEY	ncp	Rply File Search Continue HPLASIII.PRS		88
916	LINDSEY	SALES1	ncp	Req File Search Init /HOME/LINDSEY /APPS		82
917	SALES1	LINDSEY	ncp	Rply File Search Init		64
918	LINDSEY	SALES1	ncp	Req File Search Continue WPLAC}.SET		74
919	SALES1	LINDSEY	ncp	Rply File Search Continue WPLAC}.SET		88
920	LINDSEY	SALES1	ncp	Req Open File /HOME/LINDSEY /APPS/WP51/		94
921	SALES1	LINDSEY	ncp	Rply Open File WPLAC}.SET		92
922	LINDSEY	SALES1	ncp	Req Get Current Size of File WPLAC}.SET		64
923	SALES1	LINDSEY	ncp	Rply Get Current Size of File		64
924	LINDSEY	SALES1	ncp	Req Close File WPLAC}.SET		64
925	SALES1	LINDSEY	ncp	Rply Close File		64
926	LINDSEY	SALES1	ncp	Req File Search Init /HOME/LINDSEY /APPS		82
927	SALES1	LINDSEY	ncp	Rply File Search Init		64
928	LINDSEY	SALES1	ncp	Req File Search Continue WPLAC}.SET		74
929	SALES1	LINDSEY	ncp	Rply File Search Continue WPLAC}.SET		88
930	LINDSEY	SALES1	ncp	Req Open File /HOME/LINDSEY /APPS/WP51/		94
931	SALES1	LINDSEY	ncp	Rply Open File WPLAC}.SET		92
932	LINDSEY	SALES1	ncp	Req Get Current Size of File WPLAC}.SET		64
933	SALES1	LINDSEY	ncp	Rply Get Current Size of File		64
934	LINDSEY	SALES1	ncp	Req Read WPLAC}.SET; 50 bytes		68
935	SALES1	LINDSEY	ncp	Rply Read; 50 bytes		110
936	LINDSEY	SALES1	ncp	Req Read WPLAC}.SET; 50 bytes		68
937	SALES1	LINDSEY	ncp	Rply Read; 50 bytes		108
938	LINDSEY	SALES1	ncp	Req Close File WPLAC}.SET		64
939	SALES1	LINDSEY	ncp	Rply Close File		64

Packet: 934   Unfiltered: 939

Now let's examine some unique packets you are certain to find on your
network.

Special Packets on the Network

NETWARE LAN has special needs that are handled using some
unique packets that do not fit into the previously defined protocols. These unique packets include

- Watchdog packets

- Serialization packets

- Message packets

Up to this point you have seen how workstations communicate with
servers. However, it is necessary to maintain an active network connection in

order to communicate. This connectivity is held in check by NetWare's Watchdog protocol.

Watchdog Protocol

The Watchdog protocol provides constant validation of active workstation connections and notifies the NetWare operating system when a connection may be terminated as a result of lengthy periods without communicating.

When a workstation is logged in but is not being used, the Watchdog continuously questions the workstation to ensure that the connection is still valid. Workstations are queried according to their connection number, given during the login process. If a workstation does not transmit any packets to a server within 4 minutes 56.6 seconds (a settable parameter), a Watchdog packet will be transmitted to the station, as shown in Figure 15.14.

FIGURE 15.14

Watchdog queries include a station's connection number.

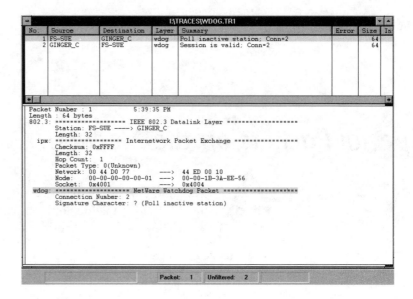

Watchdog Frame Format

As shown in Figure 15.15, only two fields are contained in a Watchdog packet after the IPX header: Connection Number and Signature Character.

FIGURE 15.15

Watchdog packet
structure

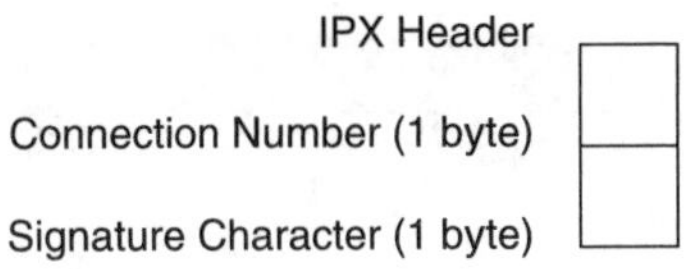

IPX Header

Connection Number (1 byte)

Signature Character (1 byte)

The Connection Number field indicates the connection number given to the station during the login process. The Signature Character field contains the value 0x3F (ASCII character ?), which is used to poll an inactive station.

If no response is received from the workstation, the server transmits ten additional Watchdog Query packets at 59.3-second intervals. If the workstation still does not respond, the server terminates the workstation's connection. It is possible to modify the Watchdog timings and retry count.

The Watchdog parameters are set at the NetWare 3.x and 4.x file server prompt, using the following syntax:

SET NUMBER OF WATCHDOG PACKETS=n

SET DELAY BETWEEN WATCHDOG PACKETS=n

SET DELAY BEFORE FIRST WATCHDOG PACKET=n

The number of Watchdog packets set defaults to 10 but can be set for 5 to 100 packets. The delay between Watchdog packets defaults to 59.3 seconds but can be set from 9.9 seconds up to 10 minutes 26.2 seconds. The delay before transmitting the first Watchdog packet defaults to 4 minutes 56.6 seconds but can be set from 15.7 seconds up to 20 minutes 52.3 seconds.

When an active workstation responds to the server, it sends a Watchdog Response packet indicating that the workstation connection is still in use. Figure 15.16 depicts a Watchdog Response packet.

NetWare 4.x servers can also display a console message reporting all Watchdog logouts. To enable this reporting feature, type

```
SET CONSOLE DISPLAY WATCHDOG LOGOUTS=ON
```

at the NetWare 4.x console.

FIGURE 15.16

Watchdog Response
packet

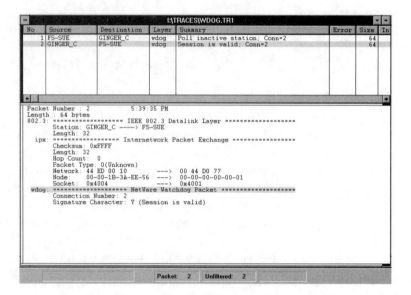

In the Signature Character field, the value 0x59 (ASCII Y) indicates that the connection is still valid although it hasn't transmitted data for the amount of time indicated in the Delay Before First Watchdog Packet parameter.

The Watchdog feature ensures that workstation connections are tested for validity if they have not transmitted recently. Definable parameters allow Net-Ware v3.x networks to determine how the Watchdog feature performs. If connections are a precious resource, the Watchdog feature can be tuned to be more aggressive and wait shorter periods of time before terminating a station's connection.

Serialization Packets

NetWare is sold in "per server" versions. Each version of NetWare can be loaded on only one file server. To ensure that a single version of NetWare is not being loaded on multiple servers, the operating system broadcasts copy-protection packets, called Serialization packets, to determine whether there are multiple copies of the same operating system on the network.

Serialization packets are 36 bytes in length (including the IPX header), as shown in Figure 15.17.

FIGURE 15.17

Serialization packets use IPX for transport.

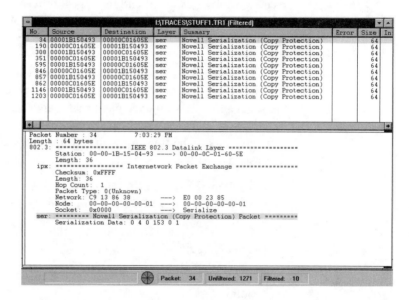

These Serialization packets are transmitted approximately every 66 seconds. Figure 15.18 shows the Serialization packet structure.

FIGURE 15.18

Serialization packet structure

IPX Header (Destination Socket 0x0457)

Serialization Data (6 bytes)

Serialization packets are transmitted to another file server's internal IPX address. Serialization packets contain only one field, the Serialization Data field. This information is used to notify other servers of the operating system serialization number. These packets are always addressed to the serialization socket number 0x0457.

If multiple servers use the same operating system, the servers will broadcast "Copyright violation" messages to all users.

Sending Messages

NetWare allows users to send messages from stations and the console to specific stations, groups, users, or the console. To the user, NetWare's messaging system appears to be a peer-to-peer operation, bypassing the NetWare server. It is not.

NetWare reserves a message buffer for each attached workstation. The console, however, displays the message received immediately. The buffer stores messages and notifies the recipient that a message is pending. Users receive a banner on their screen that displays the message sent to them.

Following are the steps for transmitting a message from a user named Jane to a user named Fred:

1. Send the message addressed to a user, group, or connection number: SEND "Backup at 7:00 P.M." to Fred [Enter].

2. Get Jane's login information and then scan the bindery for the login name "Fred."

3. Get Fred's connection number and transmit the message to his message buffer.

4. The server notifies Fred that he has a message waiting, and if Fred has not run CASTOFF, he requests the message from the server.

The packets shown in Figures 15.19 through 15.22 are seen when executing the preceding steps.

The Watchdog and Serialization packets are unique because they do not fit into the standard SAP, RIP, or NCP structure and format. NetWare's messaging is also unique in that it doesn't use the true NCP structure when notifying users that a message is waiting.

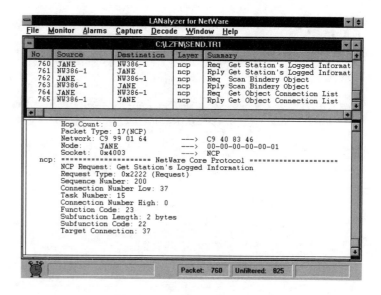

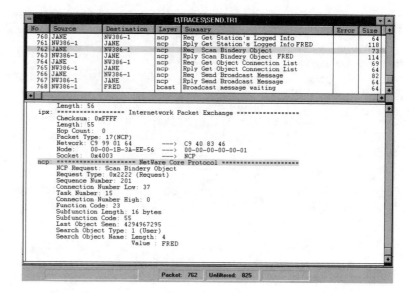

FIGURE 15.21

Transmit the message to
the server.

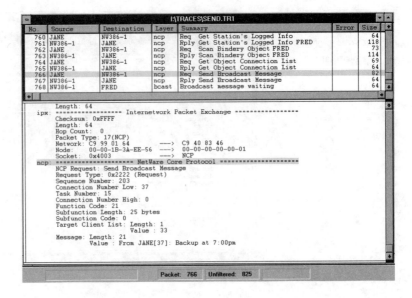

FIGURE 15.22

The server notifies Fred's
station of a message
waiting.

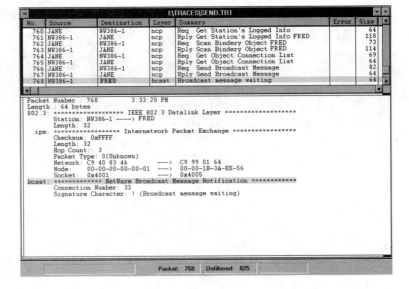

This chapter has defined the NCP header types, Read and Reply, and the Type field values used with NCP communications. You have viewed common NCP function and subfunction types for operations such as file reads, file writes, and logging in and out of a NetWare server.

The next chapter focuses on Novell's Burst Mode protocol, which increases the efficiency of file reads and writes.

Large Internet
Packet (LIP)
and Burst
Mode Protocol

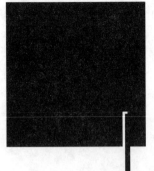

F YOU ARE using an older version of the NetWare shell (such as version 3.22), you may notice that your packets are only about 576 bytes long—even if your frame size is 1518 bytes. These older versions of the NetWare shell defaulted to a maximum of 576 bytes for all communications across a router. Imagine trying to transfer a relatively large file across a WAN link when only 576 bytes can be transferred at a time. This chapter briefly examines the functionality of Novell's Large Internet Packet (LIP) protocol, which allows you to utilize maximum frame sizes when communicating with a server across a router.

In Chapter 15, you learned that for every NCP request made by a workstation, an NCP reply is expected. This single-request/single-response (ping-pong) type of communication does not permit a multiple packet response from a single request from the client. For example, if you requested a large file from the server, you must submit a request for the first part of the file and wait for the response. After receiving the first response, you can ask for the second part of the file. Once you've received the second part, you request the third, and so on. It would be much more efficient if you could make your request once and receive a response of multiple packets in sequence without making another request.

The Burst Mode protocol was designed to make file reads and file writes more efficient. This chapter discusses the key benefits of Burst Mode and defines how to implement it. It also examines the Burst Mode communications using Novell's BNETX technology and VLM technology.

Finally, this chapter includes a listing of the changes that have been made to the NetWare client (NETX.COM). When you review the client history, you'll notice that additional functionality has been added to the shell with each revision and new NET.CFG parameters have been defined for Large Internet Packet and Burst Mode communications.

Large Internet Protocol (LIP)

I N NOVEMBER 1992, Novell released a new version of the shell (NETX) that dramatically enhanced performance by including the LIP capability. Prior to this version of the shell (version 3.31), workstations and servers were typically communicating at very small packet sizes (576 bytes)—even if the server and workstation negotiated a large packet size during the attachment process. The problem occurred when the workstation was creating an attachment to a server located on the other side of a router.

Figure 16.1 shows the typical attachment NCP calls used by a client and the corresponding reply by a NetWare server.

FIGURE 16.1

NetWare client attachment process

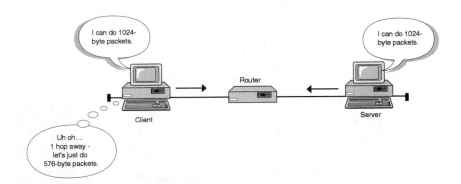

Initially, we see the client negotiating a maximum packet size of 1024 bytes. The server is on the other side of a router, but it responds with its maximum packet size, 1024 bytes. Earlier versions of the client (prior to version 3.31) looked at the Hop Count field in the IPX header of the server's response, and if the count was 1 or greater, packet sizes automatically dropped to a maximum of 576 bytes for all communications to that server.

Imagine trying to transfer files across a wide area network when you have to use 576-byte packets. Version 3.31 of the NetWare shell offered a tremendous improvement in performance by allowing clients and servers to use their maximum packet sizes for communications.

Next, we'll look at Novell's Burst Mode protocol implementation using BNETX and the VLMs.

Burst Mode Features

T HE BURST MODE protocol was designed to allow multiple responses to a single request for file reads and writes. Burst Mode increases the efficiency of client/server communications by allowing workstations to submit a single file read or write request and receive up to 64 kilobytes of data without submitting another request. The primary advantages of Burst Mode include the following:

- Large amounts of data can be transferred from a single request.

- Applications do not need to be "burst aware."

- A burst session is configured based on transmission success.

Figure 16.2 compares the performance increase of BNETX and the VLMs to the NETX shell.

FIGURE 16.2

Comparing BNETX and the VLMs to the NETX shell

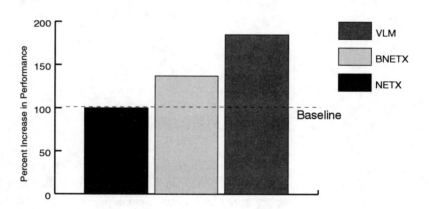

Transferring Large Amounts of Data from a Single Request

Using Burst Mode, a BNETX or VLM client makes a single file request of the server and can receive back up to 64K of data from that single request. This value is dependent on the capability of the client and network to support this large file transfer without receive congestion or lost packets.

Applications Do Not Need to Be Burst Aware

When a Burst Mode connection is established between a client and server, the workstation shell automatically uses the Burst Mode service whenever an application requests a read or write. Applications do not need to be adjusted to support Burst Mode.

The Burst Mode Session Is Based on Successful Transactions

BNETX and the VLMs increase in efficiency with each successful transaction. However, they handle this increased efficiency in different ways. In fact, there are many differences between the Burst Mode protocol implementation in BNETX and the VLMs.

BNETX Functionality

BNETX WAS RELEASED in February 1992 with the NetWare 3.26 shell. The promise of a more efficient, effective transfer of data was welcomed by all. Unfortunately, the Burst Mode BNETX shell fell short of expectations for many when it was credited with causing data corruption in some situations. Many people, however, the authors included, have used BNETX successfully and have been impressed by its performance.

Because so many people still use the BNETX shell, we have decided to give it some coverage before examining VLM-based Burst Mode communications.

BNETX enables clients and servers to read and write files using a Burst Mode window. The Burst Mode window is the number of unacknowledged bytes of data outstanding from a file read or write. The minimum window size is based on the maximum packet size allowed and the number of workstation packet burst buffers. In Figure 16.3, you are viewing a Burst Mode transaction where the window size is increasing from 7600 bytes to 7900 bytes per burst.

FIGURE 16.3

The BNETX Burst Mode window size increases based on successful transactions.

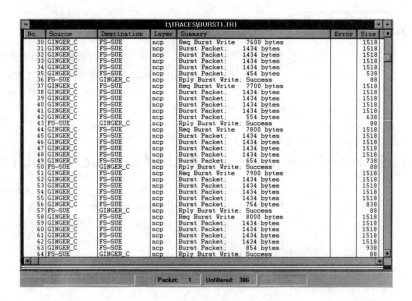

Implementing the Packet Burst Protocol with BNETX

Now let's look at how Burst Mode is implemented, beginning with the use of special client and server software.

In order to use BNETX Burst Mode protocol, both the client and server must be "burst enabled." NetWare 3.11 and earlier must have the Burst Mode NLM (PBURST.NLM) loaded at the server. Burst Mode has been integrated into NetWare 3.12 and NetWare 4.x.

Unless you are using the VLMs, the Burst Mode shell (BNETX.EXE) must be loaded at the workstation. In addition, clients must include a Burst Mode parameter in the NET.CFG file indicating the number of packet burst buffers available at the client:

pb buffers = n

This NET.CFG parameter denotes the number of packet receive buffers the workstation will allot to the packet burst. The variable n is a number between 0 and 10. If n is set to 0, Burst Mode is disabled. With BNETX, packet burst buffers are kept in conventional memory, even if the expanded or extended shell is loaded.

The packet size is negotiated when the Burst Mode shell requests a connection from a server. For example, on an Ethernet NetWare LAN, the client may negotiate a packet size of 1024 bytes. Therefore, each Burst Mode buffer requires 1126 bytes (the packet size plus the 102-byte Burst Mode header).

Initiating a **BNETX Burst Mode Connection**

When a client using the BNETX Burst Mode shell requests a connection to a Burst Mode enabled server, it negotiates the buffer size as usual and then requests a Packet Burst connection.

The Burst Mode connection NCP function number is 101 and does not require or use a subfunction code, as shown in Figure 16.4. When requesting the Burst Mode connection, the client states its maximum packet size, as well as the maximum send and receive size. If the server is Burst Mode enabled, it will respond with a Burst Mode Connection reply, as shown in Figure 16.5.

FIGURE 16.4

Burst Mode Connection request

```
                                          I:\TRACES\PBURST1.TR1
      Packet Number : 14            1:29:24 PM
      Length : 74 bytes
802.3: ================== IEEE 802.3 Datalink Layer ==================
      Station: GINGER_C ----> 00-00-1B-1E-CC-57
      Length: 56
  ipx: ================== Internetwork Packet Exchange ==================
      Checksum: 0xFFFF
      Length: 55
      Hop Count:  0
      Packet Type: 17(NCP)
      Network: 01 CA FF 03      --->  01 CA FF CB
      Node:    00-00-1B-1B-09-FB  --->  00-00-00-00-00-01
      Socket:  0x4013           --->  NCP
  ncp: ================== NetWare Core Protocol ==================
      NCP Request: Packet Burst Connection
      Request Type: 0x2222 (Request)
      Sequence Number: 2
      Connection Number Low: 5
      Task Number: 0
      Connection Number High: 0
      Function Code: 101
      Local Connection ID: 0x01272701
      Local Max Packet Size: 1500
      Local Target Socket: 0x4016
      Local Max Send Size: 268441600
      Local Max Receive Size: 268484608




                        Packet:  14   Unfiltered:  32
```

```
                                          I:\TRACES\PBURST1.TR1
Packet Number : 26              1:29:24 PM
Length : 64 bytes
802.3: ═════════════════ IEEE 802.3 Datalink Layer ══════════════════
        Station: FS-SUE ----> GINGER_C
        Length: 46
  ipx: ═════════════════ Internetwork Packet Exchange ═════════════════
        Checksum: 0xFFFF
        Length: 46
        Hop Count:  0
        Packet Type: 17(NCP)
        Network: 01 CA FF CA        --->  01 CA FF 03
        Node:    00-00-00-00-00-01  --->  00-00-1B-1B-09-FB
        Socket:  NCP                --->  0x4013
  ncp: ═════════════════ NetWare Core Protocol ═════════════════
        NCP Reply: Packet Burst Connection
        Reply Type: 0x3333 (Reply)
        Sequence Number: 2
        Connection Number Low: 4
        Task Number: 1
        Connection Number High: 0
        Completion Code: 0 (Success)
        Connection Status: 0x00
        Remote Target ID: 0x01000400
        Remote Max Packet Size: 1500




                                  Packet:  26    Unfiltered:  32
```

If, however, a BNETX client attempts to establish a Burst Mode connection with a server that is not Burst Mode enabled, the server will answer back with an indication that "No Such Property" exists, as shown in Figure 16.6.

```
                                          I:\TRACES\PBURST1.TR1
Packet Number : 15              1:29:24 PM
Length : 64 bytes
802.3: ═════════════════ IEEE 802.3 Datalink Layer ══════════════════
        Station: 00-00-1B-1E-CC-57 ----> GINGER_C
        Length: 38
  ipx: ═════════════════ Internetwork Packet Exchange ══════════════════
        Checksum: 0xFFFF
        Length: 38
        Hop Count:  0
        Packet Type: 17(NCP)
        Network: 01 CA FF CB        --->  01 CA FF 03
        Node:    00-00-00-00-00-01  --->  00-00-1B-1B-09-FB
        Socket:  NCP                --->  0x4013
  ncp: ═════════════════ NetWare Core Protocol ═════════════════
        NCP Reply: Packet Burst Connection
        Reply Type: 0x3333 (Reply)
        Sequence Number: 2
        Connection Number Low: 5
        Task Number: 1
        Connection Number High: 0
        Completion Code: 251 (No Such Property)
        Connection Status: 0x00




                                  Packet:  15    Unfiltered:  32
```

If the server does not allow Burst Mode file transfers, the communications will use the standard request/response method of NCP.

VLM *Burst Mode Functionality*

O NE MAJOR DIFFERENCE between the BNETX and VLM implementations of Burst Mode is the way the two executables handle windowing. As mentioned earlier, BNETX increases the window size based on successful communications.

The VLM versions 1.02 and earlier, however, adjust the Interpacket Gap (IPG)—the time between packets transmitted on the network—to increase the burst efficiency. VLM versions 1.03 and later adjust both the window size and the IPG.

The VLMs do not have a maximum window size limitation, as does BNETX. There are, however, default values for outstanding Burst Read packets (16) and Burst Write packets (10). The window size is calculated as follows:

Burst reads	Maximum number of reads × frame size
Burst writes	Maximum number of writes × frame size

How do the Burst read and Burst write defaults work? Let's assume a client wants to read a 56K file. On an Ethernet network, the workstation requests two windows of 16 packets (24K each) and one window of 6 packets (8K), for a total of 56K. On a Token Ring network that supports 4K packets, the workstation requests only one window of 14 packets, for a total of 56K.

How does the VLM use the IPG to optimize Burst Mode communications? The VLM first needs to determine the round-trip time to the destination. When establishing a connection to the server, the VLMs transmit multiple pings to the destination and determine the fastest round-trip time. One-half of this time becomes the maximum interpacket gap time.

In VLM versions 1.02 and earlier, the Burst Mode IPG begins at zero, and after a series of failures occurs, the IPG is increased until communications are successful or until the predetermined maximum IPG is reached.

In VLM versions 1.03 and later, the Burst Mode IPG begins at one-half of the maximum IPG time (or one-quarter of the fastest round-trip time determined in the ping session).

Implementing the Packet Burst Protocol with VLM.EXE

The VLMs enable the Burst Mode feature through the FIO.VLM (File Input/Output VLM). VLMs also enable Burst Mode through a "pb buffers =" statement in the NET.CFG file; however, this value is interpreted differently with the VLMs. As mentioned earlier in this chapter, BNETX uses this number to set aside buffer space. The VLMs, however, interpret the value 0 as Burst Mode disabled; any other number indicates that Burst Mode should be enabled.

The server that the VLM is communicating with must support Burst Mode. NetWare 3.12 and 4.x servers are enabled by default. If you are using a NetWare 3.11 server, you must load the PBURST.NLM to support Burst Mode.

In the next section, we'll examine the Burst Mode frame formats.

Burst Mode Frame Format

A S MENTIONED EARLIER in this chapter, when a Burst Mode client wishes to perform file reads or writes, the shell automatically uses Burst Mode services.

Burst Mode communications require an NCP Burst header after the IPX header and before the burst data, as shown in Figure 16.7.

The fields of the Burst Mode header are detailed in the following sections.

Request Type (2 bytes)

Flags (1 byte)

Stream Type (1 byte)

Source Connection ID (4 bytes)

Destination Connection ID (4 bytes)

Packet Sequence (4 byte)

Send Delay Time (usec) (4 byte)

Burst Sequence Number (2 bytes)

ACK Sequence Number (2 bytes)

Total Burst Length (4 bytes)

Burst Offset (4 bytes)

Burst Length (2 bytes)

Fragment List Entries (2 bytes)

Function (4 bytes)

File Handle (4 bytes)

Starting Offset (4 bytes)

Bytes to Write (4 bytes)

TYPE FIELD The Type field is the NCP Request/Reply Type field. When a client is using Burst Mode, the Type field will contain the value 0x7777, indicating that the packet is a burst packet.

FLAGS The flags available include the following:

Flag	Description
SYS	Setting this bit indicates that the burst is a system packet and does not have any burst data associated with it
SAK	This bit function is not currently implemented but will eventually be set to indicate that the sender would like the receiver to transmit its missing fragment list
EOB	Setting this bit indicates that this packet contains the last of the burst data that the sender will transmit
BSY	This field is not currently implemented but will eventually notify a requester that the server is busy and it should wait
ABT	Setting this bit indicates to the client that the session is no longer valid

STREAM TYPE The stream type is used by the server, and the only current value is 0x02, which indicates "Big send burst."

SOURCE CONNECTION ID The source connection ID is a random number that is generally formed from the current time of day and provides a unique identifier for a burst connection. This number is generated by the sender and cannot contain the value 0.

DESTINATION CONNECTION ID The destination connection ID is a random number similar to the source connection ID, but it is defined by the receiver. The value cannot be 0.

PACKET SEQUENCE NUMBER The packet sequence number tracks the current burst transaction and is incremented by 1 for every new packet a node transmits in each service transaction.

SEND DELAY TIME The Send Delay Time field identifies the delay time between each of the sender's packet transmissions and is specified in units of approximately 100 microseconds.

Burst Sequence Number

All replies in response to a single request are members of a burst set. Each packet in the set contains the same burst sequence number. When a client and server set up the burst connection, this sequence number is 0 and will increment with each successive burst sent.

ACK SEQUENCE NUMBER The ACK sequence number is the burst sequence number the node expects to receive next; it determines whether the last burst transmitted was successfully received.

All packets of a burst set will have the same burst sequence and ACK sequence number until the last packet of the burst set. The last packet will contain an ACK sequence number equal to the current burst sequence number plus 1. This indicates the number of the next burst sequence expected.

TOTAL BURST LENGTH The Total Burst Length field defines the length of the entire burst transaction (in actual data bytes). This will be the sum of all burst sets.

BURST OFFSET The burst offset field defines where in the burst this packet's data will fit. If the offset is 0, this is the first packet of the burst transaction.

BURST LENGTH The Burst Length field specifies the total length of the burst being transmitted (in bytes).

FRAGMENT LIST ENTRIES The Fragment List Entries field defines the number of elements missing from the burst transaction. The missing fragment list will follow this number, if applicable. The value 0 indicates that there are no missing fragments.

FUNCTION The Function field defines whether the current burst transaction is a read or write.

Analyzing the Benefits of Burst Mode

THE FOLLOWING SESSION was captured using the LANalyzer for Windows. A workstation using the Burst Mode shell (BNETX) has connected to a server that has Burst Mode enabled.

In this example, a large file write has been requested, copying the contents of the local drive, C, up to the file server. This is illustrated in Figure 16.8.

FIGURE 16.8

Burst Mode file write session

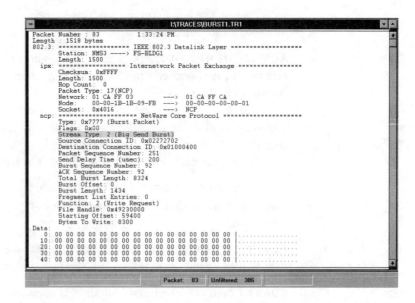

```
                                      I:\TRACES\BURST1.TR1
Packet Number : 83              1:33:24 PM
Length : 1518 bytes
802.3: ================= IEEE 802.3 Datalink Layer ==================
          Station: NMS3 ----> FS-BLDG1
          Length: 1500
   ipx: ================ Internetwork Packet Exchange =================
          Checksum: 0xFFFF
          Length: 1500
          Hop Count: 0
          Packet Type: 17(NCP)
          Network: 01 CA FF 03       ---> 01 CA FF CA
          Node:    00-00-1B-1B-09-FB ---> 00-00-00-00-00-01
          Socket:  0x4016            ---> NCP
   ncp: ================= NetWare Core Protocol =====================
          Type: 0x7777 (Burst Packet)
          Flags: 0x00
          Stream Type: 2 (Big Send Burst)
          Source Connection ID: 0x02272702
          Destination Connection ID: 0x01000400
          Packet Sequence Number: 251
          Send Delay Time (usec): 200
          Burst Sequence Number: 92
          ACK Sequence Number: 92
          Total Burst Length: 8324
          Burst Offset: 0
          Burst Length: 1434
          Fragment List Entries: 0
          Function: 2 (Write Request)
          File Handle: 0x49230000
          Starting Offset: 59400
          Bytes To Write: 8300
Data:
   0: 00 00 00 00 00 00 00 00 00 00 00 00 00 00 00 00   |...............
  10: 00 00 00 00 00 00 00 00 00 00 00 00 00 00 00 00   |...............
  20: 00 00 00 00 00 00 00 00 00 00 00 00 00 00 00 00   |...............
  30: 00 00 00 00 00 00 00 00 00 00 00 00 00 00 00 00   |...............
  40: 00 00 00 00 00 00 00 00 00 00 00 00 00 00 00 00   |...............

                              Packet: 83    Unfiltered: 386
```

Figure 16.9 shows a Burst Mode Write request from the workstation labeled NMS3 to the server named FS-BLDG1.

FIGURE 16.9

Burst Mode Write request

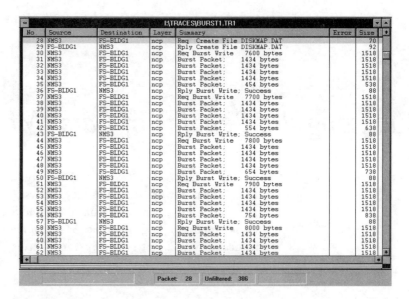

```
                                      I:\TRACES\BURST1.TR1
No.  Source     Destination   Layer  Summary                          Error  Size
 28  NMS3       FS-BLDG1      ncp    Req  Create File DISKMAP.DAT               70
 29  FS-BLDG1   NMS3          ncp    Rply Create File DISKMAP.DAT               92
 30  NMS3       FS-BLDG1      ncp    Req Burst Write   7600 bytes             1518
 31  NMS3       FS-BLDG1      ncp    Burst Packet;    1434 bytes             1518
 32  NMS3       FS-BLDG1      ncp    Burst Packet;    1434 bytes             1518
 33  NMS3       FS-BLDG1      ncp    Burst Packet;    1434 bytes             1518
 34  NMS3       FS-BLDG1      ncp    Burst Packet;    1434 bytes             1518
 35  NMS3       FS-BLDG1      ncp    Burst Packet;     454 bytes              538
 36  FS-BLDG1   NMS3          ncp    Rply Burst Write; Success                 88
 37  NMS3       FS-BLDG1      ncp    Req Burst Write   7700 bytes             1518
 38  NMS3       FS-BLDG1      ncp    Burst Packet;    1434 bytes             1518
 39  NMS3       FS-BLDG1      ncp    Burst Packet;    1434 bytes             1518
 40  NMS3       FS-BLDG1      ncp    Burst Packet;    1434 bytes             1518
 41  NMS3       FS-BLDG1      ncp    Burst Packet;    1434 bytes             1518
 42  NMS3       FS-BLDG1      ncp    Burst Packet;     554 bytes              638
 43  FS-BLDG1   NMS3          ncp    Rply Burst Write; Success                 88
 44  NMS3       FS-BLDG1      ncp    Req Burst Write   7800 bytes             1518
 45  NMS3       FS-BLDG1      ncp    Burst Packet;    1434 bytes             1518
 46  NMS3       FS-BLDG1      ncp    Burst Packet;    1434 bytes             1518
 47  NMS3       FS-BLDG1      ncp    Burst Packet;    1434 bytes             1518
 48  NMS3       FS-BLDG1      ncp    Burst Packet;    1434 bytes             1518
 49  NMS3       FS-BLDG1      ncp    Burst Packet;     654 bytes              738
 50  FS-BLDG1   NMS3          ncp    Rply Burst Write; Success                 88
 51  NMS3       FS-BLDG1      ncp    Req Burst Write   7900 bytes             1518
 52  NMS3       FS-BLDG1      ncp    Burst Packet;    1434 bytes             1518
 53  NMS3       FS-BLDG1      ncp    Burst Packet;    1434 bytes             1518
 54  NMS3       FS-BLDG1      ncp    Burst Packet;    1434 bytes             1518
 55  NMS3       FS-BLDG1      ncp    Burst Packet;    1434 bytes             1518
 56  NMS3       FS-BLDG1      ncp    Burst Packet;     754 bytes              838
 57  FS-BLDG1   NMS3          ncp    Rply Burst Write; Success                 88
 58  NMS3       FS-BLDG1      ncp    Req Burst Write   8000 bytes             1518
 59  NMS3       FS-BLDG1      ncp    Burst Packet;    1434 bytes             1518
 60  NMS3       FS-BLDG1      ncp    Burst Packet;    1434 bytes             1518
 61  NMS3       FS-BLDG1      ncp    Burst Packet;    1434 bytes             1518
 62  NMS3       FS-BLDG1      ncp    Burst Packet;    1434 bytes             1518

                              Packet: 28    Unfiltered: 386
```

The first packet in this trace is a request from the workstation, NMS3, to the server, FS-BLDG1, to create a file named DISKMAP.DAT. This is the file that will next be copied up to the server—you are viewing the 28th packet in the trace.

After the server replies that the file has been created successfully, the workstation begins the file transfer, allowing a total of 7600 bytes transmitted to be outstanding (without acknowledgment). As each transfer proceeds successfully, the number of outstanding bytes increments by 100 throughout the burst transaction.

History of the NetWare Shell

THE NETWARE NETX.COM file has undergone numerous changes since its release in May 1990. Novell has maintained a file called HISTORY.DOC that lists all changes implemented in the shell since its release. When you download a new version of the shell from NetWire, Novell's forum structure on CompuServe, this file is generally included as a Word for Windows document in the new shell software. Additional DOC files list changes that have been made to the VLM-based DOS Requester as well.

The following sections describe changes that have been made to the shell between May 1990 and June 1993. Information regarding more recent changes to the shell can be found in a DOC file with the workstation software.

Shell v3.01 Rev A

The initial release of the v3.01 shell files (5-8-90) forms the beginning of the DOS shell history file. The release included the following files:

NETx.COM

EMSNETx.COM

XMSNETx.COM

Shell v3.01 Rev B

The second release of the v3.01 shell (6-6-90) corrected a problem with the Rev A shell in which loading SiteLock by Brightworks would fail, thus causing the DOS workstation to hang. The release included the following files:

NETx.COM

EMSNETx.COM

XMSNETx.COM

Shell v3.01 Rev C

The NetWare DOS Shell v3.01 Rev C was made available only to NetWare developers and included the following files:

NETx.COM

EMSNETx.COM

XMSNETx.COM

(These changes were all incorporated into the Rev D release dated 9-7-90.) V3.01 Rev C corrected the following problems with the Rev B shell:

- Using the Preferred Server option with the Rev B shell caused the network response time to be functionally slower than if the user did not use this option.

- When using DOS 4.0 with the EMSNETx and XMSNETx shells, the DOS directories would not display correctly under Windows.

- The enhanced memory shells were not sending header information when using print job configurations that included escape codes. For example, a print job that should have printed landscape printed using the default mode (portrait).

- When printing to a captured LPT device, a "Device not ready" error message appeared. A retry allowed the job to continue.

- Fake roots were being deleted on paths with volume names before the path was determined valid; for example, CD PRN: would delete the fake root.

- On NetWare v2.x-based servers, memory in Dynamic Memory Pool 1 (DMP 1) was not being released properly with the XMSNETx and EMSNETx shells, eventually causing the server to hang. With the v3.01 Rev C shell, the memory is released when the user exits the Windows DOS prompt.

Shell v3.01 Rev D

The NetWare DOS shell v3.01 Rev D (9-7-90), was released to users and contains all the changes listed above for the Rev C shell.

Another release of the Rev D shell occurred on 9-18-90 and included the following files:

NETx.COM

EMSNETx.COM

XMSNETx.COM

This release corrected the following problems:

- When running the v3.01 Rev D shell with a NetWare v2.15 or previous OS, external program execution from the login script (using the # command) did not work unless the user had Open privileges at the volume root.

- The NVER command returned Rev C instead of Rev D.

Shell v3.01 Rev E

Rev 8 of the shell (11-27-90) included the following files:

NETx.COM

EMSNETx.COM

XMSNETx.COM

This revision corrected the problems and added the enhancements listed here:

- When using the DOS 4.0 "TrueName" command (an undocumented DOS command), invalid data was returned to the shell. This invalid data caused Emerald's System's backup to function improperly.

- Microsoft Link was reporting a scratched file error when linking a large number of files.

- The rename function returned the wrong error code to applications such as Platinum Accounting by Advanced Business Microsystems. This error was also exhibited with the NETGEN message "Cannot find DRVRDATA.DAT."

- The shell was not correctly maintaining the default server after logout when an X.25 bridge was used.

- On ELS NetWare servers, you would get one less connection than the maximum when using remote boot. The v3.01 Rev E shell allows the maximum number of server connections.

- This release enabled file caching in EMSNETx and XMSNETx shells; file caching was not enabled in earlier releases of the enhanced memory shells.

- It added support for the VERSION.EXE utility.

- It added the "/?" option to the command line, to display version and usage information.

- It added a feature that informs the user if a terminate-and-stay-resident (TSR) program is loaded above the shell when the user is trying to unload the shell.

Shell v3.02

Version 3.02 of the NetWare DOS shell (2-6-91) included the following files:

NETx.COM

EMSNETx.COM

XMSNETx.COM

This release contained the following fixes and enhancements:

- It corrected a problem that caused some applications that use EMS or XMS (such as DESQview, NetRemote, and so on) to occasionally hang when using the enhanced memory shells.

- It corrected a problem where capturing to a file would result in truncated print files.

- Unloading the shell now relinquishes all connections. (Previously, it retained one connection.)

- This release corrected a problem with the file caching introduced with the NetWare shell v3.01 Rev E. Users were experiencing problems when running Paradox, Quattro, and Lotus 1-2-3 with the extended memory shells.

- It enhanced the speed of file caching, which improves the speed of file read and writes.

- Setting the parameter "CACHE BUFFERS = 0" in the NET.CFG file now turns off the shell's file caching.

- It added two new NET.CFG parameters, DOS NAME and ENVIRONMENT PAD.

DOS NAME = NAME The DOS NAME = *name* option specifies the name of the DOS version used by the workstation. This name could be something like MSDOS, PCDOS, or DRDOS and should correspond to the %OS name in the login script and the name of the DOS directory. The maximum length of the DOS NAME is five characters.

ENVIRONMENT PAD = NUMBER The ENVIRONMENT PAD = *number* option specifies the number of bytes that can be added to the DOS environment space for storing search drive path names. If you are specifying many long path names for search drives with the MAP command, you may need to add extra environment space to hold those names. The number of bytes can be anywhere from 17 to 512 (17 is the default). Novell recommends that you leave this option at the default value unless you are encountering environment space problems.

Shell v3.10

Version 3.10 of the NetWare DOS shell (3/7/91) included the following files:

NETx.COM

EMSNETx.COM

XMSNETx.COM

The new NET5.COM, XMSNET5.EXE, and EMSNET5.EXE files work with DOS 5.0.

Shell v3.21

Starting with the v3.21 (7-18-91) release of the NetWare DOS shell, the same three files—NETX.COM, XMSNETXEXE, and EMSNETXEXE—work with DOS 3.x, 4.x, and 5.x. This is the so-called "generic" shell.

In addition, the v3.21 shell contained the following corrections and enhancements:

- It fixed a problem with the Preferred Server function that caused some machines to hang randomly.

- It fixed a problem with being denied simultaneous access to a shared file.

- It corrected "call 5" functions for programs ported from CP/M to DOS.

- It resolved a problem where Btrieve files were being corrupted when the server was downed improperly.

- It fixed a cache problem that was causing a WordPerfect disk-full error.

- It fixed the DOS NAME parameter problem that was causing the EMS and XMS shells to hang when loading.

- It fixed the problem with the P_STATION variable's returning bad information in the login script. (This problem occurred only with the v3.2 shell.)

- It fixed a problem that was causing DOS 5.0 "Load High" not to work properly with NET5.COM. (DOS "Load High" works with NETX.COM v3.21 and later.)

- It fixed a problem that caused the DOS 5.0 MEM program to display program names improperly after the shell was loaded.

- It fixed a problem that made the DOS ATTRIB command unable to find hidden directories on network drives.

- It fixed a problem with improper remote booting on workstations with hard drives.

- It added the /C = *filename* option to allow flexible naming of the shell configuration file (for instance, /C NET.CFG).

- It added the /F option to allow the shell to be unloaded after it has been loaded high.

- It added a date code to the shell. The command

  NETX i

  now displays the shell's date of creation along with the version and copyright information.

- It added a feature to display the version of DOS that is currently running when the shell is loaded.

- It enhanced the shell to be able to locate the master environment, regardless of its location.

- It added support for EMS memory handle names.

- It added support for international date and time formats.

Shell v3.22

V3.22 of the NetWare DOS shell (7-31-91) corrected a problem with remote boot and DOS 5.0. Previously, the shell looked to the F drive rather than the A (virtual) drive. This release included the following files:

NETX.COM

EMSNETX.EXE

XMSNETX.EXE

Shell v3.26

V3.26 of the NetWare DOS shell (2-11-92) included the following files:

NETX.COM

BNETX.COM

EMSNETX.EXE

XMSNETX.EXE

BNETX.COM is the new Burst Mode (Packet Burst) shell. This version incorporated the following corrections and enhancements:

- It corrected a problem where CAPTURE would return "garbage" characters to the screen when capturing without a specified queue name.

- It corrected a problem in which COMSPEC was not being reset to the local drive when the shell was unloaded with COMSPEC set to a network drive.

- It corrected a problem where the MS-DOS DOSNAME was not working properly with EMSNETX.EXE and XMSNETX.EXE.

- It corrected a problem with certain database applications that issue the Commit File command. (The file is now properly updated on the file server disk.)

- It corrected network errors resulting from a packet size negotiation problem. This problem occurred when using the Preferred Server option on a workstation with a packet size greater than that of the preferred server, when the initial server also had a packet size greater than the preferred server.

- It enhanced the shell so memory display applications such as the MS-DOS MEM program displayed the name of the shell, as well as its size and location.

- It added a procedure to check whether the total of "FILE HANDLES=" in NET.CFG and "FILES=" in CONFIG.SYS exceeds 254. If so, an error is returned and the shell is not loaded.

- It added two new NET.CFG parameters: SEARCH DIR FIRST and NCP TIMEOUT FLAG

SEARCH DIR FIRST = ON/OFF The SEARCH DIR FIRST option determines the order in which the shell searches files and directories on a NetWare file server. If SEARCH DIR FIRST = ON, the shell searches for directories first. If SEARCH DIR FIRST = OFF, the shell searches for files first. The default is OFF.

SEARCH DIR FIRST applies only to handle-oriented directory searches, as from within the Windows File Manager, not to FCB directory searches, as in DOS's DIR command.

NCP TIMEOUT OPTIONS The NCP TIMEOUT options add the ability to change the default timeout value of the shell. Three options need to be set:

NCP TIMEOUT FLAG = ON (default is OFF)

NCP TIMEOUT BASE = n (default is 10; range is 1–255)

NCP TIMEOUT MULTIPLIER = n (default is 4; range 1–255)

If only NCP TIMEOUT FLAG = ON is set, the shell uses the default values for the NCP timeout base and multiplier. Setting the base and multiplier lower than these default values reduces the shell's timeout. Setting the values too low will cause an excessive number of network errors.

Increasing the base by increments of 1 increases the NCP timeout by 1 tick. The shell multiplies the NCP TIMEOUT BASE number by the value set for NCP TIMEOUT MULTIPLIER. The result should not exceed 255.

The NCP timeout option was added for unusual circumstances and may cause unpredictable results when used incorrectly! Novell recommends that these values not be changed from the defaults except in special circumstances.

Shell v3.30

V3.30 of the NetWare DOS client software was not released. The following files were included:

NETX.EXE

BNETX.EXE

EMSNETX.EXE

XMSNETX.EXE

The changes and enhancements detailed in this section were all incorporated into the v3.31 release dated 11-12-92.

V3.30 of the shell incorporates the following significant enhancements that enable it to work with upcoming products such as SFT Level III and NetWare v4.0. (A v3.30 client can attach to a NetWare v4.0 server, but the shell does not support any Directory Services functionality.)

- The v3.30 shell has been language enabled so that all initialization and run-time messages are accessed from the NETX.MSG file. This file must be located in the same directory as NETX.EXE.

- NETX and BNETX are now .EXE files. This makes it easier to load them high, since the message file is appended and doesn't affect the load image size. It now takes a 60K contiguous upper memory block (UMB) to load NETX.EXE high.

*If *NETX.COM files reside in the same directory as *NETX.EXE files, users must rename or remove the *.COM files to be able to run the *.EXE files.*

- This version fixed the shell to allow it to be unloaded when it has been loaded into a UMB.

- It modified the shell so it can correctly handle double-byte and foreign characters in path and file names, and it removed support for the SPECIAL UPPERCASE keyword in NET.CFG.

- It enhanced the shell to handle broadcast messages that, when translated, are longer than the current maximum 22-character clear text message. When the user presses Ctrl+Enter, the remainder of the message is displayed.

- It enhanced the shell so that broadcast messages are always displayed at the bottom of the screen. The shell now reads the number of active display rows before displaying the broadcast message.

- It enhanced the shell's ability to adapt to network changes by renegotiating packet size when a router or an SFT III mirrored server goes down.

- It added Large Internet Packet (LIP) capability for routers that are enabled for large packets. (Refer to the documentation that accompanies the LIP software.)

- In light of Novell's change of the default Ethernet frame type from 802.3 to 802.2, this release added support for IPX checksumming on 802.2 frames.

- It changed how the shell looks for its configuration file:

    1. It first looks for a NET.CFG file in the current working directory.

    2. If no NET.CFG file is found, it looks for this file in the directory the LSL was loaded from, or in the current working directory at the time the LSL was loaded, in that order.

    3. If a NET.CFG file is still not found, it looks for a SHELL.CFG file in the current working directory.

- This release fixed a memory allocation error caused when the ENVIRONMENT PAD variable in NET.CFG was set below the minimum of eleven decimals.

- It fixed a problem where the shell was printing out the "Pipe not found in transient portion of COMMAND.COM" warning when the shell had already patched the pipe string. It now prints the warning only if the shell couldn't find a pipe string, either modified or not.

- It fixed a bug that was causing the shell, when used with IPXODI, to hang after receiving a broadcast.

- It fixed a problem where the shell was changing the value of the stack pointer without disabling interrupts first, which caused occasional lock-ups.

Shell v3.31

The 3.31 release of the NetWare DOS client software (11-12-92) supports the NCP Packet Signature security enhancement for NetWare v3.11. This release included the following files:

NETX.EXE

BNETX.EXE

EMSNETX.EXE

XMSNETX.EXE

It incorporated the following corrections and enhancements:

- It enhanced all shell files to perform NCP packet signing. This feature is enabled through the following NET.CFG setting:

  SIGNATURE LEVEL = n

  The default value for n is one, which means the client signs packets only if the server requests it. Other valid values are

0	Client does not sign packet
2	Client signs packets if the server is capable of signing
3	Client signs packets and requires the server to sign packets (or logging in will fail)

  Refer to the documentation file that comes with the security enhancement for more information.

- It added two new NET.CFG parameters to limit packet sizes:

  LI FRAME MAX = n

  This parameter sets the maximum frame size when using Large Internet Packet (LIP). The default is 8192 bytes (8K). The valid range for n is 512 to 16,384 bytes.

  PB FRAME MAX = n

  This parameter sets the maximum frame size when using Burst Mode (Packet Burst). The default is 2112 bytes. The valid range for n is 576 to 8256 bytes.

WARNING   *In almost all cases, the default values are the best ones to use. Only a qualified NetWare technician should change these parameters.*

- This version fixed a problem where the shell would not unload properly under DR DOS v6.0.

- It fixed several problems with the Burst Mode shell: a memory allocation bug; an incomplete write problem; and a timing problem that was manifest in various ways, including hanging under Windows.

Shell v3.32

The v3.32 release of the NetWare DOS client software (2-17-93) has been changed to include support for DOS versions 3.0 through 6.0. It includes the following files:

NETX.EXE

BNETX.EXE

EMSNETX.EXE

XMSNETX.EXE

Shell v3.32 PTF

The ptf (product temporary fix) version (06-24-93) includes the following files:

NETX.EXE

EMSNETX.EXE

XMSNETX.EXE

This version incorporates the following corrections and enhancements:

- Interrupt 21h function 40h errors were not being passed on to application. The shell was clearing the carry flag on write errors, causing an application to believe that no write error occurred.

- Interrupt 21h function 4B01h (load but do not execute) was causing the workstation to hang.

- The stack size was increased to accommodate the PRINT TAIL parameter in NET.CFG.

- Interrupt 21h function 4409h was returning incorrect values when run on a network drive.

- The shell was returning an incorrect print job number.

- If a section of a file was locked with int 21h–5Ch, and then another workstation accessed the same file and tried to read the locked area with int 21h–3Fh, it returned successful. This version of the shell fixes the problem.

On April 20, 1993, BNETX.EXE and PBURST.NLM were removed from DOSUP7.ZIP because of a rare problem resulting in data corruption when Burst Mode was being used.

This chapter has defined the key benefits of the Burst Mode protocol and examined a Burst Mode Connection request, Burst Mode Connection reply, and Burst Mode file write session. You have examined the key differences between BNETX and the VLM implementation of Burst Mode, and you have examined the response received when a Burst Mode client attempts to make a Burst Mode connection to a server that does not have Burst Mode enabled.

The next chapter examines NetWare's Service Advertising Protocol (SAP) and the newly developed NetWare Link Services Protocol (NLSP).

Service
Advertising
Protocol (SAP)

17

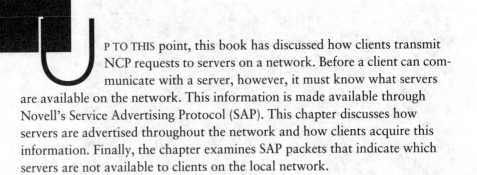

P TO THIS point, this book has discussed how clients transmit NCP requests to servers on a network. Before a client can communicate with a server, however, it must know what servers are available on the network. This information is made available through Novell's Service Advertising Protocol (SAP). This chapter discusses how servers are advertised throughout the network and how clients acquire this information. Finally, the chapter examines SAP packets that indicate which servers are not available to clients on the local network.

Throughout this chapter, the term "server" is used to identify service-oriented processes that may be running on a NetWare server, router, or workstation.

SAP Functionality

OVELL'S SAP SERVICES provide information on all the known servers throughout the entire internetwork. These servers can include file servers, print servers, NetWare access servers, remote console servers, and so on. Novell assigns a number to each server type. Many servers also have a name, assigned by the person installing or configuring the network. The server name and type number are advertised throughout the network and stored in each NetWare 2.x and 3.x server's bindery and each 4.x server's directory services database. The *bindery* is a NetWare 2.x and 3.x database of resources and clients on the network.

When a client requests information about available services, bindery-based servers use the information stored in their binderies to reply to the client, as shown in Figure 17.1.

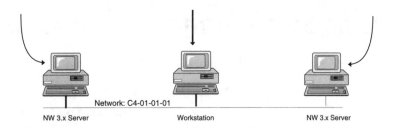

Server Name: SALES1
Server Type: 0x0004 (File Server)
Network: 0x99-00-00-01 (Internal IPX)
Node: 0x00-00-00-00-00-01

Server Name: MKTG-45
Server Type: 0x0004 (File Server)
Network: 0x88-00-00-01 (Internal IPX)
Node: 0x00-00-00-00-00-01

Server Name: PS01
Server Type: 0x0047 (Advertising Print Server)
Network: 0x99-00-00-01
Node: 0x00-00-00-00-00-01

Server Name: PS02
Server Type: 0x0047 (Advertising Print Server)
Network: C4-01-01-01
Node: 0x00-00-1B-09-81-3E

Server Name: MKTG-45
Server Type: 0x000107 (NetWare 386)
Network: 0x88-00-00-01
Node: 0x00-00-00-00-01

Network: C4-01-01-01

NW 3.x Server   Workstation   NW 3.x Server

The SAP packets use IPX for transport and are defined by the value 0x0452 in the Destination and Source Socket fields of the IPX header. As shown in Figure 17.2, you can find SAP information directly after the IPX header.

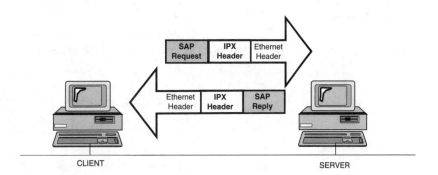

The three types of SAP packets that may be seen on a NetWare LAN are

- Periodic SAP information broadcasts

- SAP service queries

- SAP service responses

These three types of SAP packets enable up-to-date service information, as well as specific service address information, to be distributed throughout the network.

Periodic SAP Information Broadcasts

AS MENTIONED EARLIER, all servers maintain a list of available network services in their binderies. As shown in Figure 17.3, this list of services is broadcast onto locally attached networks to inform other servers and routers of network services available. Using this method, routers and servers maintain current information about network services.

FIGURE 17.3

Servers broadcast SAP packets onto all locally attached networks.

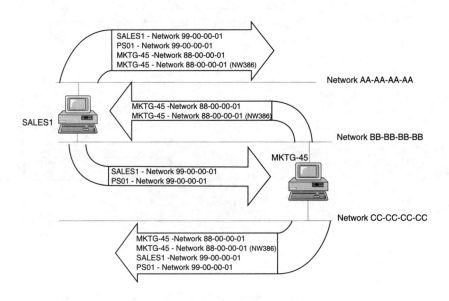

These SAP information packets are broadcast on the network every 60 seconds. They do not require a request packet before being transmitted. This differentiates SAP information broadcast packets from SAP Service Reply packets. Upon receipt of these information packets, servers update the service information contained in their binderies.

Figure 17.3 depicts how server information is propagated through an internetwork containing three separate Ethernet LANs. Server SALES1 is a file server with PSERVER.NLM loaded. This server will broadcast its services, NCP and print, on network AA-AA-AA-AA and network BB-BB-BB-BB every 60 seconds. Upon receipt of the packets, server MKTG-45 will update its bindery information and broadcast all known services onto network CC-CC-CC-CC. In that SAP broadcast, MKTG-45 will include services provided by SALES1 and its own available services, file and remote console (NetWare 386).

SAP information broadcast packets use the same structure as SAP response packets and are defined later in this chapter.

If 3 minutes pass and a server fails to broadcast SAP information, all routers and servers will assume the server is not available and remove the server from their binderies.

Each SAP information broadcast packet can contain information about up to seven servers. As shown in Figure 17.4, packets that contain information about more than one server repeat the Server Type, Server Name, Network Address, Node, Socket, and Intermediate Networks fields.

SAP Service Query

W HEN A WORKSTATION wishes to know about services available on the internetwork, it transmits a server query SAP. For example, a workstation transmits this packet when the shell (NETX.COM) is loaded in order to learn of available servers. The NetWare DOS Requester (VLM.EXE) transmits a SAP request to locate the nearest directory servers. If the VLM does not receive a response, it transmits a SAP request to locate the nearest file server. There is currently only one type of service query regularly observed on the network: the Nearest Service query.

FIGURE 17.4

SAP broadcasts can advertise up to seven servers per packet.

```
Packet Number : 151          11:48:28AM
Length : 498 bytes
802.3: =================== IEEE 802.3 Datalink Layer ===================
       Station: 00-00-0C-01-60-5E ----> FF-FF-FF-FF-FF-FF
       Length: 480
  ipx: =================== Internetwork Packet Exchange =================
       Checksum: 0xFFFF
       Length: 480
       Hop Count:  0
       Packet Type: 4(IPX)
       Network: DE AD BE EF          --->  DE AD BE EF
       Node:    00-00-1B-00-14-5E  --->  FF-FF-FF-FF-FF-FF
       Socket:  SAP                 --->  SAP
  sap: ============== NetWare Service Advertising Protocol =============
       Type: 2 (General Service Response)
       Server Name: IBM95
           Server Type: 0x0004 (File Server)
           Network: 84 07 00 95
           Node:    00-00-00-00-00-01
           Socket:  NCP
           Intermediate Networks: 2
       Server Name: MKTG-45
           Server Type: 0x0004 (File Server)
           Network: 88-00-00-01
           Node:    00-00-00-00-00-01
           Socket:  NCP
           Intermediate Networks: 2
       Server Name: SALES1
           Server Type: 0x0004 (File Server)
           Network: 99-00-00-01
           Node:    00-00-00-00-00-01
           Socket:  NCP
           Intermediate Networks: 2
       Server Name: ADMIN1
           Server Type: 0x0004 (File Server)
           Network: 00 20 82 73
           Node:    00-00-00-00-00-01
           Socket:  NCP
           Intermediate Networks: 2
       Server Name: SALES2
           Server Type: 0x0004 (File Server)
           Network: 00 20 82 83
           Node:    00-00-00-00-00-01
           Socket:  NCP
           Intermediate Networks: 2
       Server Name: BACKUP1
           Server Type: 0x0004 (File Server)
           Network: 00 10 86 51
           Node:    00-00-00-00-00-01
           Socket:  NCP
           Intermediate Networks: 2
       Server Name: ADMIN2
           Server Type: 0x0004 (File Server)
           Network: 00 10 02 22
           Node:    00-00-00-00-00-01
           Socket:  NCP
           Intermediate Networks: 2
```

Although contained in various technical documents, the General Service query is not currently implemented by Novell and is not discussed in detail in this chapter. The format for General Service Query packets is identical to that of the Nearest Service Query packets, except that the Service Type field contains the value 0×0001.

The Nearest Service query finds a particular server type on the network. For example, as shown in Figure 17.5, to find the nearest (most quickly responding) file server, NETX transmits a Nearest Service query for server type 0x0004.

FIGURE 17.5

A station uses a Nearest Service query to determine the nearest file server.

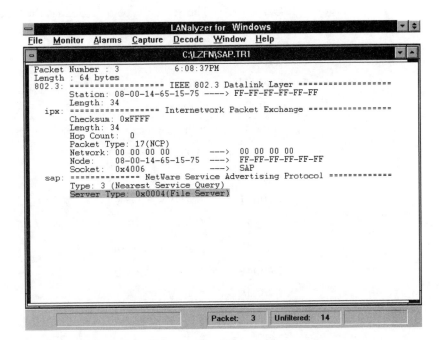

Contrary to popular belief, when a Nearest Service Query packet is transmitted, the station will receive responses from *each* server on the network that provides the service type requested by the client, not just the nearest one. As shown later in this chapter, you can use the Nearest Service query to build a list of available servers on the network.

The Nearest Service Query packet format is shown in Figure 17.6.

FIGURE 17.6

Service Query packet
format

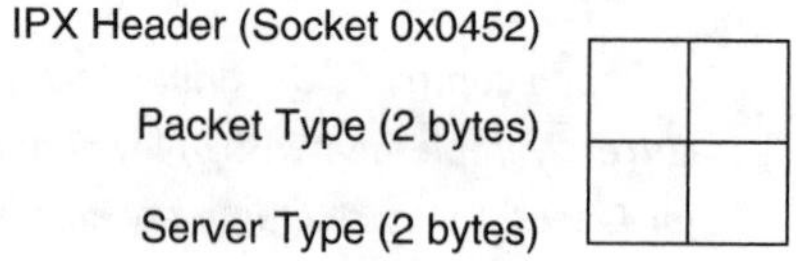

IPX Header (Socket 0x0452)

Packet Type (2 bytes)

Server Type (2 bytes)

PACKET TYPE The Packet Type field defines whether the packet is a General Service query or Nearest Service query. The packet type for the Nearest Service query is 0x0003. The packet type for the General Service query is 0x0001.

SERVER TYPE The Server Type field defines the type of service desired. The server types are defined by Novell and include the following:

Type	Description
0x0004	File server
0x0005	Job server
0x0007	Print server
0x0009	Archive server
0x000A	Job queue
0x0021	NAS SNA gateway
0x002E	Dynamic SAP
0x0047	Advertising print server
0x004B	Btrieve VAP 5.0
0x004C	SQL VAP
0x007A	TES—NetWare VMS
0x0098	NetWare access server
0x009A	Named Pipes server
0x009E	Portable NetWare—UNIX
0x0107	NetWare 386
0x0111	Test server

Type	Description
0x0166	NetWare management
0x026A	NetWare management
0x026B	Time synchronization
0x278	NetWare Directory server

So far, this chapter has described two of the three available types of Net-Ware SAP packets: SAP information broadcasts and service queries. The third type of SAP packet is service responses.

SAP Service Response Types

HERE ARE TWO types of service response packets: General Service responses (discussed earlier in this chapter) and Nearest Service responses. Both response types use the same format, as shown in Figure 17.7.

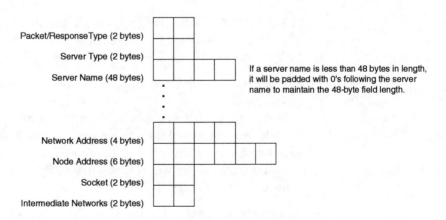

FIGURE 17.7

SAP Response packet format

Packet/ResponseType (2 bytes)
Server Type (2 bytes)
Server Name (48 bytes)

If a server name is less than 48 bytes in length, it will be padded with 0's following the server name to maintain the 48-byte field length.

Network Address (4 bytes)
Node Address (6 bytes)
Socket (2 bytes)
Intermediate Networks (2 bytes)

Note: SAP responses can contain information for up to seven servers by repeating the server type through Intermediate Networks fields in a single SAP response.

General Service responses are currently used only for the service information broadcasts. Each of these SAP responses can contain information about up to seven servers.

The Nearest Service Response packets are sent in reply to Nearest Service queries and can contain information about only one server—the server with the least number of intermediate networks that matches the server type in the SAP Service Query packet. For example, if a server contains bindery entries for three known servers, FS1, FS2, and FS3, that are located one, two, and three hops away, respectively, the server will report information only about the closest one, FS1.

SAP Service Response Packet Format

BOTH GENERAL AND Nearest Service responses use the same packet structure. The packets are differentiated within the Response Type field.

RESPONSE TYPE The Response Type field contains either 0x0002, for SAP General Service responses, or 0x0004, for Nearest Service responses.

SERVER TYPE The Server Type field identifies the type of service available. The server type numbers for responses are the same as the server types defined for queries.

SERVER NAME The Server Name field contains the object name of the server. This name can be up to 48 bytes long and must be unique within each server type. For example, you can have a print server (type 0x0047) and file server (type 0x0004) that have the name SALES1, but you cannot have two file servers named SALES1. NetWare server names are assigned when the operating system is configured or installed; print server names are defined within PCONSOLE.

NETWORK ADDRESS The network address is a 4-byte number that identifies the network address of the server listed.

NODE ADDRESS The node address number identifies the node address of the server. NetWare 3.x- and 4.x-based services will advertise 0x00-00-00-00-00-01 as the service node address.

SOCKET The Socket field identifies the socket number on which the server will receive all service requests. For example, a server type 0x0004 will receive NCP requests on socket 0x0451.

For additional information on socket numbers, refer to Chapter 14.

INTERMEDIATE NETWORKS The Intermediate Networks field identifies the number of routers between a server and the client (the hop count). Net-Ware 3.x-based servers will advertise NCP services with the value of 1 in the Intermediate Networks field when broadcasting on the local network. This is because of the internal IPX network upon which NCP services reside. The network extending from the LAN adapter is one hop away from the internal IPX LAN. (This concept is covered in more detail toward the end of this chapter.)

Monitoring Excessive SAP Traffic

A S NETWARE LANS expand to include additional servers, SAP traffic also increases. Since each server must transmit a server information broadcast every 60 seconds, a network with many servers will experience a large amount of SAP traffic.

If a server supports multiple frame types and IPX is bound to each, the server will SAP once for each logical LAN driver that is linked to IPX. A server may have to transmit more than one SAP packet if it has more than seven services in its server information tables.

Using a filtering mechanism, such as the NetWare MultiProtocol Router's SAP filter, you can restrict which services are advertised across routers throughout the internet. This technique reduces the overall SAP traffic. This filter may also restrict the servers a client can access, thus providing additional network security. Plan carefully before installing the SAP filter to ensure that users can still access all required servers. Third-party routers, such as Cisco routers, also offer the ability to filter SAP traffic on the network using an Access List. Novell has also released an IPX Router enhancement package on NetWire. Download the IPXRT3.EXE file to add SAP filtering capabilities to your NetWare 3.1x servers.

What about reducing the number of SAPs that cross a WAN link? Novell's NetWare MultiProtocol Router and some third-party routers can be configured to SAP on update only. This reduces the need for periodic broadcasts; SAP information crosses the WAN link only when changes on the network have occurred. Of course, you must ensure that each router is completely interoperable and that you use identical configurations on each router on each side of the WAN link.

Using the IPX Router enhancements (included with Novell's MPR and available on NetWire as IPXRT3.EXE), you can also change the number of SAP entries per SAP update packet. Currently, the SAP update packets only hold information about 7 or fewer servers. Why the limitation in size? They are little, itty-bitty packets, assuming that ARCnet is the media access method. You can use the INETCFG utility to increase the SAP packet size to the maximum frame size supported by your server or router. Don't worry about making a packet size that is too large to cross the entire internetwork. Remember, SAP packets are only handled by the local network—they do not need to cross routers. Routers will rebuild a new SAP update packet to forward onto other networks.

How can you determine the current number of SAPs on your network? Using the LANalyzer, you can create an application that tracks the number of packets using the value 0x0452 in the Socket fields of an IPX header.

> Novell's internal network was experiencing workstation timeouts because the network was constantly flooded with SAP traffic. This prompted Novell to create the FILTER.NLM, which provides for SAP filtering. The Novell SAP filter is now available only as a feature of Novell's MultiProtocol Router.

A single SAP packet can have one of the following socket designation combinations, depending on the type of SAP packet:

- Source socket 0x0452 and destination socket 0x0452 are used for service information broadcasts.

- Dynamically assigned source socket (in the range of 0x4001– 0x7FFF) and destination socket 0x0452 are used for Nearest Service Query broadcasts.

- Source sockets of 0x0452 and client-assigned destination sockets are used for Nearest Service responses.

You need to look at both source and destination sockets to ensure that you catch all SAP packets. Figure 17.8 shows a LANalyzer application that was created to monitor all SAP traffic on the network. The first channel, SAP-SR, filters on the value 0x0452 in the Source Socket field. The second channel, SAP-DEST, filters on the value 0x0452 in the Destination Socket field.

FIGURE 17.8

Filtering on both source and destination sockets ensures that you capture all SAP packets.

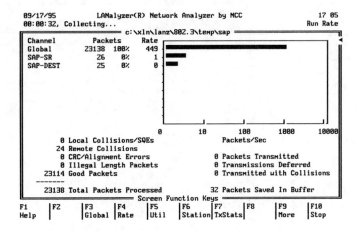

In Figure 17.8, the peak number of SAP packets per second is less than 1% of the total number of packets on the network. Excessive SAP traffic is not yet a concern on this network. Monitoring SAP traffic on a growing network will help determine when SAP filtering becomes necessary.

Next, you will use SAP information to determine the types of services that are currently available on a network.

Identifying Servers and Availability

USING THE LANALYZER for Windows, you can capture SAP information broadcast packets (General Service responses) on a NetWare LAN to identify all services available on the network. If a workstation is unable to connect to a server, you may wish to verify the server's availability first. In Figure 17.9, you are viewing a SAP information broadcast from the server, TRAIN1.

FIGURE 17.9

SAP information broadcasts identify servers available on the network.

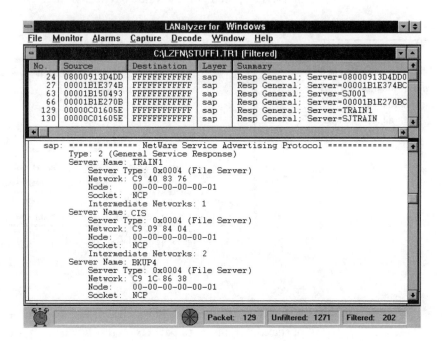

The Intermediate Networks field indicates the number of hops to the service. As shown in Figure 17.10, if the value in this field is 16, the service is not available; it is considered unreachable.

Unreachable services may be an indication of network problems. If a router goes down, you may see a sudden increase in unreachable services. A little later in this chapter, you will learn about the "server shutdown" packets that also contain the "unreachable" designation in the Intermediate Networks field.

FIGURE 17.10

Services that are 16 hops
away are considered
unreachable.

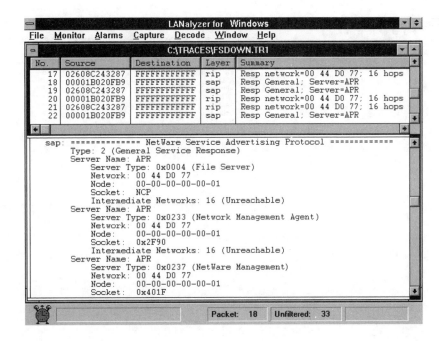

FIGURE 17.10

Services that are 16 hops
away are considered
unreachable.

Actively Gathering Service Information

U SING THE LANALYZER, you can actively determine the services available on the network. LANalyzer contains a predefined application, SERVERVU, for finding the network services. By broadcasting a Nearest Service Request packet, as shown in Figure 17.11, you can receive information of the nearest servers on the network. All servers on the local network will respond. This application is configured to capture routing information packets, as well. The routing packets contain information about other networks that can be explored.

FIGURE 17.11

Results of the SERVERVU
application

```
09/17/95        LANalyzer(R) Network Analyzer by NCC              19 09
00:00:32, Collecting...                                     Run Station
          c:\xln\lanz\802.3\netware\802.3\servervu
Stations seen: 7
                     Packet Rate    Total Packets    Avg. Size    Errors
No.  Station Address  Rcv   Xmt      Rcv      Xmt    Rcv   Xmt   Rcv   Xmt
1    exos651575        1     0       140       0     114    -                ◄
2    SALES1            0     0        0        7      -    114
3    ADMIN-02          0     0        0        7      -    114
4    MKTG-45           0     0        0        7      -    114
5    SALES2            0     0        0        7      -    114
6    BKUP-FS1          0     0        0        7      -    114
7    OPS-01            0     0        0        7      -    114
8
9
10
11
12
13
14
15
16
                      Screen Function Keys
F1      |F2      |F3     |F4    |F5    |F6      |F7      |F8    |F9    |F10
Help    |        |Global |Rate  |Util  |Station |TxStats |      |More  |Stop
```

"Server Shutdown" Packets

T HE SAP ALSO allows servers to announce that they are going down. A
properly downed server will broadcast a "server shutdown" packet
to notify all routers and servers on the network that it will no longer
be available. This information is propagated throughout the network, and the
server and router tables are updated to reflect the server's absence.

As shown in Figure 17.12, a "server shutdown" packet is simply a response
packet indicating that the server is now considered unreachable, 16 hops
away. A server will also broadcast RIP packets announcing that networks
cannot be reached through it in a similar way (see Chapter 18).

Servers transmit a "server shutdown" packet when they are brought down.

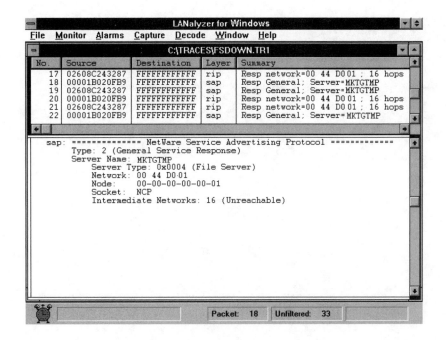

SAP Intermediate Networks Field

AS YOU WORK more in depth with analyzers, you may notice a strange feature of NetWare 3.x that is viewed in SAP packets sent from the servers. As shown in Figure 17.13, LANalyzer for Windows has been placed on network C9-99-01-64.

Earlier, this chapter discussed the internal IPX network and indicated that NetWare 3.x and NetWare 4.x file servers advertise NCP services as one network away because of the internal IPX network address (the virtual LAN within the 3.x and 4.x server).

For example, in Figure 17.14, a NetWare 3.x server broadcasts a SAP that states

- The file server (NCP) is one hop away.

- The print server is two hops away.

FIGURE 17.13

Viewing local SAP packets

Server Name: SF-01
Type: 0x0004 (File Server)
Socket: 0x451 NCP
Hops: 1

Server Name: PS01
Server Type: 0x0047 (Advertising Print Server)
Socket: 0x8060 (Print Server)
Hops: 2

LANalyzer for
Windows

Network: C9-99-01-64

NW 3.x Server

FIGURE 17.14

An NLM-based service
will advertise itself as
two hops away on
the local LAN.

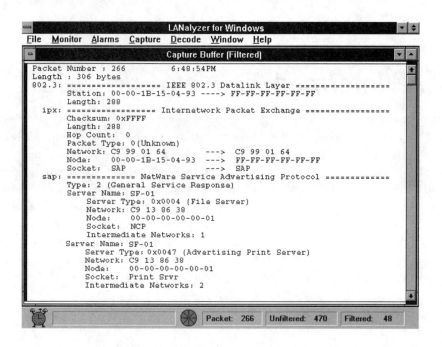

```
                              LANalyzer for Windows
 File   Monitor   Alarms   Capture   Decode   Window   Help
                         Capture Buffer (Filtered)
 Packet Number : 266            6:48:54PM
 Length : 306 bytes
 802.3: ================== IEEE 802.3 Datalink Layer ==================
         Station: 00-00-1B-15-04-93 ----> FF-FF-FF-FF-FF-FF
         Length: 288
    ipx: ================= Internetwork Packet Exchange =================
         Checksum: 0xFFFF
         Length: 288
         Hop Count: 0
         Packet Type: 0(Unknown)
         Network: C9 99 01 64        --->  C9 99 01 64
         Node:    00-00-1B-15-04-93  --->  FF-FF-FF-FF-FF-FF
         Socket:  SAP                --->  SAP
    sap: ============== NetWare Service Advertising Protocol =============
         Type: 2 (General Service Response)
         Server Name: SF-01
             Server Type: 0x0004 (File Server)
             Network: C9 13 86 38
             Node:    00-00-00-00-00-01
             Socket:  NCP
             Intermediate Networks: 1
         Server Name: SF-01
             Server Type: 0x0047 (Advertising Print Server)
             Network: C9 13 86 38
             Node:    00-00-00-00-00-01
             Socket:  Print Srvr
             Intermediate Networks: 2

                                      Packet:  266    Unfiltered:  470    Filtered:   48
```

Although the network and node addresses reflect that the file server and print server are on the same network, the print server is actually considered one network farther away—remote to the file server itself. Figure 17.15 illustrates the logical interpretation of this SAP anomaly.

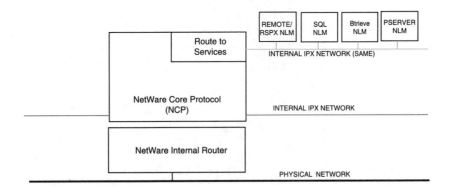

As discussed in this chapter, the Service Advertising Protocol is used by NetWare servers and routers to exchange information about available servers on the internetwork and their distance from the local network. With LAN-alyzer for windows, you have examined these packets and differentiated between SAP information broadcasts and Nearest Service Query and Response packets. You have also actively gathered a listing of services available on the network by using a SAP broadcast.

Typically, a client transmits a SAP request to identify a specific service on the network. Once the client knows the service name and address, it must determine which routes are available to access these services. The next chapter examines the Routing Information Protocol (RIP), which provides the client with this information.

Routing Information Protocol (RIP) and NetWare Link Services Protocol (NLSP)

HE PREVIOUS CHAPTERS have discussed how packets are addressed before being transmitted. Two distinct address types are used on NetWare LANs: the hardware address and the software address.

The *hardware address* is specified in the Ethernet, Token Ring, ARCnet, or FDDI header Source and Destination fields. This address corresponds to the address on the local network interface card. Providing this address alone, however, can get packets routed only through the local LAN, not through the Internet. Nor can this information alone allow you to cross from one network type to another (between ARCnet and Ethernet, for example).

You therefore need to assign software addresses, as well. *Software addresses* are independent of the media on which they rely. They are the same, regardless of whether a packet is traveling across an Ethernet, a Token Ring, or an ARCnet LAN. In NetWare, the software address is called the *internetwork address*. The internetwork address includes a 4-byte network address (assigned during installation of the operating system) and a 6-byte node address. The node address portion is "borrowed" from the node's physical hardware address. In the case of physical addresses that are shorter than 6 bytes (such as ARCnet), the address is padded with preceding 0's.

The IPX header defined in Chapter 6 contains the internetwork address (network address and node address) and indicates the final destination network of the packet. This information is used for routing purposes. Routers must also provide information about the networks to which they are directly attached or to which they may route packets. This way, when a client transmits a packet across the network, it can address the packet to the closest router, which, in turn, forwards the packet on to the next router, and so on, until the packet reaches the final destination network.

Routing information is passed between servers and routers by Novell's Routing Information Protocol (RIP). This routing information is contained in routing information tables located at each router and server on the network.

This chapter explains the functionality of Novell's current routing protocol, NetWare's RIP; examines the packet structure used; and provides several analysis techniques for viewing and streamlining routing networks. This chapter also defines the steps required to test routing efficiencies on a NetWare LAN. Finally, this chapter addresses Novell's new approach to internetworking using a new routing protocol called the NetWare Link Services Protocol (NLSP), which is a link-state protocol. The current routing protocol, (RIP) is a vector-based protocol. The difference between vector-based and link-state protocols is also discussed in this chapter.

Routing Information Protocol Functionality

 S SHOWN IN Figure 18.1, RIP packets use the IPX protocol for transport and designate the value 0x0453 in the IPX Socket field.

FIGURE 18.1

RIP uses IPX for transport.

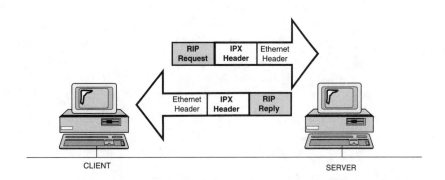

IPX routers will transmit their routing information on the network in five specific circumstances:

- **When a router initializes:** When you bring up a new router, it broadcasts a RIP packet to inform other network routers that it is available to forward packets between networks.

- **When a router requires initial routing information:** Besides presenting information of routes it is making available, routers request information of all other routers on the network so they can configure their routing information tables.

- **Periodically, to maintain current routing tables:** Every 60 seconds, Net-Ware IPX routers transmit a RIP broadcast packet to ensure that all routers maintain current routing information tables.

- **To notify routers of a change in routing configurations:** When a router has changed any information in its routing information tables, it broadcasts the new information to guarantee that all routers have correct information in their tables.

- **To notify other routers that they are going down:** If a router is being properly "downed," it broadcasts routing information indicating that all routes through it are unreachable so other routers can find alternate routes.

If a router shuts down from loss of power or because of malfunctions, it may not be able to transmit a "going down" packet. Because of this possibility, all routers maintain a timeout mechanism. If an entry in the routing information table is not verified through routing broadcasts within three minutes, it is purged from the table. It is assumed that the route is no longer available.

When IPX routers transmit their routing information, they must follow specific rules. Their broadcasts must be local broadcasts only, and they must use the Best Information Algorithm (BIA). To understand the RIP packets that traverse the local system, it is necessary to first examine why these packets are local only and what the algorithm provides you.

Local Broadcasts and the Best Information Algorithm

R IP BROADCASTS ARE restricted to the local network only and allow routers to propagate the routing information onto other networks. Each router maintains a table of known routes and broadcasts this information on each locally attached segment. Other routers will receive this information, update their routing information tables, and transmit an up-to-date routing information packet.

For example, in Figure 18.2, router A is a NetWare v3.11 server (SALES1). There are two network interface cards in this server, with IPX bound to both. One network is assigned the network address AA-AA-AA-AA, the other BB-BB-BB-BB. The router will advertise any remote networks to which it provides routing services.

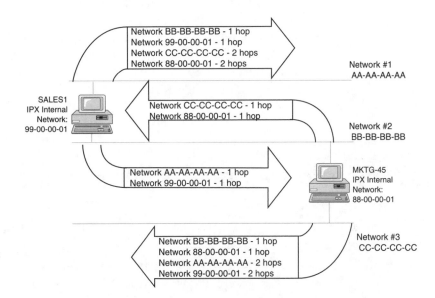

Because the server is a NetWare v3.11 operating system, it also has an IPX internal network address that will be broadcast. This is important because clients must be able to route to the internal network for services, just as they would route to LAN A on a NetWare 2.x server.

RIP packets are not allowed to cross routers. Instead, each router accepts the information, updates its tables, and transmits current information to its locally attached networks.

The Best Information Algorithm states that

- Routers may not transmit information back onto the network upon which it was received.

■ Routers may not transmit information about the network upon which they are transmitting.

For example, in Figure 18.2, SALES1 and MKTG-45 connect networks 1, 2, and 3, providing routing services. SALES1 is physically attached to networks 1 and 2. SALES1 will transmit routing information about network 1 onto network 2. According to the BIA, it cannot broadcast routing information about network 2 onto network 2. This is acceptable since nodes on network 2 do not need to route packets when communicating with local network nodes. MKTG-45 receives the RIP packet from SALES1, updates its tables, and transmits a RIP packet onto network 3, announcing that it is a router to networks 1 and 2. In accordance with the BIA, MKTG-45 does not announce this information back onto local network 2. If it did, nodes on the local segment would assume there were two routes to network 1, one through SALES1 and another through MKTG-45.

Routing Information Packet Format

NOW THAT NETWARE'S routing functionality has been defined, let's examine the Routing Information Protocol packet formats. Two types of RIP packets use the same packet formats: the request packets and the response packets. As shown in Figure 18.3, RIP packets have the value 0x0453 in the IPX Socket field.

PACKET TYPE The Type field designates whether the packet is a request for routing information or a reply containing routing information. The two Type field values are

Request	0x0001
Response	0x0002

Request packets are transmitted by workstations that want to locate a route to a network. Responses are transmitted by routers and indicate the networks to which they can route. As shown in Figure 18.3, RIP response packets are also transmitted to broadcast information about known routes. In this

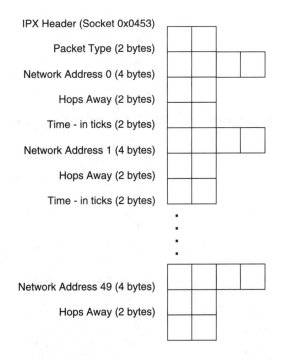

FIGURE 18.3

RIP packet format

IPX Header (Socket 0x0453)

Packet Type (2 bytes)

Network Address 0 (4 bytes)

Hops Away (2 bytes)

Time - in ticks (2 bytes)

Network Address 1 (4 bytes)

Hops Away (2 bytes)

Time - in ticks (2 bytes)

Network Address 49 (4 bytes)

Hops Away (2 bytes)

case, a RIP response packet can contain information on up to 50 networks (network 0 through network 49).

NETWORK ADDRESS If the packet is a RIP request, the Network Address field will contain the network being sought. The value 0xFF-FF-FF-FF indicates that the RIP request is for all known networks.

HOPS AWAY The Hops Away field is valid only on response-type packets and contains the number of routers a packet must cross to reach a network. For example, in Figure 18.2, SALES1 would transmit RIP response packets onto network 2, indicating that there is one hop between clients on network 2 and network 1.

On RIP requests, the hop field will contain the value 0xFFFF. (The decimal equivalent is 65535.)

TIME—IN TICKS The Time field is valid only for reply packets and indicates the time required to reach the remote network. One tick is equivalent to 1/18 of a second.

On request packets, this field is padded with 0xFFFF. (The decimal equivalent is 65535.)

Router "Going Down" Packets

WHEN ROUTERS ARE functioning properly, they broadcast RIP information every 60 seconds. If a router is being brought down, however, it will notify all other routers that it cannot provide services anymore.

In order to provide this information, routers broadcast a "going down" RIP packet on all attached networks, as shown in Figure 18.4. This function is performed by all internal and external NetWare routers (v2.x and v3.x).

FIGURE 18.4

Routers transmit a "going down" packet to all attached networks.

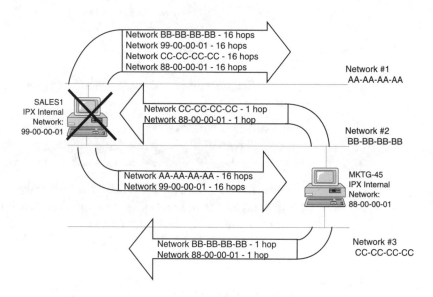

These packets contain the same routing information that is normally transmitted on the networks, but the hop count is now 16. Sixteen hops is considered unreachable. Upon receiving this new information, routers update their routing tables and remove any routes that are no longer available. Figure 18.4 shows a "going down" packet from SALES1 indicating that networks AA-AA-AA-AA and 99-00-00-01 are no longer reachable through that router. As shown in Figure 18.5, router "going down" packets indicate that attached networks are 16 hops away.

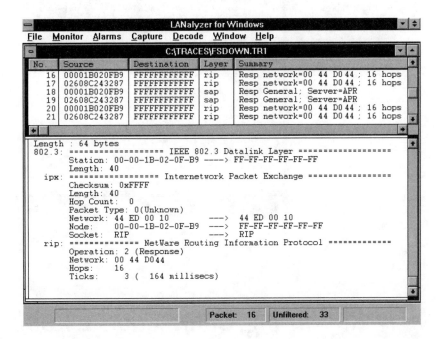

This information is useful when troubleshooting network communications that occur over a router. For example, if a particular route seems sluggish, you can track whether it is "losing" its routing tables and intermittently transmitting a "going down" packet to local networks, as shown in Figure 18.6.

During a workstation's initial network connection, the RIP also finds the route to the server responding most quickly.

FIGURE 18.6

Intermittently failing routers will broadcast "going down" packets when they lose their routing tables.

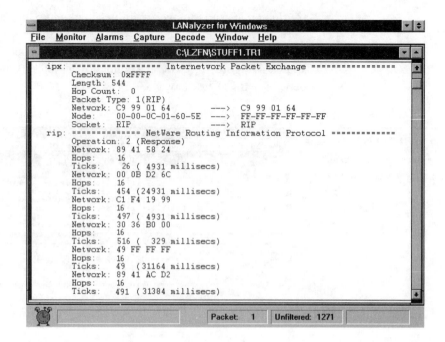

```
              LANalyzer for Windows
File   Monitor   Alarms   Capture   Decode   Window   Help
                    C:\LZFN\STUFF1.TR1
ipx: ================= Internetwork Packet Exchange =================
       Checksum: 0xFFFF
       Length: 544
       Hop Count:  0
       Packet Type: 1(RIP)
       Network: C9 99 01 64        --->  C9 99 01 64
       Node:    00-00-0C-01-60-5E  --->  FF-FF-FF-FF-FF-FF
       Socket:  RIP                --->  RIP
rip: ============= NetWare Routing Information Protocol =============
       Operation: 2 (Response)
       Network: 89 41 58 24
       Hops:      16
       Ticks:     26 ( 4931 millisecs)
       Network: 00 0B D2 6C
       Hops:      16
       Ticks:    454 (24931 millisecs)
       Network: C1 F4 19 99
       Hops:      16
       Ticks:    497 ( 4931 millisecs)
       Network: 30 36 B0 00
       Hops:      16
       Ticks:    516 (  329 millisecs)
       Network: 49 FF FF FF
       Hops:      16
       Ticks:     49  (31164 millisecs)
       Network: 89 41 AC D2
       Hops:      16
       Ticks:    491 (31384 millisecs)

                              Packet:  1     Unfiltered: 1271
```

Using RIP during Connection Establishment

WHEN A WORKSTATION launches the shell program (NETX.COM), it broadcasts a SAP packet to locate the server able to respond the most quickly. The SAP packet contains the responding server's network address. The workstation must then find a route to that server. It does this by using a RIP request broadcast. As shown in Figure 18.7, a workstation transmits a RIP request broadcast onto the local network. In this packet, the workstation indicates the network number it wishes to locate (as learned from the SAP reply, defined above). The router that provides routing services to the desired network will respond. In Figure 18.7, the client is requesting a route to network 00-00-11-62.

FIGURE 18.7

The RIP is used in obtaining the initial connection to a server.

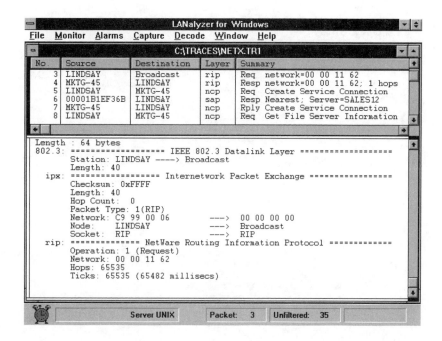

Testing Routing Efficiencies

USING THE LANALYZER, you can test network routes and determine their efficiencies. The LANalyzer contains a predefined application, ROUTVIEW, that transmits an IPX diagnostic packet (see Chapter 19) to workstations and servers on the other side of a router. The responses are time stamped upon receipt. You can use this information to determine the round-trip delay through network routers.

Figure 18.8 shows an internetwork of five LANs connected by routers. The LANalyzer is placed on network AA-AA-AA-AA. In this example, you will test the round-trip delay between network AA-AA-AA-AA and network EE-EE-EE-EE, crossing four routers.

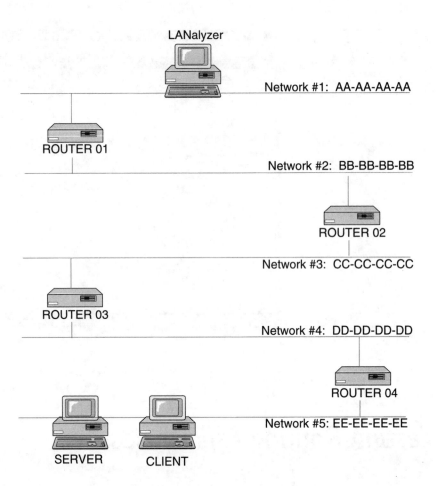

To determine available routes from the local network, you can first filter on all RIP broadcasts on the network; this provides a listing of all known networks, routers to use when accessing the remote LAN, and the distance from the local network (in hops). As shown in Figure 18.9, the router advertising services to network EE-EE-EE-EE is called ROUTER01.

Using the LANalyzer's predefined ROUTVIEW application, you can transmit diagnostic packets across the network to the remote LAN. As the active stations on the network respond, their packets are saved in the trace buffer.

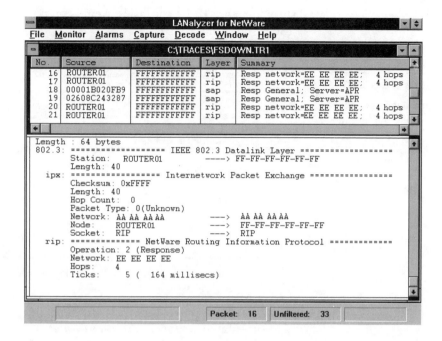

FIGURE 18.9

ROUTER01 replies that it
provides routing services
to network EE-EE-EE-EE.

Chapter 19 focuses on creating and using these diagnostic packets.

You must edit the ROUTVIEW application in order to capture and time-stamp the packet you are transmitting across the network. This will give you a reference point when determining round-trip delay time for communicating across the four routers.

The LANalyzer ROUTVIEW application should be configured to capture the following packets:

Channel router	All RIP packets
Channel nodes	Responses to test packets
Channel test	Test packets transmitted

After the application is run, the trace display provides a listing of all responding nodes and their response times. As shown in the LANalyzer trace display in Figure 18.10, the fastest round-trip time to a server on the network is 130.075ms (milliseconds).

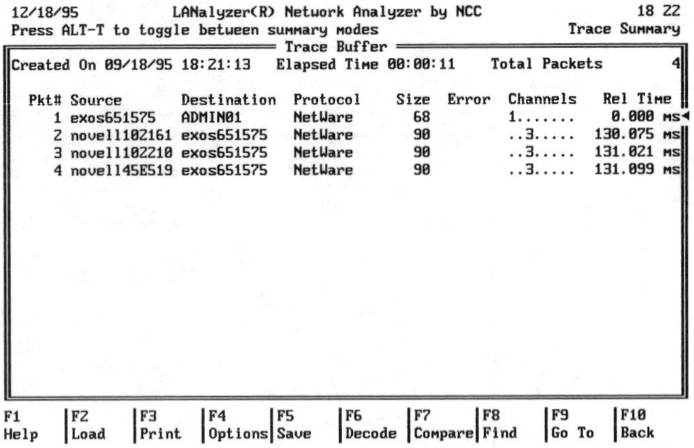

FIGURE 18.10

Time stamps provide the round-trip delay time.

```
12/18/95         LANalyzer(R) Network Analyzer by NCC              18 22
Press ALT-T to toggle between summary modes                    Trace Summary
================================= Trace Buffer =================================
Created On 09/18/95 18:21:13   Elapsed Time 00:00:11   Total Packets        4

 Pkt# Source       Destination  Protocol   Size  Error  Channels    Rel Time
    1 exos651575   ADMIN01      NetWare     68           1.......     0.000 ms◄
    2 novell102161 exos651575   NetWare     90           ..3.....   130.075 ms
    3 novell102210 exos651575   NetWare     90           ..3.....   131.021 ms
    4 novell145E519 exos651575  NetWare     90           ..3.....   131.099 ms









F1      F2      F3      F4       F5      F6      F7       F8    F9     F10
Help    Load    Print   Options  Save    Decode  Compare  Find  Go To  Back
```

The time stamp is shown in *relative format*. This format indicates the time of packet receipt based on the first packet in the buffer. When the first packet is received, it is time-stamped as 0.00ms. Another is received, and it is time-stamped based on the first packet's arrival time of 0.00ms. You can tell that the second packet (the response) arrived approximately 130ms after the test packet was sent.

If the response time is considered inadequate, there may be a problem with either the node tested or one of the routers connecting to the remote network. First, test several more nodes located on network EE-EE-EE-EE. If all nodes respond at approximately the same rate, you can rule out the possibility that the delay is isolated to the first node you tested on the network. You can now assume that the delay is caused by a router. To test this theory, you can perform the same test on network DD-DD-DD-DD and measure the average round-trip response time. You can perform this test on all the networks connecting network AA-AA-AA-AA to network EE-EE-EE-EE in order to determine which router may be causing the slow response through the network.

As is evident in Figure 18.11, the router between networks BB-BB-BB-BB and CC-CC-CC-CC seems to be introducing an unacceptable delay into the network communications. This router may be faulty or insufficient for the routing load it is required to handle.

FIGURE 18.11

Charting the response
times

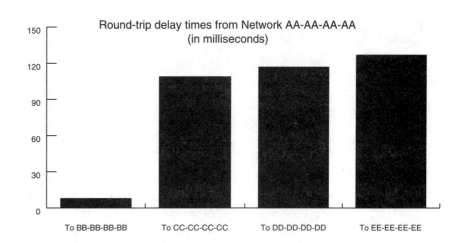

FIGURE 18.11

Charting the response
times

To test a single device's response across the network, you can address the diagnostic packet to the station's node address in the IPX header. This tests round-trip response time from a single network node, as shown in Figure 18.12. Chapter 19 contains additional details on Novell's diagnostic packets.

FIGURE 18.12

Testing the response
time of a single remote
network node

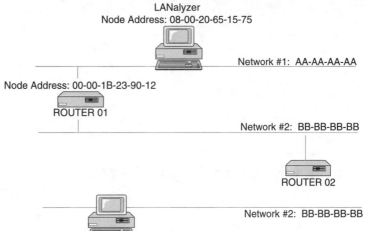

Distance-Vector and Link State Routing Protocols

NETWARE RIP IS a distance-vector routing protocol. Distance-vector routing protocols typically exchange information about the network's topology through periodic broadcasts with their immediate router neighbors. Each router then consolidates the information received and passes on the consolidated information to other routers, servers, and clients on the next network. (Review the beginning of this chapter to see how a distance-vector routing protocol, such as RIP, propagates routing information through the network.)

Novell has developed a new routing protocol. Novell's link-state protocol, called NetWare Link Services Protocol (NLSP), is offered as an enhancement that runs on NetWare 3.11 and later operating systems. To get the NLSP NLMs, download IPXRT3.EXE from NetWire. NLSP is also included in the NetWare MultiProtocol Router.

Link-state routing protocols were developed to meet the demands of larger internetworks by scaling readily to handle large, complex internetworks and adapt more quickly to network topology changes.

The following table lists common distance-vector and link-state routing protocols:

Protocol Suite	Distance-Vector Routing Protocol	Link-State Routing Protocol
IPX	RIP	NLSP
TCP/IP	RIP, IGRP	OSPF, IS-IS
OSI	—	IS-IS
AppleTalk	RTMP	—

How Does a Link-State Protocol Work?

In an internetwork that uses a link-state routing protocol, each router or server floods information about itself and its immediate neighbor routers to every router in the routing area. A *routing area* is a collection of networks sharing the same area address as part of an entire internetwork. Routing areas are created to enhance the scalability, manageability, and security of the internetwork routing system. These flooding transmissions are sent only when something changes on the network. In a link-state routed internetwork, there is no need for periodic broadcasts of routing information.

Link-state routers use the information received to build a map of the routing area. Link-state routers do not have to rely on second-hand information; distance-vector routers do. The map that link-state routers create includes the routing area's routers, servers, links connecting the routers, the operational status of the routers and links, and related parameters (hence the name "link-state").

NetWare internetworks can contain both RIP and NLSP routers, enabling you to upgrade the network at your own pace. If you upgrade your NetWare server/router to support NLSP, the device will only send RIP update packets out ports that it has heard RIP updates coming in on (indicating there is a RIP device on that network segment). Once the NLSP router no longer hears RIP packets (for a default timeout value of 4 minutes), the NLSP router begins to send out LSP (Link State Protocol) packets instead of RIP packets. Now, let's examine some of the internetworking enhancements related to NLSP.

Advantages of NLSP

NLSP replaces both RIP and SAP traffic on a NetWare internetwork and offers better performance, reliability, and management of network traffic. NLSP offers the following benefits, compared to RIP and SAP:

- Improved routing

- Reduced network overhead

- Low WAN overhead

- Increased reliability

- Less CPU usage

- Better scalability

- Better manageability

- Backward compatibility

- Manual link-cost assignment

Let's take a closer look at each of these benefits.

IMPROVED ROUTING RIP routers store only information that has been received from their neighboring routers. These routers maintain only a listing of routes based on how far away they are in hops. NLSP routers, however, store a complete map of the network layout, enabling them to make decisions based on the best route available.

REDUCED NETWORK OVERHEAD RIP routers transmit periodic route update packets onto the network to ensure that all routers have the same routing information. NLSP routers broadcast routing information only when something has changed. This method of propagating information dramatically decreases the amount of routing traffic on the network.

LOW WAN OVERHEAD NLSP replaces the SAP protocol and eliminates the need for constant SAP broadcast packets across WAN links; NLSP transmits information only when services have changed.

INCREASED RELIABILITY NLSP periodically checks links for connectivity and switches to an alternate link if a link fails. NLSP also quickly updates the topology databases, or maps, stored in each node when there are changes in the routing area. This ensures that NLSP routers can continue to select the best routing paths.

REDUCED CPU USAGE In a RIP environment, RIP and SAP information received on a periodic basis must be processed, requiring CPU time. Since NLSP transmits information only as changes to routes and services occur, it reduces the amount of CPU time needed to process route and service information.

BETTER SCALABILITY On a RIP-based network, packets cannot cross more than 15 hops; a service or network 16 hops away is considered unreachable. NLSP networks support up to 127 hops.

BETTER MANAGEABILITY NLSP maintains an NLSP MIB (Management Information Base) that can be queried by any SNMP (Simple Network Management Protocol) console, such as NetWare Management System. By querying the NLSP MIB, an administrator can obtain a map of the entire NetWare internetwork.

BACKWARD COMPATIBILITY NLSP was designed to be backward compatible with RIP-based networks. Segments can be updated one at a time. NLSP services are available immediately after the NLSP NLM has been installed and configured on a NetWare 3.11 or later server; the server does not need to be rebooted.

MANUAL LINK-COST ASSIGNMENT Although NLSP routers know the cost of every link and automatically choose the most efficient path for each packet, a manual override enables you to modify the cost of a specific route. For example, if you wanted to ensure that a NetWare server/router did not handle the routing responsibilities on a network that had a dedicated router attached, you could manually assign a greater link-cost to the server/router. Traffic would be routed through the dedicated router. If the dedicated router failed or was brought down, the traffic would be rerouted through the server/router. This feature can also be used on WAN links to ensure that traffic is routed through the most efficient link, as shown in Figure 18.13.

FIGURE 18.13

Manual link-cost assignment ensures that the most efficient WAN path is used.

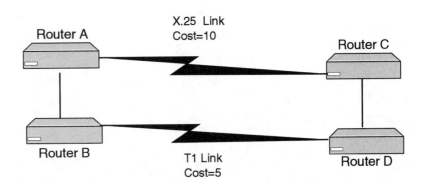

NLSP is just one of the new protocols designed to make larger internetworks more efficient, reliable, and manageable.

This chapter has examined NetWare's Routing Information Protocol functionality and packet structures. You know that by filtering on packets that contain the value 0x0453 in the IPX Socket fields, you can view RIP packets and determine available and unavailable routes. These packets will also define the distance between the current network and remote networks on the internetwork. RIP packets are also useful when testing the efficiency of a certain route. This chapter also differentiated between vector-based and link-state routing protocols and introduced you to Novell's new routing protocol, the NetWare Link Services Protocol.

Chapter 19 examines how IPX diagnostic packets can be sent across routers to test routing delays. It also examines the many uses of the Diagnostic Responder and shows how to transmit these packets using the LANalyzer.

NetWare
Diagnostic
Packets

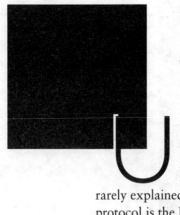

U P TO THIS point, you have examined how many of the NetWare protocols work, including IPX, SPX, SPX II, NCP, SAP, RIP, and NLSP. There is, however, one NetWare protocol that is rarely explained, although it is most useful in analyzing NetWare LANs. This protocol is the Diagnostic Responder.

This chapter examines Novell's Diagnostic Responder services and packet structures. It also reviews several ways in which you can use the Diagnostic Responder for network analysis.

On a NetWare LAN, it is helpful to be able to "ping" another network system, or transmit a single packet that requires a direct response. It is also helpful to receive workstation configuration information with the response. You can use the Diagnostic Responder for

- Connectivity testing

- Configuration information gathering

Connectivity Testing

W HEN WORKSTATIONS LOAD IPX.COM or IPXODI.COM, they automatically load the Diagnostic Responder. It is possible, however, to load IPX without the Diagnostic Responder. Figure 19.1 indicates the load options for IPX.

NetWare v2.x and later servers always have the Diagnostic Responder capability enabled.

All servers and clients that have the Responder loaded must transmit a response upon receipt of a diagnostic packet that is addressed to their node

FIGURE 19.1

Loading options for IPX

```
NetWare IPX/SPX Protocol   v2.11 (930423)
(C) Copyright 1990-1993 Novell, Inc.   All Rights Reserved.

Available command line options:
/?     Display this help screen.
/D     Eliminate Diagnostic Responder - Reduces size by 3K.
/A     Eliminate Diagnostic Responder and SPX - Reduces size by 9K.

/C=[path\]filename.ext
       Specify a configuration file to use (Default is NET.CFG).

/U     Unload resident IPXODI from memory.
/F     Forcibly unload resident IPXODI from memory, regardless of programs
       loaded above it.  Using this option can cause a machine to crash if
       applications are still using IPX/SPX.
```

address or 0xFF-FF-FF-FF-FF-FF (broadcast). This response from the server or client indicates that it can receive and transmit packets successfully. As shown in Figure 19.2, the response also contains configuration information about the server or client.

FIGURE 19.2

You can use the Diagnostic Responder to test connectivity; in addition, it provides configuration information.

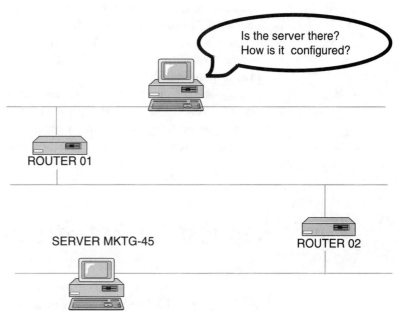

IPX Internal Network Address: 88-00-00-01
Node address: 00-00-00-00-00-01

Configuration Information Gathering

W HEN A SERVER or client replies, it transmits a Configuration Response packet that indicates the components present at the server or client. The Configuration Response packet also includes the number of instances for each component.

Servers and clients may report that they have components such as

- IPX/SPX

- Router driver

- File server/router

- LAN driver

- Shell

In order to obtain configuration information from a server or a client, an application or protocol analyzer can transmit a Configuration Request packet to the desired server or client. As shown in Figure 19.3, a single Configuration Response packet may contain a list of one or more components that are part of the responding system.

In Chapter 18, diagnostic packets were transmitted to test the round-trip delay time across routers. Although the LANalyzer includes applications that have predefined Diagnostic Request packet transmit channels, you may want to create a customized Diagnostic Request packet to meet your specific needs.

Diagnostic Request Packet Structure

A DIAGNOSTIC REQUEST packet is defined by the value 0x0456 in the IPX header Destination Socket field, as shown in Figure 19.4. The diagnostic request information follows the IPX header. The diagnostic request information may be quite simple, requesting all information from each station being addressed. It may also, however, become

FIGURE 19.3

Responding nodes supply configuration information.

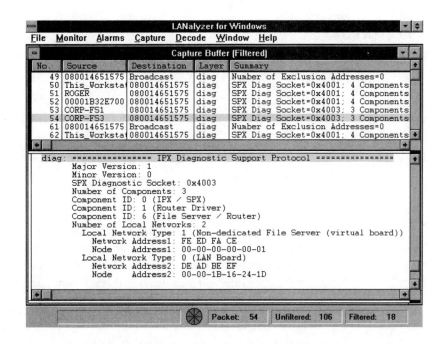

FIGURE 19.4

Diagnostic packets use the socket number 0x0456.

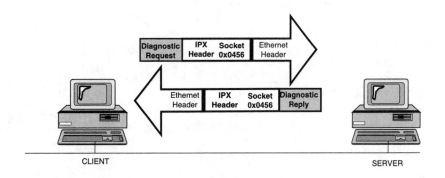

quite complex, allowing you to broadcast a Diagnostic Request packet on the network and then, within the Diagnostic Request packet, specify stations that should *not* respond. The structure of the Diagnostic Request packet is shown in Figure 19.5.

FIGURE 19.5

Diagnostic Request packet
structure

IPX Header (Socket 0x0456)

Exclusion Address Count (1 byte)

Exclusion Address 0 (6 bytes)

Exclusion Address 79 (6 bytes)

EXCLUSION ADDRESS COUNT The Exclusion Address Count field defines
the number of stations that will be requested not to respond. These are *exclusion addresses*. A 0 in this field indicates that all stations should respond. The
maximum value for this field is 80 (exclusion address 0 through 79).

EXCLUSION ADDRESS If, in the IPX header, the packet is addressed to
broadcast, all stations will respond to the packet. If you do not wish to receive
a response from a server or client, you must put its node address in the Exclusion Address field. You can exclude up to 80 stations from responding.

Figure 19.6 shows a Diagnostic Request packet that has two stations listed
in the Exclusion Address field.

FIGURE 19.6

Listing node addresses in
the Exclusion field
denotes that they should
not respond.

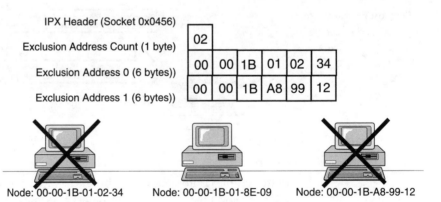

IPX Header (Socket 0x0456)

Exclusion Address Count (1 byte)

Exclusion Address 0 (6 bytes))

Exclusion Address 1 (6 bytes))

Node: 00-00-1B-01-02-34   Node: 00-00-1B-01-8E-09   Node: 00-00-1B-A8-99-12

When nodes respond, they transmit a Diagnostic Response packet. Nodes must respond within 0.5 seconds of receipt of the Diagnostic Request packet. If you are testing a large network, these responses add to the overall network utilization and may cause some sluggishness during the response phase.

Diagnostic Response Packet Structure

F A NODE receives a packet addressed to it specifically or addressed to broadcast that contains the value 0x0456 in the Destination Socket field, the node understands it is a diagnostic packet. By looking within the diagnostic packet, the station can determine whether or not it should respond. If the station's node address is not listed in the Exclusion Address field, it will respond with a Diagnostic Response packet.

The Diagnostic Response packet information follows the IPX header and is transmitted from the diagnostic configuration socket number 0x0456. LANalyzer for Windows decodes this field value as "Configure," as shown in Figure 19.7.

The packet will vary in length, depending on the number of components reported from the responding node. Figure 19.8 shows the Diagnostic Response packet structure.

MAJOR/MINOR VERSION The Major and Minor fields indicate the version of the Diagnostic Responder that is installed in the responding station. Currently, you may commonly find version 1.0 (major version 1, minor version 0) or version 1.1 from responding stations.

SPX DIAGNOSTIC SOCKET NUMBER The SPX Diagnostic Socket field identifies the socket number to which all SPX diagnostic responses can be addressed. The SPX Diagnostic Responder is available for third-party development.

COMPONENT COUNT The Component Count field defines the number of components found within this response packet.

COMPONENT TYPE The Component Type field contains information about one of the components, or active processes, at the responding node. The component structure can be either simple or extended.

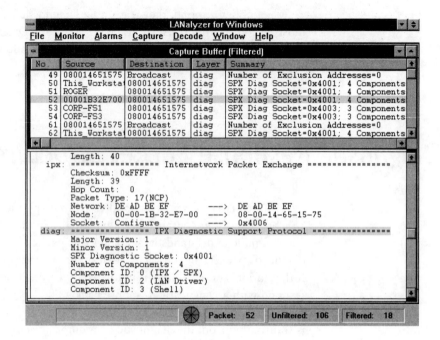

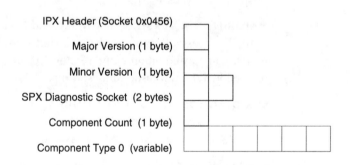

Simple Component Structures

A simple component structure contains a single, 1-byte field called the Component ID field. Simple structures are used to identify the following component types:

Type	Component
0	IPX/SPX
1	Router drivers
2	LAN drivers
3	Shells
4	VAPs

Figure 19.7, shown earlier, shows a Diagnostic Response packet that is reporting three simple components: IPX/SPX, the LAN driver (shell driver), and the shell. The packet contains only 38 bytes of data—30 bytes for the IPX header and 8 bytes for the diagnostic response information.

Extended Components

The extended component structure reports specific information about such components as routers, file servers/routers, and nondedicated IPX/SPX. A response using an extended component structure is shown in Figure 19.9.

EXTENDED COMPONENT ID The first field, Component ID, defines the component type number. Extended component type numbers include:

Type	Component
5	Router
6	File server/router
7	Nondedicated IPX/SPX

NUMBER OF LOCAL NETWORKS The Number of Local Networks field denotes the number of local networks with which this component may communicate. For example, a file server/router component will communicate with at least one network for a dedicated NetWare 2.x server (with a single network interface card). The file server/router component will communicate with

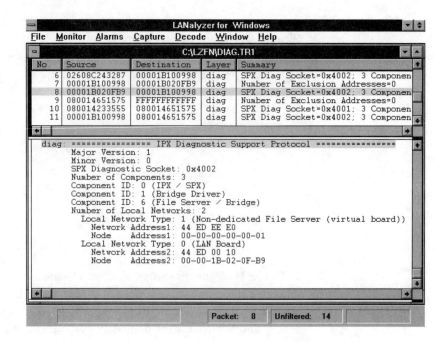

at least two networks if it is a NetWare 3.x or 4.x system; one network is the internal IPX network, and the second is the network interface card. The network type, network address, and node address will be listed for each network the component communicates with.

LOCAL NETWORK TYPE The Local Network type field contains a number indicating the type of network the component communicates with. The network types include:

Type	Component
0	LAN board
1	Nondedicated file server (virtual board)
2	Redirected remote line

NetWare 3.x and 4.x servers place their internal IPX network address and node address of 0x00-00-00-00-00-01 in IPX headers when they communicate. To find the actual network address and node address of the LANs to which the server is connected, view the Network Address field and Node Address field of the first extended component with network type 0 (LAN board).

NetWare 3.x and 4.x servers always have a nondedicated file server (virtual board) extended component listed. This is the internal IPX network defined upon installation of the server.

NETWORK ADDRESS The Network Address field contains the 4-byte network address assigned to the network listed in the local network type field.

NODE ADDRESS The Node Address field contains the 6-byte node address that accompanies the network address listed above. Redirected remote lines have a node address of 0x00-00-00-00-00-00. NetWare v3.x and 4.x IPX internal networks have a node address of 0x00-00-00-00-00-01.

Figure 19.9, shown earlier, depicts a Diagnostic Response packet from a NetWare v3.x server. Based on the response, you can determine that the server has the IPX internal network address of 44-ED-EE-E0 and the network address of 44-ED-00-10.

Component Type Descriptions

The following table provides brief descriptions of component types that can be found in Diagnostic Response packets.

Type	Component	Description
0	IPX/SPX	The actual IPX/SPX process or module in a dedicated NetWare file server, dedicated NetWare router, or NetWare client
1	Router drivers	The LAN board driver process in a file server or router, where "LAN driver" refers to the client LAN board driver

Type	Component	Description
2	LAN drivers	The client LAN board driver, such as NE2000.COM, NE1000.COM, and so on
3	Shells	The DOS shell/emulation module in the workstation (NETX.COM)
4	VAPs	The DOS shell/emulation module loaded on a NetWare v2.x server or an external router for VAP support
5	Router	The routing component in an external NetWare router
6	File server/router	The routing component in a NetWare file server (internal router)
7	Nondedicated IPX/SPX	The IPX/SPX process on a NetWare 2.x nondedicated file server, an external nondedicated router, or a NetWare v3.x or v4.x internal virtual LAN (IPX internal network)

Creating Diagnostic Tests

AS MENTIONED EARLIER in this chapter, you can use the Diagnostic Responder to test connectivity or gather configuration information about a server or client.

When creating a diagnostic test, you must first determine which network and nodes you wish to send the Diagnostic Request packet to and to whom the responses should be sent. This information will be placed in the IPX header of the Diagnostic Request packet.

Place the remote or local network address in the Destination Network Address field. You can use the value 0x00-00-00-00 to indicate the local network. Place the node address of the destination client or server in the Destination Node Address field. The value 0xFF-FF-FF-FF-FF-FF indicates that all nodes on the designated network should respond. Place your network address in the Source Network Address field. If you want the responses to be transmitted to another network, however, you can place that network address in the Source Network Address field instead. When you use the LANalyzer, the Source Node field can contain a fictitious node address. To capture the responses addressed to that node, you can configure the LANalyzer to filter for all Diagnostic Response packets sent to that node address.

Figure 19.10 shows a Diagnostic Request packet being transmitted to all nodes on network BB-BB-BB-BB.

After the IPX header, you can indicate information regarding the intended recipients. If you want all workstations (as indicated by broadcast addressing in the IPX header) to reply, the value in the Exclusion Count field should be 0x00. If, however, you do not want certain stations to reply, you can indicate an exclusion address count and then list the node addresses that should not respond. For example, perhaps you want only workstations, not servers, to respond.

In Figure 19.11, a Diagnostic Request packet is again being sent to all nodes on network BB-BB-BB-BB. Following the IPX header, however, it is specified that workstation 0x00-00-1B-03-98-3D should not respond. All other nodes on the network should respond.

As shown in Chapter 18, you can transmit diagnostic packets to test round-trip delay times across routers. You can also use it to test client and server connectivity. By simply addressing the IPX header to the desired client or server, you can test whether it is responding. Figure 19.12 shows a connectivity test transmitted directly to server SALES1, as shown in the Destination Network and Destination Node fields of the IPX header.

Since all servers have the Diagnostic Responder enabled, they should respond to the request. However, since the Diagnostic Responder is IPX based, there is no guarantee that the requests arrived on the remote network. In that case, you may wish to send a request to all nodes to ensure that you can access the remote network. If other stations reply successfully but the server does not, you can determine that it is either not connected or not running on the network.

The Diagnostic Responder can be a tremendously helpful tool for testing network response and connectivity. Since the responses provide configuration information about servers and clients, you can also use the Responder for

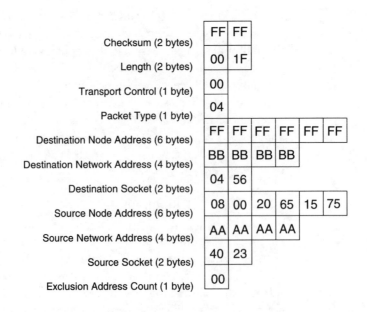

Checksum (2 bytes)

FF	FF

Length (2 bytes)

00	1F

Transport Control (1 byte)

00

Packet Type (1 byte)

04

Destination Node Address (6 bytes)

FF	FF	FF	FF	FF	FF

Destination Network Address (4 bytes)

BB	BB	BB	BB

Destination Socket (2 bytes)

04	56

Source Node Address (6 bytes)

08	00	20	65	15	75

Source Network Address (4 bytes)

AA	AA	AA	AA

Source Socket (2 bytes)

40	23

Exclusion Address Count (1 byte)

00

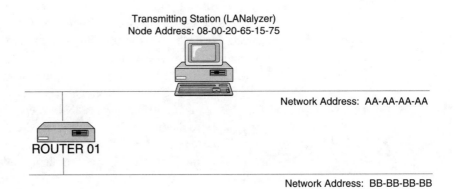

Transmitting Station (LANalyzer)
Node Address: 08-00-20-65-15-75

Network Address: AA-AA-AA-AA

ROUTER 01

Network Address: BB-BB-BB-BB

information gathering. Many third-party products also use the Diagnostic Responder to "discover" network devices.

Two LANalyzer applications are designed to transmit Diagnostic Request packets and filter for responses: NODEVIEW and ROUTVIEW.

FIGURE 19.11

Listing a node address in the Exclusion Address field indicates that a node should not respond to the Diagnostic Request packet.

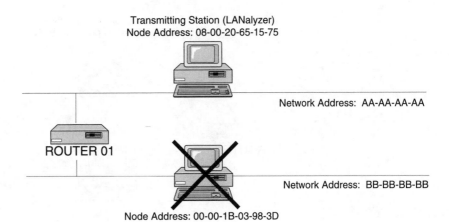

Checksum (2 bytes)	FF	FF				
Length (2 bytes)	00	25				
Transport Control (1 byte)	00					
Packet Type (1 byte)	04					
Destination Node Address (6 bytes)	FF	FF	FF	FF	FF	FF
Destination Network Address (4 bytes)	BB	BB	BB	BB		
Destination Socket (2 bytes)	04	56				
Source Node Address (6 bytes)	08	00	20	65	15	75
Source Network Address (4 bytes)	AA	AA	AA	AA		
Source Socket (2 bytes)	40	23				
Exclusion Address Count (1 byte)	01					
Exclusion Address (6 bytes)	00	00	1B	03	98	3D

Transmitting Station (LANalyzer)
Node Address: 08-00-20-65-15-75

Network Address: AA-AA-AA-AA

ROUTER 01

Network Address: BB-BB-BB-BB

Node Address: 00-00-1B-03-98-3D

You can use NODEVIEW to check the connectivity of NetWare nodes, and you can use ROUTVIEW to check nodes and servers on the other side of a router.

FIGURE 19.12

Testing the connectivity of
server SALES1

Checksum (2 bytes)	FF	FF				
Length (2 bytes)	00	1F				
Transport Control (1 byte)	00					
Packet Type (1 byte)	04					
Destination Node Address (6 bytes)	00	00	00	00	00	01
Destination Network Address (4 bytes)	C9	00	00	01		
Destination Socket (2 bytes)	04	56				
Source Node Address (6 bytes)	08	00	20	65	15	75
Source Network Address (4 bytes)	AA	AA	AA	AA		
Source Socket (2 bytes)	40	23				
Exclusion Address Count (1 byte)	00					

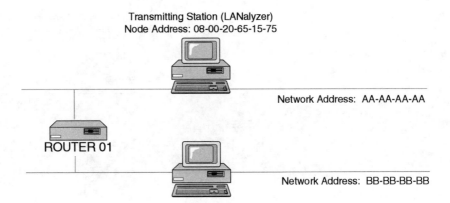

Transmitting Station (LANalyzer)
Node Address: 08-00-20-65-15-75

Network Address: AA-AA-AA-AA

ROUTER 01

Network Address: BB-BB-BB-BB

Server SALES1
IPX Internal Network Address:C9-00-00-01
Node Address: 00-00-00-00-00-01

This chapter has defined several uses for the Diagnostic Responder, including connectivity testing and configuration information gathering. By looking at the Diagnostic Responder Request packet format, you have seen how to transmit to an entire network, a group of selected nodes, or specific, individual stations.

The next chapter introduces one of the newest NetWare protocols, NetWare Directory Services (NDS).

NetWare Directory Services (NDS)

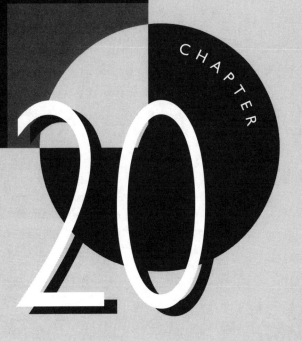

HEN NOVELL RELEASED NetWare 4.0, a new set of packets was observed on the network. These packets are required to support many NetWare 4.x features, including NetWare Directory Services (NDS). NDS is a globally distributed network database that replaces the bindery used in previous versions of NetWare.

In this chapter we examine the typical communications that occur on a network that uses NDS. This chapter also includes a list of the primary NCP function and subfunction codes that deal with NDS, as well as the NDS protocol verbs that provide NDS functionality at the NCP level.

Overview of NetWare NDS

NTIL NETWARE 4.0 was released, Novell relied on the bindery to store and provide all information necessary for the operating system and applications. NDS views the network as a unified information system rather than as a group of separate computers.

In earlier versions of NetWare, you logged in to a specific server. In an NDS-based network, you log in to the entire network. A single login provides you with access to all the network services you have rights to.

This chapter focuses on the NDS communications only. For additional information on NDS functionality and administration, refer to the materials listed in the bibliography contained in Appendix B.

NDS-Related Communications

N AN NDS network, several unique communications support the NDS database functions and time synchronization, as described in the following sections.

Replication

To enhance fault tolerance and access time to the network, the NDS database can be distributed across the network. Portions of the database can reside on all servers. Rather than keep a copy of the entire database on each server, you can partition off the database and store copies of each partition on many servers throughout the network. A *replica* is a copy of an NDS partition. These replicas are synchronized across the network to ensure accuracy.

Distribution of replicas requires additional communications on the network. NDS communications uses a new packet format that extends the existing NCP header (as defined in Chapter 15) for functions such as

- Comparing replica information

- Updating replicas

- Joining partitions

- Modifying replica entries

- Reading replica entries

- Removing replicas

- Synchronizing partitions

This chapter includes information on each of these functions. First, let's examine the type of time synchronization used on the network.

Time Synchronization

Time synchronization is important to the operation of NDS because it establishes the order in which directory events take place. For example, if you change a user password, the transaction is time stamped. This time stamp is a unique code that includes the time the event took place and identification of the replica that initiated the event. The time stamping requires that each server be identified as one type of time server. There are four types of time servers in NDS:

- Single Reference
- Primary
- Reference
- Secondary

Single Reference Time Servers

The Single Reference time server provides time to the Secondary time servers and clients. When this type of server is used, it is the sole source of time for the entire network. The supervisor sets the time on the Single Reference time server. This type of time server is the default when you install NetWare 4.x. When using a Single Reference time server, you cannot have any Primary or Reference time servers on the network.

Primary Time Servers

The Primary time server synchronizes network time with at least one other Primary or Reference time server. The Primary time server provides the time to Secondary time servers and clients. This type of server resets its internal clock to synchronize with the decided network time.

Reference Time Servers

The Reference time server provides a time for all other servers and clients to synchronize with. Reference time servers are generally synchronized with an external time source, such as a radio clock that receives time signals from the National Observatory or another accurate time source. The Reference time server polls Primary or Reference time servers and then votes with them to synchronize the time. Primary time servers must reach consensus with the time provided by the Reference time server.

Secondary Time Servers

Secondary time servers obtain the time from a Single Reference, Primary, or Reference time server. The Secondary time server provides the time to clients (such as workstations and applications). This type of server cannot vote to determine the correct network time.

New NCP and NDS Verbs

FIVE NEW NCP calls support NDS communications. Of course, five calls cannot support all the functionality defined by NDS. Hence, the need for NDS verbs. NDS verbs are nested in the NDS packets, as shown in Figure 20.1, and can be considered sub-subfunction calls.

FIGURE 20.1

NDS verbs are nested in the NDS packets.

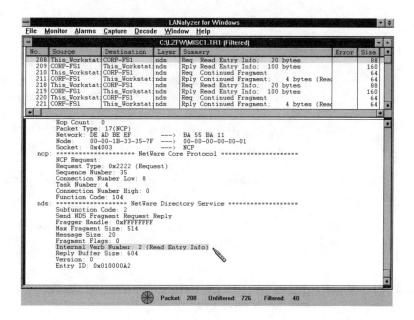

New NCP Function Calls

The following is a list of the new function calls that support NDS communications:

Service	Request Type	Function Code	Subfunction Code
Ping for NDS NCP	2222	104	01
Send NDS Fragmented Request/Reply	2222	104	02
Close NDS Fragment	2222	104	03
Return Bindery Context	2222	104	04
Monitor NDS Connection	2222	104	05

Now let's examine each of these function calls and view the structure of each packet.

Ping for NDS NCP

The Ping for NDS NCP packet allows a client to query a server to see whether it supports NCP function code 104, the NDS function code. When an NDS server is brought up, this is one of the packets it transmits, as shown in Figure 20.2.

The reply includes the tree name—T—followed by underscores, and the tree depth (root), as shown in Figure 20.3. The following completion codes are possible for this packet:

Decimal	Hexadecimal	Completion Code
0	0x00	Success
251	0xFB	NDS NCP not available
254	0xFE	Bad packet

Send NDS Fragmented Request/Reply

The Send NDS Fragmented Request/Reply NCP sends fragmented requests to a server and receives fragmented replies. For example, when a server is

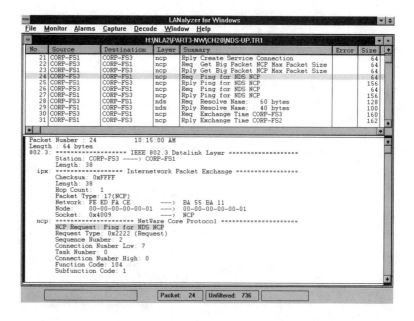

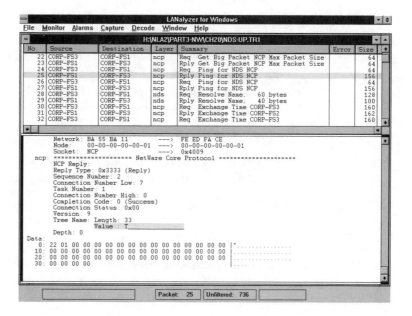

updating another server's NDS replica information, the server transmits a series of NDS fragments that contain all the update information for the packet. Figure 20.4 displays the format of this NCP.

FIGURE 20.4

Send NDS Fragmented Request/Reply packet format

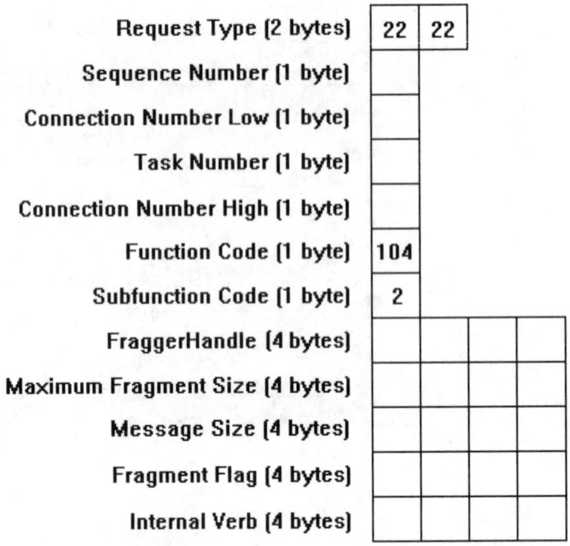

Request Type (2 bytes)	22 22
Sequence Number (1 byte)	
Connection Number Low (1 byte)	
Task Number (1 byte)	
Connection Number High (1 byte)	
Function Code (1 byte)	104
Subfunction Code (1 byte)	2
FraggerHandle (4 bytes)	
Maximum Fragment Size (4 bytes)	
Message Size (4 bytes)	
Fragment Flag (4 bytes)	
Internal Verb (4 bytes)	

MAXIMUM FRAGMENT SIZE The Maximum Fragment Size field indicates the maximum number of data bytes that can be sent as a reply. This field is the maximum size supported by the underlying media minus the 4-byte Reply Size and 4-byte FraggerHandle fields in the NDS reply.

FLAG The Flag field is always set to 0.

INTERNAL VERB The Internal Verb field contains the number of the NDS verb that should be executed. Table 20.1, presented later in this chapter, describes each NDS verb.

CLOSE NDS FRAGMENT The Close NDS Fragment packet completes an NDS fragment-based communication.

RETURN BINDERY CONTEXT The Return Bindery Context packet simply gets the NDS bindery context.

MONITOR NDS CONNECTION The Monitor NDS Connection packet monitors the validity of an NDS connection.

NDS NCP Verbs

As mentioned earlier in this chapter, NDS communications can be fragmented into a number of requests and replies. The Verb field defines the type of NDS service that is requested. For example, Figure 20.5 displays a request for a server address. Figure 20.6 displays the response, which indicates that the server name is CORP-FS2, the context is LAB.TC, and the server's address is BA-55-BA-11:00-00-00-00-00-01:4-51. This information can be interpreted as follows:

Internal IPX address	BA-55-BA-11
Internal node address	00-00-00-00-00-01
NCP socket number:	04-51

FIGURE 20.5

The verb number 53 (decimal) indicates a request to get a server address.

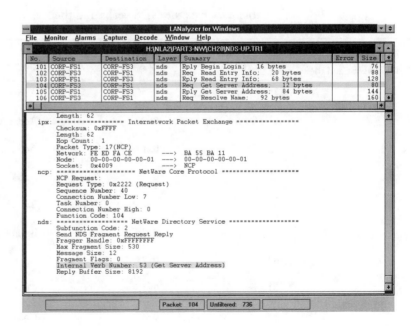

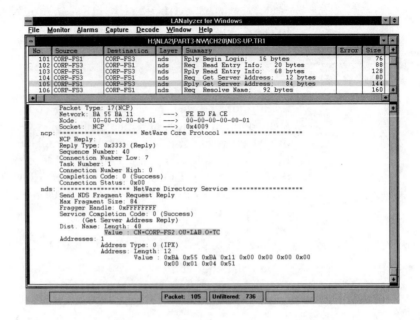

Table 20.1 lists the NDS verbs and their values.

	DECIMAL VALUE	HEXADECIMAL VALUE	DESCRIPTION
TABLE 20.1 NDS verbs and their values	76	0x4C	Abort Low Level Join
	07	0x07	Add Entry
	14	0x14	Add Partition
	25	0x19	Add Replica
	45	0x2D	Backup Entry
	59	0x3B	Begin Authentication
	42	0x2A	Begin Move Entry
	31	0x1F	Change Replica Type
	70	0x46	Change Tree Name

	DECIMAL VALUE	HEXADECIMAL VALUE	DESCRIPTION
TABLE 20.1 NDS verbs and their values (continued)	72	0x48	Check Login Restrictions
	50	0x32	Close Iteration
	04	0x04	Compare
	64	0x40	Create Back Link
	67	0x43	Create Entry Directory
	29	0x1D	Create Subordinate Reference
	11	0x0B	Define Attribute
	14	0x0E	Define Class
	65	0x41	Delete External Reference
	69	0x45	Designate New Master
	36	0x24	End Update Replica
	33	0x21	End Update Schema
	60	0x3C	Finish Authentication
	43	0x2B	Finish Move Entry
	77	0x4D	Get All Servers
	19	0x13	Get Effective Rights
	41	0x29	Get Replica Root ID
	53	0x35	Get Server Address
	24	0x18	Join Partitions
	30	0x1E	Link Replica
	05	0x05	List
	18	0x12	List Containable Classes

	DECIMAL VALUE	HEXADECIMAL VALUE	DESCRIPTION
TABLE 20.1 NDS verbs and their values (continued)	22	0x16	List Partitions
	75	0x4B	Low Level Join
	74	0x4A	Low Level Split
	16	0x10	Modify Class Definition
	09	0x09	Modify Entry
	10	0x0A	Modify Relative Distinguished Name
	27	0x1B	Open Stream
	71	0x47	Partition Entry Count
	3	0x03	Read
	12	0x0C	Read Attribute Definition
	15	0x0F	Read Class Definition
	2	0x02	Read Entry Information
	44	0x2C	Release Moved Entry
	13	0x0D	Remove Attribute Definition
	17	0x11	Remove Class Definition
	8	0x08	Remove Entry
	68	0x44	Remove Entry Directory
	21	0x15	Remove Partition
	26	0x1A	Remove Replica
	66	0x42	Rename External Reference
	63	0x3F	Repair Timestamps
	1	0x01	Resolve Name

TABLE 20.1	DECIMAL VALUE	HEXADECIMAL VALUE	DESCRIPTION
	46	0x2E	Restore Entry
NDS verbs and their	6	0x06	Search Entries
values	54	0x36	Set Keys
(continued)	23	0x17	Split Partition
	73	0x49	Start Join
	35	0x23	Start Update Replica
	32	0x20	Start Update Schema
	38	0x26	Synchronize Partition
	39	0x27	Synchronize Schema
	37	0x25	Update Replica
	34	0x22	Update Schema

Replica updates occur transparently on the network. Let's take a look at one part of a replica update, shown in Figure 20.7. In packet 436, the server CORP-FS3 transmits a fragment request packet to a server named CORP-FS1. Packet 437 is the response packet that contains the replica update information.

As you can see, in packet 437, the response contains information regarding a network print queue (Q1 and CN=LAZER1.OU=LAB.O=TC), queue directory (SYS:QUEUES\AB000002.QDR), print server (CN=PS1.OU=LAB.O=TC), host server (CN=CORP-FS2.OU=LAB.O=TC), and volume (CN=CORP-FS2_SYS.OU=LAB.O=TC).

FIGURE 20.7

NDS replication
information is exchanged
using the NDS fragment
Request/Reply NCP.

```
Packet Number : 436           10:19:31 AM
Length : 64 bytes
802.3: =================== IEEE 802.3 Datalink Layer ===================
          Station: CORP-FS3 ----> CORP-FS1
          Length: 46
    ipx: ================= Internetwork Packet Exchange =================
          Checksum: 0xFFFF
          Length: 46
          Hop Count:  0
          Packet Type: 17(NCP)
          Network: FE ED FA CE        --->  BA 55 BA 11
          Node:    00-00-00-00-00-01  --->  00-00-00-00-00-01
          Socket:  NCP                --->  0x4006
    ncp: ==================== NetWare Core Protocol ====================
          NCP Reply:
          Reply Type: 0x3333 (Reply)
          Sequence Number: 48
          Connection Number Low: 2
          Task Number: 1
          Connection Number High: 0
          Completion Code: 0 (Success)
          Connection Status: 0x00
    nds: =================== NetWare Directory Service ==================
          Send NDS Fragment Request Reply
          Max Fragment Size: 4
          Fragger Handle: 0x0
                (Continued Fragment Reply)

Packet Number : 437           10:19:31 AM
Message Fragment List :
433, 435, 437
Length : 1424 bytes
802.3: =================== IEEE 802.3 Datalink Layer ===================
          Station: CORP-FS1 ----> CORP-FS3
          Length: 360
    ipx: ================= Internetwork Packet Exchange =================
          Checksum: 0xFFFF
          Length: 360
          Hop Count:  1
          Packet Type: 17(NCP)
          Network: BA 55 BA 11        --->  FE ED FA CE
          Node:    00-00-00-00-00-01  --->  00-00-00-00-00-01
          Socket:  0x4006             --->  NCP
    ncp: ==================== NetWare Core Protocol ====================
          NCP Request:
          Request Type: 0x2222 (Request)
          Sequence Number: 49
          Connection Number Low: 2
          Task Number: 0
          Connection Number High: 0
          Function Code: 104
    nds: =================== NetWare Directory Service ==================
          Subfunction Code: 2
          Send NDS Fragment Request Reply
          Fragger Handle: 0x0
          Version: 2
          Flags: 0x00000001
          Iteration Handle: 0xFFFFFFFF
          Replica Handle: 0x00000002
          Replica Type: 1
          Parent ID: 0x0100009D
          Replica Name: Length: 12
                        Value : CN=Q1
          Whole Seconds:  754713136 (02:32:16 December  1, 1993 GMT)
          Replica Number: 1
          Event ID: 0
          Base Class: Length: 12
                        Value : Queue
```

FIGURE 20.7

NDS replication
information is exchanged
using the NDS fragment
Request/Reply NCP
(continued).

```
Chunk Size: 1296
        Attribute Info Entrys: 11
        Attribute Name: Length: 8
                        Value : ACL
     Attribute Value Entrys: 4
     Flags: 0x00000008
     Whole Seconds:  754713136 (02:32:16 December  1, 1993 GMT)
     Replica Number: 1
     Event ID: 4
     Length of ACL Entry: 76
     Protected Attr Name: Length: 48
                        Value : [All Attributes Rights]
        Subject Name: Length: 14
                   Value : [Root]
        Privileges: 2


        Flags: 0x00000008
        Whole Seconds:  754713137 (02:32:17 December  1, 1993 GMT)
        Replica Number: 1
        Event ID: 0
        Length of ACL Entry: 72
        Protected Attr Name: Length: 30
                        Value : [Entry Rights]
        Subject Name: Length: 28
                   Value : CN=Admin.O=TC
        Privileges: 1F


        Flags: 0x00000008
        Whole Seconds:  754713137 (02:32:17 December  1, 1993 GMT)
        Replica Number: 1
        Event ID: 1
        Length of ACL Entry: 88
        Protected Attr Name: Length: 48
                        Value : [All Attributes Rights]
        Subject Name: Length: 28
                   Value : CN=Admin.O=TC
        Privileges: 2F


        Flags: 0x00000008
        Whole Seconds:  754713137 (02:32:17 December  1, 1993 GMT)
        Replica Number: 1
        Event ID: 2
        Length of ACL Entry: 60
        Protected Attr Name: Length: 30
                        Value : [Entry Rights]
        Subject Name: Length: 14
                   Value : [Root]
        Privileges: 1


        Attribute Name: Length: 6
                   Value : CN
        Attribute Value Entrys: 1
        Flags: 0x00000009
        Whole Seconds:  754713136 (02:32:16 December  1, 1993 GMT)
        Replica Number: 1
        Event ID: 6
        Length: 6
        Value : Q1


        Attribute Name: Length: 24
                   Value : Description
        Attribute Value Entrys: 1
        Flags: 0x00000008
        Whole Seconds:  754713136 (02:32:16 December  1, 1993 GMT)
        Replica Number: 1
        Event ID: 12
        Length: 4
        Value :
```

FIGURE 20.7

NDS replication
information is exchanged
using the NDS fragment
Request/Reply NCP
(continued).

```
Attribute Name: Length: 24
               Value : Host Server
Attribute Value Entrys: 1
Flags: 0x00000008
Whole Seconds:  754713136 (02:32:16 December  1, 1993 GMT)
Replica Number: 1
Event ID: 8
Length: 48
Value : CN=CORP-FS2.OU=LAB.O=TC


Attribute Name: Length: 26
               Value : Object Class
Attribute Value Entrys: 3
Flags: 0x0000000A
Whole Seconds:  754713136 (02:32:16 December  1, 1993 GMT)
Replica Number: 1
Event ID: 1
Length: 12
Value : Queue


Flags: 0x00000008
Whole Seconds:  754713136 (02:32:16 December  1, 1993 GMT)
Replica Number: 1
Event ID: 2
Length: 18
Value : Resource


Flags: 0x00000008
Whole Seconds:  754713136 (02:32:16 December  1, 1993 GMT)
Replica Number: 1
Event ID: 3
Length: 8
Value : Top


Attribute Name: Length: 18
               Value : Operator
Attribute Value Entrys: 1
Flags: 0x00000008
Whole Seconds:  754713138 (02:32:18 December  1, 1993 GMT)
Replica Number: 1
Event ID: 0
Length: 28
Value : CN=Admin.O=TC


Attribute Name: Length: 32
               Value : Queue Directory
Attribute Value Entrys: 1
Flags: 0x00000008
Whole Seconds:  754713136 (02:32:16 December  1, 1993 GMT)
Replica Number: 1
Event ID: 11
Length: 48
Value : SYS:QUEUES\AB000002.QDR


Attribute Name: Length: 14
               Value : Server
Attribute Value Entrys: 1
Flags: 0x00000008
Whole Seconds:  754777637 (20:27:17 December  1, 1993 GMT)
Replica Number: 1
Event ID: 0
Length: 38
Value : CN=PS1.OU=LAB.O=TC
```

FIGURE 20.7

NDS replication
information is exchanged
using the NDS fragment
Request/Reply NCP
(continued).

```
Attribute Name: Length: 10
                Value : User
Attribute Value Entrys: 3
Flags: 0x00000008
Whole Seconds:  754713137 (02:32:17 December  1, 1993 GMT)
Replica Number: 1
Event ID: 3
Length: 24
Value : OU=LAB.O=TC

Flags: 0x00000008
Whole Seconds:  754713137 (02:32:17 December  1, 1993 GMT)
Replica Number: 1
Event ID: 4
Length: 48
Value : CN=Everyone.OU=LAB.O=TC

Flags: 0x00000008
Whole Seconds:  754713138 (02:32:18 December  1, 1993 GMT)
Replica Number: 1
Event ID: 1
Length: 28
Value : CN=Admin.O=TC

Attribute Name: Length: 14
                Value : Device
Attribute Value Entrys: 1
Flags: 0x00000008
Whole Seconds:  754713153 (02:32:33 December  1, 1993 GMT)
Replica Number: 1
Event ID: 5
Length: 44
Value : CN=LAZER1.OU=LAB.O=TC

Attribute Name: Length: 14
                Value : Volume
Attribute Value Entrys: 1
Flags: 0x00000008
Whole Seconds:  754713136 (02:32:16 December  1, 1993 GMT)
Replica Number: 1
Event ID: 10
Length: 56
Value : CN=CORP-FS2_SYS.OU=LAB.O=TC
```

The NDS verbs are the heart of all NDS database replication for distribution of directory services information.

Classifying Your NDS Traffic Level

We are constantly asked about the effect of NDS traffic on overall traffic requirements. There is no single answer to this question—the packets per second requirement depends on your NDS replication definition and the size of your NDS tree.

You can use the LANalyzer for Windows to quickly determine how much current bandwidth is required by NDS by following these simple steps:

Step 1: Increase your Packet Receive buffer size to the largest possible setting. Select Capture > Options and select a setting that matches the amount of memory in your LZFW station.

Step 2: Define a Capture Filter for NetWare traffic only. Select Capture > Filter and double-click on the NetWare entry in the protocols list.

Step 3: Start the Capture by clicking on the Start button under the Capture buffer dial.

Step 4: Let the Capture buffer fill up completely. You can tell when the buffer is full by looking at the Capture buffer dial. When the dial is colored in completely (in turquoise, not gray), this indicates the buffer is full.

Step 5: View the Capture buffer by clicking on the View button under the Capture buffer dial.

Step 6: Scroll through the Summary window until you find a packet that has the entry "NDS" in the Layer column. Click on the NDS packet in the Summary window; the packet decode window now shows the contents of the selected packet.

Step 7: Inside the packet decode window, double-click the Function Code field that contains the value "104." The Display Filter window appears with the filter set to look for all packets with the value 104 in the Function Code field offset. Click OK.

LZFW is now sorting through all the packets in your Capture buffer to isolate and display only NDS packets. Record the number in the Unfiltered Packets field at the bottom of the screen. Record the number in the Filtered Packets field at the bottom of the screen. The filtered packets are NDS traffic; the unfiltered packets are all NetWare packets. If you captured 1000 packets (unfiltered) and have 50 NDS packets (filtered), then NDS traffic comprises approximately 5% of all NetWare traffic at the current time.

This provides you with a quick look at the percentage of packets on the wire that are NDS packets. Hopefully in the future, LANalyzer for Windows will have more sophisticated Capture Filters that allow us to define a capture filter on a function code field. This would enable us to use the trending abilities of the statistics graphs to determine overall NDS traffic levels (based on bandwidth utilization and packets per second) over time.

In this chapter, we examined the new NCP calls that support NetWare Directory Services, the verb listing used for fragmented reads of the directory services replicas, sample NetWare Directory NCP calls, and finally, a portion of the replica update process. Part IV of this book examines how to create a network baseline, stress-test network cabling systems and components, test NCP communications, and characterize server performance.

Performance Benchmarking, Testing, and Optimization

Creating and Using a Network Baseline

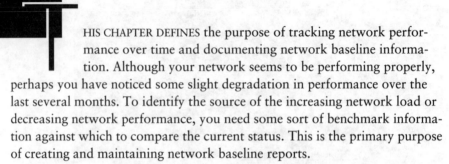

THIS CHAPTER DEFINES the purpose of tracking network performance over time and documenting network baseline information. Although your network seems to be performing properly, perhaps you have noticed some slight degradation in performance over the last several months. To identify the source of the increasing network load or decreasing network performance, you need some sort of benchmark information against which to compare the current status. This is the primary purpose of creating and maintaining network baseline reports.

A baseline is simply a "snapshot" of network health. As your network grows in complexity and size, you can refer back to your baseline report to chart its growth and performance.

What Is Included in a Baseline Report?

BASELINE REPORTS CAN include specialized information about a network, such as router statistics, LAN driver statistics, and so on. However, several key characteristics of network performance should be included in all baseline reports. These key characteristics include

- Utilization

- Error rates

- Packets per second

- Kilobytes per second

- Most active servers

- Request Being Processed packets

Within practical limits, this information could be tracked for mission-critical servers and clients on the network, as well.

Utilization Trends

Utilization increase is a common characteristic of a network that has grown over time. As new workstations and applications are added to the network, more users and more data are dependent on the cabling system for transport. By documenting this change, you can prepare for further growth and justify the expense required to enhance the network.

When charting utilization statistics, it is a good idea to create a utilization trend graph. A trend graph plots information over a certain time period, such as a week or month. A statistics graph that provides only 20 minutes of utilization information would be misleading for later comparisons. Perhaps the utilization was being charted at a time when the network was busier than normal, such as during the morning hours when everyone is logging in to the network, or when backups are being performed across the network. Figure 21.1 shows a utilization trend graph as it appears on the LANalyzer for Windows screen.

FIGURE 21.1

Utilization trend graph

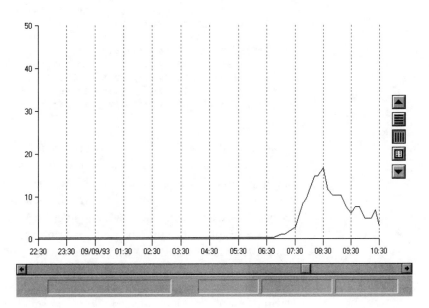

Analyzers generally allow you to export network statistics in various formats. You can then import the information to a spreadsheet program to provide further analysis. When exporting statistics for use in a spreadsheet, be certain to select the proper delimiter value for the spreadsheet program you are using. A delimiter such as a comma or tab will separate the fields of the information for proper interpretation by a spreadsheet program. Figure 21.2 shows a file that has been exported using comma separation.

FIGURE 21.2

File exported with comma-separated fields

```
"Date","Time","Pkts/Sec","Avg. Errors","Util","Kb/Sec"
"7/9/93","3:15:03AM","687","1","13","161"
"7/9/93","3:30:03AM","444","1","7","93"
"7/9/93","3:45:03AM","808","1","14","167"
"7/9/93","4:00:03AM","515","1","9","108"
"7/9/93","4:15:03AM","787","1","15","183"
"7/9/93","4:30:03AM","723","1","14","172"
"7/9/93","4:45:03AM","616","1","11","136"
"7/9/93","5:00:04AM","546","1","10","123"
"7/9/93","5:15:03AM","607","1","10","125"
"7/9/93","5:30:03AM","427","1","7","89"
"7/9/93","5:45:04AM","387","1","7","84"
"7/9/93","6:00:04AM","381","1","7","83"
"7/9/93","6:15:03AM","401","1","7","85"
"7/9/93","6:30:03AM","401","1","7","85"
"7/9/93","6:45:03AM","437","1","7","88"
"7/9/93","7:00:03AM","395","1","7","85"
"7/9/93","7:15:03AM","420","1","7","85"
"7/9/93","7:30:04AM","361","1","6","75"
"7/9/93","7:45:04AM","349","1","6","76"
"7/9/93","8:00:04AM","329","1","6","74"
"7/9/93","8:15:04AM","363","1","6","80"
"7/9/93","8:30:04AM","342","1","6","74"
```

Notice that the fields are separated by commas. The titles are also separated by commas. Figure 21.3 shows how the data can be plotted. This example uses a bar graph to display the utilization trend information. By viewing Figure 21.3, you can see several characteristics of your network's performance, such as peak load times and idle times.

On the graph, notice that the peak load times are from 8:00 A.M. to 9:00 A.M., 5:00 P.M., and 12:00 A.M. These are the times when people are logging in to and out of the network and when backup is being performed, respectively.

Based on the information presented, you may decide to set your utilization alarm threshold at 25%, since you do not normally exceed 21% utilization at the peak time of the day.

FIGURE 21.3

A comma-separated file can be imported by many spreadsheet programs.

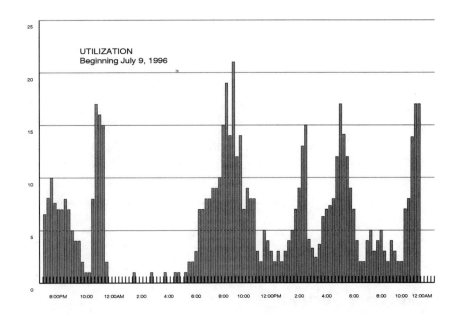

Error Rates

You should also include error rate trend information in the baseline report. This ensures that you are aware of your typical error rates over time. As the network grows, the error rates may also increase. As discussed in Parts I and II of this book, increased errors may be a symptom of network growth, cabling bottlenecks or miswiring, or possibly a component failure.

Figure 21.4 shows a trend graph for error rates. This trend information has been exported and plotted on a line graph. The typical number of errors on this network ranges from 0 to 4 errors in every 15-minute period.

Based on this graph and the preceding utilization graph, you can see that your errors are closely related to network utilization. As the network grows, both utilization and errors will most likely increase. If, however, errors increase and utilization does not, you have a possible component problem, such as a faulty network interface card or transceiver.

FIGURE 21.4

Error rate trend
information plotted on
a line graph

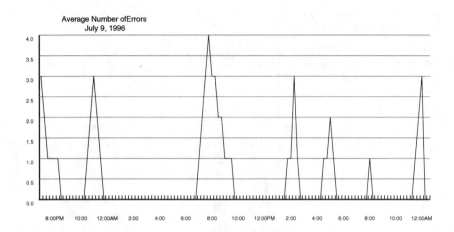

FIGURE 21.4

Error rate trend
information plotted on
a line graph

Packets per Second

Tracking the number of packets per second on the network will give you a general idea of the amount of traffic on the wire. This is not the same as utilization, since utilization is based on the number of kilobytes on the wire per second. Packets can range in size and do not directly correspond with utilization. Utilization may increase as the result of an increase in either the number of packets on the wire or the size of packets.

On a NetWare LAN, the number of packets per second indicates the number of requests, replies, and information packets that are typically serviced by the network. If the number of packets increases but the utilization does not, you can assume that the number of small packets has increased, which causes no increase in bandwidth utilization.

Figure 21.5 shows a trend graph for packets per second in an area graph. You can easily see the peak times for requests, replies, and information packets on the network.

As you add NetWare servers to your network, you may see the number of packets per second steadily rise. Part of the increase is a result of the number of SAP and RIP broadcasts that are propagated throughout the network. The excessive number of SAP packets often seen on large NetWare LANs prompted the creation of Novell's RESTRICT.NLM product, designed to limit SAP packets passed by NetWare routers. This product has evolved into the SAP filtering ability in NetWare 4.x and the MultiProtocol Router. As

FIGURE 21.5

Packets-per-second trend graph

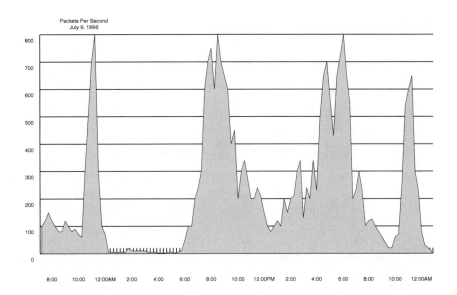

mentioned in Chapter 17, some third-party routers, such as Cisco routers, also have the ability to filter SAP traffic.

Kilobytes per Second

By tracking kilobytes per second, you can determine the actual throughput of your network—the number of kilobytes transmitted per second.

The utilization statistics are based on kilobytes per second and determine a percentage of bandwidth in use compared to the maximum possible for Ethernet (10Mb/s) and Token Ring (4 or 16Mb/s).

Most Active Servers

Be aware of the most active servers on the network. Maintaining a list of the top three servers will help you distribute the load among them as you add applications and users. To measure server activity, track the number of packets per second from the server over several days or a week. If you place too many users on a single server, the server may begin transmitting Request Being Processed packets. By keeping an eye on the servers most often used, you may be able to avoid server overload. If performance decreases but

Request Being Processed packets are not observed, the server's LAN card may be the bottleneck.

In Chapter 24, you will graph server performance statistics.

Request Being Processed Packets

If a server cannot reply to a client because it is busy performing other tasks, it transmits a Request Being Processed packet. A few of these packets may not signal a problem, but a constantly increasing number is a sign that the server is being overloaded.

In Chapter 24, you will look more closely at the cause of Request Being Processed packets.

When Should a Baseline Be Created?

BASELINE INFORMATION SHOULD be gathered on a healthy network during a time in which conditions are normal. In order to create a baseline indicative of normal network activity, the baseline information should be gathered when the network is performing under normal conditions. You can recompile baseline information after adding a new server, workstation, router, or application, if desired. As mentioned earlier in this chapter, the purpose of a baseline is to provide a "snapshot" of normal network activity. You can contrast future network reports against the baseline for comparative purposes. This historical data, viewed in total, shows the "evolution" of your network and may indicate future trends.

An additional use of baselining is the prediction of network performance based on planned changes. For example, if a client GUI (graphical user interface) were being considered for all stations on the network, a typical station using the new GUI could be tested. The station's increased traffic could be multiplied by the anticipated total number of stations in the implementation planned and then added to the baseline to define estimated performance:

Baseline + (new traffic × number of stations) = estimated future baseline

Comparing Current Network Performance against the Baseline

N ORDER TO track network growth and health, you can gather statistics months later than the baseline was created and compare the information against the baseline.

For example, in Figure 21.6, you can see a graph of the current network utilization in comparison to a network baseline created in January 1993. The network administrator wanted to know how the network had been affected by the addition of several workstations and a database server.

FIGURE 21.6

Comparing utilization information in September 1993 against the baseline of daily activity created in January

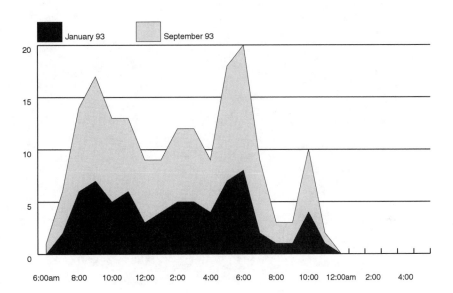

By appending September's utilization information to January's baseline information, a comparative chart of utilization growth has been created. The utilization chart is for a 24-hour period beginning at 6:00 A.M. Although the idle times have not changed significantly—from midnight to 5:30 A.M., the network goes unused—overall utilization during the work hours has increased quite a bit.

This chapter has examined some key elements that should be included in a baseline report, such as utilization, error rate, and packets per second. You also viewed a comma-separated trend file and the charts that were created from the data. Finally, you compared current network activity against the baseline to verify that bandwidth utilization has increased over an eight-month period.

In the next chapter, you will stress-test the network cabling system and an individual component.

Stress-Testing Techniques

22

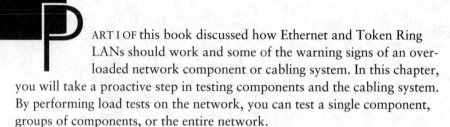

ART I OF this book discussed how Ethernet and Token Ring LANs should work and some of the warning signs of an over-loaded network component or cabling system. In this chapter, you will take a proactive step in testing components and the cabling system. By performing load tests on the network, you can test a single component, groups of components, or the entire network.

Two types of loads can be generated onto the network:

- Dumb loads

- Intelligent loads

Before you begin generating load tests on the network, a word of warning: be very selective of when you perform load tests, because they will most likely degrade network performance. The tests are designed to find the point at which a component or network cabling system becomes the bottleneck for communications. You should perform these tests during the evenings or on a weekend, when the network is less actively used.

Dumb Loads

UMB LOADS ARE designed to test the cabling system bandwidth and determine how much additional load the media can sustain without performance degradation.

When you are generating traffic that is not addressed to any particular device and that contains no meaningful information, it is called a dumb load. You can use these loads to test the network cabling system. In Chapter 3, you used a dumb load (GENLOAD test) to test access to the network cabling system. As shown in Figure 22.1, the GENLOAD application can be configured to transmit packets to an invalid node address of 0x00-00-00-00-00-00. No station will respond to this address; therefore, you are not testing a component.

FIGURE 22.1

The GENLOAD application is designed to generate a dumb load.

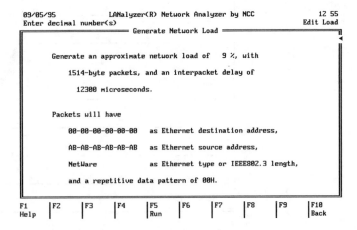

```
09/05/95              LANalyzer(R) Network Analyzer by NCC          12 55
Enter decimal number(s)                                          Edit Load
                        ═══ Generate Network Load ═══

         Generate an approximate network load of   9 %, with

            1514-byte packets, and an interpacket delay of

              12300 microseconds.

         Packets will have

              00-00-00-00-00-00    as Ethernet destination address,

              AB-AB-AB-AB-AB-AB    as Ethernet source address,

              NetWare             as Ethernet type or IEEE802.3 length,

              and a repetitive data pattern of 00H.


F1     |F2    |F3    |F4    |F5    |F6    |F7    |F8    |F9    |F10
Help   |      |      |      |Run   |      |      |      |      |Back
```

Using the GENLOAD application, you can generate varying amounts of load onto the network and view your transmission statistics to evaluate network access. In Figure 22.2, the results of running a GENLOAD test on an Ethernet network have been plotted. During the test, the percentage of transmissions that were successfully transmitted on the first attempt has been noted. As the load increases on the network, successful first attempts decrease.

It is clear from the graph that access to the medium begins to decline when there is a network load of approximately 35% to 40%. From 40% to 50%, the decline in performance is quite noticeable. The following table lists the statistics for Figure 22.2.

Ethernet Network Load	Successful Transmissions
10%	100%
20%	98%
30%	97%
40%	90%
50%	58%
60%	46%
70%	44%

FIGURE 22.2

Results of testing the
Ethernet network access
under various loads

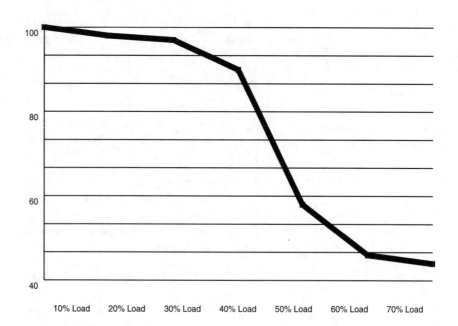

Many people stress-test their networks based on user response. This method requires you to generate a reasonable load onto the network for a full work day and wait for any network users to complain about network performance. If the load is unacceptable, the symptoms encountered may include workstation timeouts and/or slow file transfers. If, however, no users complain, you know there is some margin for growth on the network.

You can also test your expansion capabilities by loading an application during the stress test. Pay particular attention to the response time as the load increases on the network.

Now that you know your margin for growth, you can determine whether network sluggishness is due to a bottleneck in the cabling system. If, at a later date, users begin to complain of slow file transfers, check the utilization. If you are within your acceptable bandwidth utilization amount, some other problem may be causing the slowness, such as an overloaded server or router.

Although not a very scientific method for stress-testing the network cabling system, testing acceptable bandwidth utilization based on user response gives a realistic measure of how much performance degradation users will permit.

Intelligent Loads

OU USE *INTELLIGENT LOADS* to test a particular device on a network, such as a router, server, or network interface card. When you generate an intelligent load, the packets are addressed to a particular device, often with some reply requested, as shown in Figure 22.3.

NetWare v3.x and 4.x servers will adjust parameters, such as packet receive buffers, in response to load demands. This type of "regulation" should be considered when drawing conclusions from your tests.

FIGURE 22.3

Intelligent loads are transmitted to a particular device on the network.

An intelligent load may be used to test individual components.

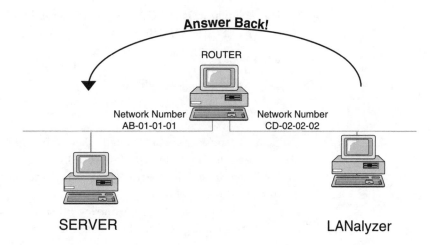

One example of using an intelligent load test is when you are testing the response from a server's network interface card. By transmitting various loads consisting of SAP requests to a NetWare server, you can test the server card's ability to buffer packets and respond.

For example, you can perform an intelligent load test on a NetWare v3.x server that has a 16-bit card installed. By transmitting gradually increasing loads of SAP packets, you can determine at what point the card is unable to keep up. If, however, you substitute a 32-bit card in the server, you should see a dramatic increase in performance. This increase in performance is not due to any changes in the server except the 32-bit network interface card. You can use this type of load test to justify the purchase of a faster card for the server or a router.

Stress Tests

TWO LANALYZER APPLICATIONS are designed specifically for stress testing. The first one, GENLOAD, has been covered in this chapter and in Chapter 3.

The second test, VARLOAD, generates a random load between 1% and 7%. As shown in Figure 22.4, three transmit channels are defined in VARLOAD:

- 64-byte packets

- 633-byte packets

- 1082-byte packets

Each transmit channel is defined as a dumb load by default, transmitting to destination address 0x-00-00-00-00-00-00. To make the application transmit an intelligent load, edit the transmit channel and provide a destination address, as shown in Figure 22.5.

In this example, you are transmitting Ethernet packets to a file server. Since the packets are addressed to the server, the server will attempt to process the packet.

As you can see in Figure 22.6, once VARLOAD is running, the Global screen shows the packet size distribution on the network and the current load.

Bridges and routers are good candidates for testing. Use multiple tests with various size packets to determine whether bridging/routing efficiency is affected by packet size. Many internetworking devices have built-in error

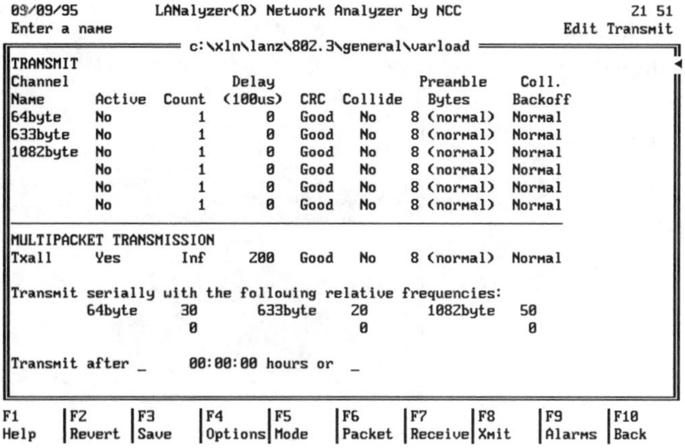

FIGURE 22.4

The VARLOAD application for Ethernet has three predefined channels to transmit 64-, 633-, and 1082-byte packets.

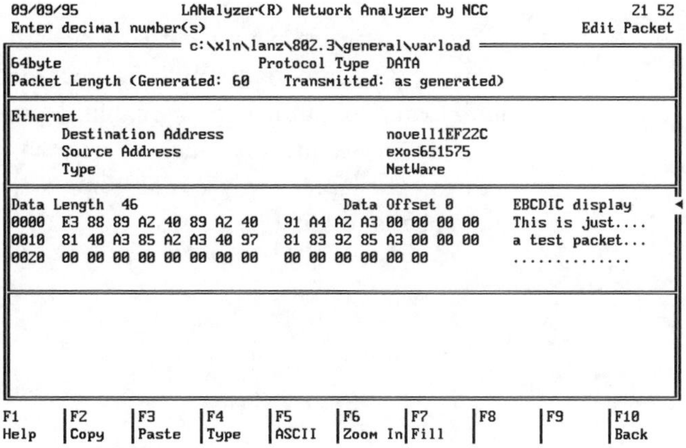

```
09/09/95           LANalyzer(R) Network Analyzer by NCC              21 51
Enter a name                                                    Edit Transmit
              ═══════ c:\xln\lanz\802.3\general\varload ═══════
TRANSMIT
Channel                    Delay                   Preamble    Coll.
Name       Active  Count  (100us)  CRC  Collide    Bytes       Backoff
64byte     No      1       0       Good  No        8 (normal)  Normal
633byte    No      1       0       Good  No        8 (normal)  Normal
1082byte   No      1       0       Good  No        8 (normal)  Normal
           No      1       0       Good  No        8 (normal)  Normal
           No      1       0       Good  No        8 (normal)  Normal
           No      1       0       Good  No        8 (normal)  Normal
──────────────────────────────────────────────────────────────────────
MULTIPACKET TRANSMISSION
Txall      Yes     Inf     200     Good  No        8 (normal)  Normal

Transmit serially with the following relative frequencies:
           64byte     30        633byte    20       1082byte   50
                       0                    0                   0

Transmit after _    00:00:00 hours or  _


F1    |F2     |F3   |F4      |F5   |F6     |F7     |F8   |F9     |F10
Help  |Revert |Save |Options |Mode |Packet |Receive|Xmit |Alarms |Back
```

FIGURE 22.5

Using VARLOAD for Ethernet to transmit a particular device

```
09/09/95           LANalyzer(R) Network Analyzer by NCC              21 52
Enter decimal number(s)                                         Edit Packet
              ═══════ c:\xln\lanz\802.3\general\varload ═══════
64byte                        Protocol Type   DATA
Packet Length (Generated: 60    Transmitted: as generated)

Ethernet
     Destination Address              novell1EF22C
     Source Address                   exos651575
     Type                             NetWare

Data Length  46                     Data Offset 0    EBCDIC display
0000  E3 88 89 A2 40 89 A2 40   91 A4 A2 A3 00 00 00 00   This is just....
0010  81 40 A3 85 A2 A3 40 97   81 83 92 85 A3 00 00 00   a test packet...
0020  00 00 00 00 00 00 00 00   00 00 00 00 00 00         ..............




F1    |F2   |F3    |F4   |F5    |F6      |F7   |F8   |F9   |F10
Help  |Copy |Paste |Type |ASCII |Zoom In |Fill |     |     |Back
```

monitoring that may supply useful information for test results. If two LAN-alyzers are available, monitor the generated load on the far side of the inter-networking device to ensure accurate packet bridged/routed rates and observe any bridge- or router-induced errors.

Whenever possible, try to add intelligence to your load test by emulating the type of traffic that will most likely occur on your network. For example, if you wish to simulate graphics users, transmit large packet sizes.

FIGURE 22.6

The VARLOAD application defaults to displaying the Global screen.

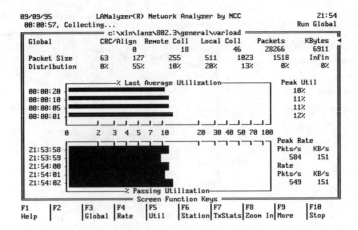

This chapter has examined two types of loads that can be transmitted onto the network: dumb loads and intelligent loads. You learned that you can use dumb loads to test the network cabling system and that intelligent loads are best suited to testing a particular device on the network.

The next chapter analyzes NetWare NCP communications, such as the attachment and login processes.

Testing and
Optimizing NCP
Communications

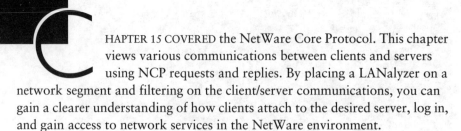

HAPTER 15 COVERED the NetWare Core Protocol. This chapter views various communications between clients and servers using NCP requests and replies. By placing a LANalyzer on a network segment and filtering on the client/server communications, you can gain a clearer understanding of how clients attach to the desired server, log in, and gain access to network services in the NetWare environment.

This chapter covers four specific topics:

- Connection procedure for NETX, NETX with Preferred Server, and VLMs

- Login procedure

- NetWare security

- Directory access/rights

The Connection Procedure Using NETX.COM

HEN A CLIENT executes NETX.COM, it generates a Get Nearest Server SAP broadcast on the local network. Either a server on the local network or a NetWare router can reply to this request. The replies provide the name and network address of the nearest server. In Figure 23.1, you can see the NETX sequence.

FIGURE 23.1

NETX sequence

No.	Source	Destination	Layer	Size	Summary
1	LAURA	Broadcast	sap	0064	Query Nearest File Server
2	FS-BOZO1	LAURA	sap	0114	Resp Nearest; Server=FS-BOZO1
3	LAURA	Broadcast	rip	0064	Req network=00 00 11 62
4	FS-BOZO1	LAURA	rip	0064	Resp network=00 00 11 62; 1 hops
5	LAURA	FS-BOZO1	ncp	0064	Req Create Service Connection
6	FS-BOZO1	LAURA	ncp	0064	Rply Create Service Connection
7	LAURA	FS-BOZO1	ncp	0064	Req Get File Server Info
8	FS-BOZO1	LAURA	ncp	0184	Rply Get File Server Info FS-BOZO1
9	LAURA	FS-BOZO1	ncp	0064	Req Negotiate Buffer Size;1024 bytes
10	FS-BOZO1	LAURA	ncp	0064	Rply Negotiate Buffer Size;1024 bytes
11	LAURA	FS-BOZO1	ncp	0064	Req Logout
12	FS-BOZO1	LAURA	ncp	0064	Rply Logout
13	LAURA	FS-BOZO1	ncp	0064	Req Get File Server Date and Time
14	FS-BOZO1	LAURA	ncp	0064	Rply Get File Server Date and Time

A client performs the following steps to create an attachment to a NetWare server using the NETX shell:

1. Find the nearest file server (primary) and the route to it.

2. Create the connection and negotiate the buffer size.

3. Issue the logout command to the preferred server.

Let's examine each of these steps.

Step 1: Find the Nearest File Server (Primary) and the Route to It

In packet 1, the client, LAURA, transmits a SAP request for the Nearest File Server. This is the first packet transmitted when NETX.COM is loaded, requesting the nearest server. Packet 2 shows that FS-BOZO1 responded first. Packet 3 depicts the station, LAURA, requesting the route to the server FS-BOZO1's internal IPX address, 00-00-11-62.

Step 2: Create the Connection and Negotiate the Buffer Size

In packet 5, the client requests a connection to the server. In packet 7, the client requests basic file server information, and in packet 9, the client starts the buffer negotiation process to determine the maximum packet size the client can use for communications.

Step 3: Issue the Logout Command to the Preferred Server

To ensure that any past connections are clear for the client, the client issues a Logout command to the server (packet 11).

The entire NETX sequence requires 14 packets. Now let's examine the communications of the Preferred Server option.

The Connection Procedure Using NETX.COM with the Preferred Server Option

F YOU WANT to be connected automatically to a specific server, you can include the Preferred Server parameter when you type NETX (NETX PS = *servername*) or include the Preferred Server information in your NET.CFG file (PREFERRED SERVER = *servername*).

The Preferred Server option does not work intuitively. You might think that since you explicitly specified your preferred server, that server would be the one you connect to by default, and you might assume that no additional packets are generated by using this option. Not true.

In a preferred server environment, you actually follow the general rules of NETX first by creating an attachment to the first server that responds to your Get Nearest Server SAP request. Once you have established a connection with this server, you query the bindery to locate your preferred server's address.

The NETX sequence follows seven steps:

1. Find the nearest server (primary) and the route to it.

2. Create the connection and negotiate the buffer size.

3. Query the primary server's bindery for the network address to the preferred server.

4. Locate the route to the preferred server.

5. Create a connection to the preferred server and negotiate the buffer size.

6. Destroy the connection to the primary server.

7. Issue the Logout command to the preferred server.

Figure 23.2 shows a trace of a preferred server connection being established between the client, LINDSAY, the default server, FS2, and the preferred server, SALES1.

FIGURE 23.2

NETX sequence using the Preferred Server option

No.	Source	Destination	Layer	Size	Summary
1	LINDSAY	Broadcast	sap	0064	Query Nearest File Server
2	FS2	LINDSAY	sap	0114	Resp Nearest;Server=FS2
3	LINDSAY	Broadcast	rip	0064	Req network=00 00 11 62
4	FS2	LINDSAY	rip	0064	Resp network=00 00 11 62; 1 hops
5	LINDSAY	FS2	ncp	0064	Req Create Service Connection
6	FS2	LINDSAY	ncp	0064	Rply Create Service Connection
7	LINDSAY	FS2	ncp	0064	Req Get File Server Information
8	FS2	LINDSAY	ncp	0184	Rply Get File Server Information
9	00001B110014	LINDSAY	sap	0114	Resp Nearest; Server=SANFRAN1
10	LINDSAY	FS2	ncp	0064	Req Negotiate Buffer Size
11	FS2	LINDSAY	ncp	0064	Rply Negotiate Buffer Size
12	LINDSAY	FS2	ncp	0084	Req Read Property Value
13	FS2	LINDSAY	ncp	0186	Rply Read Property Value
14	LINDSAY	Broadcast	rip	0064	Req network=C9 40 83 46
15	00001B15089F	LINDSAY	sap	0114	Resp Nearest; Server=TOM-P-SERVER
16	00001B331232	LINDSAY	sap	0114	Resp Nearest; Server=PETESERVER
17	00001B03F363	LINDSAY	sap	0114	Resp Nearest; Server=ADMINISTRAT
18	00001B1EF36B	LINDSAY	sap	0114	Resp Nearest; Server=FS1
19	00001B1E1047	LINDSAY	sap	0114	Resp Nearest; Server=PURCHASING
20	00001B3321C3	LINDSAY	sap	0114	Resp Nearest; Server=SW-FS02
21	00001B1E5CCD	LINDSAY	sap	0114	Resp Nearest; Server=SW-FS01
22	00001B32EE91	LINDSAY	sap	0114	Resp Nearest; Server=SW-FS04
23	00001B1E5CD8	LINDSAY	sap	0114	Resp Nearest; Server=SW-FS05
24	00001B036448	LINDSAY	sap	0114	Resp Nearest; Server=SW-FS06
25	00001B036448	LINDSAY	rip	0064	Resp network=C9 40 83 46; 1 hops
26	LINDSAY	SALES1	ncp	0064	Req Create Service Connection
27	SALES1	LINDSAY	ncp	0064	Rply Create Service Connection
28	LINDSAY	SALES1	ncp	0064	Req Get File Server Information
29	SALES1	LINDSAY	ncp	0184	Rply Get File Server Information
30	LINDSAY	SALES1	ncp	0064	Req Negotiate Buffer Size
31	SALES1	LINDSAY	ncp	0064	Rply Negotiate Buffer Size
32	LINDSAY	SALES1	ncp	0064	Req Destroy Service Connection
33	SALES1	LINDSAY	ncp	0064	Rply Destroy Service Connection
34	LINDSAY	SALES1	ncp	0064	Req Logout
35	SALES1	LINDSAY	ncp	0064	Rply Logout
36	LINDSAY	SALES1	ncp	0064	Req Get File Server Date and Time
37	SALES1	LINDSAY	ncp	0064	Rplyy Get File Server Date and Time

Step 1: Find the Nearest Server (Primary) and the Route to It

In packet 1, the client, LINDSAY, is requesting the nearest server. Packet 2 shows that FS2 responded the most quickly. Even though other servers will reply to the Get Nearest Server request (packets 9 and 15–24), the client will ignore these responses. Packet 3 depicts that the client is requesting the route to the server FS2.

Step 2: Create the Connection and Negotiate the Buffer Size

In packets 5, 7, and 10, the client is creating the connection, obtaining information about the server, and negotiating the buffer size.

Step 3: Query the Primary Server's Bindery for the Network Address to the Preferred Server

If the Preferred Server option is placed in the client's NET.CFG file or at the command line (NETX PS = *server name*), the client will query the server that responded first to the Get Nearest Server SAP for the network address of the preferred server. This query (packet 12) is made through the use of a Get Property Value NCP. However, if the client did not request a specific server, it will retain a connection to the original server that answered the Get Nearest Server query.

By viewing packet 12, as shown in Figure 23.3, you can see that the client is requesting the network address of server SALES1.

Step 4: Locate the Route to the Preferred Server

In packet 14 of the trace shown in Figure 23.2, the client is requesting the route to the network on which the preferred server is located, C9-40-83-46.

Step 5: Create a Connection to the Preferred Server and Negotiate the Buffer Size

Next, the client creates the connection to the preferred server, obtains server information, and negotiates the buffer size. The client and server will agree to use the lowest buffer size negotiated. This occurred in packets 26 to 31 of the trace in Figure 23.2.

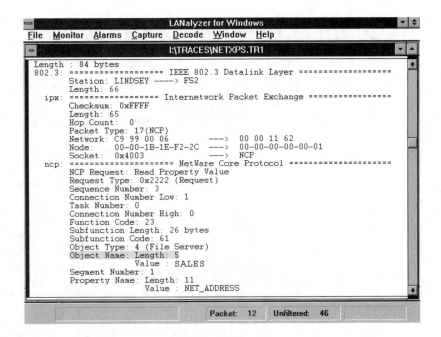

FIGURE 23.3

The client requests the
network address of its
preferred server.

Step 6: Destroy the Connection to the Primary Server

Because the original server is no longer required, the client destroys the connection (packets 32 and 33).

Step 7: Issue the Logout Command to the Preferred Server

To ensure that any past connections are clear for the client, it issues a Logout command to the server (packets 34 and 35).

The Connection Procedure Using VLMs

HERE ARE SOME significant differences in the network communications when you use the NetWare 4.x DOS Requester (VLM) to attach to the network, as shown in Figure 23.4.

FIGURE 23.4

Connecting to the network using the DOS Requester VLM.

No.	Source	Destination	Layer	Size	Summary
1	FRED	Broadcast	sap	0064	Query Nearest Directory Server
2	CORP-FS1	FRED	sap	0114	Resp Nearest; Server=TC_____
3	FRED	Broadcast	rip	0064	Req network=BA 55 BA 11
4	CORP-FS1	FRED	rip	0064	Resp network=BA 55 BA 11; 2 hops
5	FRED	CORP-FS1	ncp	0064	Req Create Service Connection
6	CORP-FS1	FRED	ncp	0064	Rply Create Service Connection
7	FRED	CORP-FS1	ncp	0064	Req Get File Server Info
8	CORP-FS1	FRED	ncp	0184	Rply Get File Server Info CORP-FS1
9	FRED	CORP-FS1	ncp	0064	Req Get Big Packet NCP Max Packet
10	CORP-FS1	FRED	ncp	0064	Rply Get Big Packet NCP Max Packet
11	FRED	CORP-FS1	ncp	1518	Req Create Service Connection
12	FRED	CORP-FS1	ncp	1518	Req Create Service Connection
13	FRED	CORP-FS1	ncp	1518	Req Create Service Connection
14	CORP-FS1	FRED	ncp	1518	Req Create Service Connection
15	FRED	CORP-FS1	ncp	1518	Req Create Service Connection
16	CORP-FS1	FRED	ncp	1518	Req Create Service Connection
17	CORP-FS1	FRED	ncp	1518	Req Create Service Connection
18	CORP-FS1	FRED	ncp	1518	Req Create Service Connection
19	FRED	CORP-FS1	ncp	0074	Req Packet Burst Connection
20	CORP-FS1	FRED	ncp	0064	Rply Packet Burst Connection
21	FRED	CORP-FS1	ncp	1518	Req Create Service Connection
22	FRED	CORP-FS1	ncp	1518	Req Create Service Connection
23	CORP-FS1	FRED	ncp	1518	Req Create Service Connection
24	CORP-FS1	FRED	ncp	1518	Req Create Service Connection
25	FRED	CORP-FS1	ncp	1518	Req Create Service Connection
26	FRED	CORP-FS1	ncp	1518	Req Create Service Connection
27	CORP-FS1	FRED	ncp	1518	Req Create Service Connection
28	CORP-FS1	FRED	ncp	1518	Req Create Service Connection
29	FRED	CORP-FS1	ncp	1518	Req Create Service Connection
30	FRED	CORP-FS1	ncp	1518	Req Create Service Connection
31	CORP-FS1	FRED	ncp	1518	Req Create Service Connection
32	CORP-FS1	FRED	ncp	1518	Req Create Service Connection
33	FRED	CORP-FS1	ncp	0064	Req Get File Server Date and Time
34	CORP-FS1	FRED	ncp	0064	Rply Get File Server Date and Time

The sequence of events follows these steps:

1. Find the nearest directory server and the route to it.

2. Create the connection and negotiate the maximum packet size.

3. Request a Burst Mode connection and determine round-trip transmission time.

4. Get the file server date and time.

Step 1: Find the Nearest Directory Server and the Route to It

In packet 1, the client, FRED, transmits a SAP request for the Nearest Directory Server. This is the first packet transmitted when VLM is loaded. Packet 2 is the response that indicates TC is the Nearest Directory Server. Packet 3 depicts FRED's station requesting the route to the directory server's internal IPX address, BA-55-BA-11.

Step 2: Create the Connection and Negotiate the Maximum Packet Size

In packet 5, the client requests a connection to the directory server. Packet 7 is a request for basic file server information. Packet 9 is FRED's request to find the maximum packet size that can be used for the NCP communications. Packets 11 through 18 are used to verify the maximum packet size of 1518 bytes. These packets are actually buffered to meet the 1518-byte packet size. If a communication cannot be completed, the sender drops down to a smaller size. This ensures that a maximum packet size is supported by all the links between the source client and the destination server.

Step 3: Request a Burst Mode Connection and Determine Round-Trip Transmission Time

Packet 19 is a request for a Packet Burst Connection; packet 20 is the reply granting the connection. Once a Packet Burst Connection has been granted, the client (using the DOSUP9.EXE version of the VLMS) transmits three pairs of packets to determine how much time it takes for the communications between the client and server. This is how the newer VLM client determines the interpacket gap to be used for Burst Mode communications, as discussed in Chapter 16.

Step 4: Get the File Server Date and Time

Finally, the VLM requests the file server date and time. The entire VLM sequence requires 34 packets.

Netware Server Connection Priorities

HEN YOU ARE connecting to a NetWare bindery-based LAN, three server connection priorities are available:

- Primary server
- Preferred server
- Default server

The *primary server* is the one you attached to during the NETX sequence. Even if you included a Preferred Server= command in your NET.CFG file, you can still attach initially to another server.

The *preferred server* is the one that you explicitly logged in to by typing **LOGIN** *server name/user name* or that you placed in your NET.CFG file by using the PS= option.

The *default server* is the server implied by the client's default drive.

Now that you have established a connection with the primary server, the preferred server, or a directory server, you can begin the login process.

The Login Process without Burst Mode Support

SERS ARE OFTEN surprised at the number of packets required to complete the login process. However, several files are downloaded to the workstation during the login process. These files can include

LOGIN.EXE (login executable file)

NET$LOG.DAT (system login script)

LOGIN.DAT (user login script)

CAPTURE.EXE (port redirection executable file)

PRINTCON.DAT (print job configuration file)

NET$PRN.DAT (printer device definition file)

Figure 23.5 shows some of the NCP calls used during the login process. Remember, the NETX sequence has already occurred and the user has a connection to the server (see Figure 23.1).

FIGURE 23.5

NCP calls during the login process

No.	Source	Destination	Layer	Size	Summary
1	LINDSAY	FS2	ncp	0064	Req Open File LOGIN
2	FS2	LINDSAY	ncp	0064	Rply Open File; Failure
3	LINDSAY	FS2	ncp	0064	Req Get Directory Path
4	FS2	LINDSAY	ncp	0066	Rply Get Directory Path SYS:LOGIN
5	LINDSAY	FS2	ncp	0064	Req File Search Initialize /LOGIN
6	FS2	LINDSAY	ncp	0064	Rply File Search Initialize
7	LINDSAY	FS2	ncp	0074	Req File Search Continue LOGIN.COM
8	FS2	LINDSAY	ncp	0064	Rply File Search Continue; Failure
9	LINDSAY	FS2	ncp	0064	Req File Search Initialize /LOGIN
10	FS2	LINDSAY	ncp	0064	Rply File Search Initialize
11	LINDSAY	FS2	ncp	0074	Req File Search Continue LOGIN.EXE
12	FS2	LINDSAY	ncp	0088	Rply File Search Continue LOGIN.E
13	LINDSAY	FS2	ncp	0076	Req Open File /LOGIN/LOGIN.EXE
14	FS2	LINDSAY	ncp	0092	Rply Open File LOGIN.EXE
15	LINDSAY	FS2	ncp	0068	Req Read LOGIN.EXE; 30 bytes
16	FS2	LINDSAY	ncp	0088	Rply Read; 30 bytes
17	LINDSAY	FS2	ncp	0068	Req Read LOGIN.EXE; 512 bytes
18	FS2	LINDSAY	ncp	0570	Rply Read; 512 bytes
19	LINDSAY	FS2	ncp	0068	Req Read LOGIN.EXE; 1024 bytes
	(Download LOGIN.EXE to the client)				
253	LINDSAY	FS2	ncp	0068	Req Read LOGIN.EXE; 30 bytes
254	FS2	LINDSAY	ncp	0088	Rply Read; 30bytes
255	LINDSAY	FS2	ncp	0064	Req Close File LOGIN.EXE
256	FS2	LINDSAY	ncp	0064	Rply Close File
257	LINDSAY	FS2	ncp	0064	Req Get Bindery Access Level
258	FS2	LINDSAY	ncp	0064	Rply Get Bindery Access Level
259	LINDSAY	FS2	ncp	0084	Req Read Property Value
260	FS2	LINDSAY	ncp	0186	Rply Read Property Value
261	LINDSAY	Broadcast	rip	0064	Req network=C9 40 83 46
262	SALES1	LINDSAY	rip	0064	Resp network=C9 40 83 46; 1 hops
263	LINDSAY	SALES1	ncp	0064	Req Create Service Connection
264	SALES1	LINDSAY	ncp	0064	Rply CreateService Connection
265	LINDSAY	SALES1	ncp	0064	Req Get FileServer Information
266	SALES1	LINDSAY	ncp	0184	Rply Get FileServer Information
267	LINDSAY	SALES1	ncp	0064	Req Negotiate Buffer Size
268	SALES1	LINDSAY	ncp	0064	Rply Negotiate Buffer Size
269	LINDSAY	FS2	ncp	0064	Req End Of Job
270	FS2	LINDSAY	ncp	0064	Rply End Of Job
271	LINDSAY	SALES1	ncp	0064	Req End Of Job
272	SALES1	LINDSAY	ncp	0064	Rply End Of Job
273	LINDSAY	FS2	ncp	0064	Req Logout
274	FS2	LINDSAY	ncp	0064	Rply Logout
275	LINDSAY	SALES1	ncp	0064	Req Logout
276	SALES1	LINDSAY	ncp	0064	Rply Logout
277	LINDSAY	FS2	ncp	0064	Req Destroy Service Connection
278	FS2	LINDSAY	ncp	0064	Rply Destroy Service Connection
279	LINDSAY	SALES1	ncp	0070	Req Get Bindery Object ID
280	SALES1	LINDSAY	ncp	0110	Rply Get Bindery Object ID
281	LINDSAY	SALES1	ncp	0064	Req Get Log Key
282	SALES1	LINDSAY	ncp	0064	Rply Get Log Key

FIGURE 23.5

NCP calls during the
login process
(continued)

283	LINDSAY	SALES1	ncp	0070	Req	Get Bindery Object ID
284	SALES1	LINDSAY	ncp	0110	Rply	Get Bindery Object ID
285	LINDSAY	SALES1	ncp	0078	Req	Keyed Login
286	SALES1	LINDSAY	ncp	0064	Rply	Keyed Login; Failure
287	LINDSAY	SALES1	ncp	0064	Req	Get Log Key
288	SALES1	LINDSAY	ncp	0064	Rply	Get Log Key
289	LINDSAY	SALES1	ncp	0070	Req	Get Bindery Object ID
290	SALES1	LINDSAY	ncp	0110	Rply	Get Bindery Object ID
291	LINDSAY	SALES1	ncp	0078	Req	Keyed Login
292	SALES1	LINDSAY	ncp	0064	Rply	Keyed Login
293	LINDSAY	SALES1	ncp	0066	Req	Alloc Permanent Directory Ha
294	SALES1	LINDSAY	ncp	0064	Rply	Alloc Permanent Directory Ha
295	LINDSAY	SALES1	ncp	0064	Req	Deallocate Directory Handle
296	SALES1	LINDSAY	ncp	0064	Rply	Deallocate Directory Handle
297	LINDSAY	SALES1	ncp	0066	Req	Set Directory Handle LOGIN
298	SALES1	LINDSAY	ncp	0064	Rply	Set Directory Handle
299	LINDSAY	SALES1	ncp	0064	Req	Get File Server Date and Tim
300	SALES1	LINDSAY	ncp	0064	Rply	Get File Server Date and Tim
301	LINDSAY	SALES1	ncp	0064	Req	Get Bindery Access Level
302	SALES1	LINDSAY	ncp	0064	Rply	Get Bindery Access Level
303	LINDSAY	SALES1	ncp	0064	Req	Get Station's Logged Informa
304	SALES1	LINDSAY	ncp	0118	Rply	Get Station's Logged Informa
305	LINDSAY	SALES1	ncp	0064	Req	Get Internet Address
306	SALES1	LINDSAY	ncp	0068	Rply	Get Internet Address
307	LINDSAY	SALES1	ncp	0086	Req	Read Property Value
308	SALES1	LINDSAY	ncp	0186	Rply	Read Property Value
309	LINDSAY	SALES1	ncp	0082	Req	Search for File SYS:PUBLIC/N
310	SALES1	LINDSAY	ncp	0088	Rply	Search for File NET$LOG.DAT
311	LINDSAY	SALES1	ncp	0082	Req	Open File SYS:PUBLIC/NET$LOG
312	SALES1	LINDSAY	ncp	0092	Rply	Open File NET$LOG.DAT
313	LINDSAY	SALES1	ncp	0068	Req	Read NET$LOG.DAT; 512 bytes

The number of packets required for the login process is dependent on commands within the login scripts. Each executable command within a login script may require another file to be downloaded to the client's station. For example, if you place two capture statements within the login script, the CAPTURE.EXE file will be downloaded twice, once for each statement.

The following is the general sequence for logging in to a NetWare server:

1. Locate and download the LOGIN.EXE file from the server to which you attached (primary server).

2. Find out your privileges in the LOGIN directory.

3. Locate the server to which you wish to log in (preferred server).

4. Create the service connection and obtain information about the server.

5. Negotiate the buffer size.

6. End the job with both the servers and log out from each.

7. Destroy your connection with the primary server.

8. Submit your password.

9. Allocate a directory handle for LOGIN.

10. Get additional information regarding bindery access and client/server information.

Let's examine each of these steps.

Step 1: Locate and Download the LOGIN.EXE File from the Server to Which You Attached (Primary Server)

In Figure 23.5, note in packet 2 an Open File; Failure response from the server. This response is common in NetWare when you are opening a file; it indicates that either the file is not in the directory where you are located or you haven't typed the entire file name. The system must attempt to execute the file name you typed by first placing a .COM extension at the end. If that fails, it then places an .EXE extension at the end of the file name. Finally, it attempts to open the file with .BAT as the extension.

In packet 13, the client has found the LOGIN.EXE file and is requesting to open it. Packets 15 through 254 were used to download the file LOGIN.EXE to the client.

Step 2: Find Out Your Privileges in the LOGIN Directory

In packet 257, Get Bindery Access Level is the NCP call to get your privileges in the LOGIN directory. By default, you are given "anyone read, anyone write" privileges to the LOGIN directory. After you log in, you are granted "logged read, logged write" privileges to the LOGIN directory.

Step 3: Locate the Server to Which You Wish to Log In (Preferred Server)

If the server you are attached to (the primary server) is not the one you requested in your login argument, you query the server bindery for the network address of the server you want to log in to (your preferred server; packets 259 and 260).

Even though you do not specify "preferred server" when loading the shell, the server you explicitly log in to becomes your preferred server.

Step 4: Create the Service Connection and Obtain Information about the Server

In packet 263, you can see that the Create Service Connection (NCP type 1111) is issued to the preferred server.

Step 5: Negotiate the Buffer Size

Next, the station and the server negotiate buffer sizes. Once they each report their maximum buffer sizes, their communications will occur using the lowest buffer size negotiated during this phase (packets 267 and 268). If they are not using Novell's Large Internet Packet (LIP) protocol and there is a router between the client and the server, they will default to 576-byte packets.

Step 6: End the Job with Both the Servers and Log Out from Each

The client then ends the job with both servers and sends a Logout NCP request to each (packets 269–276). This ensures that any connections previously held open for the client are terminated.

Step 7: Destroy Your Connection with the Primary Server

Now that the client has connected to the preferred server, it sends a Destroy Service Connection NCP (NCP request type 5555) to the primary server (packets 277 and 278). The client no longer has any connection or association with that server until it explicitly requests it or reloads NETX.

Step 8: Submit Your Password

Packets 285 through 292 consist of an exchange of a *log key*—the specific encryption sequence—from the server and the encrypted password from the client.

Step 9: Allocate a Directory Handle for LOGIN

In packet 297, the client requests that a directory handle be set for the login directory. The client is now prepared to use a directory handle for the LOGIN directory of its preferred server.

Step 10: Get Additional Information Regarding Bindery Access and Client/Server Information

In packets 299 through 308, the client is requesting information regarding rights, internet address, and logged information. The rights granted at this time are "logged read, logged write"; these are the privileges required to access the system login script. The Internet Address includes the network number and workstation node address. The station's logged information is a synopsis of station information such as login name, login time, and user ID (\MAIL*user ID*).

Once the client has completed the preceding steps, it can begin to read the system login script (NET$LOG.DAT), user login script (\MAIL\\*user ID*\LOGIN.DAT), CAPTURE.EXE file, print job configuration file (PRINTCON.DAT), and printer device definitions (NET$PRN.DAT).

The Login Process to NetWare 4.x with Burst Mode Support

F YOU ARE logging in to a NetWare 4.x server using the VLMs, the login process is quite different, as shown in Figure 23.6.

As you will notice, the primary difference is the number of packets it takes to log in to the network. Using NetWare VLMs to log in to a NetWare 4.x server, your station and the server exchange almost 1000 packets (on an Ethernet LAN with a maximum packet size of 1518 bytes).

```
No.   Source        Destination    Layer  Size  Summary
  1 This_Worksta    CORP-FS1       ncp    0064  Req  File Search Init
  2 CORP-FS1        This_Worksta   ncp    0064  Rply File Search Init
  3 This_Worksta    CORP-FS1       ncp    0071  Req  File Search Continue LOGIN.?
  4 CORP-FS1        This_Worksta   ncp    0088  Rply File Search Continue LOGIN.EXE
  5 This_Worksta    CORP-FS1       ncp    0071  Req  File Search Continue LOGIN.?
  6 CORP-FS1        This_Worksta   ncp    0064  Rply File Search Continue; Failur
  7 This_Worksta    CORP-FS1       ncp    0071  Req  File Search Continue LOGIN.?
  8 CORP-FS1        This_Worksta   ncp    0064  Rply File Search Continue; Failure
  9 This_Worksta    CORP-FS1       ncp    0068  Req  Open File LOGIN.EXE
 10 CORP-FS1        This_Worksta   ncp    0092  Rply Open File LOGIN.EXE
 11 This_Worksta    CORP-FS1       ncp    0108  Req Burst Read    1462 bytes
 12 CORP-FS1        This_Worksta   ncp    1488  Burst Packet;    1404 bytes
 13 CORP-FS1        This_Worksta   ncp    0150  Burst Packet;      66 bytes
 14 This_Worksta    CORP-FS1       ncp    0108  Req Burst Read   22456 bytes
 15 CORP-FS1        This_Worksta   ncp    1488  Burst Packet;    1404 bytes
 16 CORP-FS1        This_Worksta   ncp    0320  Burst Packet;     236 bytes
 17 CORP-FS1        This_Worksta   ncp    1488  Burst Packet;    1404 bytes
 18 CORP-FS1        This_Worksta   ncp    1488  Burst Packet;    1404 bytes
 19 CORP-FS1        This_Worksta   ncp    1488  Burst Packet;    1404 bytes
 20 CORP-FS1        This_Worksta   ncp    1488  Burst Packet;    1404 bytes
 21 CORP-FS1        This_Worksta   ncp    1488  Burst Packet;    1404 bytes
 22 CORP-FS1        This_Worksta   ncp    1256  Burst Packet;    1172 bytes
 23 CORP-FS1        This_Worksta   ncp    1488  Burst Packet;    1404 bytes
 24 CORP-FS1        This_Worksta   ncp    1488  Burst Packet;    1404 bytes
 25 CORP-FS1        This_Worksta   ncp    1372  Burst Packet;    1288 bytes
 26 CORP-FS1        This_Worksta   ncp    1488  Burst Packet;    1404 bytes
 27 CORP-FS1        This_Worksta   ncp    1488  Burst Packet;    1404 bytes
 28 CORP-FS1        This_Worksta   ncp    1372  Burst Packet;    1288 bytes
 29 CORP-FS1        This_Worksta   ncp    1488  Burst Packet;    1404 bytes
 30 CORP-FS1        This_Worksta   ncp    1488  Burst Packet;    1404 bytes
 31 CORP-FS1        This_Worksta   ncp    1372  Burst Packet;    1288 bytes
 32 CORP-FS1        This_Worksta   ncp    0428  Burst Packet;     344 bytes
 33 This_Worksta    CORP-FS1       ncp    0108  Req Burst Read   22456 bytes
 34 CORP-FS1        This_Worksta   ncp    1488  Burst Packet;    1404 bytes
 35 CORP-FS1        This_Worksta   ncp    1488  Burst Packet;    1404 bytes

(Download LOGIN.EXE to the client)

322 This_Worksta    CORP-FS1       ncp    0108  Req Burst Read    1584 bytes
323 CORP-FS1        This_Worksta   ncp    1488  Burst Packet;    1404 bytes
324 CORP-FS1        This_Worksta   ncp    0274  Burst Packet;     190 bytes
325 This_Worksta    CORP-FS1       ncp    0064  Req  Close File LOGIN.EXE
326 CORP-FS1        This_Worksta   ncp    0064  Rply Close File
327 This_Worksta    CORP-FS1       ncp    0064  Req  File Search Init
328 CORP-FS1        This_Worksta   ncp    0064  Rply File Search Init
329 This_Worksta    CORP-FS1       ncp    0071  Req  File Search Continue LOGIN.MSG
330 CORP-FS1        This_Worksta   ncp    0064  Rply File Search Continue; Failure
331 This_Worksta    CORP-FS1       ncp    0064  Req  File Search Init
332 CORP-FS1        This_Worksta   ncp    0064  Rply File Search Init
333 This_Worksta    CORP-FS1       ncp    0071  Req  File Search Continue LOGIN.MSG
334 CORP-FS1        This_Worksta   ncp    0064  Rply File Search Continue; Failure
335 This_Worksta    CORP-FS1       ncp    0069  Req  Search for File LOGIN.MSG
336 CORP-FS1        This_Worksta   ncp    0064  Rply Search for File; Failure
337 This_Worksta    CORP-FS1       ncp    0069  Req  Search for File LOGIN.MSG
338 CORP-FS1        This_Worksta   ncp    0064  Rply Search for File; Failure
339 This_Worksta    CORP-FS1       ncp    0069  Req  Search for File LOGIN.MSG
340 CORP-FS1        This_Worksta   ncp    0064  Rply Search for File; Failure
341 This_Worksta    CORP-FS1       ncp    0069  Req  Search for File LOGIN.MSG
342 CORP-FS1        This_Worksta   ncp    0064  Rply Search for File; Failure
343 This_Worksta    CORP-FS1       ncp    0064  Req  File Search Init NLS
344 CORP-FS1        This_Worksta   ncp    0064  Rply File Search Init
345 This_Worksta    CORP-FS1       ncp    0065  Req  File Search Continue *.*
346 CORP-FS1        This_Worksta   ncp    0088  Rply File Search Continue 1252_UNI
```

FIGURE 23.6

The login process using VLMs and Netware 4.x (continued)

(Download directory information for SYS:\PUBLIC\NLS)

```
635 This_Worksta  CORP-FS1       ncp   0065  Req  File Search Continue *.*
636 CORP-FS1      This_Worksta   ncp   0088  Rply File Search Continue ENGLISH
637 This_Worksta  CORP-FS1       ncp   0068  Req  File Search Init NLS\ENGLISH
638 CORP-FS1      This_Worksta   ncp   0064  Rply File Search Init
639 This_Worksta  CORP-FS1       ncp   0071  Req  File Search Continue LOGIN.MSG
640 CORP-FS1      This_Worksta   ncp   0088  Rply File Search Continue LOGIN.MSG
641 This_Worksta  CORP-FS1       ncp   0065  Req  File Search Continue *.*
642 CORP-FS1      This_Worksta   ncp   0064  Rply File Search Continue; Failure
643 This_Worksta  CORP-FS1       ncp   0080  Req  Open File NLS\ENGLISH\LOGIN.MSG
644 CORP-FS1      This_Worksta   ncp   0092  Rply Open File LOGIN.MSG
645 This_Worksta  CORP-FS1       ncp   0081  Req  Search for File NLS\ENGLISH\LOGIN.MSG
646 CORP-FS1      This_Worksta   ncp   0088  Rply Search for File LOGIN.MSG
647 This_Worksta  CORP-FS1       ncp   0108  Req Burst Read  12230 bytes
648 CORP-FS1      This_Worksta   ncp   1488  Burst Packet;    1404 bytes
649 CORP-FS1      This_Worksta   ncp   1488  Burst Packet;    1404 bytes
650 CORP-FS1      This_Worksta   ncp   1380  Burst Packet;    1296 bytes
651 CORP-FS1      This_Worksta   ncp   1488  Burst Packet;    1404 bytes
652 CORP-FS1      This_Worksta   ncp   1488  Burst Packet;    1404 bytes
653 CORP-FS1      This_Worksta   ncp   1372  Burst Packet;    1288 bytes
654 CORP-FS1      This_Worksta   ncp   1488  Burst Packet;    1404 bytes
655 CORP-FS1      This_Worksta   ncp   1282  Burst Packet;    1198 bytes
656 This_Worksta  CORP-FS1       ncp   0064  Req  Close File LOGIN.MSG
657 CORP-FS1      This_Worksta   ncp   0064  Rply Close File
658 This_Worksta  CORP-FS1       ncp   0064  Req  Ping for NDS NCP
659 CORP-FS1      This_Worksta   ncp   0156  Rply Ping for NDS NCP
660 This_Worksta  CORP-FS1       ncp   0070  Req  Open File UNI_437.001
661 CORP-FS1      This_Worksta   ncp   0064  Rply Open File; Failure
662 This_Worksta  CORP-FS1       ncp   0074  Req  Open File NLS\UNI_437.001
663 CORP-FS1      This_Worksta   ncp   0092  Rply Open File UNI_437.001
664 This_Worksta  CORP-FS1       ncp   0064  Req  Close File UNI_437.001
665 CORP-FS1      This_Worksta   ncp   0064  Rply Close File
666 This_Worksta  CORP-FS1       ncp   0074  Req  Open File NLS\UNI_437.001
667 CORP-FS1      This_Worksta   ncp   0092  Rply Open File UNI_437.001
668 This_Worksta  CORP-FS1       ncp   0108  Req Burst Read   1564 bytes
669 CORP-FS1      This_Worksta   ncp   1116  Burst Packet;    1032 bytes
670 CORP-FS1      This_Worksta   ncp   0624  Burst Packet;     540 bytes
671 This_Worksta  CORP-FS1       ncp   0108  Req Burst Read   2708 bytes
```

(Read Unicode Rules Tables for enabled language)

```
716 This_Worksta  CORP-FS1       ncp   0108  Req Burst Read   1564 bytes
717 CORP-FS1      This_Worksta   ncp   0752  Burst Packet;     667 bytes
718 This_Worksta  CORP-FS1       ncp   0064  Req  Close File 437_UNI.001
719 CORP-FS1      This_Worksta   ncp   0064  Rply Close File
720 This_Worksta  CORP-FS1       ncp   0064  Req  Logout
721 CORP-FS1      This_Worksta   ncp   0064  Rply Logout
722 This_Worksta  CORP-FS1       ncp   0064  Req  Logout
723 CORP-FS1      This_Worksta   ncp   0064  Rply Logout
724 This_Worksta  CORP-FS1       ncp   0064  Req  Get Directory Path
725 CORP-FS1      This_Worksta   ncp   0066  Rply Get Directory Path SYS:LOGIN
726 This_Worksta  CORP-FS1       ncp   0064  Req  Get Directory Path
727 CORP-FS1      This_Worksta   ncp   0066  Rply Get Directory Path SYS:LOGIN
728 This_Worksta  CORP-FS1       ncp   0064  Req  Get Directory Path
729 CORP-FS1      This_Worksta   ncp   0066  Rply Get Directory Path SYS:LOGIN
730 This_Worksta  CORP-FS1       ncp   0064  Req  Deallocate Directory Handle
731 CORP-FS1      This_Worksta   ncp   0064  Rply Deallocate Directory Handle
732 This_Worksta  CORP-FS1       nds   0156  Req  Resolve Name;   88 bytes
733 CORP-FS1      This_Worksta   nds   0100  Rply Resolve Name;   40 bytes
734 This_Worksta  CORP-FS1       nds   0088  Req  Begin Login;    20 bytes
735 CORP-FS1      This_Worksta   nds   0076  Rply Begin Login;    16 bytes
736 This_Worksta  CORP-FS1       nds   0080  Req  Get Server Address;   12 bytes
737 CORP-FS1      This_Worksta   nds   0144  Rply Get Server Address;   84 bytes
738 This_Worksta  CORP-FS1       nds   0160  Req  Resolve Name;   92 bytes
```

FIGURE 23.6

The login process using VLMs and Netware 4.x (continued)

```
739 CORP-FS1       This_Worksta   nds   0100   Rply Resolve Name;    40 bytes
740 This_Worksta   CORP-FS1       nds   0130   Req  Read;    62 bytes
741 CORP-FS1       This_Worksta   nds   0496   Rply Read;   436 bytes
742 This_Worksta   CORP-FS1       nds   0064   Req  Continued Fragment
743 CORP-FS1       This_Worksta   nds   0064   Rply Continued Fragment;     4 bytes
744 This_Worksta   CORP-FS1       nds   0088   Req  Read Entry Info;   20 bytes
745 CORP-FS1       This_Worksta   nds   0142   Rply Read Entry Info;    82 bytes
746 This_Worksta   CORP-FS1       nds   0577   Req  Finish Login; 1200 bytes
747 CORP-FS1       This_Worksta   nds   0064   Rply Finish Login;    4 bytes
748 This_Worksta   CORP-FS1       nds   0577   Req Continued Fragment(Finish Login)
749 CORP-FS1       This_Worksta   nds   0064   Rply Continued Fragment;     4 bytes
750 This_Worksta   CORP-FS1       nds   0234   Req Continued Fragment(Finish Login)
751 This_Worksta   CORP-FS1       nds   0234   Req Continued Fragment(Finish Login)
752 CORP-FS1       This_Worksta   ncp   0064   Rply Rqst Being Processed; Conn=7
753 CORP-FS1       This_Worksta   nds   0412   Rply Continued Fragment;   352 byt
754 This_Worksta   CORP-FS1       nds   0064   Req Continued Fragment(Finish Login)
755 CORP-FS1       This_Worksta   nds   0064   Rply Continued Fragment;     4 bytes
756 This_Worksta   CORP-FS1       nds   0130   Req  Read;    62 bytes
757 CORP-FS1       This_Worksta   nds   0490   Rply Read;   430 bytes
758 This_Worksta   CORP-FS1       nds   0064   Req  Continued Fragment
759 CORP-FS1       This_Worksta   nds   0064   Rply Continued Fragment;     4 bytes
760 This_Worksta   CORP-FS1       nds   0080   Req  Get Server Address;   12 bytes
761 CORP-FS1       This_Worksta   nds   0144   Rply Get Server Address;   84 bytes
762 This_Worksta   CORP-FS1       nds   0160   Req  Resolve Name;    92 bytes
763 CORP-FS1       This_Worksta   nds   0100   Rply Resolve Name;    40 bytes
764 This_Worksta   CORP-FS1       nds   0130   Req  Read;    62 bytes
765 CORP-FS1       This_Worksta   nds   0496   Rply Read;   436 bytes
766 This_Worksta   CORP-FS1       nds   0064   Req  Continued Fragment
767 CORP-FS1       This_Worksta   nds   0064   Rply Continued Fragment;     4 bytes
768 This_Worksta   CORP-FS1       nds   0156   Req  Resolve Name;    88 bytes
769 CORP-FS1       This_Worksta   nds   0100   Rply Resolve Name;    40 bytes
770 This_Worksta   CORP-FS1       nds   0092   Req  Begin Authentication;   24 bytes
771 This_Worksta   CORP-FS1       nds   0092   Req  Begin Authentication;   24 bytes
772 CORP-FS1       This_Worksta   ncp   0064   Rply Rqst Being Processed; Conn=7
773 CORP-FS1       This_Worksta   nds   0192   Rply Begin Authentication; 132 bytes
774 This_Worksta   CORP-FS1       nds   0064   Req  Continued Fragment
775 CORP-FS1       This_Worksta   nds   0064   Rply Continued Fragment;     4 bytes
776 This_Worksta   CORP-FS1       nds   0508   Req  Finish Authentication; 440 bytes
777 This_Worksta   CORP-FS1       nds   0508   Req  Finish Authentication; 440 bytes
778 CORP-FS1       This_Worksta   ncp   0064   Rply Rqst Being Processed; Conn=7
779 CORP-FS1       This_Worksta   nds   0068   Rply Finish Authentication;  8 bytes
780 This_Worksta   CORP-FS1       ncp   0064   Req Change Conn Authentic. SYS:LOGIN
781 CORP-FS1       This_Worksta   ncp   0064   RplyChange Conn Authentic. SYS:LOGIN
782 This_Worksta   CORP-FS1       ncp   0064   Req  Get Station Logged Info
783 CORP-FS1       This_Worksta   ncp   0118   Rply Get Station Logged Info LAURA
784 This_Worksta   CORP-FS1       ncp   0073   Req  Scan Bindery Object CORP-FS2
785 CORP-FS1       This_Worksta   ncp   0114   Rply Scan Bindery Object CORP-FS2
786 This_Worksta   CORP-FS1       ncp   0064   Req  Ping for NDS NCP
787 CORP-FS1       This_Worksta   ncp   0156   Rply Ping for NDS NCP
788 This_Worksta   CORP-FS1       ncp   0064   Req  Ping for NDS NCP
789 CORP-FS1       This_Worksta   ncp   0156   Rply Ping for NDS NCP
790 This_Worksta   CORP-FS1       ncp   0064   Req  Get Internet Address
791 CORP-FS1       This_Worksta   ncp   0070   Rply Get Internet Address
792 This_Worksta   CORP-FS1       nds   0156   Req  Resolve Name;    88 bytes
793 CORP-FS1       This_Worksta   nds   0100   Rply Resolve Name;    40 bytes
794 This_Worksta   CORP-FS1       nds   0156   Req  Resolve Name;    88 bytes
795 CORP-FS1       This_Worksta   nds   0100   Rply Resolve Name;    40 bytes
796 This_Worksta   CORP-FS1       nds   0124   Req  Read;    56 bytes
797 CORP-FS1       This_Worksta   nds   0116   Rply Read;    56 bytes
798 This_Worksta   CORP-FS1       nds   0156   Req  Resolve Name;    88 bytes
799 CORP-FS1       This_Worksta   nds   0100   Rply Resolve Name;    40 bytes
800 This_Worksta   CORP-FS1       nds   0140   Req  Read;    72 bytes
801 CORP-FS1       This_Worksta   nds   0176   Rply Read;   116 bytes
802 This_Worksta   CORP-FS1       nds   0064   Req  Continued Fragment
803 CORP-FS1       This_Worksta   nds   0064   Rply Continued Fragment;     4 bytes
```

FIGURE 23.6

The login process using
VLMs and Netware 4.x
(continued)

```
804 This_Worksta  CORP-FS1      nds   0156  Req  Resolve Name;    88 bytes
805 CORP-FS1      This_Worksta  nds   0100  Rply Resolve Name;    40 bytes
806 This_Worksta  CORP-FS1      nds   0128  Req  Read;   60 bytes
807 CORP-FS1      This_Worksta  nds   0140  Rply Read;   80 bytes
808 This_Worksta  CORP-FS1      nds   0136  Req  Resolve Name;    68 bytes
809 CORP-FS1      This_Worksta  nds   0100  Rply Resolve Name;    40 bytes
810 This_Worksta  CORP-FS1      nds   0122  Req  Open Stream;   54 bytes
811 CORP-FS1      This_Worksta  nds   0068  Rply Open Stream; No Such Value;
812 This_Worksta  CORP-FS1      nds   0156  Req  Resolve Name;    88 bytes
813 CORP-FS1      This_Worksta  nds   0100  Rply Resolve Name;    40 bytes
814 This_Worksta  CORP-FS1      nds   0124  Req  Read;   56 bytes
815 CORP-FS1      This_Worksta  nds   0068  Rply Read; No Such Attribute;
816 This_Worksta  CORP-FS1      nds   0156  Req  Resolve Name;    88 bytes
817 CORP-FS1      This_Worksta  nds   0100  Rply Resolve Name;    40 bytes
818 This_Worksta  CORP-FS1      nds   0122  Req  Open Stream;   54 bytes
819 CORP-FS1      This_Worksta  nds   0068  Rply Open Stream; No Such Value;
820 This_Worksta  CORP-FS1      ncp   0064  Req  Get Directory Path
821 CORP-FS1      This_Worksta  ncp   0066  Rply Get Directory Path SYS:LOGIN
822 This_Worksta  CORP-FS1      ncp   0064  Req  Get Directory Path
823 CORP-FS1      This_Worksta  ncp   0066  Rply Get Directory Path SYS:LOGIN
824 This_Worksta  CORP-FS1      ncp   0064  Req  Get Directory Path
825 CORP-FS1      This_Worksta  ncp   0066  Rply Get Directory Path SYS:LOGIN
826 This_Worksta  CORP-FS1      ncp   0064  Req  Get Directory Path
827 CORP-FS1      This_Worksta  ncp   0066  Rply Get Directory Path SYS:LOGIN
828 This_Worksta  CORP-FS1      ncp   0064  Req  Get Directory Path
829 CORP-FS1      This_Worksta  ncp   0066  Rply Get Directory Path SYS:LOGIN
830 This_Worksta  CORP-FS1      nds   0168  Req  Resolve Name;   100 bytes
831 CORP-FS1      This_Worksta  nds   0076  Rply Resolve Name; No Such Entry;
832 This_Worksta  CORP-FS1      ncp   0064  Req  Get Station Logged Info
833 CORP-FS1      This_Worksta  ncp   0118  Rply Get Station Logged Info LAURA
834 This_Worksta  CORP-FS1      ncp   0073  Req  Scan Bindery Object CORP-FS2
835 CORP-FS1      This_Worksta  ncp   0114  Rply Scan Bindery Object CORP-FS2
836 This_Worksta  CORP-FS1      ncp   0064  Req  Get Directory Path
837 CORP-FS1      This_Worksta  ncp   0066  Rply Get Directory Path SYS:LOGIN
838 This_Worksta  CORP-FS1      ncp   0064  Req  Deallocate Directory Handle
839 CORP-FS1      This_Worksta  ncp   0064  Rply Deallocate Directory Handle
840 This_Worksta  CORP-FS1      ncp   0065  Req  Alloc Permanent Dir Handle SYS
841 CORP-FS1      This_Worksta  ncp   0064  Rply Alloc Permanent Dir Handle
842 This_Worksta  CORP-FS1      ncp   0065  Req  Alloc Permanent Dir Handle SYS
843 CORP-FS1      This_Worksta  ncp   0064  Rply Alloc Permanent Dir Handle
844 This_Worksta  CORP-FS1      ncp   0064  Req  Get Directory Path
845 CORP-FS1      This_Worksta  ncp   0064  Rply Get Directory Path SYS:
846 This_Worksta  CORP-FS1      ncp   0064  Req  Get Directory Path
847 CORP-FS1      This_Worksta  ncp   0064  Rply Get Directory Path SYS:
848 This_Worksta  CORP-FS1      ncp   0064  Req  Get Directory Path
849 CORP-FS1      This_Worksta  ncp   0064  Rply Get Directory Path SYS:
850 This_Worksta  CORP-FS1      ncp   0064  Req  Get Directory Path
851 CORP-FS1      This_Worksta  ncp   0064  Rply Get Directory Path SYS:
852 This_Worksta  CORP-FS1      ncp   0064  Req  Get Directory Path
853 CORP-FS1      This_Worksta  ncp   0064  Rply Get Directory Path SYS:
854 This_Worksta  CORP-FS1      nds   0168  Req  Resolve Name;   100 bytes
855 CORP-FS1      This_Worksta  nds   0076  Rply Resolve Name; No Such Entry;
856 This_Worksta  CORP-FS1      ncp   0064  Req  Get Station Logged Info
857 CORP-FS1      This_Worksta  ncp   0118  Rply Get Station Logged Info LAURA
858 This_Worksta  CORP-FS1      ncp   0073  Req  Scan Bindery Object CORP-FS2
859 CORP-FS1      This_Worksta  ncp   0114  Rply Scan Bindery Object CORP-FS2
860 This_Worksta  CORP-FS1      ncp   0064  Req  Get Directory Path
861 CORP-FS1      This_Worksta  ncp   0064  Rply Get Directory Path SYS:
862 This_Worksta  CORP-FS1      ncp   0064  Req  Deallocate Directory Handle
863 CORP-FS1      This_Worksta  ncp   0064  Rply Deallocate Directory Handle
864 This_Worksta  CORP-FS1      ncp   0064  Req  Deallocate Directory Handle
865 CORP-FS1      This_Worksta  ncp   0064  Rply Deallocate Directory Handle
866 This_Worksta  CORP-FS1      ncp   0065  Req  Alloc Permanent Dir Handle SYS:
867 CORP-FS1      This_Worksta  ncp   0064  Rply Alloc Permanent Dir Handle
868 This_Worksta  CORP-FS1      ncp   0065  Req  Alloc Permanent Dir Handle SYS:
```

FIGURE 23.6

The login process using
VLMs and Netware 4.x
(continued)

```
869 CORP-FS1      This_Worksta   ncp   0064  Rply Alloc Permanent Dir Handle
870 This_Worksta  CORP-FS1       ncp   0065  Req  Get Effective Dir Rights LAURA
871 CORP-FS1      This_Worksta   ncp   0064  Rply Get Effective Dir Rights
872 This_Worksta  CORP-FS1       nds   0168  Req  Resolve Name;  100 bytes
873 CORP-FS1      This_Worksta   nds   0076  Rply Resolve Name; No Such Entry;
874 This_Worksta  CORP-FS1       ncp   0064  Req  Get Station Logged Info
875 CORP-FS1      This_Worksta   ncp   0118  Rply Get Station Logged Info LAURA
876 This_Worksta  CORP-FS1       ncp   0073  Req  Scan Bindery Object CORP-FS2
877 CORP-FS1      This_Worksta   ncp   0114  Rply Scan Bindery Object CORP-FS2
878 This_Worksta  CORP-FS1       ncp   0065  Req  Alloc Permanent Dir Handle SYS
879 CORP-FS1      This_Worksta   ncp   0064  Rply Alloc Permanent Dir Handle
880 This_Worksta  CORP-FS1       ncp   0065  Req  Alloc Permanent Dir Handle SYS
881 CORP-FS1      This_Worksta   ncp   0064  Rply Alloc Permanent Dir Handle
882 This_Worksta  CORP-FS1       ncp   0066  Req  Get Effective Dir Rights PUBLIC
883 CORP-FS1      This_Worksta   ncp   0064  Rply Get Effective Dir Rights
884 This_Worksta  CORP-FS1       ncp   0067  Req  Set Dir Handle PUBLIC
885 CORP-FS1      This_Worksta   ncp   0064  Rply Set Dir Handle
886 This_Worksta  CORP-FS1       nds   0168  Req  Resolve Name;  100 bytes
887 This_Worksta  CORP-FS1       nds   0168  Req  Resolve Name;  100 bytes
888 CORP-FS1      This_Worksta   nds   0076  Rply Resolve Name; No Such Entry;
889 CORP-FS1      This_Worksta   nds   0076  Rply Resolve Name; No Such Entry;
890 This_Worksta  CORP-FS1       sap   0064  Query Nearest  File Server
891 CORP-FS1      This_Worksta   sap   0114  Resp Nearest; Server=CORP-FS1
892 This_Worksta  CORP-FS1       ncp   0064  Req  Get Station Logged Info
893 CORP-FS1      This_Worksta   ncp   0118  Rply Get Station Logged Info LAURA
894 This_Worksta  CORP-FS1       ncp   0073  Req  Scan Bindery Object CORP-FS2
895 CORP-FS1      This_Worksta   ncp   0114  Rply Scan Bindery Object CORP-FS2
896 This_Worksta  CORP-FS1       ncp   0064  Req  Get Directory Path
897 CORP-FS1      This_Worksta   ncp   0064  Rply Get Directory Path SYS:
898 This_Worksta  CORP-FS1       ncp   0065  Req  Alloc Permanent Dir Handle SYS
899 CORP-FS1      This_Worksta   ncp   0064  Rply Alloc Permanent Dir Handle
900 This_Worksta  CORP-FS1       ncp   0065  Req  Alloc Permanent Dir Handle SYS
901 CORP-FS1      This_Worksta   ncp   0064  Rply Alloc Permanent Dir Handle
902 This_Worksta  CORP-FS1       ncp   0085  Req  Get Effective Dir Rights
PUBLIC\IBM_PC\MSDOS\V6.20
903 CORP-FS1      This_Worksta   ncp   0064  Rply Get Effective Dir Rights; Invalid
Path
904 This_Worksta  CORP-FS1       ncp   0064  Req  Get Directory Path
905 CORP-FS1      This_Worksta   ncp   0064  Rply Get Directory Path SYS:
906 This_Worksta  CORP-FS1       ncp   0064  Req  Get Directory Path
907 CORP-FS1      This_Worksta   ncp   0064  Rply Get Directory Path SYS:
908 This_Worksta  CORP-FS1       ncp   0064  Req  Get Directory Path
909 CORP-FS1      This_Worksta   ncp   0064  Rply Get Directory Path SYS:
910 This_Worksta  CORP-FS1       ncp   0064  Req  Get Station Logged Info
911 CORP-FS1      This_Worksta   ncp   0118  Rply Get Station Logged Info LAURA
912 This_Worksta  CORP-FS1       ncp   0073  Req  Scan Bindery Object CORP-FS2
913 CORP-FS1      This_Worksta   ncp   0114  Rply Scan Bindery Object CORP-FS2
914 This_Worksta  CORP-FS1       ncp   0064  Req  Get Volume Number SYS
915 CORP-FS1      This_Worksta   ncp   0064  Rply Get Volume Number
916 This_Worksta  CORP-FS1       ncp   0064  Req  Get Extended Vol Info
917 CORP-FS1      This_Worksta   ncp   0194  Rply Get Extended Vol Info
918 This_Worksta  CORP-FS1       nds   0088  Req  Read Entry Info;   20 bytes
919 CORP-FS1      This_Worksta   nds   0160  Rply Read Entry Info;  100 bytes
920 This_Worksta  CORP-FS1       nds   0064  Req  Continued Fragment
921 CORP-FS1      This_Worksta   nds   0064  Rply Continued Fragment;    4 bytes
922 This_Worksta  CORP-FS1       ncp   0064  Req  Get Directory Path
923 CORP-FS1      This_Worksta   ncp   0064  Rply Get Directory Path SYS:
924 This_Worksta  CORP-FS1       ncp   0064  Req  Get Directory Path
925 CORP-FS1      This_Worksta   ncp   0064  Rply Get Directory Path SYS:
926 This_Worksta  CORP-FS1       ncp   0064  Req  Get Directory Path
927 CORP-FS1      This_Worksta   ncp   0064  Rply Get Directory Path SYS:
928 This_Worksta  CORP-FS1       ncp   0064  Req  Get Directory Path
929 CORP-FS1      This_Worksta   ncp   0064  Rply Get Directory Path SYS:
930 This_Worksta  CORP-FS1       ncp   0064  Req  Get Station Logged Info
931 CORP-FS1      This_Worksta   ncp   0118  Rply Get Station Logged Info LAURA
```

FIGURE 23.6

The login process using
VLMs and Netware 4.x
(continued)

```
932 This_Worksta  CORP-FS1      ncp   0073  Req  Scan Bindery Object CORP-FS2
933 CORP-FS1      This_Worksta  ncp   0114  Rply Scan Bindery Object CORP-FS2
934 This_Worksta  CORP-FS1      ncp   0064  Req  Get Volume Number SYS
935 CORP-FS1      This_Worksta  ncp   0064  Rply Get Volume Number
936 This_Worksta  CORP-FS1      ncp   0064  Req  Get Extended Vol Info
937 CORP-FS1      This_Worksta  ncp   0194  Rply Get Extended Vol Info
938 This_Worksta  CORP-FS1      nds   0088  Req  Read Entry Info;   20 bytes
939 CORP-FS1      This_Worksta  nds   0160  Rply Read Entry Info;  100 bytes
940 This_Worksta  CORP-FS1      nds   0064  Req  Continued Fragment
941 CORP-FS1      This_Worksta  nds   0064  Rply Continued Fragment;    4 bytes
942 This_Worksta  CORP-FS1      ncp   0064  Req  Get Directory Path
943 CORP-FS1      This_Worksta  ncp   0064  Rply Get Directory Path SYS:
944 This_Worksta  CORP-FS1      ncp   0064  Req  Get Directory Path
945 CORP-FS1      This_Worksta  ncp   0064  Rply Get Directory Path SYS:
946 This_Worksta  CORP-FS1      ncp   0064  Req  Get Station Logged Info
947 CORP-FS1      This_Worksta  ncp   0118  Rply Get Station Logged Info LAUR
948 This_Worksta  CORP-FS1      ncp   0073  Req  Scan Bindery Object CORP-FS2
949 CORP-FS1      This_Worksta  ncp   0114  Rply Scan Bindery Object CORP-FS2
950 This_Worksta  CORP-FS1      ncp   0064  Req  Get Volume Number SYS
951 CORP-FS1      This_Worksta  ncp   0064  Rply Get Volume Number
952 This_Worksta  CORP-FS1      ncp   0064  Req  Get Extended Vol Info
953 CORP-FS1      This_Worksta  ncp   0194  Rply Get Extended Vol Info
954 This_Worksta  CORP-FS1      nds   0088  Req  Read Entry Info;   20 bytes
955 CORP-FS1      This_Worksta  nds   0160  Rply Read Entry Info;  100 bytes
956 This_Worksta  CORP-FS1      nds   0064  Req  Continued Fragment
957 CORP-FS1      This_Worksta  nds   0064  Rply Continued Fragment;    4 bytes
958 This_Worksta  CORP-FS1      ncp   0064  Req  Get File Server Date and Time
959 CORP-FS1      This_Worksta  ncp   0064  Rply Get File Server Date and Time
960 This_Worksta  CORP-FS1      ncp   0064  Req  Get Directory Path
961 CORP-FS1      This_Worksta  ncp   0064  Rply Get Directory Path SYS:
962 This_Worksta  CORP-FS1      ncp   0064  Req  End Of Job
963 CORP-FS1      This_Worksta  ncp   0064  Rply End Of Job
964 This_Worksta  CORP-FS1      ncp   0064  Req  End Of Job
965 CORP-FS1      This_Worksta  ncp   0064  Rply End Of Job
```

Three large transfers have been removed from the trace file shown in Figure 23.6. The first section (packets 36 to 321) is the download of the LOGIN.EXE file from the server to the client's memory. The second is the viewing of the NetWare Language Support (NLS) directory in the server's SYS:PUBLIC\NLS directory. The third large transfer is the download of the Unicode Rules Tables for the enabled language.

For additional information on the NCP calls shown in Figure 23.6, refer to the tables in Chapter 15.

Now let's examine NetWare's security process and how you can use the LANalyzer to detect intruders on the network.

An Example of NetWare Security

NETWARE'S SECURITY CANNOT be broken into by using a protocol analyzer. Passwords are encrypted with a one-way encryption scheme. The encryption scheme is dynamic, constantly changing the key, so a password is never encrypted the same way twice. In fact, if you provide the wrong password when logging in, the server will give a second login key for your second attempt at the password.

As shown during the login procedure, the client requests the log key from the server. It then applies the key to the password before sending it to the server. Figure 23.7 shows a client requesting the encryption key (packet 275), receiving the encryption key (packet 276), and transmitting the encrypted password to the server (packet 279).

FIGURE 23.7

Keyed Login; failure indicates that the password is incorrect.

```
271     LINDSAY      SALES1    ncp    0064    Req  Logout
272     SALES1       LINDSAY   ncp    0064    Rply Logout
273     LINDSAY      SALES1    ncp    0070    Req  Get Bindery Object ID
274     SALES1       LINDSAY   ncp    0110    Rply Get Bindery Object ID
275     LINDSAY      SALES1    ncp    0064    Req  Get Log Key
276     SALES1       LINDSAY   ncp    0064    Rply Get Log Key
277     LINDSAY      SALES1    ncp    0070    Req  Get Bindery Object ID
278     SALES1       LINDSAY   ncp    0110    Rply Get Bindery Object ID
279     LINDSAY      SALES1    ncp    0078    Req  Keyed Login
280     SALES1       LINDSAY   ncp    0064    Rply Keyed Login; Failure
281     LINDSAY      SALES1    ncp    0064    Req  Get Log Key
282     SALES1       LINDSAY   ncp    0064    Rply Get Log Key
283     LINDSAY      SALES1    ncp    0070    Req  Get Bindery Object ID
284     SALES1       LINDSAY   ncp    0110    Rply Get Bindery Object ID
285     LINDSAY      SALES1    ncp    0078    Req  Keyed Login
286     LINDSAY      SALES1    ncp    0078    Req  Keyed Login
287     SALES1       LINDSAY   ncp    0064    Rply Rqst Being Processed; Conn=1
288     LINDSAY      SALES1    ncp    0078    Req  Keyed Login
289     SALES1       LINDSAY   ncp    0064    Rply Rqst Being Processed; Conn=1
290     SALES1       LINDSAY   ncp    0064    Rply Keyed Login; Failure
```

If the password is incorrect, the server replies with a Keyed Login; Failure response, as shown in Figure 23.7.

When a user attempts to log in, the client process (shell) makes two attempts to supply a password to the server before informing the user of a failure. When the first attempt to supply an encrypted password fails (packet 280), the client asks for a second log key (packet 281) and resubmits the password with the new key (packet 285). If this second attempt also fails, the message "Access to server denied" is displayed and the user must reissue the LOGIN.EXE command.

Now let's see how to tell if the user name was incorrectly entered at the workstation.

Incorrect User Name

If the client types the wrong user name, the server notifies the client that the object is not in the bindery, as shown in Figure 23.8.

FIGURE 23.8

The response No Such Object indicates that the user name does not exist in the bindery.

```
Packet Number : 285          5:26:17PM
Length : 66 bytes
802.3: =================== IEEE 802.3 Datalink Layer ==================
       Station: LINDSAY ----> SALES1
       Length: 48
   ipx: =================== Internetwork Packet Exchange =================
       Checksum: 0xFFFF
       Length: 48
       Hop Count:  0
       Packet Type: 17(NCP)
       Network: C9 99 00 06        --->  C9 40 83 46
       Node:    LINDSAY            --->  00-00-00-00-00-01
       Socket:  0x4003             --->  NCP
   ncp: =================== NetWare Core Protocol ====================
       NCP Request: Get Bindery Object ID
       Request Type: 0x2222 (Request)
       Sequence Number: 5
       Connection Number Low: 11
       Task Number: 1
       Connection Number High: 0
       Function Code: 23
       Subfunction Length: 9 bytes
       Subfunction Code: 53
       Object Type: 1 (User)
       Object Name: Length: 5
                    Value : LAURA

Packet Number : 286          5:26:17PM
Length : 64 bytes
802.3: =================== IEEE 802.3 Datalink Layer ==================
       Station: SALES1 ----> LINDSAY
       Length: 38
   ipx: =================== Internetwork Packet Exchange =================
       Checksum: 0xFFFF
       Length: 38
       Hop Count:  0
       Packet Type: 17(NCP)
       Network: C9 40 83 46        --->  C9 99 00 06
       Node:    00-00-00-00-00-01  --->  LINDSAY
       Socket:  NCP                --->  0x4003
   ncp: =================== NetWare Core Protocol ====================
       NCP Reply: Get Bindery Object ID
       Reply Type: 0x3333 (Reply)
       Sequence Number: 5
       Connection Number Low: 11
       Task Number: 1
       Connection Number High: 0
       Completion Code: 252 (No Such Object)
       Connection Status: 0x00
```

The user will still be prompted to enter the password, however. This has always been considered a security feature since it masks whether the user name was wrong or the password was wrong.

As shown in this section, if users complain that they cannot access the NetWare server, you can simply view the packets transmitted during the login process to determine whether they are submitting the wrong password or the wrong user name.

Watching for Unauthorized Network Users

S OME PROTOCOL ANALYZERS can alert you to unauthorized users even before they execute LOGIN.EXE. As shown earlier in Figure 23.1, when a client issues NETX.COM, it begins transmitting SAP and RIP packets on the wire. Analyzers such as the LANalyzer have a "new station" alarm that can be triggered each time a new node address is discovered.

In Figure 23.9, you are viewing a LANalyzer log file listing the users that have been discovered and the detection dates and times. If desired, you can have an audible alarm or an alarm banner (visual alarm) notify you of a new user, as well.

This tracking method has become a fairly common procedure for network security enhancements. The administrator can set up the application to run in the evening and log all new station access information to a single file. If a new station is detected at midnight, when no one should be accessing the network, the log file provides the node address of the user, as shown in Figure 23.9.

Although NetWare's time restrictions are generally sufficient for keeping users off the network during certain off-business hours, you can use the LANalyzer to track attempts by unknown stations, such as portables, to gain access to the network at any time.

A relatively new feature called packet signing was added to NetWare to enhance security, as well. In a network that supports packet signing, each client transmits a unique code "signature" with each communication to the server. The server matches the information received to verify that the client is the true owner of a valid network connection.

FIGURE 23.9

LANalyzer alarm log file

```
Log : 09/10/93 19:26:16 New station with address exosC16258 detected
Log : 09/10/93 19:26:16 New station with address novell34230F detected
Log : 09/10/93 19:26:16 New station with address novell1E8667 detected
Log : 09/10/93 19:26:16 New station with address cisco021602 detected
Log : 09/10/93 19:26:16 New station with address novell33E9BD detected
Log : 09/10/93 19:26:16 New station with address exosC14126 detected
Log : 09/10/93 19:26:16 New station with address exos556013 detected
Log : 09/10/93 19:26:16 New station with address novell02A4A2 detected
Log : 09/10/93 19:26:17 New station with address novell1E8474 detected
Log : 09/10/93 19:26:17 New station with address novell31D74B detected
Log : 09/10/93 19:26:17 New station with address novell1E5188 detected
Log : 09/10/93 19:26:17 New station with address novell1E5A6C detected
Log : 09/10/93 19:26:17 New station with address novell15199C detected
Log : 09/10/93 19:26:17 New station with address novell315391 detected
Log : 09/10/93 19:26:17 New station with address novell03E112 detected
Log : 09/10/93 19:26:17 New station with address novell190ED5 detected
Log : 09/10/93 19:26:17 New station with address novell032464 detected
Log : 09/10/93 19:26:17 New station with address novell326EE6 detected
Log : 09/10/93 19:26:17 New station with address hp13F8E4 detected
Log : 09/10/93 19:26:17 New station with address novell30C4D3 detected
Log : 09/10/93 19:26:18 New station with address novell1E1BD9 detected
Log : 09/10/93 19:26:18 New station with address novell3458DF detected
Log : 09/10/93 19:26:18 New station with address novell1E8456 detected
Log : 09/10/93 19:26:19 New station with address novell1E375D detected
Log : 09/10/93 19:26:19 New station with address novell31B695 detected
Log : 09/10/93 19:26:20 New station with address novell31AA8F detected
Log : 09/10/93 19:26:21 New station with address novell1E248D detected
Log : 09/10/93 19:26:21 New station with address novell350774 detected
Log : 09/10/93 19:26:21 New station with address novell1E866A detected
Log : 09/10/93 19:26:23 New station with address novell351DC3 detected
Log : 09/10/93 19:26:25 New station with address novell02F04E detected
Log : 09/10/93 19:26:25 New station with address intel0C759F detected
Log : 09/10/93 19:26:25 New station with address novell315410 detected
Log : 09/10/93 19:26:26 New station with address novell1E8631 detected
Log : 09/10/93 19:26:27 New station with address intel0C76F4 detected
Log : 09/10/93 19:26:27 New station with address novell1E85E6 detected
Log : 09/10/93 19:26:29 New station with address novell315092 detected
Log : 09/10/93 19:26:29 New station with address novell1E1047 detected
Log : 09/10/93 19:26:29 New station with address novell1EF36B detected
Log : 09/10/93 19:26:29 New station with address novell1E5987 detected
Log : 09/10/93 19:26:29 New station with address novell30FF9B detected
Log : 09/10/93 19:26:29 New station with address novell31A234 detected
Log : 09/10/93 19:26:29 New station with address 00-00-0E-1A-CE-46 detected
Log : 09/10/93 19:26:29 New station with address novell318E7E detected
Log : 09/10/93 19:26:29 New station with address intel044E1C detected
Log : 09/10/93 19:26:29 New station with address novell35040D detected
Log : 09/10/93 19:26:29 New station with address novell41C057 detected
Log : 09/10/93 19:26:30 New station with address novell1E1AA5 detected
Log : 09/10/93 19:26:31 New station with address exosF10530 detected
Log : 09/10/93 19:26:32 New station with address novell1E119E detected
Log : 09/10/93 19:26:34 New station with address novell30386A detected
Log : 09/10/93 19:26:34 New station with address novell03CEC1 detected
Log : 09/10/93 19:26:34 New station with address exosC40940 detected
Log : 09/10/93 19:26:34 New station with address exosC38746 detected
Log : 09/10/93 19:26:34 New station with address exos565529 detected
Log : 09/10/93 19:26:35 New station with address novell19101A detected
```

If a client does not have packet signing enabled in its NET.CFG file on a network that requires signing, the login attempt will fail. Figure 23.10 depicts the communications that occur when a station fails to make a connection because of packet signing.

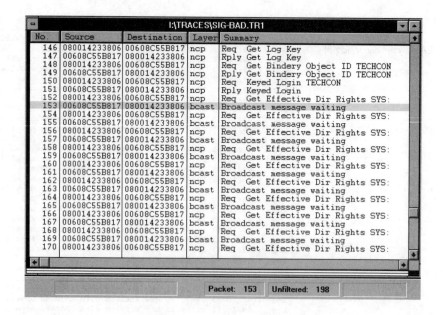

As you can see in Figure 23.10, if the client attempts to find out its directory rights, it is denied access with a blast of broadcast beeps and messages indicating invalid or absent signature information.

Next, you will see how the server replies to stations attempting to read or write files without the appropriate directory or file privileges.

Viewing Access Rights/Privileges

WHEN A CLIENT attempts to write a file to the server, the client must first determine what rights it has to the directory in which it is located. This information is supplied through the Get Bindery Access Level NCP call. The client wishing to write to the directory will request its bindery privilege information, and the server will supply it.

In Figure 23.11, the station is attempting to write a file, TEMP.BAT, to the PUBLIC directory. Packet 5 is the NCP request, Create File. Packet 6 is the NCP reply.

FIGURE 23.11

The user attempts to
write to the PUBLIC
directory.

```
                              C:\TRACES\NOCREATE.TR1
Packet Number : 5              6:15:39PM
Length : 66 bytes
802.3: =================== IEEE 802.3 Datalink Layer ===================
       Station: LINDSAY ----> SALES1
       Length: 48
  ipx: =================== Internetwork Packet Exchange =================
       Checksum: 0xFFFF
       Length: 48
       Hop Count:  0
       Packet Type: 17(NCP)
       Network: C9 99 00 06          --->  C9 40 83 46
       Node:    LINDSAY              --->  00-00-00-00-00-01
       Socket:  0x4003               --->  NCP
  ncp: =================== NetWare Core Protocol ===================
       NCP Request: Create File
       Request Type: 0x2222 (Request)
       Sequence Number: 10
       Connection Number Low: 9
       Task Number: 1
       Connection Number High: 0
       Function Code: 67
       Directory Handle: 0x08
       File Attributes: 0x00
       File Name: Length: 8
                  Value : TEMP.BAT


                                        Packet:  5    Unfiltered:  8
```

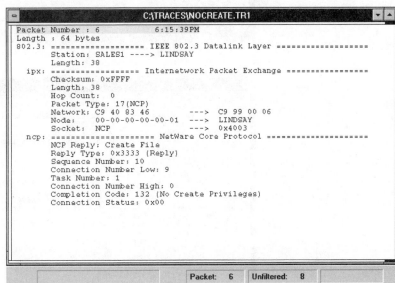

```
                              C:\TRACES\NOCREATE.TR1
Packet Number : 6              6:15:39PM
Length : 64 bytes
802.3: =================== IEEE 802.3 Datalink Layer ===================
       Station: SALES1 ----> LINDSAY
       Length: 38
  ipx: =================== Internetwork Packet Exchange =================
       Checksum: 0xFFFF
       Length: 38
       Hop Count:  0
       Packet Type: 17(NCP)
       Network: C9 40 83 46          --->  C9 99 00 06
       Node:    00-00-00-00-00-01     --->  LINDSAY
       Socket:  NCP                   --->  0x4003
  ncp: =================== NetWare Core Protocol ===================
       NCP Reply: Create File
       Reply Type: 0x3333 (Reply)
       Sequence Number: 10
       Connection Number Low: 9
       Task Number: 1
       Connection Number High: 0
       Completion Code: 132 (No Create Privileges)
       Connection Status: 0x00


                                        Packet:  6    Unfiltered:  8
```

In packet 6, you can see the server returning the NCP Create File reply with
a completion code of 132 (no create privileges). This is why the user cannot
save the file to the PUBLIC directory.

In Figure 23.12, you are viewing a user's attempt to delete a file from the PUBLIC directory.

FIGURE 23.12

A user without rights attempts to delete a file.

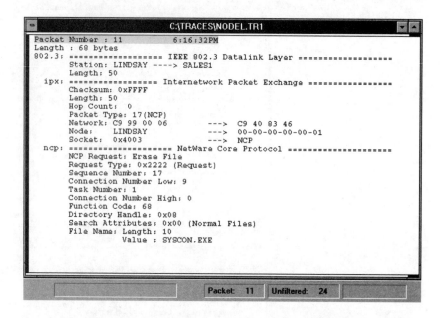

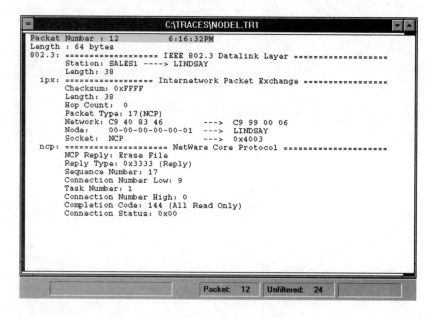

Packet 11 is the user's request to delete the file SYSCON.EXE. In packet 12, the server replies, stating that the request is denied because the file is flagged Read Only. Using the LANalyzer, you can set up an application that filters on requests to delete files (function code 68) if you are concerned about the integrity and safety of data.

This chapter has examined the NETX sequence (including the Preferred Server option) and the VLM attachment sequence and has differentiated among the three server connection priorities (primary, preferred, and default). You viewed the login procedure for NetWare 3.x bindery-based servers and NetWare 4.x NDS networks. You also viewed an attempt to create and delete a file without proper access privileges.

The next chapter focuses on characterizing NetWare server performance.

Characterizing
Server
Performance

CHAPTER

24

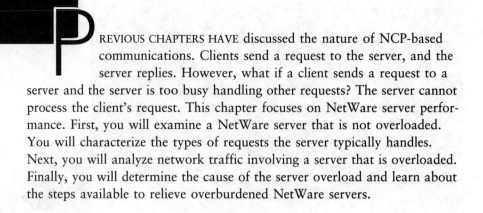

REVIOUS CHAPTERS HAVE discussed the nature of NCP-based communications. Clients send a request to the server, and the server replies. However, what if a client sends a request to a server and the server is too busy handling other requests? The server cannot process the client's request. This chapter focuses on NetWare server performance. First, you will examine a NetWare server that is not overloaded. You will characterize the types of requests the server typically handles. Next, you will analyze network traffic involving a server that is overloaded. Finally, you will determine the cause of the server overload and learn about the steps available to relieve overburdened NetWare servers.

Setting Up a Server Workload Test

N ORDER TO characterize the server's workload, you must follow these steps:

1. Identify the server to examine.

2. Create an application to filter on NCP traffic.

3. Plot the data.

Step 1: Identify the Server to Examine

Unless you specify a single server within the application you create, you will be characterizing all servers' performance information. To characterize traffic from a single NetWare v3.x server, filter on the server's internal IPX address in the IPX header. Figure 24.1 shows a packet that has been received from a NetWare v3.x server. Note that the address in the IPX header differs from the address in the Ethernet header. Remember, if a packet has crossed a router, the Ethernet source address will be the physical address of the router, not the server. Therefore, the server's address must go in the IPX header's Source Address (or Destination Address) field, not the Ethernet header's Source Address (or Destination Address) field.

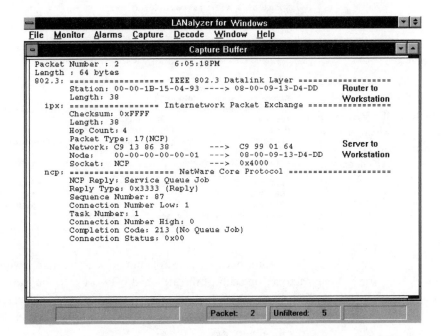

If you do not know the internal IPX address of the server on a 3.x-based network, log in to the network and type **SLIST**. You will receive a listing of all server names, internal IPX addresses (or LAN card A addresses for NetWare 2.x servers), and node addresses, as shown in Figure 24.2.

If you have a mapping to the PUBLIC directory on a NetWare 4.x server, you must use the NLIST SERVER /B command, as shown in Figure 24.3.

You can identify NetWare 3.x and 4.x servers by the node address 0x00-00-00-00-00-01. Once you have determined the server whose local traffic you would like to characterize, place your analyzer on that server's network, as shown in Figure 24.4. This ensures that you are viewing all traffic to and from that server; routers and bridges are not filtering out traffic. If a server is acting

FIGURE 24.2

The SLIST command lists all known servers on the network, as well as their network and node addresses.

```
Known NetWare File Servers                    Network   Node Address Status
FS1                                          [  A87666] [           1]
FS2                                          [A190FF9A] [           1]
FS3                                          [A88AA88A] [           1]
FS4                                          [CC007000] [           1]
MKTG-45                                      [C9408346] [           1]
MKTG-SE                                      [C0000016] [           1]
SALES1                                       [C9138638] [           1]
SALES2                                       [C0CB4117] [           1]
SALES3                                       [ 1020001] [           1]

Total of 9 file servers found.
```

FIGURE 24.3

Use the NLIST SERVER /B command when you have a mapping to a NetWare 4.x PUBLIC directory.

```
Object Class: server
Known to Server: CORP-FS2
Active NetWare Server= The NetWare Server that is currently running
Address              = The network address
Node                 = The network node
Status               = The status of your connection

Active NetWare Server                         Address   Node      Status
CORP-FS1                                      [      99] [        1]Attached
CORP-FS2                                      [BA55BA11] [        1]Default
CORP-FS3                                      [FEEDFACE] [        1]
A total of 3 server objects was found.
```

as a router between multiple networks, you may wish to examine the server's activity on each of the attached networks. If you examine only one of the networks to which the server is attached, you are not creating a complete report of the server's activity; you are only gathering server activity information for the local network.

In the example, you can place your LANalyzer on either side of the repeater on the same network as the server SALES1, the server for which you are going to characterize local traffic.

Step 2: Create an Application to Filter on NCP Traffic

Set up an application that filters on specific NCP function codes. The application should also capture broadcast packets (addressed to FF-FF-FF-FF-FF-FF in the Ethernet header), routed packets (greater than 0 in the Transport Control field), and Request Being Processed packets (NCP type 9999). The application

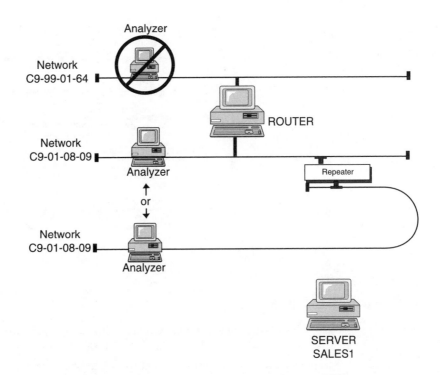

FIGURE 24.4

Place your analyzer on the server's network.

must filter on these Request Being Processed packets in order to locate potentially overloaded servers. Later in this chapter, you will examine the implications of these Request Being Processed packets.

You must also determine the collection time and sampling period for your application. For how long do you want to collect data, and at what frequency? For example, perhaps you want to characterize server traffic at 2:00 P.M. You may wish to collect data for 15 minutes, sampling every 20 seconds.

In Figure 24.5, the LANalyzer's predefined application, PERFORM, is being used to characterize the performance of the server SALES1. The PERFORM application is filtering on delay (Request Being Processed packets), broadcasts, logins, file reads/writes, messages, queues, bridge (routed packets), and all NetWare traffic in general.

FIGURE 24.5

The LANalyzer PERFORM
application characterizes
server performance.

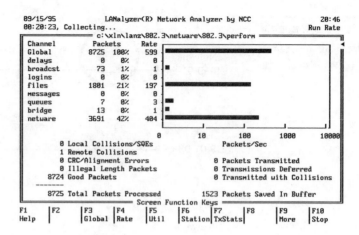

FIGURE 24.5

The LANalyzer PERFORM
application characterizes
server performance.

Step 3: Plot the Data

To obtain a clear view of server performance, you can plot the data using a
spreadsheet program. In Figure 24.6, the data was exported in CSV (comma-
separated value) format. Next, the data was imported into the spreadsheet
and a line graph format was selected to graph the data.

FIGURE 24.6

The data is plotted in a
line graph format.

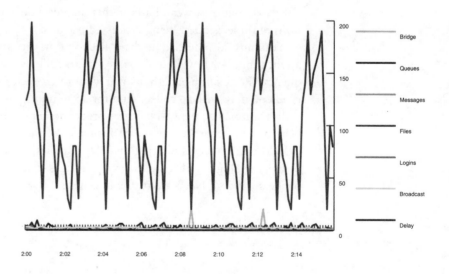

By viewing this graph, you can see that most requests made from server SALES1 are file requests. In this application, the server SALES1 is not transmitting any Request Being Processed packets. You can determine, therefore, that the server is keeping up with client requests. If users are complaining of slow responses from the network, you can determine that the server is not at fault. After doing so, you can look at other sources for the network delay, such as an overloaded cabling system. The next step would be to test the utilization on the server's segment and the client's segment, as defined in Chapter 3.

Next, you will locate an overloaded server, characterize the traffic, and determine the possible cause of the overload condition.

Locating an Overloaded Server

T O LOCATE A server that is not keeping up with client requests, you must look for Request Being Processed packets on the network. NetWare servers include a flow-control mechanism that enables them to report an overload condition to client shells. When a client sends requests to a server, the client shell expects a response within the IPX timeout period.

When a workstation does not receive a response within the timeout period, it assumes the server has not received the original request. It reexecutes the request. This retransmission function is useful if packets are lost or network access is interrupted, perhaps as the result of an overloaded cabling segment—the server may not be able to access the medium to reply. This reexecution process, however, does not indicate an overloaded server. To help control workstation requests to an overloaded server, Novell has created the unique NCP type 9999, Request Being Processed, to indicate an overloaded server.

When a client transmits a request to an overloaded server, the server replies with a Request Being Processed packet, as shown in Figure 24.7.

These Request Being Processed packets are a clear indication that the server cannot keep up with all the work it is currently handling. However, it is not necessarily the fault of the workstation that received the Request Being Processed packet. It may be due to other processes the server is handling. Later in this chapter, you will determine the cause of a server overload condition. First,

FIGURE 24.7

A client requests services, but the server replies that it is busy.

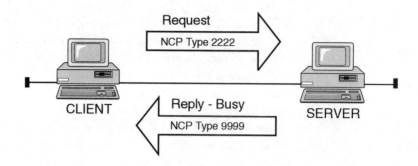

let's continue to examine the communications between a client and an over-loaded server.

Upon receipt of a Request Being Processed packet, the workstation resets its IPX timeout timer and continues to wait for a reply. If the client does not receive any reply within the timeout value, it reexecutes the request. The server can either execute the request and transmit a reply or, if it is busy, transmit another Request Being Processed packet.

A client can reexecute a request up to 20 times without receiving any reply (including a Request Being Processed packet) before giving up. This amount is configurable, however, in the NET.CFG file. For example, you can add the line "IPX RETRY = 50" to make the client more persistent on a busy or problem network segment. When the retry count is reached, the user receives a network error message indicating that the station experienced an "Error Receiving from Server *server name*," indicating that the server did not reply within the timeout value. Remember, however, that you are looking for Request Being Processed packet responses to indicate an overloaded server.

To locate a server that is overloaded, you must create an application that filters on the Request Being Processed NCP type 9999, as shown in Figure 24.8.

When viewing the trace, the NetWare v3.x or 4.x server that is sending the Request Being Processed packet places its internal IPX address in the IPX header Source Address field, as shown in Figure 24.9.

Many analyzers provide a name table that allows substitution of the server's name for the internal IPX address. If, however, the server name is not shown within the IPX header, you can use the SLIST command to determine the server name, as discussed earlier in this chapter. In Figure 24.9, a server with the internal IPX network address of C9-40-83-46 has been identified as

FIGURE 24.8

A filter is set up to look for Request Being Processed packets.

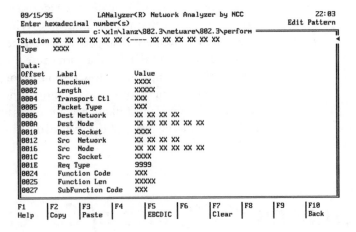

FIGURE 24.9

A Request Being Processed packet contains the server's internal IPX address.

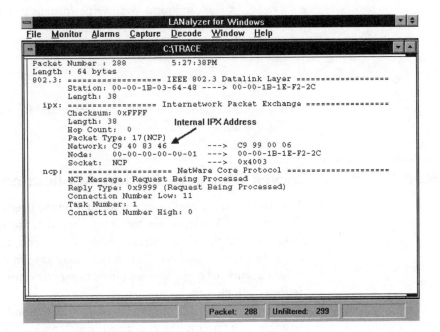

an overloaded server. By reviewing Figure 24.2, you will discover that it is the MKTG-45 server that is indicating an overload condition.

How many Request Being Processed packets are too many? A few overload packets throughout the day may not cause noticeable delay to the users. When users begin to complain of slow response from the server, however, and the server is indicating an overload condition, the number of Request Being Processed packets has most likely become excessive for your network. Next, you will determine the cause of the overload condition.

Determining the Cause of Server Overload

WHEN AN OVERLOADED server has been located, you can determine the cause of the overload and take corrective action to improve performance. These are the steps for characterizing an overloaded server's traffic:

1. Run the server characterization application.

2. Plot the results.

3. Look for relationships between traffic and Request Being Processed packets.

Step 1: Run the Server Characterization Application

A characterization application must filter on the overloaded server's address (the internal IPX address for NetWare 3.x and 4.x servers). The analyzer should also be placed on the segment the server is on, as shown in Figure 24.10. It should be noted that NetWare servers may have multiple network segments attached; only delay packets sent from the server onto the network local to the analyzer will be seen.

Next, define an appropriate length for the test and sampling rate. In this example, you will run the characterization application for 15 minutes, sampling every 20 seconds.

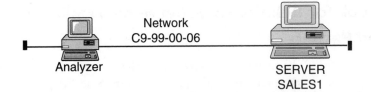

FIGURE 24.10

Filter on SALES1's traffic
on the local segment

Step 2: Plot the Results

After running the application, plot the results using a spreadsheet program.
Figure 24.11 shows the results plotted using a line graph.

FIGURE 24.11

The results are plotted
using a line graph.

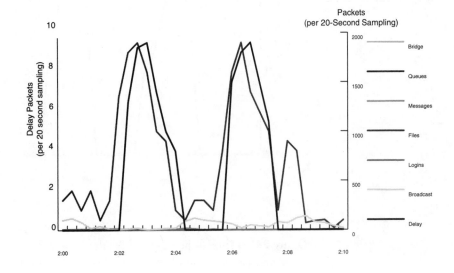

Step 3: Look for Relationships between Traffic and Request Being Processed Packets

The final step in determining the cause of the overload condition requires interpretation of the plotted results. Since Request Being Processed packets are sent when servers are busy, look for a correlation between the Request Being Processed packets and a specific type of activity, such as printing requests or file activity. For example, Figure 24.12 shows only the broadcast packets and the Request Being Processed packets being plotted. You can see there is no relationship between the increase in broadcasts and the Request Being Processed packets. Therefore, you can state that the broadcasts are not causing the server overload.

FIGURE 24.12

Broadcast requests compared with Request Being Processed packets

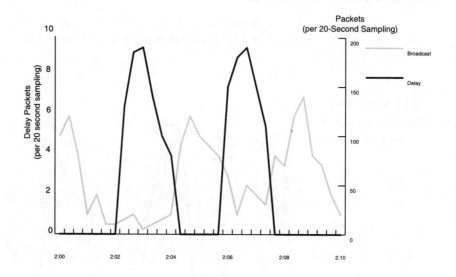

Next, you will compare file activity to Request Being Processed packets. Figure 24.13 shows the graphed results.

As you can see, the file requests show a direct relationship to the Request Being Processed packets. This indicates that they are causing the server overload condition.

Now let's examine the possible solutions to various server overload conditions.

FIGURE 24.13

File activity compared with Request Being Processed packets

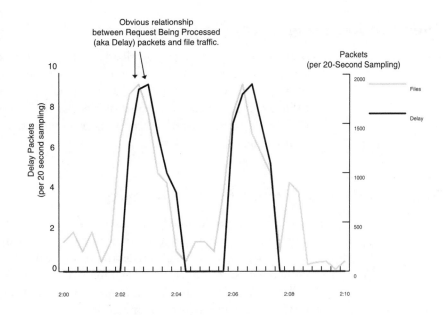

Obvious relationship between Request Being Processed (aka Delay) packets and file traffic.

Packets (per 20-Second Sampling)

Delay Packets (per 20 second sampling)

Files

Delay

Balancing Server Loads

B ASED ON THE results of the server workload test, you can take several steps to remedy performance problems, as described in the following sections.

Overload Resulting from Broadcast Activity

If the server is being overloaded because of an extreme number of broadcast requests, track down the source of the requests. For example, if a server begins to report an overload condition at the same time a high number of broadcasts occurs, view the trace to determine who is sending the broadcasts onto the network. Perhaps a workstation has a corrupt shell, causing it to send repeated Get Nearest Server packets onto the LAN. The server will respond to each of these packets, eventually causing an overload situation. Replace the faulty shell.

Overload Resulting from File Activity

If the server is reporting an overload associated with extremely high file activity, check the server to determine whether it has enough memory. Most file requests should be serviced from cache on a NetWare server. Check the Monitor screen to see the number of requests being serviced from cache. Chances are that an overload resulting from file activity indicates a need to increase the server memory.

Overload Resulting from Routed Activity

If a server cannot handle requests because it is busy routing packets, consider moving the routing responsibility from the server to an external router or another server. You can also redistribute applications or user accounts to minimize the need to route traffic. Upgrading to a faster bus and network adapter will also help. For example, upgrading from an ISA bus to an EISA, MCA, or PCI bus will increase performance.

Overload Resulting from Print Activity

If the server is reporting an overload because of excessive print activity, consider moving the queues to another server, or find out which users are most actively sending queue requests. Determine whether they can submit jobs to queues on another server.

Another option involves reviewing the queue system and determining whether too many users are spooling to a single queue on the network. Redistribute queues across the network, if desired.

You can use this same type of approach to troubleshoot overload resulting from other NCP request types, as well.

In this chapter, you have characterized performance on a server that is not overloaded by creating an application filtering on certain NCP function and subfunction codes. This application helped you locate an overloaded server. After plotting the results, you determined the cause of the overload on the network.

Part V of this book focuses on the features and benefits provided by protocol analyzers.

Protocol Analyzers— Overview and Features

PART

V

Overview of Protocol Analyzers

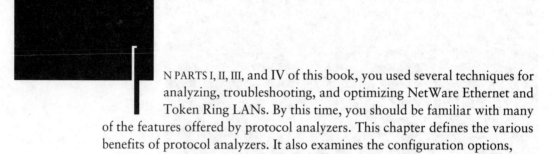

I N PARTS I, II, III, and IV of this book, you used several techniques for analyzing, troubleshooting, and optimizing NetWare Ethernet and Token Ring LANs. By this time, you should be familiar with many of the features offered by protocol analyzers. This chapter defines the various benefits of protocol analyzers. It also examines the configuration options, such as hardware and software or software only.

Protocol analyzers offer a tremendous amount of information about network performance, and you can use them to analyze networks from the physical-layer through the upper-layer protocols. This chapter begins by examining protocol analyzer features for physical-layer analysis.

Physical-Layer Analysis

M ANY ANALYZERS HAVE the capability to test the cabling system on the network. Although a TDR (time domain reflectometer) has been the standard industry tool for testing cabling, many analyzers now include this feature, as well. Figure 25.1 shows the LANalyzer's cable check being run on a network.

The LANalyzer uses the rudimentary TDR functionality built into the Ethernet chipset to determine opens (cable breaks) or shorts (contact between the conductor and the ground). By sending a signal down the cabling system, timing the return signal (if any), and determining whether the return signal was in phase or out of phase, the LANalyzer can determine whether the cable is experiencing a short or an open condition. You can use analyzers that provide this type of functionality to troubleshoot network backbones and segments, as well as drop cables.

FIGURE 25.1

LANalyzer cable check

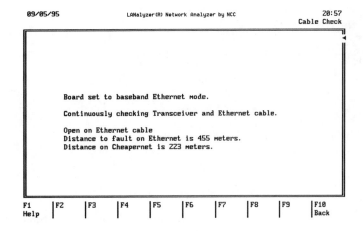

```
09/05/95               LANalyzer(R) Network Analyzer by NCC              20:57
                                                                    Cable Check



            Board set to baseband Ethernet mode.

            Continuously checking Transceiver and Ethernet cable.

            Open on Ethernet cable
            Distance to fault on Ethernet is 455 meters.
            Distance on Cheapernet is 223 meters.




    F1     |F2    |F3    |F4    |F5    |F6    |F7    |F8    |F9    |F10
    Help   |      |      |      |      |      |      |      |      |Back
```

Data Link–Layer Analysis

C HAPTERS 4 AND 5 of this book were dedicated to data link-layer analysis for Ethernet, and Chapter 11 discussed data link-layer analysis of Token Ring. In these chapters, you viewed several methods for determining frame errors. Analyzers provide a method for looking beyond the workstation error messages to the traffic on the wire.

Analyzers can report an assortment of Ethernet errors, such as the following:

- Local collisions

- Late collisions

- Remote collisions

- Short packets

- Long packets

- CRC/alignment errors

- Jabber

Many analyzer vendors use the term "fragments" to define collisions.

Analyzers can generally report an assortment of Token Ring errors, such as the following:

- Line errors

- Burst errors

- Beaconing

- Receiver congestion

Of course, you must understand the implications of each error to determine the cause of the network errors.

Many analyzers do not report all the errors listed above. When purchasing an analyzer, determine which errors it will report and how it defines each error.

As shown in Figure 25.2, you can use an analyzer to determine the source of errors, as well. This provides a streamlined method for catching hardware or software errors on the network.

FIGURE 25.2

You can use the analyzer to determine the source of errors.

```
09/05/95              LANalyzer(R) Network Analyzer by NCC              21 24
Press ALT-T to toggle between summary modes                        Trace Summary
                          b:\crc
Created On 09/05/95 20:15:32   Elapsed Time 00:00:19   Total Packets    2600
  Pkt# Source     Destination  Protocol  Size  Error  Channels IntPkt Time
  344 novell1EF22C BLDG4        NetWare    74   CRC    12......  0.403 MS◄
  345 novell1EF22C BLDG4        NetWare    74   CRC    12......  0.403 MS◄
  346 novell1187450 MKTG        NetWare    64          1.......  0.475 MS
  347 MKTG         novell1EF22C NetWare   184          1.......  0.770 MS
  348 MKTG         novell1EF22C NetWare   184          1.......  0.770 MS
  349 exos8e4501   SALES        NetWare    64          1.......  0.561 MS
  350 BLDG4        novell1EF22C NetWare    64          1.......  0.671 MS
  351 3com90d0b5   SALES        NetWare    64          1.......  0.412 MS
  352 SALES        novell1EF22C NetWare   184          1.......  0.756 MS
  353 novell1897612 ADMIN1      NetWare    64          1.......  0.559 MS
  354 novell1897612 ADMIN1      NetWare    64          1.......  0.559 MS
  355 novell1EF22C SALES        NetWare    64   CRC    12......  0.392 MS
  356 SALES        novell1EF22C NetWare    64          1.......  0.545 MS
  357 novell1EF22C BLDG4        NetWare   568   CRC    12......  1.002 MS
  358 BLDG4        novell1EF22C NetWare   390          1.......  1.343 MS
  359 novell1674590 BLDG4       NetWare    64          1 ......  0.521 MS
  360 BLDG4        novell1EF22C NetWare   184          1.......  0.733 MS

F1      F2      F3      F4      F5      F6      F7      F8      F9      F10
Help    Load    Print   Options Buffer  Decode  Compare Find    Go To   Back
```

Network-Layer Analysis

THE NETWORK LAYER provides routing information for the internetwork. In a NetWare environment, the IPX header provides routing information and is used to send a packet throughout a large NetWare internet. At this layer, you can use analyzers to determine the distance between clients and servers. This information helps you determine whether a network cabling system needs reconfiguration or whether applications or clients should be moved to other networks because of routing inefficiencies.

In Figure 25.3, you are viewing a LANalyzer application called HOP-COUNT that registers all traffic based on the number of hops seen in the Transport Control field of the IPX header.

FIGURE 25.3

You can use the HOPCOUNT application to find routing inefficiencies.

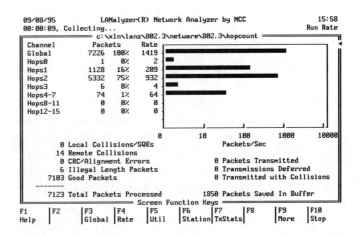

Generally, most troubleshooting analysis happens at the network layer and below. The errors found there are those an administrator can usually handle, such as swapping out a bad network interface card, reloading a LAN driver, and distributing resources or clients to another network or segment.

However, when a problem does occur above the network layer, you can use analyzers to interpret the communications occurring on the wire. For example, if an application does not load properly from the server, you may wish to use a protocol analyzer to see the downloading process on the wire.

Upper-Layer Protocol Analysis

U PPER-LAYER PROTOCOL analysis deals with the transport-, session-, presentation-, and application-layer protocols. In the NetWare environment, these include

- SPX/SPX II

- Packet Burst

- Large Internet Packet

- NLSP

- NCP

- NDS

- RIP

- SAP

Analysis at this level requires a solid understanding of the protocol's method of communicating. For example, if you wanted to determine whether a network was utilizing the Packet Burst protocol when it should, you would need a general understanding of how Packet Burst connections are created, as shown in Figure 25.4. This, in turn, would help you understand why connections may be getting refused by the servers.

Another example involves the analysis of an SPX session between a client and the server. To understand why the SPX session is aborting, you can use an analyzer to "listen" to the connection-oriented services on the wire.

You can also use analyzers to measure performance of an upper-layer protocol, such as NCP. After installing a new NetWare shell (NETX) or the DOS Requester (VLM), if you wished to determine whether they were enhancing performance, you could create an application that filters on the station using the new shell or requester. Comparing current performance against the previous shell or requester's performance can help determine whether the new shell is more efficient than its predecessor.

You can also examine applications with analyzers. When the workstation loads an application from the server, analyzers can capture the traffic between

FIGURE 25.4

You can use analyzers to determine why a Packet Burst connection is being refused at the server.

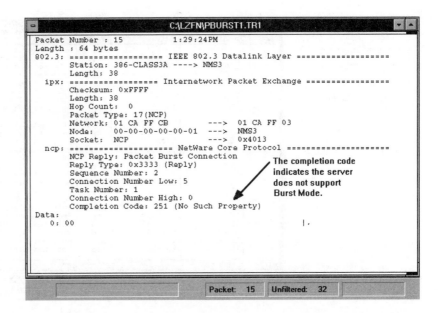

```
                              C:\LZFN\PBURST1.TR1
Packet Number : 15              1:29:24PM
Length : 64 bytes
802.3: ================== IEEE 802.3 Datalink Layer ==================
       Station: 386-CLASS3A ----> NMS3
       Length: 38
  ipx: ================== Internetwork Packet Exchange ================
       Checksum: 0xFFFF
       Length: 38
       Hop Count:  0
       Packet Type: 17(NCP)
       Network: 01 CA FF CB      ---> 01 CA FF 03
       Node:    00-00-00-00-00-01 ---> NMS3
       Socket:  NCP               ---> 0x4013
  ncp: ================= NetWare Core Protocol ====================
       NCP Reply: Packet Burst Connection      The completion code
       Reply Type: 0x3333 (Reply)              indicates the server
       Sequence Number: 2                      does not support
       Connection Number Low: 5                Burst Mode.
       Task Number: 1
       Connection Number High: 0
       Completion Code: 251 (No Such Property)
Data:
     0: 00                                              | .

                                    Packet:  15   Unfiltered:  32
```

the server and workstation to see the application download to the client system, as well as any supplemental files the application relies on. For example, if a WordPerfect user continuously complains of having the wrong working environment (such as an unusual color scheme or units instead of points for measurement), you can view the download sequence to determine which .SET file is being loaded with the application, as shown in Figure 25.5.

Preceding chapters provided other examples of how you can use analyzers to troubleshoot and optimize the network. These include

- Creating a baseline

- Stress-testing the cabling system

- Stress-testing a component

- Route testing

- Utilization gauging

- Growth planning

FIGURE 25.5

The analyzer interprets downloading of an application and any supplemental files.

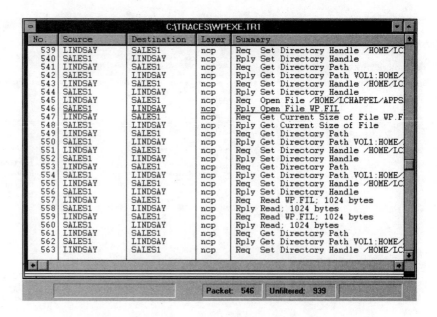

Besides reviewing the features and capabilities of analyzers, you need to be aware that analyzers are available in two standard configurations:

- Hardware/software

- Software only

Hardware/Software Analyzer Kits

HARDWARE/SOFTWARE SOLUTIONS are generally more expensive than software-only solutions because of the cost of the interface board (and sometimes the PC) that accompanies the software.

The analyzer features defined in this book are based on the capability of NCC LANalyzer and LANalyzer for Windows products. Check with your analyzer vendor to determine product capabilities.

The specialized cards that are included with the system can provide additional functionality, such as the following:

- An on-board buffer

- An on-board processor

- Greater transmit capabilities

The specialized cards often include an on-board buffer for packet capture. This type of buffering is generally faster than saving packets to a disk or system memory, and it allows the analyzer to keep up with higher traffic network systems.

The on-board processor included on these cards frees the PC from handling all the processing required for capturing packets and maintaining statistics information. On a higher traffic network system, these on-board processors provide a more powerful analyzer system.

The specialized hardware systems also provide greater transmit capabilities. For example, the LANalyzer allows users to simultaneously transmit and receive packets. The ability to capture and decode improperly framed data and transmit errors onto the network is also a capability enabled by hardware/software solutions.

One drawback of hardware/software solutions is cost. Hardware/software solutions are generally more expensive than software-only solutions because of the specialized hardware prices. Prices for hardware/software systems generally start at around $10,000.

Another drawback of hardware/software solutions is the lack of portability of these systems. In order to analyze a network with a hardware/software system, you must take to the site either a portable system with the hardware installed or the specialized card and software in hopes of finding a system to use on site.

Software-Only Solutions

SOFTWARE-ONLY SOLUTIONS are becoming more popular because of their cost (they do not require expensive specialized boards) and portability. Prices for software-only solutions start at around $900. For smaller networks and cost-conscious users, the software-only option allows access to a protocol analyzer without the high price tag.

The software-only solutions offer greater portability, as well. To analyze a network, it is possible with a software-only solution to take just a set of disks to a customer site. However, it may still be more convenient to carry a portable unit with the software preinstalled.

These systems rely on the processing power of the PC they are installed in and are dependent on the LAN driver that accompanies the software. As an example, the LANalyzer for Windows includes the latest drivers from Novell (drivers for NetWare 4.0). These drivers can operate in "promiscuous" mode, allowing all errors seen on the wire to be filtered up to the LANalyzer for Windows application for statistics gathering. You should select a network card for your analyzer that supports full promiscuous mode and is high performance, as well.

Stand-Alone and Distributed Solutions

UNTIL RECENTLY, ALL network analyzers were stand-alone solutions—the analyzer was placed on a single network segment and had to be moved from segment to segment to gather statistics and packets throughout the network. LANalyzer and LANalyzer for Windows are stand-alone network analyzers.

However, several distributed network analyzers have recently been released to an anxiously waiting group of network administrators and technicians. Distributed analyzers are the most exciting network management and troubleshooting products to emerge in many years. These analyzers allow you to monitor all network segments and traffic from a single management console.

For example, Novell's NetWare Management System supports distributed network analysis using the NetWare LANalyzer Agents (NLM-based analyzer modules that are loaded on NetWare servers, NetWare RunTime, or NetWare MultiProtocol Routers throughout the network).

Using the NetWare Management System with NetWare LANalyzer Agents, you can access and obtain the same network communications information that is provided by LANalzyer for Windows, without leaving your desk. Whether you have 3 network segments or 300, you should seriously consider using a distributed solution to save precious time and energy when you are analyzing the network.

This chapter has covered the general features of analyzers, from the ability to analyze physical-layer protocols to the ability to analyze upper-layer protocols. Analyzers—whether hardware/software or software only, and whether stand-alone or distributed—offer the network administrator or support technician a variety of options.

The next chapter focuses on statistics gathering options for short-term or trend information.

Trend and Current Statistics (Baseline Information)

CHAPTER

26

N THIS BOOK you have viewed a variety of statistics regarding network performance. For example, you looked at utilization trend information that indicates typical network utilization. You also looked at error trends on the network. This chapter examines how statistics are gathered and the types of data that can be saved in statistics files.

Statistics are created from the packets viewed on the wire by the analyzer, as shown in Figure 26.1.

FIGURE 26.1

Statistics are created from the activity seen by the analyzer.

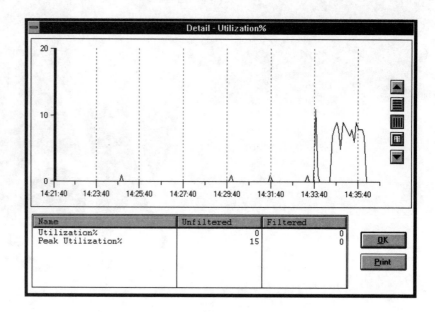

Incrementing Statistics Counters

W HEN A PACKET is viewed, the analyzer can determine the type of packet—error packet, broadcast, and so on—and increment the appropriate statistics counter. You can configure the analyzer to track the types of packets you are most interested in. For example, if the analyzer sees a NetWare broadcast packet, the following counters may be affected:

- NetWare packets
- Good packets (packets that comply with Ethernet standards)
- Broadcast packets (all)
- SAP broadcast packets
- Packets between 64 and 127 bytes
- Packets per second
- Kilobytes per second
- Current bandwidth utilization

Statistics can be presented in many different ways, including bar graphs, line graphs, gauges, and digital counters. In Figure 26.2, you are viewing LANalyzer's Global Statistics screen on an Ethernet LAN. This screen displays information on all network activity.

On the Global Statistics screen, you are presented with statistics information such as

- Packet size distribution
- Total number of packets
- Total number of kilobytes
- Average utilization over sampling periods
- Utilization for the current sampling period
- Average kilobytes per second
- Peak kilobytes per second

FIGURE 26.2

LANalyzer's Global
Statistics screen

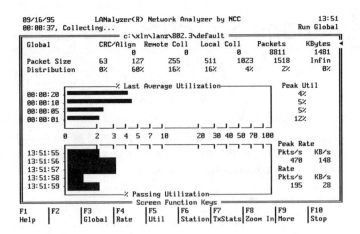

The packet size distribution is listed across the top of the screen. The size columns are interpreted as follows:

Heading	Interpretation
63	Between 0 and 63 bytes, inclusive (short packets)
127	Between 64 and 127 bytes, inclusive
255	Between 128 and 255 bytes, inclusive
511	Between 256 and 511 bytes, inclusive
1023	Between 512 and 1023 bytes, inclusive
1518	Between 1024 and 1518 bytes, inclusive
Inf	Packets greater than 1518 bytes (long packets)

Packet size distribution is dependent on the type of network you are analyzing.

You can use this packet size distribution information for network optimization purposes. If a network is consistently using smaller packets when the protocol supports larger packets, you may wish to investigate the reason for using the smaller packet size (such as a NetWare router that does not support larger packet sizes). By increasing packet sizes, you can reduce the amount of overhead required for communications and, ultimately, increase network efficiency. Databases can be tuned so that record sizes support more efficient data transfer to the client.

The total number of packets and kilobytes is also listed across the top of the screen. The number under the Packets heading indicates the total number of packets that have occurred on the network since the test began. As activity increases, the total number of packets also increases. Comparing this number for a one-hour test period against an earlier one-hour test period provides a quick determination of recent network traffic patterns.

The KBytes column indicates the total number of kilobytes that have traversed the network since the application began. This number indicates the network throughput—how much information is being transmitted on the wire during the time period. Once again, you can compare this information against earlier statistics to determine whether the network throughput has increased.

The average utilization over sampling periods is recorded on the graph at the top center of the screen (see the upper bar graph in Figure 26.2).

The sampling periods are listed on the left side of the bar graph: 1 second, 5 seconds, 10 seconds, and 20 seconds. The utilization is averaged over each of the time periods and plotted on the bar graph. These sampling periods can be changed to reflect 1, 5, 10, and 20 times a selected sampling period. For example, you can configure the application to gather statistics each minute instead of each second. In that case, this column would include sampling averages for the last 1 minute, 5 minutes, 10 minutes, and 20 minutes.

On the right side of the screen, the average kilobytes per second (for the time the application has been running) are recorded. Below this indicator are the peak kilobytes per second during the application time period. You can use these indicators to determine whether the current throughput is typical.

The utilization for the current sampling period is listed below the average utilization bar graph. This graph indicates the bandwidth utilization for the last 5 seconds, 1 second at a time. You can compare this information to the average listed above it to determine whether utilization is increasing or decreasing. On small percentages that do not show up on the graph, the LANalyzer provides the ability to "zoom in" on the graph, as shown in Figure 26.3.

Statistics you can gather over time on a network include the following:

- Utilization

- Kilobytes/second

- Packets/second

- Errors/second

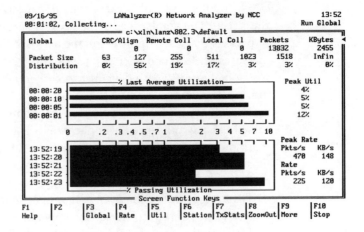

The total packets and total kilobytes may also be useful in situations in which you are benchmarking or testing the network or network component, such as bridge or router throughput. It is important to know current utilization when troubleshooting, but it is also important to note how bandwidth utilization has increased or decreased over time. Figure 26.4 shows the LANalyzer for Windows Detail Utilization screen. You can notice a dramatic increase in utilization.

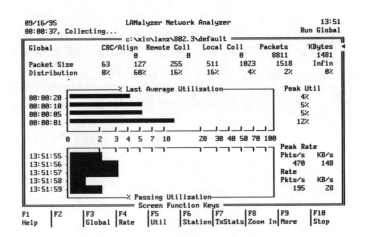

Kilobytes-per-second statistics indicate the increase or decrease in throughput on the network, as shown in Figure 26.5.

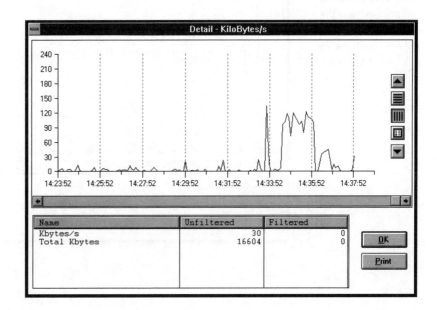

Packets-per-second statistics indicate the number of packets that have been transmitted on the network over time, as shown in Figure 26.6.

Errors-per-second statistics illustrate the increase or decrease in the errors occurring on the network, as shown in Figure 26.7.

The errors table provides a detailed breakdown of the number of fragments, short packets, long packets, CRC/Alignment errors, and so on. As shown in Figure 26.8, statistics tables accompany the line graphs and provide peak and average information.

Analyzers also provide information for troubleshooting and optimizing the network with short-term and long-term, or trend, statistics.

FIGURE 26.6

Packets-per-second statistics indicate the number of packets on the network for each sampling period.

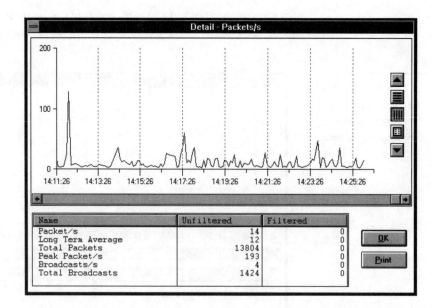

FIGURE 26.7

Errors-per-second statistics indicate increasing or decreasing errors on the LAN.

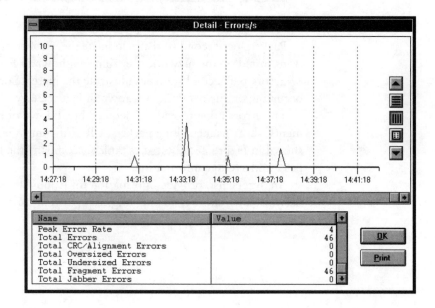

Short-Term Statistics

S HORT-TERM STATISTICS provide a "snapshot" of network performance in real time. These statistics are generally plotted each second and can be compared against the long-term statistics to determine whether current network activity is typical.

In Figure 26.8, you are viewing a LANalyzer for Windows screen that depicts short-term utilization statistics. This screen indicates that the network bandwidth utilization has increased dramatically over the last 15 minutes.

FIGURE 26.8

Short-term utilization statistics indicate a steady increase in bandwidth utilization over the last 15 minutes.

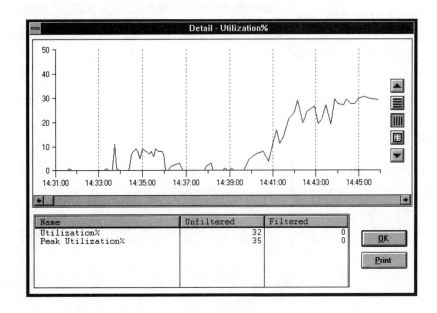

In order to provide a comparative graph, it is important to create a baseline report, as defined in Chapter 21.

Long-Term (Trend) Statistics

BASELINE REPORTS INCLUDE trend information on utilization, kilobytes per second, errors per second, and packets per second. The long-term (or trend) statistics indicate typical network performance over time. These statistics can span several days, weeks, or months. In Figure 26.9, you are viewing long-term statistics for network errors. As you can see, this network typically experiences an insignificant number of errors.

FIGURE 26.9

Trend statistics on network errors

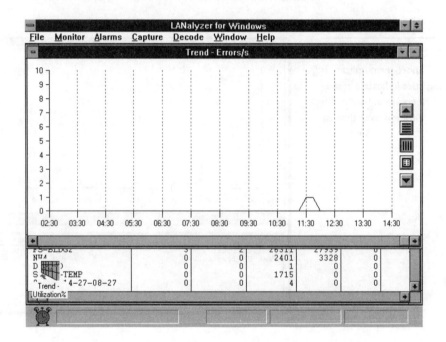

You can use this information for comparison with short-term statistics. If the short-term statistics show a dramatic rise in errors, you can see—based on the trend information—that this is not typical. Some error has occurred on the network recently. The next step for troubleshooting is to identify the type of error and the source.

You can use trend information for utilization to determine whether the current utilization is typical. For example, if utilization has risen over the last 30 minutes, you can compare this current information against your long-term statistics. You may find that this is typical because network backup is being performed at this time or because large files are being printed for the end-of-month reports.

You can also use trend information to determine the most appropriate time to back up the network. For example, in Figure 26.10, you are viewing trend statistics indicating that the best time for backup would be between 9:00 P.M. (21:00 hours) and 8:00 A.M.

FIGURE 26.10

Trend statistics provide an indication of the best time to back up the network.

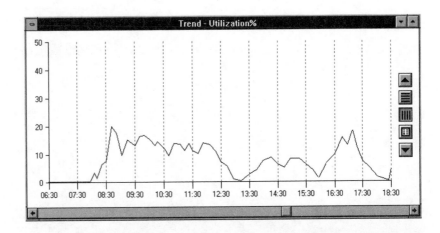

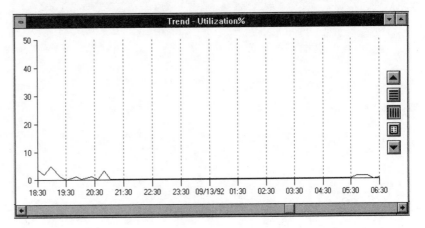

You can export trend and short-term statistics into spreadsheet format. You can then import this information into spreadsheets and plot it for further analysis.

In this chapter you have learned that you can use trend statistics, in conjunction with short-term, real-time statistics, for troubleshooting. In addition, you learned that trend statistics are also an important part of a baseline report and that short-term statistics provide a "snapshot" of current network health.

In addition to these network statistics and trends, it is useful to have information on specific network stations. The next chapter discusses station monitoring on the network.

Station Monitoring/ Tracking

27

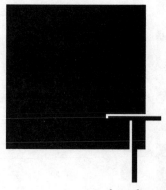

HE LAST CHAPTER reviewed some of the statistical information available for networks. If a problem on a network becomes evident when you are viewing this statistical information, you need to isolate the station or stations causing the problem. It may be necessary to determine which stations are responsible for utilization overload, errors, or excessive requests to the NetWare server. Once a station has been identified as causing a network problem, you can examine the error and take corrective action.

This chapter uses station monitoring to locate the following stations:

- Most active clients and/or servers

- Stations using the most bandwidth

- Stations generating errors on the network

The chapter also looks at name-gathering (collecting workstation and/or server names) features that are available. First, let's take a look at the network characterization and troubleshooting uses of station monitoring.

Determining the Most Active Clients/Servers on the Network

Y FILTERING ON traffic between a server and any station on the network, you can determine which client is communicating with the server most often. This requires the following steps:

1. Record all traffic to the NetWare server.

2. Sort the station names based on the total number of packets transmitted.

In Figure 27.1, you are viewing a network that supports 16 users and a single NetWare server. This is the server whose address you will filter on to determine the most active users.

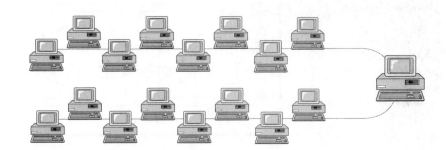

Step 1: Record All Traffic to the NetWare Server

If your NetWare server is a router—that is, it has more than one network interface board installed with attached segments—traffic from a station on one network segment to the server will not be routed to the other network segment. When you are baselining or troubleshooting, the analyzer should be placed at a strategic location to avoid having packets filtered out before being seen by the analyzer.

Filtering is covered in detail in Chapter 29.

To determine which workstations are sending the most requests to the server, you will run the LANalyzer for Windows and filter on any traffic to the server. You can do this by filtering on the Ethernet source address. The Source Address field should contain the physical address of the server's network interface card. You could also filter on the server's internal IPX address (in the Destination Network Address field of the IPX headers).

Figure 27.2 depicts the LANalyzer for Windows Capture Filter dialog box, which you can use to capture all traffic to the server. You use the top portion of the dialog box to create a filter between stations.

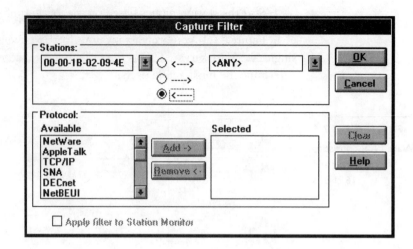

At the bottom of this dialog box is the option Apply Filter to Station Monitor. If this box is checked, only stations that are communicating with the server will show up on the LANalyzer for Windows Station Monitor screen, shown in Figure 27.3. Check this box to ensure that you are viewing only clients that are communicating with the server you specified. While the application runs, the Station Monitor screen is displayed.

Across the top of the Station Monitor screen is a count of the number of stations the LANalyzer for Windows has "seen" on the network. Stations are added to the Station Monitor screen each time their node address is contained in either the Source or Destination Address field of a properly formed frame that fits your filter criteria. If a new station enters the network and transmits an improperly formed frame on the network, it will not be added to the Station Monitor screen. This ensures that malformed or corrupt packets on the wire do not cause erroneous station numbers to be added to the Station Monitor table.

All stations listed in the Station Monitor screen are communicating with the server, based on the filter you defined earlier. In the next step, you will determine which station is communicating with the server most often, based on the number of packets sent to the server.

FIGURE 27.3

LANalyzer for Windows
Station Monitor screen

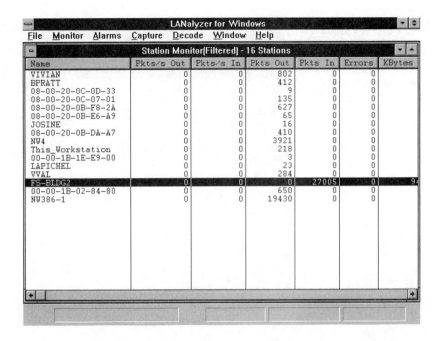

FIGURE 27.3

LANalyzer for Windows
Station Monitor screen

Step 2: Sort the Station Names Based on the Total Number of Packets Transmitted

You can sort any column of the LANalyzer for Windows Station Monitor screen. Since you know that all stations listed are communicating with the server, the next step is to determine who is sending the most requests to the server. By sorting on the Packets Out column, you can determine the most active client, as shown in Figure 27.4.

Figure 27.5 shows the graphed results of the test. Users are plotted based on the total number of packets sent to the server during a 20-minute sampling. The graph has plotted only the top ten workstations communicating with FS-BLDG2.

Based on the results of sorting the Station Monitor screen, you can see that Vivian is communicating with the server most often. If the server indicates it is overloaded by transmitting a Request Being Processed packet, you can use this method of sorting the station monitor table to determine which workstation is

FIGURE 27.4

Sorting the Packets Out column leaves the most active client at the top of the list.

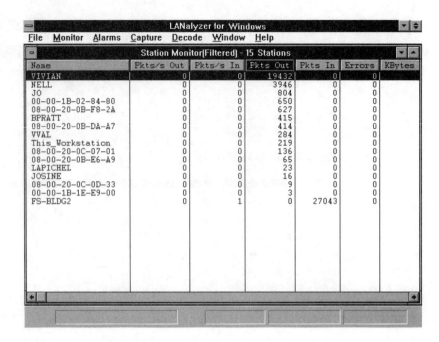

FIGURE 27.4

Sorting the Packets Out column leaves the most active client at the top of the list.

making the most requests of the server. If the server indicates an overload condition, you may decide to move Vivian's applications to a less-burdened server on the network.

Using the Station Monitor screen, you have identified the client making the most requests of a particular server. Next, you will determine which client is using most of the bandwidth.

Determining the Stations Using the Most Bandwidth

N A HEAVILY loaded network cabling system, you can determine which user is using up the most bandwidth on the network and, if possible, transfer that user to another network

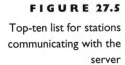

FIGURE 27.5

Top-ten list for stations communicating with the server

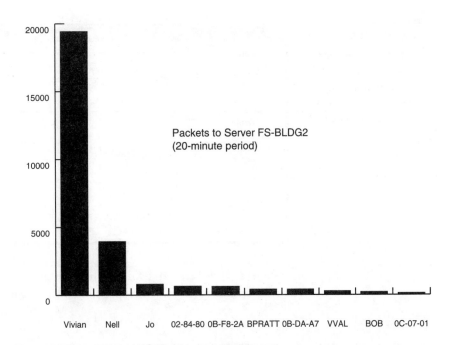

that is relatively idle and able to support such use. The following steps are required to determine the client using most of the bandwidth:

1. Remove any station filters.

2. Sort the Station Monitor screen by kilobytes out.

Step 1: Remove Any Station Filters

Since you want to determine which user on the entire network is using up most of the bandwidth, you do not want any station filters, such as FS1 to FRED, defined. To set up the LANalyzer for Windows to perform the utilization test, the station option <ANY> has been selected for the Source and Destination fields, as shown in Figure 27.6.

Step 2: Sort the Station Monitor by Kilobytes Out

Because bandwidth in use is based on the number of kilobytes transmitted from each station, sorting on the Kilobytes Out column provides you with a

FIGURE 27.6

To find the station using
the most bandwidth
on the network, accept
traffic from any station
to any station.

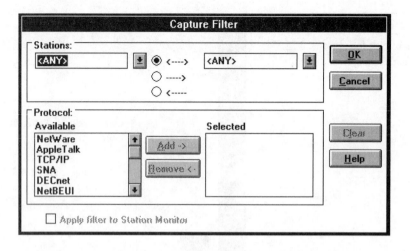

list of clients and their bandwidth utilization. For example, in Figure 27.7, you can see that NW386-1 is responsible for using most of the bandwidth.

FIGURE 27.7

Sorting the Station
Monitor screen by
kilobytes out

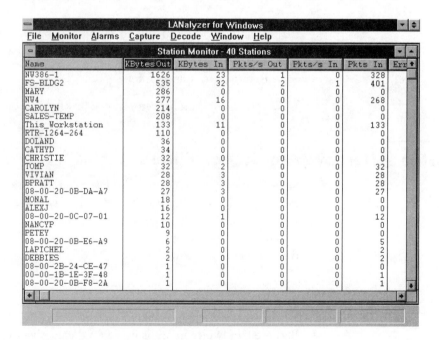

It is expected that servers and routers will use most of the bandwidth on the network since they answer requests from a number of stations. Be certain to scroll past any servers and routers to find the first network user name. In this example, Mary is the first user name. Mary is the user who is using the most bandwidth on the network.

If the cabling system becomes overloaded—if utilization and local collisions are high—you may wish to move Mary to another network that can support the bandwidth requirements.

Locating Stations Generating Errors on the Network

THE STATION MONITOR screen of the LANalyzer for Windows also provides an Errors column. This column "credits" errors to the station that transmitted them.

Refer to Chapters 5 and 11 for a listing of errors and possible causes.

Sorting the station monitor information by the errors count will determine which station is responsible for transmitting most of the errors on the network. By capturing some of the packets from this station, you can determine the type of errors the station is generating, as shown in Figure 27.8.

Because CRC errors from a single workstation indicate a problem with the workstation's network interface card, you should replace the card and monitor the network again for errors. If CRC errors were seen from several stations, it most likely indicates a problem with the cable or segment the stations are on.

You have now determined the most active network stations based on packets addressed to a server, their bandwidth utilization, and stations generating errors. Next, you will examine the name-gathering features you can use for simplified interpretation of network communications.

FIGURE 27.8

Station NW4 is intermittently transmitting CRC errors onto the network.

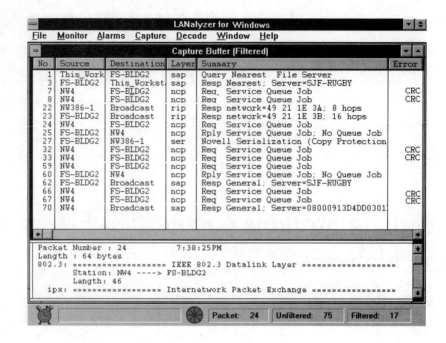

Name Gathering

THROUGHOUT THIS BOOK you have been presented with screen shots of the LANalyzer and LANalyzer for Windows products. In many screens, a name has been substituted in place of the 6-byte node address of a station. Server names have also appeared in many of the screens.

These names are kept in a name file, and when activated, the name file allows for substitute identifications (such as login names or server names) to replace physical node addresses displayed. Since an entire screen of node addresses can be somewhat difficult to interpret, the name-gathering feature simplifies the communication interpretation process.

Figure 27.9 shows a LANalyzer for Windows Station Monitor screen that has names substituted for some of the node addresses on the network.

FIGURE 27.9

Names replace node
addresses if they are
contained in the
name table.

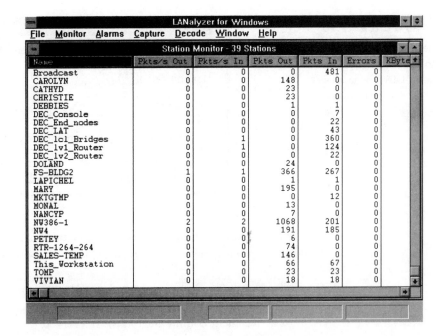

In the NetWare environment, you can perform name gathering by sending a SAP to servers on the network. NetWare 3.x and 4.x servers reply with the name that is in their AUTOEXEC.NCF file. NetWare 2.x servers respond with the name assigned to them during the NETGEN process. Each server that replies is then listed in a name table that provides a translation to the server name. However, if you use this SAP method, NetWare client names cannot be gathered for the name file, since NetWare clients do not advertise as servers.

When Novell released the LANalyzer for Windows, they took the name-gathering feature a step further. Using LANalyzer for Windows' Active Name Gathering feature, you actually attach to a server by a specified user name, such as GUEST. Figure 27.10 shows the LANalyzer's name-gathering dialog box.

Once you are attached to a server, the application obtains the list of users and their node addresses. This is the same information received when you type **USERLIST /A** at the command line when logged in to a NetWare 3.x server or **NLIST /A /B** when logged in to a NetWare 4.x server. Each known server is queried and all user names are automatically entered in to the name table. This

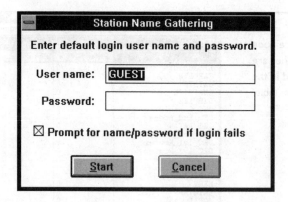

FIGURE 27.10

The application will log in
to servers as the default
user, GUEST, or another
user, if desired.

feature has added significantly to the name table capabilities, since you may
now have user names listed instead of just station physical (node) addresses.

This chapter has covered the benefits of station monitoring and name gathering. You should now be familiar with the steps required to determine the
most active client communicating with a server, the client using the most
bandwidth, and stations that are generating errors.

The next chapter views alarms and alarm thresholds.

Alarms and Alarm Thresholds

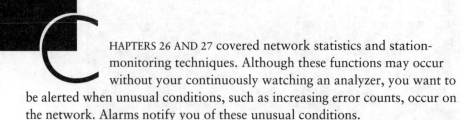

HAPTERS 26 AND 27 covered network statistics and station-monitoring techniques. Although these functions may occur without your continuously watching an analyzer, you want to be alerted when unusual conditions, such as increasing error counts, occur on the network. Alarms notify you of these unusual conditions.

This chapter discusses the two types of alarm threshold definitions: pre-defined and user defined. When you work with user-defined alarm thresholds, you will set thresholds in accordance with the baseline information gathered for a network. You will also select actions to be taken when alarm thresholds are reached.

Alarm thresholds are most commonly set based on statistics gathered, such as utilization, packets per second, or errors. As statistics are calculated, they are constantly checked to see whether they have met the alarm threshold value. In Figure 28.1, you are viewing the general functions of a protocol analyzer.

As shown in Figure 28.1, the first step an analyzer performs upon receipt of a packet is processing the global statistics. *Global statistics* include information about all the packets seen on the network, regardless of any filtering you may have set up.

Filtering is covered later in this chapter.

The second step is applying a pre-filter that defines the type of packet you want to copy into your trace buffer and calculate statistics for. The third step is copying the packets into the buffer. If the buffer is full, you can configure the analyzer to remove the oldest packets to make room for the newest packets (first in, first out). The final step is to apply a post-filter, if one has been defined. The results of these four steps provide two sets of statistics (global and specifically defined) and a buffer filled with packets defined by a pre-filter.

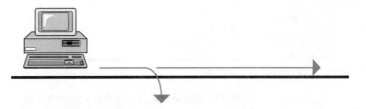

FIGURE 28.1

Basic functions of a
protocol analyzer

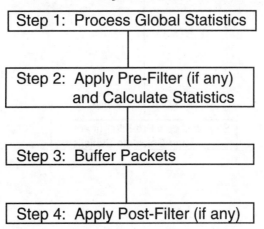

Protocol Analyzer Basic Functions

Step 1: Process Global Statistics

Step 2: Apply Pre-Filter (if any)
and Calculate Statistics

Step 3: Buffer Packets

Step 4: Apply Post-Filter (if any)

Global statistics that are calculated include the following:

- Utilization percentage

- Kilobytes per second

- Errors per second

- Packets per second

- Packet-size distribution

As shown in Figure 28.2, a 64-byte NetWare broadcast packet has been
copied into the analyzer's buffer. Before being copied, however, it was calculated into the global statistics and met the pre-filter criteria. Global statistics
that were affected include utilization, kilobytes per second, packets per second,
and the appropriate packet size distribution counter (64- to 127-byte packets).

FIGURE 28.2

Counters are incremented based on the packet received.

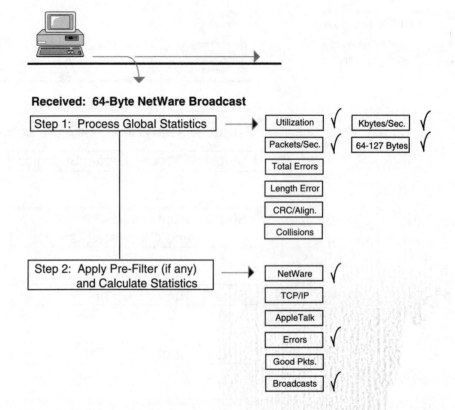

When an error packet is received, the Ethernet chipset reports the error. The LANalyzer, in turn, increments the errors-per-second counter as well as other affected global statistics counters. Global statistics can be tracked for the following errors:

- Local collisions

- Remote collisions

- Length errors

- CRC/Alignment errors

In Figure 28.3, a NetWare packet longer than 1518 bytes has been seen by the analyzer on the local network. The long packet has incremented the associated statistics counters, including errors (general), NetWare packets, and Length errors.

FIGURE 28.3

A long packet will increment several counters, including errors (general), NetWare packets, and Length errors.

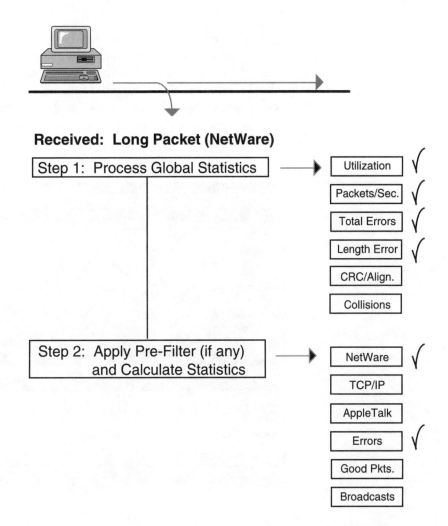

Alarm thresholds can be set on these counter values. If the value of 1 is set as an alarm threshold and a single long packet is received, an alarm is triggered. Alarm thresholds can be either predefined or user defined.

Predefined Alarm Thresholds

*P*REDEFINED ALARM THRESHOLDS are transparently set on an analysis product and generally cannot be changed by the user. For example, the LANalyzer for Windows includes a predefined server alarm threshold. The server alarm threshold is defined to trigger an alarm when a server no longer responds on the network. At the present time, this alarm threshold cannot be set by the user. In Figure 28.4, the server alarm has been triggered.

FIGURE 28.4

The LANalyzer for Windows' server alarm has been triggered.

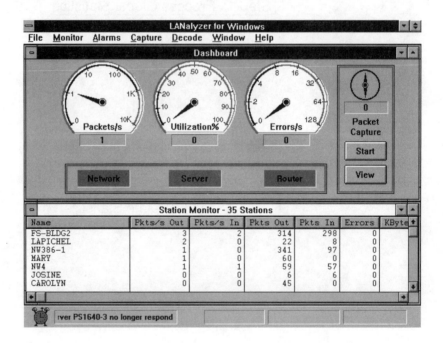

The alarm has caused an alarm clock icon and ticker-tape message to appear in the lower left-hand corner of the screen, an audible beep to sound, and an entry to be placed in the alarm log. The ticker-tape message states that server PS1640-3 no longer responds on the network. The server or an intermediary bridge or repeater may be down.

Figure 28.5 shows the alarm log that maintains a listing of alarms that have been triggered since the LANalyzer for Windows was started. The alarm log indicates that the server has not been responding since 8:58 P.M. You can print the alarm log, if desired.

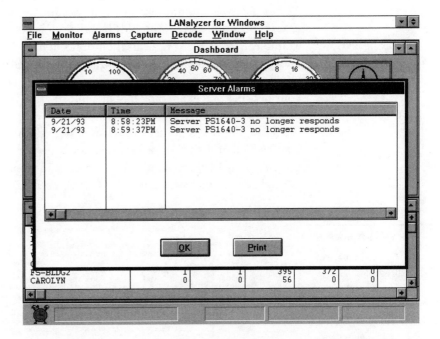

For users who are new to protocol analysis, predefined alarm thresholds ensure that the user is notified of potential problems without having to learn to set the alarm thresholds. For experienced users, however, user-defined alarm thresholds allow more flexibility and customization for alarm triggering.

User-Defined Alarm Thresholds

USER-DEFINED ALARM THRESHOLDS can be set to trigger alarms when an unusual condition occurs on the network. You can determine these thresholds based on normal network operation. For example, if your network utilization peaks at around 23%, you may wish to set an alarm threshold at 27% utilization. If the utilization reaches 27%, an alarm will be triggered, indicating that an unusual condition is occurring on your network. By examining baseline information for your network, you can determine what thresholds are appropriate.

Alarm thresholds are set in various ways, depending on the analysis tool. Figures 28.6 and 28.7 show two separate ways for defining alarm thresholds. Once again, you must examine your baseline information to determine what is normal activity on your network before you set alarms.

FIGURE 28.6

You can set alarm thresholds on each receive channel of the LANalyzer based on utilization or packets per second.

```
09/21/95            LANalyzer(R) Network Analyzer by NCC          20 49
Press + or - to toggle                                      Edit Alarms
╔═══════════════════ c:\xln\lanz\802.5\default ═══════════════════╗
║Channel    Utilization Threshold   Action   Packet Rate Threshold   Action ◄
║Global            30 %             Alarm         1000 Pkts/s         Alarm ║
║GoodPkts      Disabled %           Alarm     Disabled Pkts/s         Alarm ║
║Broadcas           1 %             Alarm           50 Pkts/s         Alarm ║
║Promiscu      Disabled %           Alarm     Disabled Pkts/s         Alarm ║
║MACpkts       Disabled %           Alarm     Disabled Pkts/s         Alarm ║
║ErrMon             1 %             Alarm            2 Pkts/s         Alarm ║
║NetBeui       Disabled %           Alarm     Disabled Pkts/s         Alarm ║
║NetWare       Disabled %           Alarm     Disabled Pkts/s         Alarm ║
║SNA           Disabled %           Alarm     Disabled Pkts/s         Alarm ║
║                                                                          ║
║When a new station is detected      take no action                        ║
║                                                                          ║
║Log alarms into file                                                      ║
║                                                                          ║
║Execute the following file when an alarm occurs and the action is Execute:║
║                                                                          ║
║                                                                          ║
║Ring bell when alarm is generated   Yes                                   ║
╚══════════════════════════════════════════════════════════════════════════╝
F1     F2     F3    F4     F5    F6    F7      F8    F9      F10
Help   Revert Save  Options Mode       Receive Xmit  Alarms  Back
```

There are also various ways of indicating that an alarm threshold has been set. These indicators depend on the analysis tool you are using. In Figures 28.8 and 28.9, you see the LANalyzer and LANalyzer for Windows screens indicating that alarm thresholds have been set.

FIGURE 28.7

You can set six user-defined alarm thresholds on the LANalyzer for Windows.

Thresholds

Alarm Name	Alarm Threshold	
Packets/s	1000	OK
Utilization%	30	Cancel
Broadcasts/s	100	Defaults
Fragments/s	5	Advanced...
CRC Errors/s	5	Help
Server Overloads/min	15	

FIGURE 28.8

The LANalyzer displays a musical note at the value of the alarm threshold.

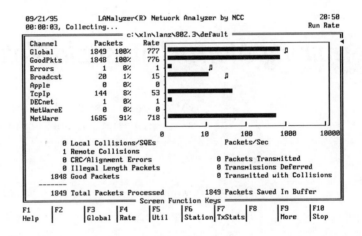

```
09/21/95        LANalyzer(R) Network Analyzer by NCC              20:50
00:00:03, Collecting...                                        Run Rate
                        c:\xln\lanz\802.3\default
Channel      Packets     Rate
Global       1849  100%   777
GoodPkts     1848  100%   776
Errors          1    0%     1
Broadcst       20    1%    15
Apple           0    0%     0
TcpIp         144    8%    53
DECnet          1    0%     1
NetWareE        0    0%     0
NetWare      1685   91%   718
                         0      10     100    1000   10000
                                       Packets/Sec
         0 Local Collisions/SQEs
         1 Remote Collisions
         0 CRC/Alignment Errors          0 Packets Transmitted
         0 Illegal Length Packets        0 Transmissions Deferred
      1848 Good Packets                  0 Transmitted with Collisions
   -------
      1849 Total Packets Processed    1849 Packets Saved In Buffer
                         Screen Function Keys
F1     |F2   |F3     |F4   |F5   |F6     |F7     |F8   |F9   |F10
Help   |     |Global |Rate |Util |Station|TxStats|     |More |Stop
```

The LANalyzer also allows thresholds to be set on testing applications that are included with the product or that you have created. For example, perhaps you have recently given users the option of using the Burst Mode shell at their workstations. You created an application that filters on Burst Mode reads and writes (NCP type 7777). The results of the application will allow you to determine the average bandwidth used by Burst Mode reads and writes. If the current bandwidth used by Burst Mode transactions is 10%, you may wish to set an alarm threshold at 15%. This will alert you to increased bandwidth use by Burst Mode transactions.

FIGURE 28.9

The LANalyzer for
Windows displays alarm
threshold limits in red
(shown here with arrows)
on the dashboard gauges.

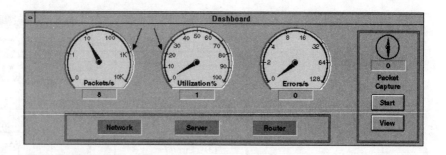

The flexibility inherent in the LANalyzer product allows alarm thresholds to be set on any defined receive channel, including the Global channel. Now, let's look at how to define typical alarm threshold values.

Determining Alarm Threshold Values

AS MENTIONED EARLIER, alarm thresholds are set in accordance with baseline information. For example, perhaps the following peaks were observed when you documented your baseline information:

Peak utilization	22%
Peak packets per second	500
Peak errors per second	2

Based on these peak values, you may wish to set the following alarm thresholds:

Utilization alarm threshold	25%
Packets-per-second alarm threshold	600
Errors-per-second alarm threshold	3

When any of these thresholds is reached, an alarm is triggered. Since users may run tests unattended, a variety of alarm actions can be defined, including those generating alarm logs or audible beeps.

Alarm Actions

OU CAN CUSTOMIZE the alert mechanism so one or more of the following actions occur when an alarm is triggered:

- The alarm is logged to a file.

- A visual alarm notification appears.

- An audible alarm signal occurs.

- An executable file is launched.

The following sections examine each of these methods to help you determine which is most appropriate for various situations.

Alarm Log File

An *alarm log file* maintains a listing of alarms that have been triggered, as well as the date and time they were triggered. In Figure 28.10, you are viewing the alarm log file created by the LANalyzer.

As you can see from the alarm log, the network has exceeded several alarm thresholds: global utilization, broadcast packet rate, and errors packet rate. The alarm log provides the value of the alarm threshold, as well as the value that triggered the alarm. Based on the information contained in the log, you can see that the errors packet alarm threshold is set extremely low: 1 error packet per second. If this condition is not causing communications difficulties or sluggishness, you may wish to raise the alarm threshold to a more reasonable number, such as 5.

This alarm file is an ASCII text file that can be imported into a word processing program for formatting and printing. Some analyzers, such as the

FIGURE 28.10

The alarm log file lists the alarm triggered, as well as the date and time the entry was made.

```
Alarm: 09/21/93 07:58:59 Broadcst packet rate of 24 pkts/s exceeded threshold of 10
Alarm: 09/21/93 08:52:03 Broadcst packet rate of 13 pkts/s exceeded threshold of 10
Alarm: 09/21/93 08:52:57 Global packet rate of 725 pkts/s exceeded threshold of 500
Alarm: 09/21/93 08:52:59 Broadcst packet rate of 23 pkts/s exceeded threshold of 10
Alarm: 09/21/93 09:13:02 Global packet rate of 566 pkts/s exceeded threshold of 500
Alarm: 09/21/93 03:53:07 Broadcst packet rate of 15 pkts/s exceeded threshold of 10
Alarm: 09/21/93 03:53:16 Errors packet rate of 45 pkts/s exceeded threshold of 1
Alarm: 09/21/93 05:00:17 Global utilization of 47% exceeded threshold of 20%
Alarm: 09/21/93 05:03:19 Broadcst packet rate of 11 pkts/s exceeded threshold of 10
Alarm: 09/21/93 05:53:26 Errors packet rate of 3 pkts/s exceeded threshold of 1
Alarm: 09/21/93 05:53:30 Errors packet rate of 2 pkts/s exceeded threshold of 1
Alarm: 09/22/93 07:53:33 Broadcst packet rate of 42 pkts/s exceeded threshold of 10
Alarm: 09/22/93 07:53:36 Broadcst packet rate of 25 pkts/s exceeded threshold of 10
Alarm: 09/22/93 07:53:38 Errors packet rate of 2 pkts/s exceeded threshold of 1
Alarm: 09/22/93 07:53:40 Errors packet rate of 2 pkts/s exceeded threshold of 1
Alarm: 09/22/93 07:53:45 Errors packet rate of 3 pkts/s exceeded threshold of 1
```

LANalyzer for Windows, allow you to view an alarm log file from within the application, as shown in Figure 28.11.

FIGURE 28.11

The LANalyzer for Windows allows you to view the alarm log file from within the application.

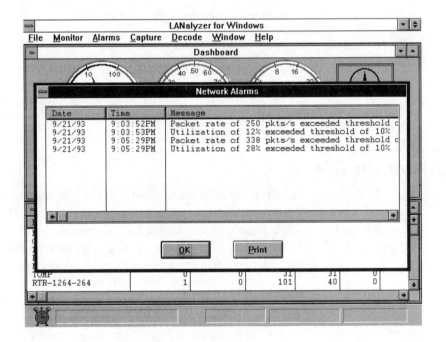

As shown in Figure 28.11, alarms have been logged for the packet rate and utilization counters. Each has exceeded the alarm threshold. You can select the Print option in order to maintain a hard-copy version of the log file.

Visual Alarm Notification

If you leave the analyzer running unattended, you can set up alarm notification to be visual so when you return to the system, you can see that an alarm has been triggered.

For example, the LANalyzer displays a banner across the top of the screen that defines the alarm triggered. As shown earlier in Figure 28.4, the LANalyzer for Windows also displays an alarm clock and a ticker-tape message that defines the alarm.

Audible Alarm Signal

Analyzers often provide an option for audible alarms (beeps) to alert the user when an alarm has been triggered. In a Windows-based product, such as the LANalyzer for Windows, that is running in the background, an alarm will cause an audible beep, even if LANalyzer for Windows is not the active screen. In Figure 28.12, alarms have been configured to generate an audible alarm.

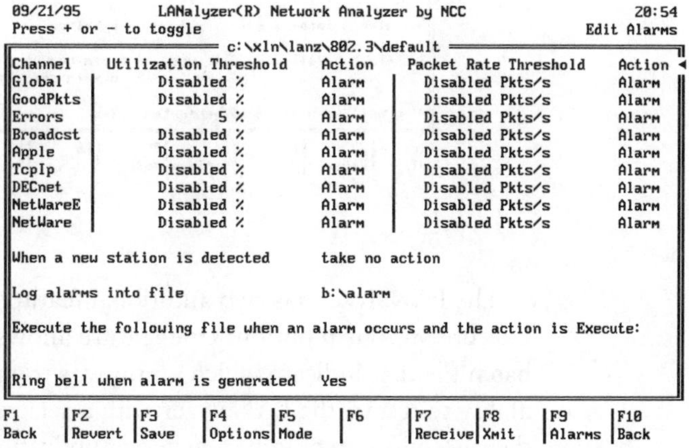

FIGURE 28.12

You can specify audible alarms in the Edit Alarms screen of the LANalyzer.

```
09/21/95        LANalyzer(R) Network Analyzer by NCC                 20:54
Press + or - to toggle                                        Edit Alarms
═══════════════════ c:\xln\lanz\802.3\default ═══════════════════
Channel    Utilization Threshold   Action    Packet Rate Threshold    Action ◄
Global         Disabled %          Alarm       Disabled Pkts/s        Alarm
GoodPkts       Disabled %          Alarm       Disabled Pkts/s        Alarm
Errors              5 %            Alarm       Disabled Pkts/s        Alarm
Broadcst       Disabled %          Alarm       Disabled Pkts/s        Alarm
Apple          Disabled %          Alarm       Disabled Pkts/s        Alarm
TcpIp          Disabled %          Alarm       Disabled Pkts/s        Alarm
DECnet         Disabled %          Alarm       Disabled Pkts/s        Alarm
NetWareE       Disabled %          Alarm       Disabled Pkts/s        Alarm
NetWare        Disabled %          Alarm       Disabled Pkts/s        Alarm

When a new station is detected       take no action

Log alarms into file                 b:\alarm

Execute the following file when an alarm occurs and the action is Execute:


Ring bell when alarm is generated    Yes

F1      F2      F3      F4      F5    F6    F7      F8      F9      F10
Back    Revert  Save    Options Mode        Receive Xmit    Alarms  Back
```

Executable Files

Many analyzers allow you to specify an executable file to be launched when an alarm is triggered. This capability adds to the effectiveness of the alarm notification system. For example, if the errors-per-second threshold is reached, perhaps you want the analyzer to launch an application that sends a message to the supervisor stating "Utilization high!"

Using the LANalyzer, you must specify the alarm that will trigger the executable and the file name. In Figure 28.13, the batch file SEND.BAT will be launched when errors reach 5%. The LANalyzer can execute .COM, .EXE, and .BAT files.

FIGURE 28.13

The file SEND.BAT will execute when the errors reach 5% on the network.

```
09/21/95        LANalyzer(R) Network Analyzer by NCC              20:54
Press + or - to toggle                                      Edit Alarms
═══════════════════ c:\xln\lanz\802.3\default ═══════════════════
Channel    Utilization Threshold   Action   Packet Rate Threshold   Action ◄
Global         Disabled %          Alarm      Disabled Pkts/s       Alarm
GoodPkts       Disabled %          Alarm      Disabled Pkts/s       Alarm
Errors            5 %              Execute    Disabled Pkts/s       Alarm
Broadcst       Disabled %          Alarm      Disabled Pkts/s       Alarm
Apple          Disabled %          Alarm      Disabled Pkts/s       Alarm
TcpIp          Disabled %          Alarm      Disabled Pkts/s       Alarm
DECnet         Disabled %          Alarm      Disabled Pkts/s       Alarm
NetWareE       Disabled %          Alarm      Disabled Pkts/s       Alarm
NetWare        Disabled %          Alarm      Disabled Pkts/s       Alarm

When a new station is detected      take no action

Log alarms into file                b:\alarm

Execute the following file when an alarm occurs and the action is Execute:
                                    c:\xln\send.bat

Ring bell when alarm is generated   Yes

F1     F2      F3     F4     F5     F6     F7      F8     F9     F10
Help   Revert  Save   Options Mode         Receive Xmit   Alarms Back
```

The LANalyzer has two additional features that give great flexibility to the Execute on Alarm option. One feature allows parameters to be passed to the batch file that indicate which alarm was triggered. The other feature is the ability to restart the LANalyzer with a selected application. An example of their usefulness would be a general application such as the LANalyzer default application, which, when an alarm is set on a channel, such as the TCP/IP channel, would execute a batch file. This batch file could have the parameter indicate that the TCP/IP channel upon which the alarm was triggered restarts the LANalyzer running a TCP/IP-specific application.

This chapter has examined the types of alarm definitions available: predefined and user defined. You have also looked at some of the options for alarm notification, such as alarm logs, audible alarms, visual alarms, and executable files.

The next chapter examines the packet capture and filtering features available with many analyzers.

Packet Capture

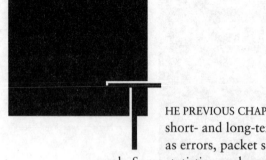

HE PREVIOUS CHAPTERS discussed the fact that you can create short- and long-term statistics to document network events such as errors, packet size distribution, and protocol types on the network. Some statistics, such as global utilization and errors, are calculated based on all packets seen. You can calculate other statistics, such as NetWare SAP traffic, RIP broadcasts, and Ethernet_802.2 frames, by applying a filter to the receive channels.

This chapter focuses on packet-capturing capabilities of analyzers and defines the filtering options available: pre-filtering (capture filtering) and post-filtering (display filtering). The chapter also discusses the advantages and simplicity of point-and-click filtering. Finally, the chapter presents the purpose and advantages of enhanced filtering (filtering with Boolean operands).

Let's begin with an overview of packet-capturing abilities. Figure 29.1 depicts the general functions of a protocol analyzer.

FIGURE 29.1

General functions of a protocol analyzer that allows both pre- and post-filtering

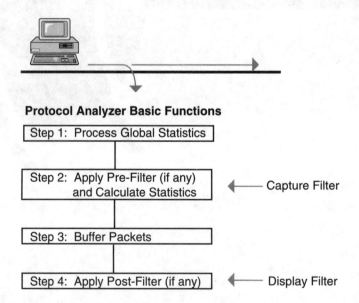

When a packet is seen on the network, the appropriate global statistics are calculated. In order to narrow the scope of packets that are being captured and saved in the buffer, however, a filter can be applied: the *pre-filter*. Packets that meet the criteria defined in the pre-filter will be buffered either on the card or in system memory (product dependent). You can also capture the packets to disk if desired.

If no pre-filter is defined and an analyzer is configured to capture all packets, the resulting packet buffer may be quite large and contain packets that do not relate to the information being sought. In this case, it may be difficult to view the important or problem packets because they are obscured by the large amount of extraneous traffic. In this situation, if the analyzer has been run without the isolating pre-filters applied, you can filter the packets that are displayed from the buffer using a *post-filter*.

As shown in Figure 29.2, packets must meet the pre-filter criteria before being buffered. Packets must then meet the post-filtering criteria in order to be displayed.

FIGURE 29.2

Packets must meet both pre- and post-filtering definitions before being displayed.

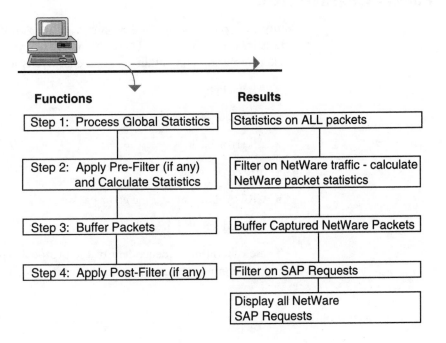

Functions

Step 1: Process Global Statistics

Step 2: Apply Pre-Filter (if any) and Calculate Statistics

Step 3: Buffer Packets

Step 4: Apply Post-Filter (if any)

Results

Statistics on ALL packets

Filter on NetWare traffic - calculate NetWare packet statistics

Buffer Captured NetWare Packets

Filter on SAP Requests

Display all NetWare SAP Requests

Figure 29.2 shows an application that has been configured with a pre-filter for NetWare packets. Although all packets will be calculated into the global statistics, only NetWare packets will be saved in the trace buffer. A post-filter has then been applied to the packets in the trace buffer. The post-filter allows only NetWare SAP packets to be displayed.

Pre-Filtering Criteria

TWO TYPES OF pre-filtering criteria can be defined: packet characteristics and field values.

Packet Characteristics

Many analyzers, such as the LANalyzer, allow you to define the packet characteristics for pre-filtering. These characteristics are based on the overall packet formation and validity. Packet characteristics include

- All packets

- All good packets

- All error packets

- Size error packets

- CRC/Alignment or Line error packets

- Defined length packets

These criteria are independent of the protocol types being captured. For example, on an Ethernet network, a packet that fits the CRC/alignment definition could be a TCP/IP or NetWare packet. Table 29.1 lists the packet characteristics and definitions.

TABLE 29.1

Sample Ethernet Packet Characteristics and Definitions

PACKET CHARACTERISTIC	DEFINITION
All packets	All good and error packets
All good packets	All packets without error
Size error packets	Packets with a valid CRC that are less than 64 bytes or greater than 1518 bytes
CRC/alignment packets	Packets with invalid CRC values or packets that do not end on an 8-bit boundary (valid length)
Defined length packets	Packets that meet the defined length criteria

You configure the defined packet length criteria by selecting a minimum and maximum packet size to be captured and calculated in the statistics. You can use the packet length criteria in conjunction with other criteria.

For example, you may wish to capture all Ethernet short packets (packets less than 64 bytes with a valid CRC value). Since there is no packet characteristic called "short packets," you can use the defined length packet criteria in conjunction with the Size error packets. In Figure 29.3, a channel, SHORT, has been defined that filters only on Ethernet Size error packets that are less than 64 bytes in length.

The value Min is used to indicate 64 bytes. The value Max is used to indicate 1518 bytes. The size range specified in the application shown is 0 to 64, inclusive, yet 64 is a valid length. You want to capture only packets shorter than 64 bytes. To define this, the Packets Allowed field has been toggled to Size-Errors. This ensures that 64-byte packets will not be captured in the buffer since they are legal-sized frames. Only short packets will be saved in the trace buffer.

FIGURE 29.3

The channel SHORT captures only packets less than 64 bytes in length.

```
09/22/95              LANalyzer(R) Network Analyzer by NCC              01 23
Press + or - to toggle, or Enter decimal number(s)              Edit Receive
╔══════════════════ c:\xln\lanz\802.3\temp\temp ═══════════════════╗
║↓RECEIVE                                              Simple Filter Mode ◄
║Channel           Size Range                   Collect  Start  Stop
║Name     Active  From   To    Packets Allowed   Stats.  Count  Count
║SHORT     Yes     0    Min    Size-Errors        Yes     Off    Off
║Rx2       No     Min   Max    Good Packets       Yes     Off    Off
║Rx3       No     Min   Max    Good Packets       Yes     Off    Off
║Rx4       No     Min   Max    Good Packets       Yes     Off    Off
║Rx5       No     Min   Max    Good Packets       Yes     Off    Off
║Rx6       No     Min   Max    Good Packets       Yes     Off    Off
║Rx7       No     Min   Max    Good Packets       Yes     Off    Off
║Rx8       No     Min   Max    Good Packets       Yes     Off    Off
║
║TRIGGERS
║Start collecting at once
║Fire stop trigger never
║Once stop trigger has fired, collect an additional         0  packets.
║When the trace buffer is full, overwrite old packets.
║
║DATA COLLECTION
╚══════════════════════════════════════════════════════════════════╝
F1     |F2      |F3   |F4      |F5   |F6     |F7      |F8    |F9     |F10
Help   |Revert  |Save |Options |Mode |Filter |Receive |Xmit  |Alarms |Back
```

Field Values

In order to capture packets based on their header type, network-layer protocol, transport-layer protocol, or upper-layer protocol information, you can indicate specific field values as pre-filtering criteria. Field values are defined based on a solid knowledge of the protocols in use. For example, to capture all RIP broadcasts on a NetWare LAN, you would define the values 0x0453 in the Source Socket field (IPX header) and FF-FF-FF-FF-FF-FF in the Destination Address field (Ethernet header), as shown in Figure 29.4.

FIGURE 29.4

The LANalyzer pre-filtering criteria are defined to capture all RIP broadcasts.

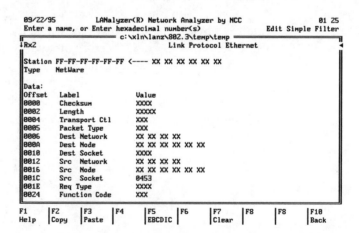

```
09/22/95              LANalyzer(R) Network Analyzer by NCC              01 25
Enter a name, or Enter hexadecimal number(s)         Edit Simple Filter
╔══════════════════ c:\xln\lanz\802.3\temp\temp ═══════════════════╗
║↓Rx2                              Link Protocol Ethernet             ◄
║
║Station FF-FF-FF-FF-FF-FF <---- XX XX XX XX XX XX
║Type    NetWare
║
║Data:
║Offset   Label            Value
║0000     Checksum         XXXX
║0002     Length           XXXXX
║0004     Transport Ctl    XXX
║0005     Packet Type      XXX
║0006     Dest Network     XX XX XX XX
║000A     Dest Node        XX XX XX XX XX XX
║0010     Dest Socket      XXXX
║0012     Src  Network     XX XX XX XX
║0016     Src  Node        XX XX XX XX XX XX
║001C     Src  Socket      0453
║001E     Req Type         XXXX
║0024     Function Code    XXX
╚══════════════════════════════════════════════════════════════════╝
F1     |F2    |F3    |F4   |F5      |F6   |F7     |F8    |F8    |F10
Help   |Copy  |Paste |     |EBCDIC  |     |Clear  |      |      |Back
```

On the LANalyzer Capture Filter screen, the value XX is a wildcard and denotes that any value will be accepted in this byte position.

The following list describes several field values that may be useful for pre-filtering on a NetWare LAN:

NetWare packets using Ethernet_802.3 frame types: Filter on the value FFFF in the Checksum field of the IPX header. You can also use a binary filter. (Binary filtering is discussed later in this chapter.)

NetWare packets using Ethernet_802.2 frame types: Filter on the value 0xE0 in both the DSAP and SSAP fields.

Source Routed Frames: Within the Token Ring header, filter on the bit value 1 in the Ring Information Indicator field.

NetWare packets using Ethernet_SNAP frame types: Within the SNAP header, filter on the value 0xAA in the DSAP and SSAP fields and the value 0x8137 in the Ethernet Type field.

NetWare packets using Ethernet_II frame types: Filter on the value 0x8137 in the Type field of the Ethernet header.

NetWare SAP broadcasts: Filter on the value 0x0452 in the Source Socket field (IPX header) and FF-FF-FF-FF-FF-FF in the Destination Address field (Ethernet header).

NetWare Get Nearest Server SAP requests: Filter on the value 0x0452 in the Source Socket field (IPX header), 0x0003 in the SAP Type field, and 0x0004 in the Server Type field.

Burst Mode reads/writes: Filter on the value 0x7777 in the NCP Request Type field.

You can define field values to capture a variety of NCP requests and replies on the network, as well. To filter on a specific NCP request or reply, see Table 15.1 in Chapter 15 for a listing of NCP function and subfunction codes.

Figure 29.5 shows a filter set up on NCP Erase File requests (function code 68) from the client 0x00-00-1B-09-32-8E that is using the Ethernet_802.2 frame format. The LANalyzer has substituted the word "novell" in place of

0x00-00-1B to indicate that this is the vendor ID assigned to Novell's network interface cards (NE1000, NE2000, and so on).

```
09/22/95         LANalyzer(R) Network Analyzer by NCC           01:32
   Press + or - to toggle, or Enter hexadecimal number(s)       Edit
Simple Filter
╔══════════════════════ c:\xln\lanz\802.3\temp\temp═══════════════════════╗
‡Station XX XX XX XX XX XX <---- novell09328E                              ◄
║Length  XXXXX
║DSAP NetWare                    SSAP NetWare              Control XX
║Data:
║Offset    Label              Value
║0000      Checksum           XXXX
║0002      Length             XXXXX
║0004      Transport Ctl      XXX
║0005      Packet Type        XXX
║0006      Dest Network       XX XX XX XX
║000A      Dest Node          XX XX XX XX XX XX
║0010      Dest Socket        0451
║0012      Src  Network       XX XX XX XX
║0016      Src  Node          XX XX XX XX XX XX
║001C      Src  Socket        XXXX
║001E      Req Type           XXXX
║0024      Function Code      68
║0025      Function Len       XXXXX

F1      F2      F3      F4      F5      F6      F7      F8      F9      F10
Help    Copy    Paste           EBCDIC          Clear                   Back
```

Novell has transferred ownership of network interface card manufacturing to a third-party company; however, the new manufacturer is still using the vendor ID number originally assigned to Novell by Xerox.

Some analyzers also allow binary filtering criteria to be defined. *Binary filtering* permits filtering based on bit values rather than byte values. For example, if you wish to capture all packets that have crossed between four and seven routers to reach the local network, you need to place a binary filter value in the Hop Count field of the IPX header. This bit value filter would be 00000000 000001XX (where the value of X can be either 0 or 1). This filter requires 13 0's to precede a 1 in the Hop Count field. The last two bits can contain either 0 or 1. This allows the following values to be accepted by the filter:

Binary Value	Definition
00000000 00000100	Four hops
00000000 00000101	Five hops
00000000 00000110	Six hops
00000000 00000111	Seven hops

Appendix E contains a binary-decimal-hexadecimal conversion chart that you may find helpful when assigning binary filters.

Some analyzers, such as the LANalyzer for Windows, allow field pre-filtering based on preset values, as shown in Figure 29.6. In this figure, a pre-filter on NetWare packets has been set. Packets that do not meet the criteria, such as AppleTalk or TCP/IP, will not be saved in the buffer. These pre-filter options are available and preconfigured, requiring a user to simply click on the desired pre-filtering criteria. This simplified method of pre-filtering may be more desirable for users who are new to protocol analysis.

FIGURE 29.6

The LANalyzer for Windows provides predefined protocol filters.

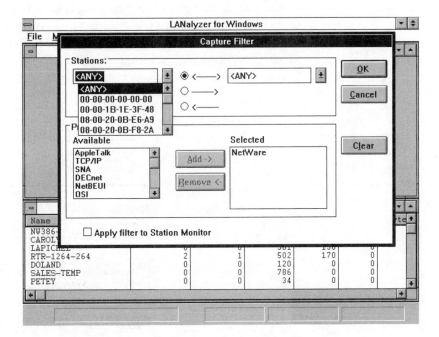

Now that you've learned about pre-filtering options for protocol analysis, let's examine the post-filtering options you can use to isolate packets in the buffer.

Post-Filtering

YOU CAN USE post-filtering (also referred to as display filtering) to apply additional filtering criteria to packets in the buffer. This ensures that packets in the buffer meet a more specific filter criterion before being displayed. For example, perhaps you have captured all NetWare packets that use the Ethernet_802.2 frame type in your buffer. The result is over 200 packets in the buffer. In order to isolate and view only NetWare SAP packets in the buffer, you can apply a NetWare SAP post-filter to the captured packets.

The packets that met the pre-filtering criteria remain in the buffer; post-filters can be changed to show different packets saved in the trace buffer.

Figure 29.7 shows the steps taken to isolate SAP Broadcast packets or Burst Mode Connection requests from a single buffer of packets that met pre-filtering criteria.

FIGURE 29.7

A variety of post-filters can be applied to the trace buffer.

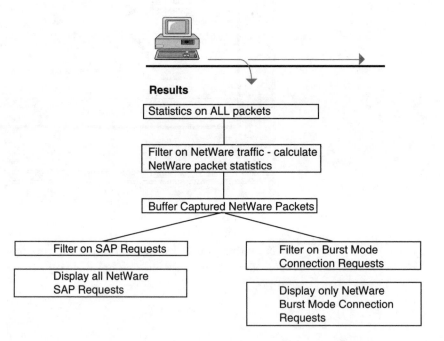

Analyzer products provide several methods for post-filtering. The LANalyzer for Windows contains preconfigured post-filters, as shown in Figure 29.8.

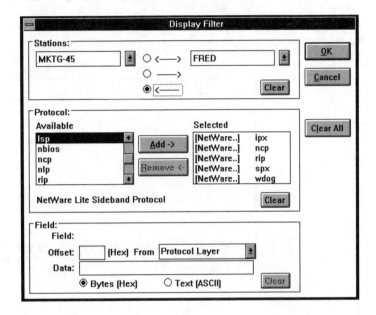

In Figure 29.8, the post-filter option NetWare has been selected; this provides you with a list of various post-filter options you can select, such as NCP, SAP, RIP, SER (Serialization packets), WDOG (Watchdog packets), and so on.

The LANalyzer for Windows also introduced a new post-filtering technique known as *point-and-click filtering*. Point-and-click filtering allows users less familiar with packet structures to use advanced post-filtering techniques.

For example, perhaps a user is viewing a Burst Mode Connection request in the buffer, as shown in Figure 29.9, and would like to filter on similar types of packets.

Using point-and-click filtering, the user need only double-click on "Function Code: 101" to automatically input the appropriate value in the post-filter. Figure 29.10 shows the values that are placed in the post-filter.

You can also use point-and-click filtering to isolate conversations between two stations. If you double-click on a line in the Summary screen that contains a packet being transmitted between the two stations, the station node addresses (or names, if a name table is used) are placed in the post-filter. As

FIGURE 29.9

Point-and-click filtering allows you to select a filter value directly from the trace buffer.

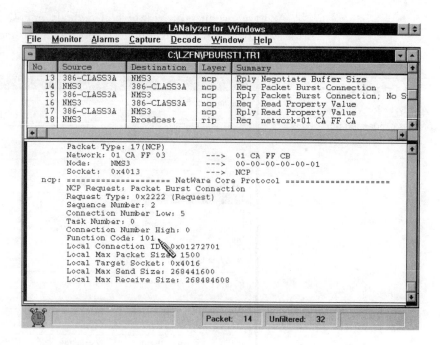

FIGURE 29.10

The value 0x65 is placed at offset 0x0006 from the protocol header to indicate that the user is looking for Burst Mode Connection request and reply packets only.

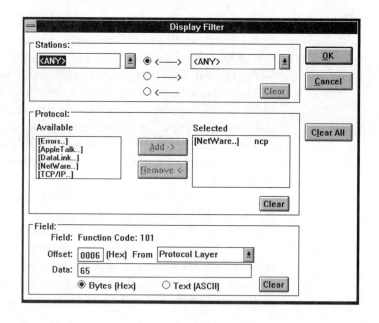

shown in the upper portion of Figure 29.11, you can use either names (contained in the name table), such as Josine and FS-BLDG2, or node addresses. You can also change the direction arrow to indicate the direction of the conversation in which you are interested.

FIGURE 29.11

If you double-click on a packet's station information, the station node addresses are placed in the post-filter.

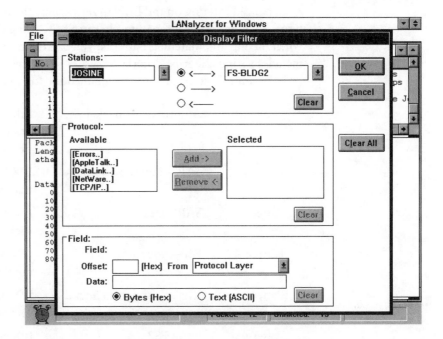

Enhanced Filtering

S SHOWN IN this chapter, you can use pre-filtering and post-filtering to isolate packets captured and displayed in the trace buffer. In addition to the basic techniques already covered, advanced users can utilize additional filtering functionality. The following is an overview of enhanced filtering capabilities.

Enhanced filtering allows the use of Boolean operands, such as AND, OR, AND NOT, and NOT, when defining filters. These operands allow more flexibility and further definition of packets to be captured or displayed. For example, perhaps you would like to capture all SAP packets on a network that supports 20 servers. You do not, however, want to capture SAP traffic from FS1 or FS2. If you did not have the option of using enhanced filtering, you would have to define a filter based on SAP traffic and then simply ignore the trace buffer entries from FS1 and FS2.

Enhanced filtering on the LANalyzer permits the use of up to 16 filter patterns. Each pattern is a separate filter itself. By using the Boolean operands when mixing and matching patterns, you can define a single channel that includes various filtering criteria.

For example, perhaps you have defined the following patterns:

Pattern 1	All broadcast packets	Ethernet header: destination address FF-FF-FF-FF-FF-FF
Pattern 2	SAP—Source Socket	IPX header: source socket number 0x0452
Pattern 3	SAP—Destination Socket	IPX header: destination socket number 0x0452
Pattern 4	RIP—Source Socket	IPX header: source socket number 0x0453
Pattern 5	RIP—Destination Socket	IPX header: destination socket number 0x0453
Pattern 6	From FS2	IPX header: source network address C9-00-00-01, node address 00-00-00-00-00-01
Pattern 7	To FS2	IPX header: destination network address C9-00-00-01, node address 00-00-00-00-00-01

By using Boolean operands, you can define the following channel filters:

- (All broadcasts) AND NOT (SAP broadcasts)

- (All broadcasts) AND NOT (RIP broadcasts)

- (All broadcasts) AND NOT (RIP broadcasts) or (SAP broadcasts)

- (All broadcasts) AND NOT (from FS2)

Figure 29.12 shows a LANalyzer application, FILEVIEW, that uses enhanced filtering. The patterns DIRECTOR, PURGE, ERASE, SRC ADDR, and DEST ADDR are associated using Boolean operands.

FIGURE 29.12

The LANalyzer application FILEVIEW is defined using enhanced filtering.

```
09/22/95              LANalyzer(R) Network Analyzer by NCC              01 34
Press + or - to toggle                                      Edit Enhanced Filter
╔══════════════ c:\xln\lanz\802.3\netware\econfig\fileview ══════════════╗
║director                                                                ◄║
║           ( director                                              )     ║
║  And Not  ( purge                                                 )     ║
║  And Not  ( erase                                                 )     ║
║      And  ( Src Addr or DestAddr                                  )     ║
║                                                                         ║
║                                                                         ║
║                                                                         ║
║                                                                         ║
║ ┌─────────────────────────────────────────────────────────────────┐   ║
║ │ Pattern Names                                                     │   ║
║ │  1: openold      2: opennew      3: create      4: creatnew       │   ║
║ │  5: read         6: write        7: search      8: erase          │   ║
║ │  9: close       10: netware     11: director   12: purge          │   ║
║ │ 13: restore     14: Src Addr    15: DestAddr   16: fltr16         │   ║
║ └─────────────────────────────────────────────────────────────────┘   ║
╚═════════════════════════════════════════════════════════════════════════╝
 F1    |F2       |F3      |F4       |F5      |F6    |F7      |F8   |F9   |F10
 Help  |AddTerm  |DelTerm |AddLine  |DelLine |      |Clear   |     |     |Back
```

The FILEVIEW application uses enhanced filtering to provide a variety of filter options by combining the patterns defined at the bottom of Figure 29.12. Each pattern is a separate filter that contains filter information in the Type, Function, Subfunction, Destination Address, or Source Address field.

Enhanced filtering is only as limited as your imagination and knowledge of the protocols. As you become more familiar with the protocols and communications, you will find that enhanced filtering permits greater flexibility in isolating specific packets on the network.

This chapter has presented two methods for isolating specific packets in a buffer: pre-filtering and post-filtering. By using pre-filtering, you can set the initial definition for packet capturing based on packet characteristics or field values. Post-filtering allows you to further define the packets to be viewed from the buffer by using techniques such as field value definition and point-and-click filtering. Enhanced filtering allows users to capture very specific information.

The next chapter focuses on packet transmission techniques.

Packet Transmission

ALTHOUGH MOST ANALYSIS techniques are based on packet receipt as defined in the previous chapter, many network tests include packet transmission to test a network cabling system or component and gather or verify network information.

This chapter examines the three primary reasons for using packet transmit tests and provides examples of manual and automatic packet transmit tests. The chapter also discusses transmit options such as building packets from scratch or copying a captured packet onto a transmit channel.

The chapter begins with an overview of the three primary uses of packet transmit tests:

- Load testing

- Component testing

- Event re-creation

Load Testing

TWO TYPES OF load tests have been defined in this book: intelligent load tests and dumb load tests. On a NetWare LAN, you can use a transmit test to determine how high bandwidth utilization can become before users complain of performance degradation. For example, in Figure 30.1, the LANalyzer GENLOAD application has been configured to generate a 9% load on the Ethernet network to a fictitious node address (0x00-00-00-00-00-00).

For more examples of load testing, see Chapter 3.

FIGURE 30.1

You can use the GENLOAD application to transmit a dumb load.

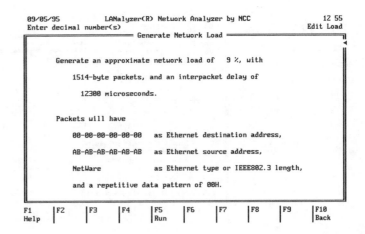

```
09/05/95          LANalyzer(R) Network Analyzer by NCC              12 55
Enter decimal number(s)                                          Edit Load
                    ═══════ Generate Network Load ═══════

      Generate an approximate network load of    9 %, with

        1514-byte packets, and an interpacket delay of

        12300 microseconds.


     Packets will have

          00-00-00-00-00-00      as Ethernet destination address,

          AB-AB-AB-AB-AB-AB      as Ethernet source address,

          NetWare                as Ethernet type or IEEE802.3 length,

          and a repetitive data pattern of 00H.


F1      |F2    |F3    |F4    |F5    |F6    |F7    |F8    |F9    |F10
Help    |      |      |      |Run   |      |      |      |      |Back
```

It has been specified that the packets being transmitted by GENLOAD will be filled with 0x00 in the data portion. Because the GENLOAD application is included with the LANalyzer, creating a dumb load test is quite simple.

Component Testing

YOU CAN USE intelligent loads to test a single component on the network, such as a server, bridge, or router. By addressing packets to a network device and, optionally, requesting a reply (using a diagnostic protocol such as the Diagnostic Responder), you can determine whether the component is able to keep up with requests under varying load conditions.

LANalyzer's SERVERVU application, shown in Figure 30.2, allows you to transmit an intelligent load to a NetWare server. The application is designed to transmit SAP requests, thereby causing the server to reply with SAP replies. If the server cannot reply because of an overload condition, the SERVERVU application can also be configured to report the number of Request Being Processed packets from the server.

In Figure 30.2, the SERVERVU application has been configured to transmit SAP broadcasts on the network. Five packets have been transmitted and 85 replies have been received. To stress-test a server, place the server's network

You can use the
SERVERVU application to
stress-test a NetWare
file server.

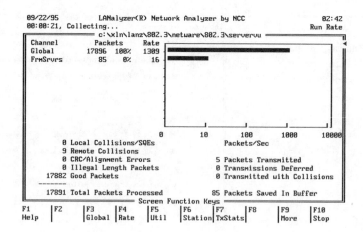

and node address in the IPX header and gradually increase the number of
packets transmitted. The server will begin replying to clients with Request
Being Processed packets when it cannot keep up.

Event Re-Creation

OU CAN ALSO use analyzers to capture and retransmit a single packet
or a sequence of packets. This is useful when an event has occurred
on the network that you must re-create in order to analyze it.

The replay technique was used when an application developer complained that his
SPX-based program was causing the NetWare server to ABEND. Because he sent
his trace to Novell, it was possible to re-create the situation and verify that the application was the cause of the server ABEND. The developer had used an unsupported
value in the SPX connection setup routine; this was evident upon examination of the
SPX header used for his connection establishment. Novell, in turn, created a patch
that would allow the server to accept these types of SPX packets without abending.

For example, perhaps you have noticed a small number of short packets on the network but have been too busy to replace the LAN drivers causing the problem. You are now installing a new bridge on the network that continues to crash intermittently throughout the day. To determine whether the bridge crashes are linked to the short packets, you can use the LANalyzer to capture a short packet, copy it into a transmit channel, change the destination address, and transmit it directly to the bridge. This enables you to test the bridge and determine whether the short packets are causing the crashes.

The LANalyzer also provides a method for replaying an entire trace buffer onto the network. For example, if an SPX-based application is suspected of causing the server to ABEND, you can capture the connection setup packets that are transmitted to the server and analyze the server's response.

When using packet transmits to test a network component or re-create an event, you can use three methods to create the test:

- Create transmit packets from scratch.

- Copy a packet from a receive channel and paste it into the transmit channel.

- Capture a sequence of packets into the buffer and replay the entire sequence.

Create Transmit Packets from Scratch

EXPERIENCED USERS MAY wish to create a transmit packet from scratch. This requires a thorough knowledge of the data link, network, transport, and upper-layer protocol structures. For example, if you wish to create a Diagnostic Request packet to send to the server on the network, you must know the length of the Diagnostic Request packet and each field value within the packet.

Figure 30.3 shows a diagnostic packet that has been created from scratch. The packet is shown in hexadecimal format.

FIGURE 30.3

A Diagnostic Request packet was built from scratch.

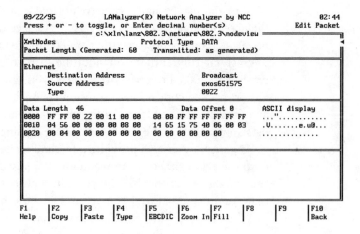

FIGURE 30.3

A Diagnostic Request packet was built from scratch.

To view the fields of the packet in their proper locations, you can apply a template to the packet. You can place templates over data to define field labels, field lengths, and field offsets. In Figure 30.4, a template called DIAG has been created and applied to the packet created earlier. As you can see from the example, this diagnostic packet contains no exclusion addresses. (Remember from Chapter 19 that the exclusion addresses specify which nodes are not required to respond.)

FIGURE 30.4

A template makes packet creation easier.

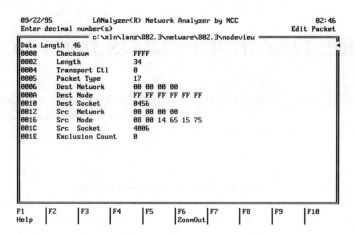

Copy-and-Paste Method

THE COPY-AND-PASTE method provides a quick way to create a packet. After capturing a packet that is similar to the type of packet you wish to send, you can copy the packet into a buffer and paste it into a transmit channel. The fields within the packet, however, may need to be changed for your test.

For example, to create a test that transmits Get Nearest Server packets, first run a LANalyzer application to capture a Get Nearest Server packet and then copy the packet from the trace buffer, as shown in Figure 30.5.

FIGURE 30.5

The Copy option allows you to copy the packet into the LANalyzer clipboard.

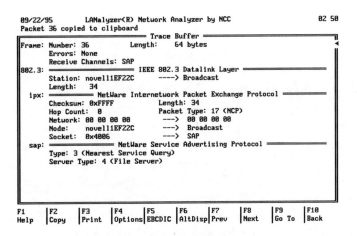

```
09/22/95         LANalyzer(R) Network Analyzer by NCC              02 50
Packet 36 copied to clipboard
                          ============= Trace Buffer ==============
Frame: Number: 36          Length:      64 bytes
       Errors: None
       Receive Channels: SAP
802.3: ============= IEEE 802.3 Datalink Layer ==============
       Station: novell1EF22C     ----> Broadcast
       Length:  34
  ipx: ========= NetWare Internetwork Packet Exchange Protocol ==========
       Checksum: 0xFFFF           Length: 34
       Hop Count:  0              Packet Type: 17 (NCP)
       Network: 00 00 00 00       --->  00 00 00 00
       Node:    novell1EF22C      --->  Broadcast
       Socket:  0x4006            --->  SAP
  sap: ============= NetWare Service Advertising Protocol ==============
       Type: 3 (Nearest Service Query)
       Server Type: 4 (File Server)



F1     |F2    |F3    |F4      |F5    |F6      |F7   |F8    |F9    |F10
Help   |Copy  |Print |Options |EBCDIC|AltDisp |Prev |Next  |Go To |Back
```

The LANalyzer screen displays a notification message in the upper left-hand corner indicating that the packet has been copied. You can then paste the packet into a transmit channel and edit the Packet fields. In Figure 30.6, the packet has been pasted into a transmit channel.

If desired, you can change the destination address to contain the node address of the device to which you want to send the packet.

FIGURE 30.6

After pasting the packet, you can edit the fields for your application.

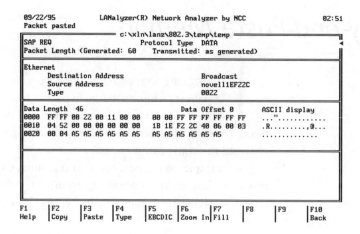

Replay Network Events

THE LANALYZER PROVIDES a utility called REPLAY, shown as the fourth utility in Figure 30.7, that allows you to retransmit the entire contents of a trace buffer or trace file onto the network. The REPLAY utility enables technicians to test various network configurations under identical conditions. The REPLAY utility is one of the many utilities included with the LANalyzer product.

The REPLAY utility does not, however, allow you to change the packets that are being transmitted onto the network. To transmit a variety of packets, you must create or edit an application and define transmit channels.

The LANalyzer has six transmit channels, allowing up to six packet types to be transmitted from a single application, as shown in Figure 30.8.

The LANalyzer also provides a variety of options for packet transmission. The options for Ethernet include

CRC Validity: The packet transmitted from that channel can have either a good or a bad CRC value. Packets with bad CRCs can be transmitted to a single network device to evaluate its handling of error packets.

Intentionally Collide: The packet can be forced to collide when transmitting. (Wait for the line to become busy, and then transmit.) You can force collisions onto the network to determine how devices are filtering (or not filtering) the collisions and their reactions to excessive network collisions.

Perform Backoff Algorithm: Once you detect a collision, you can immediately retransmit the packet, without performing the backoff algorithm and waiting. This simulates an aggressive node that does not wait the allotted time before attempting retransmission after a collision.

FIGURE 30.7

The REPLAY utility is one of the many utilities included with the LANalyzer product.

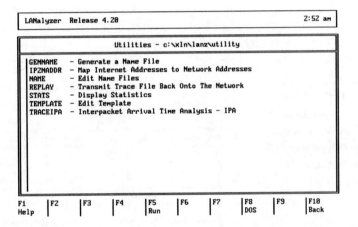

FIGURE 30.8

The LANalyzer Transmit screen supports six transmit channels.

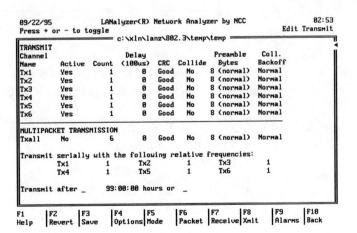

The LANalyzer provides only one option for Token Ring transmission: CRC validity. The Token Ring packet transmitted from that channel can have either a good or a bad CRC value. Packets with bad CRCs can be transmitted to a single network device to evaluate its handling of error packets.

The LANalyzer also allows you to determine the number of packets that will be transmitted from each channel. If desired, you can set the transmit number to INF (infinity). This indicates that the application will transmit packets continuously, until manually stopped.

Multipacket transmission is another feature of the LANalyzer. This option transmits the packets defined on selected channels in serial or random order. As shown in Figure 30.9, you can configure an Ethernet application to serially transmit 64-byte packets, 633-byte packets, and 1082-byte packets to create a varying load on the network.

FIGURE 30.9

An Ethernet application can serially transmit packets defined in the transmit channels.

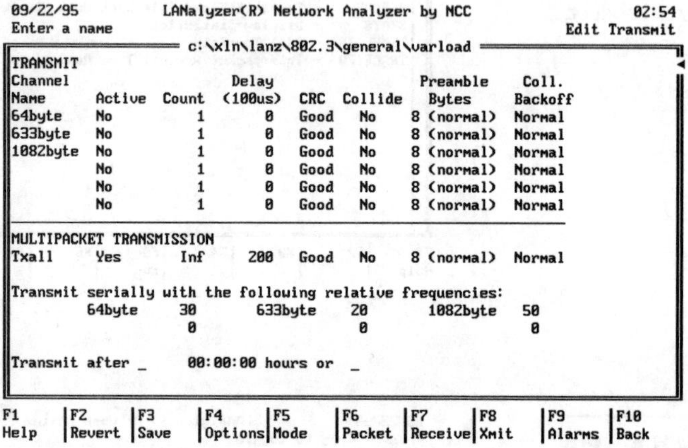

```
09/22/95              LANalyzer(R) Network Analyzer by NCC              02:54
Enter a name                                                    Edit Transmit
                    c:\xln\lanz\802.3\general\varload
TRANSMIT
Channel                   Delay                Preamble    Coll.
Name       Active  Count  (100us)  CRC  Collide  Bytes     Backoff
64byte     No      1      0        Good  No      8 (normal)  Normal
633byte    No      1      0        Good  No      8 (normal)  Normal
1082byte   No      1      0        Good  No      8 (normal)  Normal
           No      1      0        Good  No      8 (normal)  Normal
           No      1      0        Good  No      8 (normal)  Normal
           No      1      0        Good  No      8 (normal)  Normal

MULTIPACKET TRANSMISSION
Txall      Yes     Inf    200      Good  No      8 (normal)  Normal

Transmit serially with the following relative frequencies:
           64byte   30        633byte    20       1082byte   50
                    0                    0                    0

Transmit after _   00:00:00 hours or _

F1     F2     F3    F4     F5    F6     F7     F8   F9     F10
Help   Revert Save  Options Mode Packet Receive Xmit Alarms Back
```

The final option that is available on the packet transmission screen determines when packets will be transmitted. The options include

- Transmit at a certain time of day (transmit at HH:MM:SS).

- Transmit after a certain amount of time has passed (transmit after HH:MM:SS).

- Transmit when a packet has been received on one of the receive channels.

Transmit-time options allow an application to be started automatically, without operator intervention. For example, to test a router during the evening, you can elect to transmit after two hours have passed. If you start the application at 5:30 P.M., when you leave the office, the LANalyzer will begin transmitting packets at 7:30 P.M.

You can also configure a LANalyzer test to start transmitting at a specific time of day—at 8:00 A.M., for example. This time is based upon the workstation clock time.

Finally, you can choose to begin transmission after receipt on one of the application's receipt channels. For example, upon receipt of a SAP request, you can transmit a SAP reply to simulate a server answering a client that is looking for a service on the network.

These options enhance the LANalyzer's capability for testing NetWare LANs and applications.

This chapter has presented the primary reasons for using packet transmit tests: load testing, component testing, and event re-creation. You examined three options for creating transmits, including packet replay. You also learned about transmit options for multipacket and automatic transmission.

The next chapter of this book examines protocol decodes that are available for analysis tools.

Protocol
Decodes

THROUGHOUT THIS BOOK, you have seen screens that provide decodes of NetWare packets. Analyzers that can decode NetWare protocols provide an interpretation of the information within the packet. For example, function code 68 is interpreted as an Erase File NCP call.

This chapter examines decoding capabilities that are available with analysis products such as the LANalyzer and LANalyzer for Windows. The chapter also provides an overview of available decoding options and a description of templates that can be applied when no decode is available.

First, a word of warning regarding decodes. Analyzers differ in their decoding capabilities. If a product claims to decode NetWare, it may be able to decode most NetWare 2.x, NetWare 3.x, and NetWare 4.x communications but not NetWare Lite, Burst Mode, or Personal NetWare protocols. If your network uses these protocols, you will have to manually decode them from a hexadecimal display of the packet contents—a time-consuming task. Since all analyzers differ in their decoding capabilities, check with the manufacturer to ensure that the desired decodes are available.

Some analysis products also charge for decodes. When you purchase the product, you pay one flat fee for the analysis product itself; additional fees are charged for each protocol decode you wish to add to the system. For users who decode a variety of network protocols, such as AppleTalk, TCP/IP, NetWare 2.x, 3.x, 4.x, NetWare Lite, Personal NetWare, and DECnet, these types of analysis systems may not be cost efficient.

Let's begin this chapter with a comparison of a packet that has been decoded and one that has not. Figure 31.1 shows a NetWare NCP packet that has been decoded.

The decoded packet fields are interpreted and presented in English with each field labeled, such as "Hops" and "Function Code." Decodes may also change the numeric representation style from hexadecimal to decimal, ASCII, or EBCDIC when appropriate. For example, in a packet that contains data,

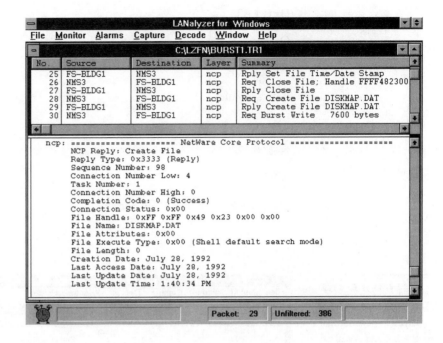

you can see hexadecimal values translated into ASCII values, as shown in Figure 31.2.

If an analyzer doesn't support decoding—or has decoding turned off, as shown in the undecoded upper layers in Figure 31.3—the packets are displayed in hexadecimal format, with no labels applied and no translations performed. In this case, you would need to manually decode the packet. Because this is a time-consuming and laborious task, it is desirable to have an analyzer that includes decodes for the protocols you will be using.

Some analyzers, such as the LANalyzer, include a large selection of decodes with the product; decodes do not need to be purchased separately. The LANalyzer product includes decodes for most of today's most popular protocols, such as

NetWare (v2.x, v3.x, v4.x, Lite, and Personal NetWare)

TCP/IP

AppleTalk (Phase I and II)

DECnet

DEC LAT

OSI

NFS

Banyan Vines

SNA

NetBEUI

XNS

SMB (LAN Manager/LAN Server)

FIGURE 31.2

The packet Data field is
displayed in hexadecimal
on the left and ASCII on
the right.

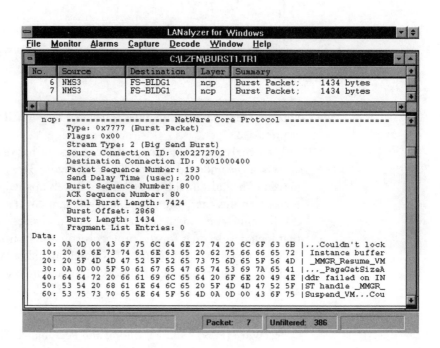

FIGURE 31.3

If no decoding is available, packet contents are shown in hexadecimal.

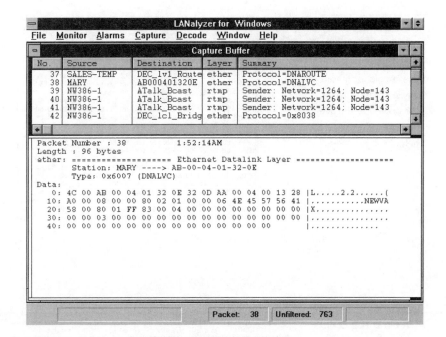

The LANalyzer provides three decoding options: No Decode, Brief Decode, and Expanded Decode. Let's look at each of these.

No Decode Option

F YOU CONFIGURE a trace buffer to use No Decode, you basically get a hexadecimal "dump" of the packet contents, as shown in Figure 31.4. This can be valuable if you want to apply a template that would display only the few fields of interest to you.

Some products, such as the LANalyzer for Windows, allow related fields of the decoded and undecoded data to be highlighted for easier correlation. As shown in Figure 31.5, the File Handle field has been highlighted in the decoded portion. The same field has automatically been highlighted in the hexadecimal representation of the packet.

FIGURE 31.4

If you elect to turn off decoding, as shown in this example, or if your analyzer cannot decide the protocol, you are presented with a hexadecimal "dump."

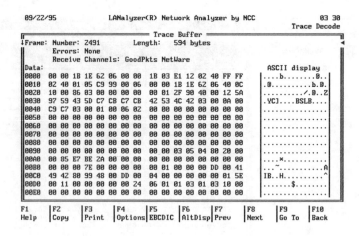

FIGURE 31.5

The File Handle field is highlighted in both the decoded and hexadecimal portions of the screen.

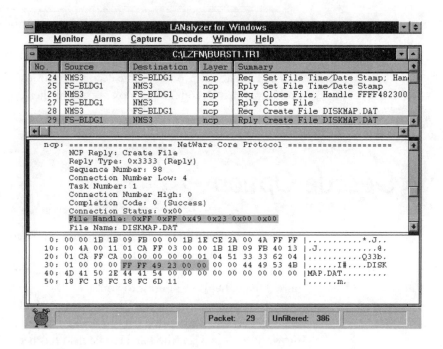

Brief Decode Option

THE LANALYZER PROVIDES a Brief Decode option that presents only the most significant fields within a packet to be shown on the Trace Decode screen, as shown in Figure 31.6.

FIGURE 31.6

A NetWare SPX packet is decoded using the Brief Decode option.

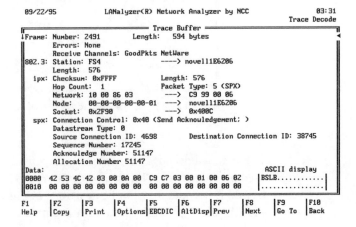

NetWare packets look the same whether you use brief or expanded decode since there are so few fields in the IPX, SPX, and NCP portions. Other protocols, such as TCP/IP, will look quite different in each decode type.

Expanded Decode Option

THE FINAL DECODE option is the Expanded Decode option. When you use expanded decode, the packet is completely decoded throughout—from the Ethernet or Token Ring header to the Data field. This is the default decode option for the LANalyzer and LANalyzer for Windows products.

Figure 31.7 shows a LANalyzer Expanded Decode screen.

FIGURE 31.7

The LANalyzer defaults to the Expanded Decode option.

```
09/22/95          LANalyzer(R) Network Analyzer by NCC            03 31
                                                            Trace Decode
╓══════════════════════════ Trace Buffer ══════════════════════════╖
↓Frame: Number: 2491        Length:    594 bytes                     ◄
       Errors: None
       Receive Channels: GoodPkts NetWare
802.3:                    ══ IEEE 802.3 Datalink Layer ══
       Station: FS4             ----> novell1E6206
       Length:  576
  ipx:            ══ NetWare Internetwork Packet Exchange Protocol ══
       Checksum: 0xFFFF         Length: 576
       Hop Count:  1            Packet Type: 5 (SPX)
       Network: 10 00 86 03   ---> C9 99 00 06
       Node:    00-00-00-00-00-01 --->  novell1E6206
       Socket:  0x2F90          --->  0x400C
  spx:           ══ NetWare Sequenced Packet Exchange Protocol ══
       Connection Control: 0x40 (Send Acknowledgement; )
       Datastream Type: 0
       Source Connection ID: 4698      Destination Connection ID: 38745
       Sequence Number: 17245
       Acknowledge Number: 51147
       Allocation Number 51147

F1   |F2   |F3    |F4      |F5    |F6      |F7    |F8   |F9    |F10
Help |Copy |Print |Options |EBCDIC|AltDisp |Prev  |Next |Go To |Back
```

Expanded decodes provide a comprehensive interpretation of the protocols used on the network. If new protocols are developed and used in the industry, however, decodes may not be available. In this case, some analyzers, such as the LANalyzer, enable you to create templates that can be placed on the packets to interpret the information.

Using Templates

UNLIKE A DECODE, a template is not an intelligent utility. Decodes interpret packet contents based on the values within a packet. For example, a packet that contains the value 0x8137 in the Type field is known to be a NetWare packet using an Ethernet_II frame. In the Destination Socket field, the value 0x0456 indicates that the packet is a diagnostic packet.

Templates, on the other hand, must be manually "placed" on a packet to provide interpretation. A template is simply an aid for viewing packets on the network. You create a template by defining a field, the field length, and the hexadecimal offset, as shown in Figure 31.8.

FIGURE 31.8

A template defines fields, field lengths, and hexadecimal offsets.

```
09/22/95        LANalyzer(R) Network Analyzer by NCC              03:34
Enter decimal number(s)                                    Template Edit
                            c:\xln\lanz\Template\nettrans
Offset from Data: 0
Byte Ordering for 'word' and 'long' Type: high, low

Offset  Label           Type        Format        Length  Bit-offset,Length
0000    Checksum        word        hexadecimal   2
0002    Length          word        decimal       2
0004    Packet Type     byte(s)     decimal       1
0005    Time To Live    byte(s)     decimal       1
0006    Source Network  byte(s)     hexadecimal   4
000A    Source Node     byte(s)     hexadecimal   6
0010    Source Socket   word        hexadecimal   2
0012    Dest Network    byte(s)     hexadecimal   4
0016    Dest Node       byte(s)     hexadecimal   6
001C    Dest Socket     word        hexadecimal   2
001E    Sequence Number byte(s)     decimal       1
001F    Fragment Number byte(s)     hexadecimal   2


F1      F2      F3      F4      F5      F6      F7   F8   F9   F10
Help    Load    Save    Insert  Delete  Append                Back
```

In Figure 31.8, a template has been created for a fictitious protocol named Network Transport Protocol. If the LANalyzer product group did not release a decode for this protocol, you could still apply the template to the packets for interpretation, as shown in Figure 31.9.

FIGURE 31.9

A template applied to the packet provides interpretation.

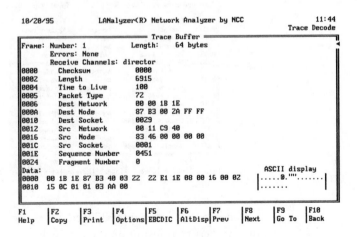

```
10/20/95        LANalyzer(R) Network Analyzer by NCC              11:44
                                                          Trace Decode
                            Trace Buffer
Frame: Number: 1           Length:    64 bytes
       Errors: None
       Receive Channels: director
0000    Checksum          0000
0002    Length            6915
0004    Time to Live      100
0005    Packet Type       72
0006    Dest Network      00 00 1B 1E
000A    Dest Node         87 B3 00 2A FF FF
0010    Dest Socket       0029
0012    Src  Network      00 11 C9 40
0016    Src  Node         83 46 00 00 00 00
001C    Src  Socket       0001
001E    Sequence Number   0451
0024    Fragment Number   0
Data:                                              ASCII display
0000 00 1B 1E 87 B3 40 03 22  22 E1 1E 08 00 16 00 02   |.....@."".......|
0010 15 0C 01 01 03 AA 00                               |.......         |


F1      F2      F3      F4      F5      F6      F7   F8   F9   F10
Help    Copy    Print   Options EBCDIC  AltDisp Prev Next Go To Back
```

The LANalyzer provides a group of template files you can use for transmit channels, receive channels, or decode screens. These template files include

NetWare

NetWare Lite

DECnet

AppleTalk

TCP/IP

ARP

RARP

OSI

SMB

ICMP

Many of these templates are shown in Figures 31.10 through 31.17.

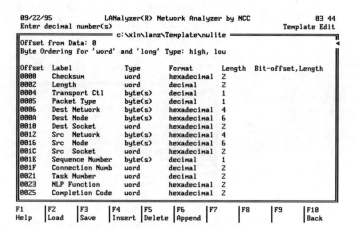

FIGURE 31.10

NetWare Lite template

As mentioned in Chapter 22, templates are also useful when you are creating packets to transmit on the network.

FIGURE 31.11

NetWare template

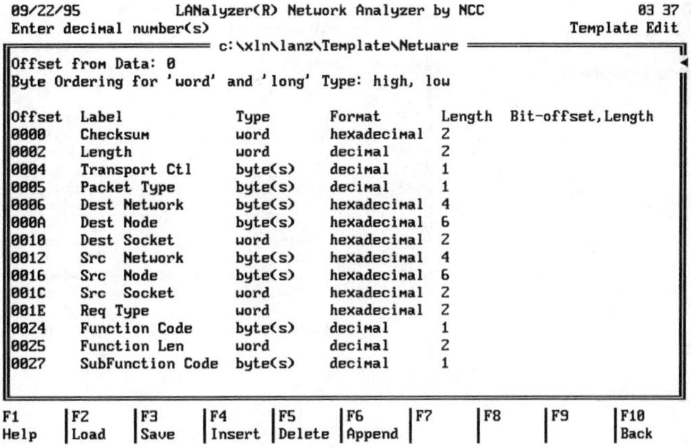

```
09/22/95          LANalyzer(R) Network Analyzer by NCC            03 37
Enter decimal number(s)                                    Template Edit
═══════════════════════ c:\xln\lanz\Template\Netware ═══════════════════
Offset from Data: 0
Byte Ordering for 'word' and 'long' Type: high, low

Offset  Label             Type       Format       Length  Bit-offset,Length
0000    Checksum          word       hexadecimal  2
0002    Length            word       decimal      2
0004    Transport Ctl     byte(s)    decimal      1
0005    Packet Type       byte(s)    decimal      1
0006    Dest Network      byte(s)    hexadecimal  4
000A    Dest Node         byte(s)    hexadecimal  6
0010    Dest Socket       word       hexadecimal  2
0012    Src  Network      byte(s)    hexadecimal  4
0016    Src  Node         byte(s)    hexadecimal  6
001C    Src  Socket       word       hexadecimal  2
001E    Req Type          word       hexadecimal  2
0024    Function Code     byte(s)    decimal      1
0025    Function Len      word       decimal      2
0027    SubFunction Code  byte(s)    decimal      1


F1     |F2    |F3    |F4     |F5     |F6     |F7   |F8   |F9   |F10
Help   |Load  |Save  |Insert |Delete |Append |     |     |     |Back
```

FIGURE 31.12

TCP/IP template

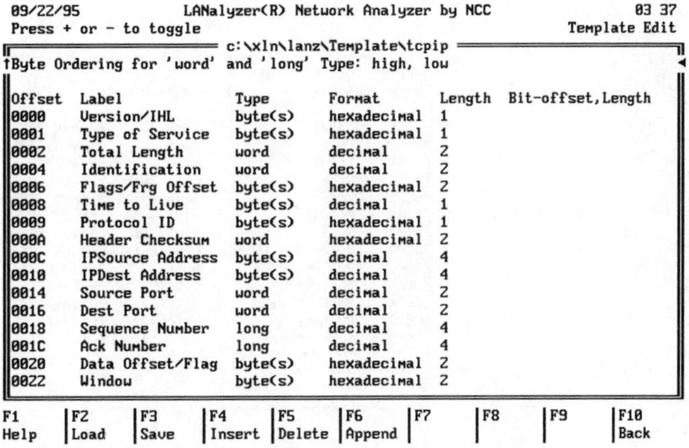

```
09/22/95          LANalyzer(R) Network Analyzer by NCC            03 37
Press + or - to toggle                                     Template Edit
═══════════════════════ c:\xln\lanz\Template\tcpip ═════════════════════
↑Byte Ordering for 'word' and 'long' Type: high, low

Offset  Label             Type       Format       Length  Bit-offset,Length
0000    Version/IHL       byte(s)    hexadecimal  1
0001    Type of Service   byte(s)    hexadecimal  1
0002    Total Length      word       decimal      2
0004    Identification    word       decimal      2
0006    Flags/Frg Offset  byte(s)    hexadecimal  2
0008    Time to Live      byte(s)    decimal      1
0009    Protocol ID       byte(s)    hexadecimal  1
000A    Header Checksum   word       hexadecimal  2
000C    IPSource Address  byte(s)    decimal      4
0010    IPDest Address    byte(s)    decimal      4
0014    Source Port       word       decimal      2
0016    Dest Port         word       decimal      2
0018    Sequence Number   long       decimal      4
001C    Ack Number        long       decimal      4
0020    Data Offset/Flag  byte(s)    hexadecimal  2
0022    Window            byte(s)    hexadecimal  2

F1     |F2    |F3    |F4     |F5     |F6     |F7   |F8   |F9   |F10
Help   |Load  |Save  |Insert |Delete |Append |     |     |     |Back
```

```
09/22/95          LANalyzer(R) Network Analyzer by NCC          03 42
Enter decimal number(s)                                   Template Edit
┌───────────────── c:\xln\lanz\Template\decnet ──────────────────────◄
│Offset from Data: 0
│Byte Ordering for 'word' and 'long' Type: low, high
│
│Offset  Label           Type       Format        Length Bit-offset,Length
│0000    Data Count      word       decimal       2
│0002    Flags           byte(s)    hexadecimal   1
│0003    Dst. Area       byte(s)    hexadecimal   1
│0004    Dst. Sub-Area   byte(s)    hexadecimal   1
│0005    Dst. ID         byte(s)    hexadecimal   6
│000B    Src. Area       byte(s)    hexadecimal   1
│000C    Src. Sub-Area   byte(s)    hexadecimal   1
│000D    Src. ID         byte(s)    hexadecimal   6
│0014    Next Lvl 2 Routr byte(s)   hexadecimal   1
│0015    Visit Count     byte(s)    hexadecimal   1
│0016    Service Class   byte(s)    hexadecimal   1
│0017    Protocol Type   byte(s)    hexadecimal   1
│
│
│
└─────────────────────────────────────────────────────────────────────
F1     F2      F3      F4      F5      F6      F7      F8      F9     F10
Help   Load    Save    Insert  Delete                                Back
```

```
09/22/95          LANalyzer(R) Network Analyzer by NCC          03 42
Enter decimal number(s)                                   Template Edit
┌───────────────── c:\xln\lanz\Template\vinesip ─────────────────────┐
│Offset from Data: 0                                                  ◄
│Byte Ordering for 'word' and 'long' Type: high, low
│
│Offset  Label           Type       Format        Length Bit-offset,Length
│0000    Checksum        word       hexadecimal   2
│0002    Length          word       decimal       2
│0004    Unused          mask byte  binary        1      0,1
│0004    Error           mask byte  binary        1      1,1
│0004    Metric          mask byte  binary        1      2,1
│0004    Redirect        mask byte  binary        1      3,1
│0004    Transport Cntrl mask byte  binary        1      4,4
│0005    Protocol Cntrl  byte(s)    hexadecimal   1
│0006    Destnetnum      byte(s)    decimal       4
│000A    Destsubnetnum   byte(s)    decimal       2
│000C    Srcnetnum       byte(s)    decimal       4
│0010    Srcsubnetnum    byte(s)    decimal       2
│
│
└─────────────────────────────────────────────────────────────────────
F1     F2      F3      F4      F5      F6      F7      F8      F9     F10
Help   Load    Save    Insert  Delete  Append                       Back
```

FIGURE 31.15

VINES SMB template

```
09/22/95          LANalyzer(R) Network Analyzer by NCC              03 43
Enter decimal number(s)                                        Template Edit
╔════════════════════ c:\xln\lanz\Template\vinessmb ════════════════════╗
║Offset from Data: 0                                                     ◄
║Byte Ordering for 'word' and 'long' Type: low, high
║
║Offset  Label            Type      Format        Length  Bit-offset,Length
║0002    Length           word      decimal       2
║0004    Transport Cntrl  byte(s)   hexadecimal   1
║0005    Protocol Cntrl   byte(s)   hexadecimal   1
║0006    Destnetnum       long      decimal       4
║000A    Destsubnetnum    word      decimal       2
║000C    Srcnetnum        long      decimal       4
║0010    Srcsubnetnum     word      decimal       2
║0012    Source Port      word      decimal       2
║0014    Destination Port word      decimal       2
║0016    Packet Type      byte(s)   decimal       1
║0017    Control Byte     byte(s)   decimal       1
║0020    Window           word      decimal       2
║0022    SMB Indicator    byte(s)   hexadecimal   4
║0026    Function         byte(s)   hexadecimal   1
║002C    Return Code      byte(s)   decimal       2
╚═══════════════════════════════════════════════════════════════════════╝
F1      F2      F3      F4      F5      F6      F7   F8   F9   F10
Help    Load    Save    Insert  Delete  Append                   Back
```

FIGURE 31.16

IP ICMP template

```
09/22/95          LANalyzer(R) Network Analyzer by NCC              03 43
Enter decimal number(s)                                        Template Edit
╔════════════════════ c:\xln\lanz\Template\ipicmp ══════════════════════╗
║Offset from Data: 0                                                     ◄
║Byte Ordering for 'word' and 'long' Type: high, low
║
║Offset  Label            Type      Format        Length  Bit-offset,Length
║0000    Version/IHL      byte(s)   hexadecimal   1
║0001    Type of Service  byte(s)   hexadecimal   1
║0002    Total Length     word      decimal       2
║0004    Identification   word      decimal       2
║0006    Flags/Frg Offset byte(s)   hexadecimal   2
║0008    Time to Live     byte(s)   decimal       1
║0009    Protocol ID      byte(s)   hexadecimal   1
║000A    Header Checksum  word      hexadecimal   2
║000C    IPSource Address byte(s)   decimal       4
║0010    IPDest Address   byte(s)   decimal       4
║0014    Type             byte(s)   hexadecimal   1
║0015    Code             byte(s)   hexadecimal   1
║0016    Checksum         word      hexadecimal   2
║0018    Identifier       word      hexadecimal   2
║001A    Sequence Number  word      hexadecimal   2
╚═══════════════════════════════════════════════════════════════════════╝
F1      F2      F3      F4      F5      F6      F7   F8   F9   F10
Help    Load    Save    Insert  Delete  Append                   Back
```

FIGURE 31.17

OSI template

```
09/22/95            LANalyzer(R) Network Analyzer by NCC              03:44
Press + or - to toggle                                      Template Edit
┌──────────────────── c:\xln\lanz\Template\osi ────────────────────────┐
│Byte Ordering for 'word' and 'long' Type: high, low                    │
│                                                                       │
│Offset  Label             Type        Format       Length Bit-offset,Length│
│0000    netwk protcol id  byte(s)     hexadecimal  1                   │
│0001    length indicator  byte(s)     decimal      1                   │
│0002    version/prot ext  byte(s)     hexadecimal  1                   │
│0003    lifetime          byte(s)     decimal      1                   │
│0004    SP/MS/ER          mask byte   binary       1       5,3         │
│0004    CLNP type         mask byte   binary       1       0,5         │
│0009    dest addr length  byte(s)     decimal      1                   │
│000A    afi               byte(s)     hexadecimal  1                   │
│000B    net entity title  byte(s)     hexadecimal  8                   │
│0013    nsap selector     byte(s)     hexadecimal  2                   │
│0015    srce addr length  byte(s)     decimal      1                   │
│0016    afi               byte(s)     hexadecimal  1                   │
│0017    net entity title  byte(s)     hexadecimal  8                   │
│001F    nsap selector     byte(s)     hexadecimal  2                   │
│0021    data unit id      word        hexadecimal  2                   │
│0025    total length      word        hexadecimal  2                   │
└───────────────────────────────────────────────────────────────────────┘
F1      |F2      |F3      |F4      |F5      |F6      |F7    |F8    |F9    |F10
Help    |Load    |Save    |Insert  |Delete  |Append  |      |      |      |Back
```

For additional reference materials on NetWare protocols, Ethernet, and protocol analysis, see Appendix B.

This chapter has illustrated the advantage of purchasing an analysis system that supports the protocols found on your network. You also examined the three decode options: No Decode, Brief Decode, and Expanded Decode. Finally, the chapter provided a listing and display of templates that are included with the LANalyzer product.

This book has explained technology, protocols, implementation, analysis techniques, and analysis features for NetWare Ethernet and Token Ring LANs. You should now have a strong foundation regarding Ethernet and Token Ring network systems, NetWare protocols, and testing strategies.

Glossary

ALARM LOG FILE   A file, generally in ASCII format, that contains a listing of alarms that have occurred, as well as the date and time each alarm occurred.

BACKOFF ALGORITHM   A computation that each Ethernet card is required to perform in order to determine available transmission times after a collision. The backoff algorithm process is formally called the "truncated binary exponential backoff."

BASELINE   The process of determining and documenting network performance characteristics under normal conditions. Network characteristics might include utilization, errors per second, kilobytes per second, packets per second, most active users/servers, and so on.

BINARY FILTERING   Filtering on bit values (0 or 1) instead of a full byte value.

BINDERY   A special-purpose database maintained by NetWare 2.*x* and 3.*x* servers. The bindery contains information about clients and resources on the network, such as passwords, client accounts, and client restrictions.

BIT STREAMING   A Token ring error caused when a token ring adapter overwrites existing data on the ring.

BRIDGE   An internetworking device that connects two network segments on the same logical LAN. A bridge filters traffic between segments based on their hardware (MAC) address and is unaware of upper-layer protocols being used.

BROADCAST   A packet type that is destined to all devices on the network.

BROADCAST ADDRESS   An address denoting that a packet is destined to all devices on the network. In Ethernet, there is one broadcast address: 0xFF-FF-FF-FF-FF-FF. In Token Ring, there are two broadcast addresses: 0xFF-FF-FF-FF-FF-FF and 0xC0-00-FF-FF-FF-FF. 0xFF-FF-FF-FF-FF-FF is for use with non-MAC frames and may traverse a bridge. 0xC0-00-FF-FF-FF-FF is used only with MAC frames; it is specific to a ring and thus not forwarded by bridges.

BURST MODE WINDOW   The Burst Mode window determines the amount of data that can be transferred in a Burst Mode session before an acknowledgment is required. The window size is dynamically adjusted based on error conditions or the lack thereof.

CARRIER OFF   The lack of a signal on an Ethernet cable. Ethernet stations can transmit when they sense that the cable condition is carrier off.

CARRIER ON   A signal on an Ethernet network cable indicating that the cable is in use.

COLLISION FRAGMENT   The result of two or more stations transmitting simultaneously on the cabling system. Fragments are defined as packets that are less than 64 bytes in length and contain an invalid CRC value. The presence or absence of a collision detection signal differentiates local collisions from remote collisions.

CROSSTALK   Interference caused by electromagnetic sources, such as a motor. Crosstalk is detected as bandwidth utilization that is not a result of packets on the wire.

CYCLICAL REDUNDANCY CHECK (CRC)   A calculation check performed by the transmitting and receiving stations to validate the integrity of frames. Transmitting stations place the CRC value in the Frame Check Sequence field; receiving stations perform the same calculation and compare the result to the value in the FCS field. The CRC is performed on all fields of the packet except the Preamble and Start Frame Delimiter fields and the Frame Check Sequence field itself.

DEAF NODE   An Ethernet node that does not adhere to the CSMA/CD requirement of "listen first, then transmit." A deaf node either will not listen to the cabling system for activity or will ignore the activity on the wire before transmitting.

DEFAULT SERVER   The server that is specified by the client's default drive mapping.

DEFERRAL TIME   The amount of time a node must wait before transmitting once it has noticed the cable is "busy." Nodes must wait 9.6 microseconds after the cable has become idle before beginning transmission.

DETERMINISTIC PROTOCOLS   Protocols that provide assurance of an opportunity to transmit on the medium. Token Ring is considered a deterministic protocol since the token (right to transmit) passes logically from one station to the next.

DISTRIBUTED FAULT   A fault that cannot be attributed to a single device on a network. For example, CRC errors associated with multiple stations are a distributed fault and may indicate a fault in the network cable.

DOWNSTREAM NEIGHBOR   A Token ring device on the transmit side of a ring station.

DUMB LOAD TEST   A test that transmits mocked-up packets for the purpose of testing a network's or component's reaction to greater network load.

DUMB LOADS   Packets that are transmitted onto the network and contain no information regarding destination or purpose. Dumb loads are used to test the network cabling system performance abilities under varying levels of utilization.

ENHANCED FILTERING   A filtering technique available with the LAN-alyzer that permits up to 16 filter patterns to be combined using Boolean operands.

EXCLUSION ADDRESS   A node address of a station that will not be required to respond to a diagnostic configuration packet (Diagnostic Responder). A maximum of 80 nodes can be excluded in each diagnostic configuration packet.

FAULT DOMAIN   The area between a ring station reporting a problem and that ring station's upstream neighbor.

FRAME STREAMING   A Token Ring hard error caused by an adapter that is transmitting random frames, tokens, abort sequences, or unintelligible data.

FRAMES   Encapsulation bits that provide synchronization services, addressing, upper-layer protocol definition, and integrity checking of information transmitted across a network.

FREQUENCY ERROR   A Token Ring hard error defined as a master ring clock that varies from the internal clock of other ring stations by more than 0.6%. Typically indicative of a bad adapter in the Active Monitor.

FUNCTIONAL ADDRESS   A multicast address that is assigned by IBM or a standards body to functional stations that are participating in management of the Token Ring network.

GLOBAL STATISTICS   Statistics regarding all the traffic on the network, including errors, utilization, kilobytes, packets per second, and so on.

HARD-ERROR RECOVERY TIMELINE   The sequence of Token Ring events used by the Token Ring network hardware in order to recover from a loss of token protocol resulting from a soft or hard error.

HARDWARE ADDRESS   An address assigned to a network interface card by either a manufacturer or, in some cases, the network administrator. The hardware address identifies the local device address to which a packet is destined. Hardware addresses can also be referred to as the physical, MAC, or Ethernet addresses.

INTELLIGENT LOADS   Packets that are transmitted to a specific device or upper-layer protocol on the network. Intelligent loads are used for component testing.

INTERNAL ERRORS   Token Ring adapter errors detected by the adapter during its self tests.

INTERNETWORK ADDRESS (NETWARE ENVIRONMENT)   A software address that consists of a 4-byte network address and 6-byte node address. A station's internetwork address denotes the network it is located on, as well as the physical address of the device.

ISOLATING ERRORS   Token Ring soft errors that provide sufficient information to identify a fault domain.

JABBER   A "packet" that is greater than the maximum size allowed (1518 bytes) and that contains a bad CRC value. A common cause of jabber on the network is a faulty transceiver.

JABBERING TRANSCEIVER   A transceiver (MAU) generating transmissions that exceed the maximum transmission time duration allowed by the 802.3 specification. The maximum transmission time cannot exceed 150 milliseconds, as defined by the IEEE 802.3. Properly functioning transceivers are required to inhibit transmission (jabber suppression) once the time duration has been exceeded.

JAM   A 32-bit transmission that follows detection of a collision by a transmitting station. Jam is used to ensure that the collision can be detected by all transmitting stations on the segment. The content of jam is unspecified but cannot be equal to the CRC value of the partial frame transmitted prior to jam.

KEY (LOGIN ENCRYPTION)   An encryption sequence provided by a Net-Ware server to clients that wish to gain access to services. A maximum of two keys is provided to clients during each NetWare login attempt.

LATE COLLISION   A collision that occurs later than 64 bytes into a packet. Late collisions indicate either a deaf node or a cabling problem, such as cable length exceeding the maximum allowable by the 802.3 specifications.

LINE ERRORS   The name for Token Ring Frame Check Sequence errors (CRC errors).

LOAD TEST   A test that is developed to determine the capabilities of either a single component on the network or the network cabling system, itself. There are two types of load tests: dumb and intelligent.

LOCAL COLLISIONS   Collisions that occur on the same network segment as the observer. Local collisions are detected by monitoring the node's collision-detect circuitry for a signal that equals or exceeds the possible signal produced by two or more MAUs.

LONG FRAMES   Frames that are greater than 1518 bytes in length and contain a valid CRC value. Long frames can be transmitted by stations that are using a faulty LAN driver.

MAJOR VECTOR   The part of Token Ring MAC data that names and describes the MAC frame command. Beacon is an example of a Token Ring major vector.

MONITOR CONTENTION   The process used by Token Ring stations to elect an Active Monitor.

MULTICAST   A frame type that is transmitted to a group of stations through the use of a multicast address.

MULTICAST ADDRESS   A special address that denotes a group of stations. For example, to address frames to all ACME routers, a frame must have the ACME router multicast address in the Destination Address field (Ethernet and Token Ring).

NEAREST ACTIVE UPSTREAM NEIGHBOR (NAUN)   *See* Upstream neighbor.

NONFUNCTIONAL ADDRESS   Token Ring name for standard multicast addresses that are not Token Ring functional addresses. *See also* Multicast address.

NONISOLATING ERROR   Token Ring soft errors that do not provide sufficient information to identify a fault domain.

PING   To transmit a packet to a defined node on the network in order to test connectivity. In the NetWare environment, a diagnostic configuration packet can be transmitted to test station connectivity and gather configuration information. The term "ping" is common in the TCP/IP environment.

PING PACKET   A packet used simply to request a reply from a station for the purpose of testing connectivity or timing round-trip delay.

POINT-AND-CLICK FILTERING   A post-filtering (display filtering) technique provided by the LANalyzer for NetWare. Point-and-click filtering allows a user to configure post-filtering values by clicking on a field shown in the decode.

POST-FILTER   A filter applied to packets that are saved in the trace buffer or on disk. Post-filters are used to focus on packets that meet a defined post-filter criterion.

PRE-FILTER   A filter applied to the packet before it is saved in the trace buffer or on disk. Pre-filters reduce the number and types of packets saved to the buffer.

PREDEFINED ALARM THRESHOLD   An alarm threshold that is determined and set by the analysis software manufacturer. These predefined alarms alert new users to potential problems before they learn how to set alarm thresholds.

PREFERRED SERVER   A NetWare server that is explicitly defined either in a NET.CFG file or at the command line during the login process.

PRIMARY SERVER   The server to which the workstation shell attached upon execution. If a preferred server has been requested, the primary server will provide routing information to the shell in order to enable the shell to request attachment of the preferred server.

RELATIVE FORMAT (TIME-STAMPING) A time-stamping format that bases all packet time stamps on the first packet within the buffer. The first packet is assumed to have been received at time 00:00:00. Each subsequent packet in the buffer will have a receipt time relative to the first.

REMOTE COLLISIONS Collisions that occur on the other side of a repeater. Remote collisions are identified as packets that are less than 64 bytes and contain an invalid CRC value. Remote collisions cannot be detected by a node's collision-detection circuitry.

REPLICA A copy of a portion of an NDS database.

RING POLL The Token Ring process that identifies each ring station's upstream neighbor.

RING RECOVERY Each time a Token Ring goes through the Monitor Contention process to elect an Active Monitor, it is considered a ring recovery.

ROOT PORT The port of a bridge from which the Bridge Protocol Data Unit is copied.

ROUTE DETERMINATION The process used by ring stations in a source-routing environment to discover the route to a target station in order to create a route entry in their source-route table.

ROUTE TABLE The table created by each ring station in a source-routing environment to store route information for each target station.

ROUTERS Devices used to connect two or more similar or dissimilar networks and provide routing services based on logical end-to-end connections. Routers utilize addressing information contained in the network header of a packet to determine the source and destination addresses on an internetwork.

ROUTING AREA An area on a large internetwork uniquely identified for NLSP use.

SHORT FRAMES Frames that are less than 64 bytes in length and contain a valid CRC value. The detection of short frames indicates that a node is using a faulty LAN driver.

SIGNAL LOSS ERROR A Token Ring hard error indicated by a loss of the data signal on the receive side of a ring station's adapter.

SIGNAL QUALITY ERROR (SQE) A signal on the collision-detection circuitry of a transceiver. An SQE signal indicates that an improper signal exists on the medium or that a collision has occurred. An SQE test is performed after each frame is transmitted to test the collision-detection circuitry of the transceiver.

SOFT ERRORS Token Ring errors that are not fatal (hard errors) but may require some recovery actions by the ring stations to reinstate the token protocol. Each ring station keeps track of and reports soft errors to the Ring Error Monitor every 2 seconds, by default.

SOFTWARE ADDRESSING Addressing that defines the logical address of a device on an internetwork and is independent of the physical address of a device. Software addresses are used by routers to forward packets through a network. On a NetWare LAN, the internetwork address is a software address.

SOURCE-ROUTE BRIDGES Data link–layer bridges used in a source-routing environment. Source-route bridges forward frames based on the route information contained within the Data field.

SPX HANDSHAKE A connection establishment sequence that must be performed before a client or server can use connection-oriented services provided by SPX.

STORED UPSTREAM ADDRESS (SUA) The upstream neighbor address saved by each ring station on a Token Ring network.

SUBVECTORS Part of the Token Ring MAC information contained in Token Ring MAC frames. Subvectors provide supporting information for the major vector command. Nearest active upstream neighbor is an example of subvector information.

TEMPLATE A defined format for protocol decoding that includes byte offset, field labels, and field lengths. When used in conjunction with packet transmission, templates label fields for easier packet creation.

TOKEN A special bit pattern used by the Token Ring protocol that, when detected by a ring station, gives that station permission to transmit data.

TOKEN CLAIMING The Monitor Contention process. *See also* Monitor Contention.

TOKEN ROTATION TIME The time, in microseconds, between free tokens on the network as detected by a ring station.

TRANSCEIVERS Chips, either internal (on the Ethernet card) or external (a separate transceiver unit), that are responsible for transmitting and receiving bits from the medium.

TRANSPARENT BRIDGES Bridges that detect the location of network devices based on the source hardware address and then build a filtering database and forward or filter frames based on this information. Transparent bridges are so named because none of the network devices are aware of their presence.

UNIVERSAL ADDRESS The name given to the hardware address that comes burned into a ROM on a network adapter from the vendor.

UPSTREAM NEIGHBOR The hardware address of the Token Ring station on the receive side of a ring station.

USER-DEFINED ALARM THRESHOLDS Alarm thresholds that can be customized based on network baseline statistics.

UTILIZATION The percentage of bandwidth currently busy handling network traffic or errors.

WIRING CLOSET The name given by IBM to the room where the Token Ring hubs and associated cabling and hardware are located.

Bibliography

Chappell, Laura, Dan Hakes, and Roger Spicer. Customized Course: *Advanced NetWare LAN Analysis*. Technology Consortium, 1994.

Comer, Douglas. *Internetworking with TCP/IP: Principles, Protocols and Architectures*. Prentice-Hall, 1989.

Day, Michael, Michael Koontz, and Dan Marshall. *NetWare 4.0 NLM Programming*. SYBEX, 1993.

Hakes, Dan. *Advanced LANalyzer Token Ring-NetWare*. Network Communications Corporation, 1994.

Hakes, Dan. *Chart of Death: Token Ring Frame Structures* (poster). Technology Consortium, 1994.

Hakes, Dan. *Chart of Death: Ethernet Frame Structures* (poster). Technology Consortium, 1994.

IEEE Standard 802.3 (ANSI): *Carrier Sense with Collision Detection (CSMA/CD) Access Method and Physical Layer Specifications*. Institute of Electrical and Electronic Engineers, 1992.

IEEE Standard 802.5 (ANSI): *Token Ring Access Method*. Institute of Electrical and Electronic Engineers, 1989.

IEEE Standard 802.5b (ANSI): *IEEE Recommended Practice for Use of Unshielded Twisted Pair Cable (UTP) for Token Ring Data Transmission at 4 Mb/s*. Institute of Electrical and Electronic Engineers, 1991.

Local Area Network: IBM Token Ring Architecture. IBM Corporation, 1992.

NetWare Link Services Protocol In-Depth. Novell, Inc., 1994.

NetWare Link Services Protocol Specification—Revision 1.0. Novell, Inc., 1994.

Novell Research. *NetWare Application Notes*, "A Comparison of NetWare IPX, SPX and NetBIOS." Novell, Inc., August 1990.

Novell Research. *NetWare Application Notes*, "NetWare Communication Processes." Novell, Inc., September 1990.

Novell Research. *NetWare Application Notes,* "Packet Burst Update: BNETX vs. VLM Implementations." Novell, Inc., November 1993.

Padiyar, Sunil, Michael Day, Michael Koontz, and Dan Marshall. *NetWare 4 Planning and Implementation.* New Riders Publishing, 1993.

Pentin, Josine and Roger Spicer. *Advanced LANalyzer Ethernet-TCP/IP.* Network Communications Corporation, 1993.

TMS380 Adapter Chipset User's Guide. Texas Instruments, 1992.

LANalyzer for Windows Product Information

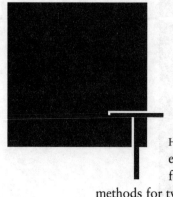

THROUGHOUT THIS BOOK you have seen screen shots and references to Novell's LANalyzer for Windows. We use LANalyzer for Windows for research and training on protocols and access methods for two primary reasons:

- LANalyzer for Windows is easy to operate.

- LANalyzer for Windows is affordable ($1,496 list price—about $1,000 street price).

If you haven't yet purchased a network analyzer, take a look at the capabilities of LANalyzer for Windows that we describe in this Appendix.

During the revision of this book, the LANalyzer for Windows product was revised and version 2.2 was announced. The new version of the product provides additional decodes and support for Novell's Client32, Windows 95, and NetWare Directory Services, as detailed below. LANalyzer for Windows v2.2 also provides "sticky tables," enhanced decodes and font change abilities.

Product Enhancements (LZFW v2.2):

Client32 Support: LZFW v2.2 provides direct support for Novell's new Client32 stack, on both Windows 3.x and Windows 95 platforms. LZFW v2.2 autodetects what client is running at the install time (Client32 on ODI, Client32 on NDIS, or VLMs (16-bit client) on ODI). LZFW v2.2 installs the correct software accordingly.

Windows 95 Support: LZFW v2.2 running on Client32 provides real Windows 95 support without the need to load any TSRs in an AUTOEXEC.BAT file.

NetWare Directory Services Support: LZFW v2.2 provides full NDS support, enabling the software to gather station names from anywhere in the NDS tree, starting from any context.

Sticky Tables: When users resize or rearrange columns within the LZFW tables, the changes will be sticky (the changes will still be in effect the next time you launch the software).

Enhanced Decodes: LZFW v2.2 includes the latest decodes for the newer Novell protocols including all the NetWare 4.1 NCPs that support NDS communications.

Font Change Abilities: Users can select which fonts and sizes to use with the LZFW displays. This is especially useful in localized (translated) versions of the product.

When you purchase LANalyzer for Windows, you receive the NetWare Expert Troubleshooting System, NetWare Expert Training, and a copy of the second edition of this book (you can never really have enough copies of this book, eh?).

Videotape Training

LANALYZER FOR WINDOWS v2.1 and earlier included a training videotape. The videotape included with the product is provided in two formats: NTSC (the first half of the tape) and PAL (the second half). I made this videotape for Novell when I worked as a technical liaison for the Network Management and Internetworking Products Division (NMIPD). The video demonstrates ways to baseline and troubleshoot Ethernet and Token Ring networks. If you have purchased LANalyzer for Windows v2.2 (or later) and are interested in video training, send an e-mail to video@imagitech.com or on CompuServe 72000,3333. We'll send you information on various network analysis and protocol stack training tapes as they become available.

NetWare Expert Troubleshooting System

T HE PRODUCT ASSUMES that most people don't memorize all the troubleshooting steps required to isolate and identify faulty or overloaded components. When an alarm is triggered and the alarm log is viewed, clicking on a "mortarboard" icon (red graduation hat) in the alarm log brings up expert advice on how to further isolate or resolve the problems. The information in the NetWare Expert Troubleshooting System was provided by the technical reviewer of this book, Roger Spicer.

NetWare Expert Training

O NE OF THE features in LANalyzer for Windows 2.0 and later is a complete computer-based, interactive, animated training program for Ethernet and Token Ring network analysis. The NetWare Expert Training includes information on baselining network performance, setting alarm thresholds, and troubleshooting network errors, as shown in Figure C.1.

NetWare Expert Training was developed by Laura A. Chappell and Roger Spicer to provide a new way of teaching analysis to users. The product also includes a comprehensive hypertext glossary and interactive quiz to test your analysis abilities. Many instructors use the training programs in their courses on network configuration and analysis.

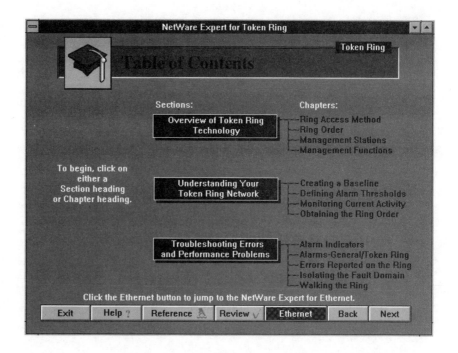

A LANalyzer for Windows Software Developers Kit (SDK) is also available for developers who want to create their own decodes for LANalyzer for Windows.

For more information on Novell's LANalyzer for Windows or LANalyzer for Windows SDK, contact your Novell Authorized Reseller. To locate the nearest reseller, call (800) NETWARE or (801) 429-5533.

Token Ring
Timers

D

N THIS APPENDIX you will find the names and descriptions of all the token ring timers as designated by IBM. All timer names are IBM. The IEEE equivalents are given where applicable.

T(any_token)

A RING STATION SETS the T(any_token) timer when it becomes the Active Monitor. This value indicates the maximum time between SDELs on the ring. This is the Active Monitor's token "Watchdog" timer.

Value	10ms
Started by	The AM when it transmits the first token
Restarted by	The AM when it detects an SDEL
Canceled by	The AM when it exits AM state
Timeout action	The AM increments the Token_Error counter and initiates the Ring Purge process
IEEE counterpart	Valid Transmission Timer (TVX)

T(attach)

THE T(ATTACH) TIMER specifies the longest a ring station can stay in the process of inserting itself onto the ring.

Value	18 seconds
Started by	Entering the Monitor Check phase of ring insertion
Restarted by	Entering Duplicate Address Check, Ring Poll, or Request Parameters phase of ring insertion
Canceled by	Removing from the ring or completing the insertion process
Timeout action	In the Monitor Check state, the station initiates Monitor Contention and enters Duplicate Address phase. In Duplicate Address Check, Ring Poll, or Request Parameters state, the station removes itself from the ring
IEEE counterpart	None

T(beacon_transmit)

AFTER A RING station recognizes a hard error and starts transmitting Beacon frames, T(beacon_transmit) is the maximum time it waits before taking itself off the ring and running a self-test.

Value	16 seconds
Started by	Start of transmission of Beacon MAC frames
Restarted by	Start of transmission of a different priority Beacon MAC frame

Canceled by	Receipt of a Beacon frame with an address not the station's own, or recovery of the ring
Timeout action	The station removes itself from the ring and runs a self-test
IEEE counterpart	none

T(claim_token)

THE T(CLAIM_TOKEN) timer is the length of time a station will stay in Monitor Contention mode and wait for an Active Monitor to be established.

Value	1 second
Started by	Entering Monitor Contention or Monitor Contention repeat mode
Restarted by	Receiving a Claim Token MAC frame
Canceled by	Winning Monitor Contention or receiving a purge MAC frame
Timeout action	In Monitor Contention mode, the station enters Beacon transmit mode with a priority of 0002, 0003, or 0004. In claim token repeat mode, the station enters Beacon transmit mode with a priority of 0004
IEEE counterpart	No Token Timer (TNT)

T(escape)

T(ESCAPE) IS THE time a station can stay in Beacon repeat mode, without receiving a Beacon frame, before it starts Monitor Contention.

Value	200ms
Started by	Receipt of a Beacon MAC frame
Restarted by	Receipt of a Beacon MAC frame
Canceled by	Receipt of a Claim Token MAC frame or entry into any mode other than Beacon
Timeout action	The station enters Monitor Contention mode
IEEE counterpart	No Token Timer (TNT)

T(good_token)

T(GOOD_TOKEN) IS THE time a station can stay in Beacon repeat mode, without receiving a Beacon frame, before it starts Monitor Contention.

Value	2.6 seconds
Started by	Activation of Standby Monitor function
Restarted by	Detection of a priority 0 token or a priority-greater-than-0 token followed by a frame
Canceled by	Deactivation of the Standby Monitor function (Monitor Contention or Beacon mode)
Timeout action	The station enters Monitor Contention mode
IEEE counterpart	No Token Timer (TNT)

T(neighbor_notification)

THE ACTIVE MONITOR uses the T(neighbor_notification) timer to indicate the time to start Ring Poll.

Value	7 seconds
Started by	Transmission of the first AMP MAC frame after becoming the Active Monitor
Restarted by	Transmission of an AMP MAC Frame
Canceled by	Deactivation of the Active Monitor function
Timeout action	Active Monitor transmits another AMP MAC frame (tries to restart Ring Poll) and then transmits a Neighbor Notification Incomplete MAC frame
IEEE counterpart	Active Monitor Timer (TAM)

T(notification_response)

(NOTIFICATION_RESPONSE) IS the time a station must wait between receipt of an AMP or SMP MAC frame with ARI and FCI set to 0 before it transmits an SMP MAC frame. It is used to prevent congestion.

Value	20ms
Started by	Receipt of an AMP or SMP MAC frame with ARI and FCI set to 0
Restarted by	Receipt of an AMP or SMP MAC frame with ARI and FCI set to 0

Canceled by	Receipt of a Ring Purge MAC frame
Timeout action	Queuing of an SMP MAC frame for transmission
IEEE counterpart	Queue PDU Timer (TQP)

T(physical_trailer)

F A STATION fails to detect the end (trailer) of a frame it transmitted, the T(physical_trailer) timer minimizes the erroneous stripping of data by the station.

Value	4.1ms
Started by	Transmitting the EDEL of a frame in which the Intermediate Frame indicator is at 0
Restarted by	Not restarted
Canceled by	Entering any mode other than strip mode; receiving, while in strip mode, a frame with a source address equal to the station's address and an EDEL; receiving, while in strip mode, an abort sequence
Timeout action	A Standby Monitor increments the Lost Frame error counter and enters normal repeat mode. An Active Monitor increments the Lost Frame counter and then purges the ring
IEEE counterpart	Queue PDU Timer (TQP)

T(receive_notification)

A STANDBY MONITOR USES the T(receive_notification) timer to make sure Ring Poll happens often enough. An Active Monitor uses this timer to ensure that the AMP MAC frame is circling the ring. Hard errors could prevent an AMP MAC frame from circling the ring.

Value	15 seconds
Started by	Activation of Active Monitor or Standby Monitor
Restarted by	Receipt of an AMP MAC Frame
Canceled by	Deactivation of Active Monitor or Standby Monitor function
Timeout action	The Active Monitor or Standby Monitor enters Monitor Contention
IEEE counterpart	Standby Monitor Timer (TSM)

T(response)

T(RESPONSE) IS THE time a ring station, ring parameter, or configuration report server should wait for a response to a request before assuming failure and repeating the request.

Value	2.5 seconds
Started by	Stripping a MAC frame that requires a response
Restarted by	Not restarted
Canceled by	Copying the necessary response MAC frame

Timeout action	Decrementing the Response Retry counter and, if the counter is not at 0, requeuing the request frame for retransmission
IEEE counterpart	none

T(ring_purge)

THE T(RING_PURGE) timer specifies how long the Active Monitor will continue to transmit Ring Purge MAC frames before assuming failure and entering Monitor Contention.

Value	1 second
Started by	Entering the Ring Purge process
Restarted by	Not restarted
Canceled by	Successful completion of the Ring Purge process
Timeout action	Active Monitor enters Monitor Contention
IEEE counterpart	No Token Timer (TNT)

T(soft_error_report)

THE T(SOFT_ERROR_REPORT) timer specifies the minimum amount of time between sending of each Report Soft Error MAC frame.

Value	2 seconds
Started by	Incrementing the soft error counter
Restarted by	Not restarted

Canceled by	Not canceled
Timeout action	Queuing of a Soft Error Report MAC frame
IEEE counterpart	None

T(transmit_pacing)

THE T(TRANSMIT_PACING) timer specifies the time the station must wait between transmission of frames. It is used to pace the transmission of Claim Token and Beacon MAC frames.

Value	20ms
Started by	Transmitting a Beacon or Claim Token MAC frame
Restarted by	Transmitting a Beacon or Claim Token MAC frame
Canceled by	Exiting Beacon or Monitor Contention mode
Timeout action	The ring station transmits a Beacon or Claim Token MAC frame, depending on the mode, followed by idles (0's). It does this without waiting for a free token
IEEE counterpart	None

Hex to Decimal ConversionChart

Dec.	Hex	Binary		Dec.	Hex	Binary		Dec.	Hex	Binary	
0	00	0000	0000	46	2E	0010	1110	92	5C	0101	1100
1	01	0000	0001	47	2F	0010	1111	93	5D	0101	1101
2	02	0000	0010	48	30	0011	0000	94	5E	0101	1110
3	03	0000	0011	49	31	0011	0001	95	5F	0101	1111
4	04	0000	0100	50	32	0011	0010	96	60	0110	0000
5	05	0000	0101	51	33	0011	0011	97	61	0110	0001
6	06	0000	0110	52	34	0011	0100	98	62	0110	0010
7	07	0000	0111	53	35	0011	0101	99	63	0110	0011
8	08	0000	1000	54	36	0011	0110	100	64	0110	0100
9	09	0000	1001	55	37	0011	0111	101	65	0110	0101
10	0A	0000	1010	56	38	0011	1000	102	66	0110	0110
11	0B	0000	1011	57	39	0011	1001	103	67	0110	0111
12	0C	0000	1100	58	3A	0011	1010	104	68	0110	1000
13	0D	0000	1101	59	3B	0011	1011	105	69	0110	1001
14	0E	0000	1110	60	3C	0011	1100	106	6A	0110	1010
15	0F	0000	1111	61	3D	0011	1101	107	6B	0110	1011
16	10	0001	0000	62	3E	0011	1110	108	6C	0110	1100
17	11	0001	0001	63	3F	0011	1111	109	6D	0110	1101
18	12	0001	0010	64	40	0100	0000	110	6E	0110	1110
19	13	0001	0011	65	41	0100	0001	111	6F	0110	1111
20	14	0001	0100	66	42	0100	0010	112	70	0111	0000
21	15	0001	0101	67	43	0100	0011	113	71	0111	0001
22	16	0001	0110	68	44	0100	0100	114	72	0111	0010
23	17	0001	0111	69	45	0100	0101	115	73	0111	0011
24	18	0001	1000	70	46	0100	0110	116	74	0111	0100
25	19	0001	1001	71	47	0100	0111	117	75	0111	0101
26	1A	0001	1010	72	48	0100	1000	118	76	0111	0110
27	1B	0001	1011	73	49	0100	1001	119	77	0111	0111
28	1C	0001	1100	74	4A	0100	1010	120	78	0111	1000
29	1D	0001	1101	75	4B	0100	1011	121	79	0111	1001
30	1E	0001	1110	76	4C	0100	1100	122	7A	0111	1010
31	1F	0001	1111	77	4D	0100	1101	123	7B	0111	1011
32	20	0010	0000	78	4E	0100	1110	124	7C	0111	1100
33	21	0010	0001	79	4F	0100	1111	125	7D	0111	1101
34	22	0010	0010	80	50	0101	0000	126	7E	0111	1110
35	23	0010	0011	81	51	0101	0001	127	7F	0111	1111
36	24	0010	0100	82	52	0101	0010	128	80	1000	0000
37	25	0010	0101	83	53	0101	0011	129	81	1000	0001
38	26	0010	0110	84	54	0101	0100	130	82	1000	0010
39	27	0010	0111	85	55	0101	0101	131	83	1000	0011
40	28	0010	1000	86	56	0101	0110	132	84	1000	0100
41	29	0010	1001	87	57	0101	0111	133	85	1000	0101
42	2A	0010	1010	88	58	0101	1000	134	86	1000	0110
43	2B	0010	1011	89	59	0101	1001	135	87	1000	0111
44	2C	0010	1100	90	5A	0101	1010	136	88	1000	1000
45	2D	0010	1101	91	5B	0101	1011	137	89	1000	1001

FIGURE E.1

Hex to decimal
conversion chart
(continued)

Dec.	Hex	Binary	Dec.	Hex	Binary	Dec.	Hex	Binary
138	8A	1000 1010	184	B8	1011 1000	230	E6	1110 0110
139	8B	1000 1011	185	B9	1011 1001	231	E7	1110 0111
140	8C	1000 1100	186	BA	1011 1010	232	E8	1110 1000
141	8D	1000 1101	187	BB	1011 1011	233	E9	1110 1001
142	8E	1000 1110	188	BC	1011 1100	234	EA	1110 1010
143	8F	1000 1111	189	BD	1011 1101	235	EB	1110 1011
144	90	1001 0000	190	BE	1011 1110	236	EC	1110 1100
145	91	1001 0001	191	BF	1011 1111	237	ED	1110 1101
146	92	1001 0010	192	C0	1100 0000	238	EE	1110 1110
147	93	1001 0011	193	C1	1100 0001	239	EF	1110 1111
148	94	1001 0100	194	C2	1100 0010	240	F0	1111 0000
149	95	1001 0101	195	C3	1100 0011	241	F1	1111 0001
150	96	1001 0110	196	C4	1100 0100	242	F2	1111 0010
151	97	1001 0111	197	C5	1100 0101	243	F3	1111 0011
152	98	1001 1000	198	C6	1100 0110	244	F4	1111 0100
153	99	1001 1001	199	C7	1100 0111	245	F5	1111 0101
154	9A	1001 1010	200	C8	1100 1000	246	F6	1111 0110
155	9B	1001 1011	201	C9	1100 1001	247	F7	1111 0111
156	9C	1001 1100	202	CA	1100 1010	248	F8	1111 1000
157	9D	1001 1101	203	CB	1100 1011	249	F9	1111 1001
158	9E	1001 1110	204	CC	1100 1100	250	FA	1111 1010
159	9F	1001 1111	205	CD	1100 1101	251	FB	1111 1011
160	A0	1010 0000	206	CE	1100 1110	252	FC	1111 1100
161	A1	1010 0001	207	CF	1100 1111	253	FD	1111 1101
162	A2	1010 0010	208	D0	1101 0000	254	FE	1111 1110
163	A3	1010 0011	209	D1	1101 0001	255	FF	1111 1111
164	A4	1010 0100	210	D2	1101 0010			
165	A5	1010 0101	211	D3	1101 0011			
166	A6	1010 0110	212	D4	1101 0100			
167	A7	1010 0111	213	D5	1101 0101			
168	A8	1010 1000	214	D6	1101 0110			
169	A9	1010 1001	215	D7	1101 0111			
170	AA	1010 1010	216	D8	1101 1000			
171	AB	1010 1011	217	D9	1101 1001			
172	AC	1010 1100	218	DA	1101 1010			
173	AD	1010 1101	219	DB	1101 1011			
174	AE	1010 1110	220	DC	1101 1100			
175	AF	1010 1111	221	DD	1101 1101			
176	B0	1011 0000	222	DE	1101 1110			
177	B1	1011 0001	223	DF	1101 1111			
178	B2	1011 0010	224	E0	1110 0000			
179	B3	1011 0011	225	E1	1110 0001			
180	B4	1011 0100	226	E2	1110 0010			
181	B5	1011 0101	227	E3	1110 0011			
182	B6	1011 0110	228	E4	1110 0100			
183	B7	1011 0111	229	E5	1110 0101			

Analysis Lab Overview

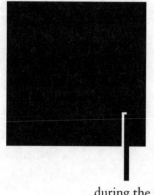

I N ORDER TO capture the traces and study Ethernet, Token Ring, and NetWare protocol performance, we had to develop a full network analysis lab. This appendix lists the lab requirements we defined during the initial development stages and details the final lab configuration. This appendix also provides details on all equipment used for development.

Lab Requirements

W E REQUIRED A number of diverse products in our network analysis lab. Of course, we could have used additional products, but these were sufficient to perform the tests required for this book. If your company manufacturers products that should be included in our analysis lab, please feel free to contact us at CompuServe 72000,3333.

The equipment we required for our research is listed here:

Ethernet Network   10BaseT cards (16-bit/32-bit), EISA, and ISA

10BaseT hubs (manageable hubs preferred)

Thinnet (10Base2) cards, cable, and connectors

NetWare 3.12-based NetWare MultiProtocol Router

NetWare 3.12 server

NetWare 4.01 server

	LANalyzer for Windows station
	NetWare Management System console
	NCC LANalyzer station
	Minimum of three client stations
Token Ring Network	4Mb/s and 16Mb/s Token Ring cards
	Dual rings supporting source routing
	8228 Multistation Access Unit
	CAU (Controlled Access Unit)
	LAM (Lobe Attachment Module)
	NetWare 4.01 server
	LANalyzer for Windows station
	NCC LANalyzer station
	Minimum of six client stations

Because a large portion of this book relates to the NetWare protocol stack, we also had to support multiple versions of the NetWare operating system, although we focused primarily on NetWare 3.x and 4.x. The following information defines the server configurations we used for development.

NetWare 3.12 Server (CORP-FS1)

The NetWare 3.12 Server (CORP-FS1) constantly complained of the load we placed on it—it has only 4MB memory. It served as a router between the Ethernet and Token Ring networks for much of the time and had to support AppleTalk, as well. Of course, now that the book is finished, we plan to add memory to it.

| Hardware Platform | Leading Edge WinPro486e (486/33) |
| Memory | 4MB |

Network interface "cards"	NE2000 supporting IPX/SPX and AppleTalk
	Madge SMART 16/4 AT Ringnode card supporting IPX/SPX and AppleTalk
Drive system	IDE controller supporting one 250MB clone drive.
Protocols loaded	IPX/SPX
	AppleTalk
Additional server applications	Print Server for Canon B600 Color Bubblejet printer

NetWare 4.01 Server (CORP-FS2)

We had two Netware 4.01 servers in the lab. These were our production servers for the entire duration of the book development. This server was our NetExplorer server for the NetWare Management System.

Hardware platform	Dominos 486/66
Memory	16MB
Network interface card(s)	Madge SMART 16/4 AT Ringnode card supporting IPX/SPX and AppleTalk
Drive system	Adaptec AHA-1522 SCSI adapter, 1GB Micropolis drive
Protocols loaded	IPX/SPX
	AppleTalk
Additional server applications	Net Explorer for NetWare Management System
	NetWare LANalyzer Agent
	NetWare Management Agent
	Print Server supporting HPIIIp and HP-4p

NetWare 4.01 Server (CORP-FS3)

Because our company, ImagiTech, Inc., develops interactive multimedia applications, we installed a video server with a lot of drive space (10GB) for video files. The disk subsystem we used was a Storage Dimensions fault-tolerant RAID disk array subsystem using RAID Level 5 architecture. This server became our video server, supporting NetWare for Video.

Hardware platform	Dominos 486/66
Memory	16MB
Network interface card	NE3200 supporting IPX/SPX and AppleTalk
Drive system	Storage Dimensions LANStor RAIDCard and LANStor ReFlex drive subsystem
Protocols loaded	IPX/SPX
	AppleTalk
Additional server applications	NetWare LANalyzer Agent
	NetWare Management Agent
	NetWare for Video 1.0

NetWare Clients

We kept a variety of client software on hand to view the different ways each shell (or DOS Requester) connected to the network and used enhanced features such as Burst Mode, Large Internet Packet, and NDS. Because this book focuses exclusively on the NetWare protocol stack, we did not document or diagram communications from Macintosh or UNIX-based stations.

Figure F.1 is a complete diagram of the LAN analysis lab at a static moment. The lab configuration changed weekly, and additional products not shown on the diagram are listed in the next section.

FIGURE F.I

The LAN analysis lab

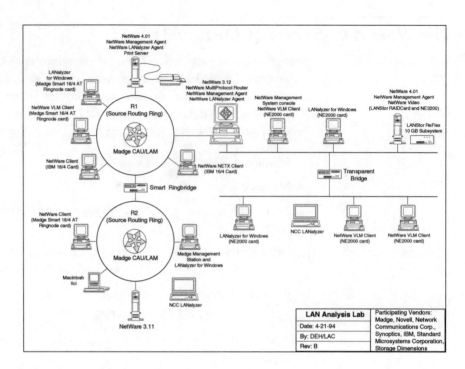

Lab Vendors and Product Information

THE PRODUCTS AND vendors listed in the following sections assisted in the development of the network analysis lab.

Madge Networks

Madge Networks joined the lab team early in the development cycle to offer assistance with the Token Ring section of this book. Madge can be contacted at:

Madge Networks
2310 North First Street
San Jose CA 95131-1011
Telephone: (408) 955-0700
Fax: (408) 955-0970

The following sections describe the various Madge products used in the LAN analysis lab.

Smart 16/4 Ringnode Card

Intelligent, full-featured Token Ring adapter cards based on the Texas Instruments TMS380 Token Ring Chipset, these cards offer switchable 4- and 16Mb/s operation and are equipped with on-board media filters and RJ45 sockets for direct connection to UTP cabling systems.

Smart LAN Support Software

The Smart LAN Support software, included with the Smart 16/4 Ringnode cards, includes a wide choice of driver modules and enables the adapter card itself to provide LAN protocol processing. This software also includes driver modules based on Madge's FastMac technology, which increases packet-processing speed and data throughput.

Smart 16/4 AT Ringnode Card

The Smart 16/4 AT Ringnode card is a fast ISA-based card that provides a choice of bus-mastering operation or programmed I/O with 8-bit or 16-bit data. The typical Smart 16/4 AT Ringnode card can drive the network at up to 1800 kilobytes per second in a NetWare server and includes an RJ45 socket for direct connection to UTP cabling systems.

Madge makes the Smart 16/4 AT Plus Ringnode card, which implements Madge's Fastmac Plus drivers and enables protocols to be downloaded to 512K of adapter memory. Protocols are actually run directly on the adapter and should enhance performance significantly. In the near future, we plan to upgrade one of the rings in our lab to new AT Plus cards to test performance and functionality.

SmartCAU

The SmartCAU, an intelligent Controlled Access Unit, is the wiring concentrator used in conjunction with the SmartLAM modules. SmartCAU supports up to 80 Token Ring stations over shielded twisted-pair and is fully compatible with IBM's 8230 Controlled Access Unit. Two ring management programs are included with the SmartCAU: TrueView CAU Manager for Windows and SmartCAU Control Program for DOS. Both programs can manage IBM CAUs as well as SmartCAUs. The TrueView CAU Manager for Windows program is an excellent addition to the product.

SmartLAM

The SmartLAM (Lobe Attachment Module) is the expansion module that provides 20 ports for connection between Token Ring stations and the SmartCAU wiring concentrator. The SmartLAM supports Token Ring stations over shielded twisted-pair wiring up to 145 meters (475 feet) at 16Mb/s.

Smart Ringbridge

The Ringbridge was our source-route bridge on the network. This bridge, capable of forwarding up to 12,500 smaller packets each second on the network, was easy to install and included the Ringbridge Control Program for remote bridge management.

Novell, Inc.

Several Novell divisions assisted the lab by providing product, configuration, and protocol information. Novell can be reached at:

Novell, Inc.
122 East 1700 South
Provo UT 84606
Telephone: (800) 453-1267 or (801) 429-7000
Fax: (801) 429-3098

The following sections list the products Novell supplied to the network analysis lab.

LANalyzer for Windows

LANalyzer for Windows is an MS Windows–based network analyzer for Ethernet and Token Ring networks. LANalyzer for Windows uses standard ODI-compliant network interface cards and drivers that support promiscuous mode operation. LANalyzer for Windows includes decodes for NetWare, TCP/IP, and AppleTalk protocol stacks.

In the final days of development of this book, Novell released the new LANalyzer for Windows v2.1, which provides support for additional protocol decodes and functionality:

- Additional protocol decodes include SNA, NFS, TELNET, FTP, TFTP, DNS, NetWare IP, and NetWare Directory Services.

- Names file entries can be marked permanent and are not overwritten during the name-gathering process.

- The Stop When capture-setting parameters can be saved for future use.

- LANalyzer for Windows can be brought automatically to the foreground in Windows when an alarm is generated.

- A new column in the Station Monitor and Station Details window displays the protocols in use by each station.

NetWare Management System (ManageWise)

NetWare Management System is an MS Windows–based, centralized management console that provides a common interface for enterprise management, including NetWare servers, hubs, routers, SNMP devices, and the network itself. We installed NetWare Management System, NetWare Management Agent, and the NetWare LANalyzer Agents to manage the entire network analysis lab from a single console.

NetWare Management Agent

NetWare Management Agent is a set of NLMs that we loaded on our Net-Ware 4.01 and NetWare 3.12 servers to provide server statistics and notify us of alarm conditions. From our NetWare Management System Console, we could track and compare statistics on each of the NetWare servers, as well as our SNMP-manageable hubs.

NetWare LANalyzer Agent

NetWare LANalyzer Agent is one of the more exciting analysis products we used. From our NetWare Management System Console, we could gather network statistics and station statistics, capture packets, and set alarms to notify us of excessive broadcasts, CRC errors, undersized/oversized packets, fragments, beaconing, receiver congestion, Line errors, Burst errors, Lost Frame errors, and Internal errors. We could simultaneously analyze all the segments on our network from a single console.

NetWare Developer Kits

We used two developer kits during the writing of this book: NetWare 3.12 Developer Kit and NetWare 4.01 Developer Kit.

NetWare Video

NetWare Video delivers compressed digital video files stored on a NetWare 3.x or 4.x server to multiple Netware clients. The compression formats supported include Indeo, Cinepak, and Microsoft Video 1.

NetWare Operating Systems

During our development, we used many versions of the NetWare operating system, including NetWare 2.2, NetWare 3.11 (with patches applied), NetWare 3.12, NetWare 4.0, NetWare 4.01, and NetWare 4.10.

NetWare MultiProtocol Router

The NetWare MultiProtocol Router software is a software-based routing solution that relies on Novell's NLM architecture and runs on either a NetWare 3.x or 4.x server or NetWare Runtime. One of the benefits of NetWare MultiProtocol Router software is the ability to filter SAP traffic on the network, as defined in Chapter 17.

Storage Dimensions, Inc.

Storage Dimensions provided us with much-needed disk storage space and high-speed controller cards for one of our NetWare 4.01 servers. Storage Dimensions can be contacted at:

Storage Dimensions, Inc.
1656 McCarthy Boulevard
Milpitas CA 95035
Telephone: (408) 954-0710
Fax: (408) 944-1203

The following sections describe the various Storage Dimensions products used in the LAN analysis lab.

LANStor RAIDCard and LANStor RAIDCard Software

The LANStor RAIDCard and LANStor RAIDCard software are part of the fault-tolerant disk array subsystem that features RAID (Redundant Array of Inexpensive Disk) level 5 architecture. The RAIDCard supports up to 14 FAST SCSI disk drives, for a total of 48GB of RAID 5 storage on a single NetWare server. The LANStor RAIDCard software provides the interface for the device driver installation and includes diagnostic and monitoring programs.

LANStor ReFlex Disk Subsystem

LANStor ReFlex is the disk subsystem that we connected to the LANStor RAIDCard in our NetWare 4.01 server. The subsystem supported 10GB of disk storage space and was essential for this server since it was also our NetWare for Video server and required massive disk space for storage of huge video files. A high-performance disk subsystem is essential to meet the streaming requirements of video on the network. The LANStor ReFlex subsystem was connected to the LANStor RAIDCard using a standard SCSI cable.

Network Communications Corporation

Network Communications Corporation (NCC) joined the lab team early in the development cycle to offer us the latest versions of the LANalyzer product for Token Ring and Ethernet analysis. NCC can be contacted at:

Network Communications Corporation
5501 Green Valley Drive
Bloomington MN 55437-1085
Telephone: (612) 844-0584
Fax: (612) 844-0487

The following sections describe the LANalyzer products used in the LAN analysis lab.

NCC LANalyzer for Token Ring

The NCC LANalyzer for Token Ring kit includes a customized, high-performance Token Ring network interface adapter with a 386 processor and 2MB memory on board. The software provides the ability to capture and analyze multiple protocols, including NetWare, TCP/IP, AppleTalk, SAA, Banyan Vines, LAN Manager, and DECnet. NCC LANalyzer has the ability to transmit packets onto the network for stress-testing components or network cabling systems. The NCC LANalyzer enables you to create very complex and sophisticated applications for testing and analyzing network performance.

NCC LANalyzer for Ethernet

The NCC LANalyzer for Ethernet kit includes a customized high-performance Ethernet network interface adapter with a 386 processor and 2MB memory on board. The same software is included in both the LANalyzer for Ethernet and LANalyzer for Token Ring products.

A number of other manufacturers were interested in participating and would have been included in the lab configuration had time permitted. We hope to work with more vendors and products in the future to enhance the lab and keep up on the latest network performance, optimization, and trouble-shooting issues.

Index

Note to the Reader: Throughout this index **boldface** page numbers indicate primary discussions of a topic. *Italic* page numbers indicate illustrations or tables.